REALISM AND CHRISTIA

God, Grammar, and Mea

The question of realism – that is, whether God exists independently of human beings – is central to much contemporary theology and church life. It is also an important topic in the philosophy of religion. This book discusses the relationship between realism and Christian faith in a thorough and systematic way, and uses the resources of both philosophy and theology to argue for a Christocentric narrative realism. Many previous defences of realism have attempted to model Christian belief on scientific theory, but Moore argues that this comparison is misleading and inadequate on both theological and philosophical grounds. In dialogue with speech act theory and critiques of realism by both non-realists and Wittgensteinians, a new account of the meaningfulness of Christian language is proposed. Moore uses this to develop a regulative conception of realism according to which God's independent reality is shown principally in Christ and then through Christian practices and the lives of Christians.

ANDREW MOORE is a Fellow of the Centre for the Study of Christianity and Culture, Regent's Park College, University of Oxford. He was formerly Chaplain of Jesus College, Oxford. He has published articles in a variety of church and academic journals, including *Religious Studies* and the *International Journal of Systematic Theology*.

REALISM
AND CHRISTIAN FAITH

God, Grammar, and Meaning

ANDREW MOORE

Regent's Park College, Oxford

CAMBRIDGE
UNIVERSITY PRESS

PUBLISHED BY THE PRESS SYNDICATE OF THE UNIVERSITY OF CAMBRIDGE
The Pitt Building, Trumpington Street, Cambridge CB2 1RP, United Kingdom

CAMBRIDGE UNIVERSITY PRESS
The Edinburgh Building, Cambridge, CB2 2RU, UK
40 West 20th Street, New York, NY 10011-4211, USA
477 Williamstown Road, Port Melbourne, VIC 3207, Australia
Ruiz de Alarcón 13, 28014 Madrid, Spain
Dock House, The Waterfront, Cape Town 8001, South Africa

http://www.cambridge.org

First Published 2003

Printed in the United Kingdom at the University Press, Cambridge

Typeface Adobe Garamond 11/12.5 pt   *System* LATEX 2ε   [TB]

A catalogue record for this book is available from the British Library

Library of Congress Cataloguing in Publication data
Moore, Andrew.
Realism and Christian faith: God, grammar, and meaning / Andrew Moore.
p.   cm.
Includes bibliographical references and index.
ISBN 0 521 81109 0 – ISBN 0 521 52415 6 (paperback)
1. God – proof, ontological.   2. Language and languages – religious
aspects – Christianity.   I. Title
BT103.M66   2002
231′.042 – dc21

ISBN 0 521 81109 0 hardback
ISBN 0 521 52415 6 paperback

The great temptation and danger consists in this, that the theologian will actually become what he seems to be – a philosopher.

Karl Barth

Contents

Preface

It was in a smoke-filled seminar room in the Philosophy Department of the University of York that I first began thinking about realism. Some of the smoke came from Martin Bell's pipe and I recall gratefully his inspiring, imaginative teaching and personal encouragement. This book has been a long time in gestation; I have incurred many debts in the process and it is a pleasure to be able to record them here. There will be those who think that this book carries with it too much of the whiff of the philosophy seminar room; others will think that there is not enough. Probably the former are right. Certainly, had I written on realism before studying theology, the argument would have been very different. For example, my views on the relationship between science and Christianity have changed significantly and positions for which I would once have argued now seem to me to be mistaken and in danger of distorting the content of Christian faith. For related reasons, I am now more sympathetic towards approaches in theology and the philosophy of religion that are indebted to Wittgenstein. As in the case of the relationship between science and Christianity, it is a better appreciation of the history of philosophy and theology in the modern period that has helped change my mind.

It is no accident, therefore, that I now try to approach the philosophical problems to do with the question of realism and Christianity from a much more theological perspective than once I might have. For encouraging me to set out on the path that led to this book, thanks are owing to Alister McGrath and Oliver O'Donovan. When I was an ordinand, the then Bishop of St Albans, John B. Taylor, firmly steered me towards doing doctoral research. I am grateful to him for his clear sense of the vital links between so-called 'academic' theology and the life of the church. The fact that I attempt to treat my themes theologically is also a result of the demands of Christian ministry. To Peter Adam, Martin Bleby, Jim Minchin, and David Warner, colleagues in the ministry, thanks for their friendship and influence during a very happy period in Melbourne, Australia. The first draft of this book was written whilst I was Chaplain of Jesus College, Oxford. I cannot imagine a setting that could manage simultaneously to be more congenial, stimulating, and challenging; many colleagues and friends there influenced and informed my thinking in relation to this project. For comments on portions of what became that first draft, thanks to Adrian Brown, Rowan Williams, Stephen N. Williams, and James Wood. For reading the whole of that draft and offering detailed suggestions for its improvement, thanks to Harriet Harris and Maurice Wiles. Many thanks also to Alan Torrance for his constructive criticism and encouraging me to bring the work to publication. I am grateful to Arthur Peacocke for making available to me otherwise hard-to-obtain works by and about him. Michael Scott read several chapters of the manuscript and I am very grateful to him for his comments on them, for hours of argument, and for advice on philosophical matters.

Suffering is part of all our lives and it is an important theme of the Christocentric argument for realism presented in this book. To Robert and Anna Booy, Kenneth Cragg, Tim and Sally Dakin, Alan Garrow, Jeremy and Ruth James, Tim Pidsley, John Roe, Adam Roberts, and Frances Whistler who have supported and encouraged me through some hard times: thank you.

I am grateful to the Principal and Fellows of Regent's Park College, Oxford for electing me a Fellow of the Centre for the Study of Christianity and Culture. Thanks especially to Nick Wood, Director of the Centre, and to Fiona Floate. My colleague John Taylor read two chapters of the manuscript and his searching comments proved most useful. Regent's is a very happy, thriving, and stimulating centre of Christian learning in the Baptist tradition, so I am specially thankful for its hospitality to a dyed-in-the-wool Anglican.

It has been a privilege to have Kevin Taylor as my editor (and occasional running partner). I am grateful for his interest in this project, for his advice, and for the professionalism with which he has seen it into print. I am grateful also to the anonymous readers appointed by Cambridge University Press for their many helpful criticisms and comments.

The argument of this book is that through their redemption in Christ human beings are granted to show the reality of the triune God. All those I have mentioned have pointed me to this; however, a few people have been special lights on the way. Oliver O'Donovan read a portion of an earlier draft and offered helpful comments. He also proved – painstakingly, tenaciously, and (to my mind) conclusively – that university bureaucrats were made for academics, not academics for them. More importantly, over the years he has kept me mindful of the fact that a theologian is called only ever to be a servant of the Word. John Webster encouraged me to publish the manuscript and has been very generous in practical help and friendship; like Oliver's, his learning and vision of the theological task have been a major inspiration. I have incurred a debt to Paul Fiddes that I shall never be able adequately to repay. He has given me extraordinary loyalty, friendship, and encouragement. He has been generous with time he did not have and read every sentence of an earlier draft, some not just once, but several times. Without his interpretative skills, perspicacious criticism, and many helpful suggestions this would be a much poorer work.

In the end, mortal words falter and then Irenaeus's dictum comes to mind: 'The Glory of God is the living human being; and the life of the human being is the Vision of God.' My parents, Dennis and Ailene, taught me to love the Word. My wife Penny has been a constant companion and friend, and her love has reflected His. Without her practical support this book could not have been written. All three have shown in their lives that of which in the following pages I have tried to speak. 'I moved in your light to see the light.'

CHAPTER I

Realism and Christian faith: towards an ontological approach

INTRODUCTION

Obituary notices announcing the death of realism continue to appear in philosophical and theological works,[1] but what is it that is supposed to have died? The philosophical doctrine known as realism can be expressed in terms of three characteristic sets of claims which, though not held by all realists and opposed by some, can serve as a preliminary formulation.[2] *Ontologically*, the realist holds that there is a reality external to human minds and that it exists as it does independently of the concepts and interpretative grids in terms of which we think about it. Its being what it is does not depend on our conceiving it (as idealists hold), or on our conceptions of it (as Kantians hold), or indeed on our conceiving it at all. Reality is there to be discovered as it objectively is; it is not subjectively invented, constructed, or projected. Hence, *epistemologically*, the realist holds that reality can be (approximately) known as it is and not just as it appears to us to be (as empiricism holds). *Semantically*, the realist holds that it is possible to refer successfully to, and so make (approximately) true statements about, reality. That is, in classical terms, the truth of a proposition is a matter of its corresponding to reality independently of our being able to verify or otherwise confirm it.[3] Thus, when Christian faith is subjected to philosophical scrutiny, typical realist claims are that (1) God exists independently of our awareness of him and of our will,[4] but that (2) despite this, we can know him and that (3) human

---

[1] See, for example, in the philosophy of science, Fine 1996²: 112, in theology, Milbank and Pickstock 2001: 1.

[2] The formulation of the philosophical position is adapted from Dalferth 1989: 16f.

[3] Although the correspondence theory of truth has been widely abandoned in philosophy, the Christian philosopher William Alston (1996) has argued for 'alethic realism' via a defence of a version of the correspondence theory of truth. In his 1995a (37ff) he briefly expounds his alethic realism to show that Christian non-realism is incoherent; regrettably he does not argue positively for the realism of the Christian faith.

[4] The need to add independence from our *will* to the definition of a Christian realism will become apparent from Cupitt's voluntarism.

language is not an inadequate or inappropriate medium for truthful speech about God.[5] This, in broad outline, is the view defended and argued for in this book.

Concerning the world of macroscopic objects such as tables, chairs, and people, the realist position might seem so obviously correct as not to need defending; for sure, in everyday life we live as realists. In this sense, realism is alive and well; to recall Mark Twain's famous cable message, reports of its death are an exaggeration. But what about the atomic and sub-atomic particles out of which present-day science tells us the tables and chairs are made up: are these real? As we shall see in chapter 3, there are philosophers of science who deny that they are. For them, proclaiming the death of realism amounts to persuading us that objects many had thought to be real never were. And then consider our moral beliefs: do we hold them in virtue of some objective moral order? Or perhaps our moral beliefs are expressions of feelings of approval or disapproval, unconnected to any independent moral reality – as Logical Positivists and others have held. For them, moral philosophy has been a long wake for a dead moral realism.[6] And, relative to the reader of these words, is the past in which they were written real? Again, there are philosophers who argue powerfully that it is not. What is more, they can consistently deny the reality of the past whilst accepting the independent reality of other people's minds. So being an anti-realist about one aspect of reality is not prima facie inconsistent with being realist about other aspects of reality.[7]

Yet it does seem prima facie inconsistent for a Christian who says the creed each Sunday, who prays to God as creator and preaches stewardship of the world as God's creation, to deny that the creator of the world exists independently of the mind and to regard the creed as 'a statement of

---

[5] It can be seen from this that the Scholastic debate between 'nominalists' and 'realists' over the status of universals is somewhat, though not wholly, remote from our present concern. Twentieth-century philosophical interest in realism received a major impetus when G. E. Moore effectively closed the nineteenth-century domination by idealism with his paper on 'External and Internal Relations' (1922: 276–309). The question of realism in something like its present form appears in Barth's 1929 lectures on 'Fate and Idea in Theology' (1986a: 25–61, cf. 1961b: 218–19). Barth influenced two of the key figures in twentieth-century discussions of the topic: T. F. Torrance (for example, in his 1969 and 1982) and Donald MacKinnon, who resolutely defended Christian realism from at least as early as his 1945 essay on 'Verifiability' (1968: 232–48; and see in particular 1979 *passim*, especially 138–65). Important and deserving of attention though his contribution is, Torrance's work lies outside the main stream of thought on which I focus. Rather unsatisfactory discussions of his realism can be found in Achtemeier 1994 and McGrath 1999: 211–20. Another tradition that has defended realism but which lies beyond the scope of this book is Transcendental Thomism, especially Bernard Lonergan's version: see, for example, his paper 'The Origins of Christian Realism' (1996: 239–61, cf. 218f).

[6] However, with Logical Positivism itself dead and buried, realism is now resurgent in moral philosophy: see Sayre-McCord 1988.

[7] This has been a major theme of Michael Dummett's work on realism: see, for example, 1991: 16.

common purpose' (David A. Hart 1993: 82) – with no ontological reference beyond those who utter it. It seems even more inconsistent for a practising Christian minister and leading non-realist seriously to declare 'I place the death of God around 1730' (Cupitt 1990: 189) and yet (one presumes) to say 'and the love of God be with us all, evermore. Amen' at the end of a funeral service for a human being. So, to announce in a theological context that realism is dead is to make a very far-reaching claim concerning not just an abstract point in philosophy with no relevance to everyday life but one whose ramifications go to the heart of Christianity.

Although Christian denials of realism about God may seem inconsistent with professing Christian faith, they reflect not just academic fashion but also lively currents of opinion in contemporary church life. The Sea of Faith Network is a religious organization embracing Christian and other faiths which has amongst its stated objects ' "to explore and promote religious faith as a human creation" '.[8] According to one of its official documents, God is not

a metaphysical entity 'out there'. Such a God is too small. 'He' is no longer credible. God is, and always was, a metaphor for the values which, though we understand them to be generated by human culture, we have come to think of as 'ultimate' and 'eternal' ... Sea of Faith suggests that it is time to 'take leave' of a real God 'out there'. (Boulton 1997: 9)

In their emphasis on the influence of culture in generating religious ideas and practices, proponents of Christian non-realism reflect the influence of the post-Structuralist stream of the phenomenological tradition. Important and rigorous versions of anti-realism have been developed in analytical philosophy, but although Kant has influenced anti-realism in analytic philosophy and Christian non-realism, his views have had less direct impact on the formulation of the latter.[9] A significant exception here is the principal and originating force behind Sea of Faith, the British philosopher of religion and Anglican priest Don Cupitt.[10] His classic statement *Taking Leave of God* (1980) has almost become a manifesto. In it he attacks realist

---

[8] Quoted in Boulton 1997: 3, no source cited. The Network has lay and ordained members in many Christian denominations. It has branches in Britain, Australia, New Zealand, and the United States.

[9] In analytic philosophy, see, for example, Goodman 1978; Rorty 1980, 1989: 3–22. Michael Dummett is generally regarded as an anti-realist (see, for example, 1978: 1–24, but cf. xxxix). Trigg 1989[2] offers a clear and forceful introduction to the debate; for his views on theological realism, see his 1992 and 1997.

Anti-realism and non-realism may be taken as cognate, though the former has a technical meaning associated with Dummett (1978: xxx, 145–6); the latter is the normal usage of Christians of that ilk.

[10] Another notable exception is the American Kantian thinker Gordon Kaufman (e.g., 1993).

Christianity on the ground that objective theism is ethically, philosophically, theologically, and culturally indefensible, and advocates its replacement by an 'expressivist' reinterpretation of Christian faith. Alvin Plantinga
has described his views as possessing 'a certain amiable dottiness' (2000:
39 n. 7), and whilst there is some truth in this, to dismiss Cupitt as an
eccentric is to miss both the depth of his learning (though this is often too
lightly worn) and the brilliance of his rhetoric, and so also the power and
impact of his opposition to religious realism.

Nevertheless, Cupitt (and many other members of Sea of Faith) is at
pains not to be seen as either anti-religious or as an atheist. Cupitt believes
that we must take leave of the God of realism for religious reasons.[11]

Religion is not metaphysics but salvation, and salvation is a state of the self. It has
to be appropriated subjectively or existentially. There is no such thing as objective
religious truth and there cannot be. The view that religious truth consists in
ideological correctness or in the objective correspondence of doctrinal statements
with historical and metaphysical facts is a modern aberration, and a product of the
decline of religious seriousness. (Cupitt 1980: 43)

Cupitt's expressivist Christianity is intended to promote salvation by liberating people from the cramped, heteronomous confines of realism's 'cosmic
Toryism' (1990: 54) and the church's 'highly bureaucratic salvation machine'
(2001: 7). Instead, he proposes an autonomous faith in which 'God *is* the
religious requirement personified and his attributes are a kind of projection of its main features as we experience them' (1980: 85).[12] 'The religious
requirement' is 'that we must become spirit' (1980: 85), and this means that
'when we choose God we choose a demand upon ourselves which is *a priori*
and overriding, namely the demand that we shall become individuated,
free, responsive and purely spiritual subjects' (1980: 88).[13]

Cupitt is a prolific writer and his position has changed over the years,
but its broad moral and philosophical outlines have not.[14] Thus, in his
agenda-setting book *Reforming Christianity* (2001), he reaffirms that 'we
are thoroughgoing anti-realists, to the point of nihilism' (39) and advocates
a return to 'religious immediacy' and the Kingdom teaching of a Jesus
unencumbered by ecclesiastical dogma. We must 'give up ... the old belief
in objective truth'. We need to

---

[11] The phrase *Taking Leave of God* is adapted from Meister Eckhart, and Cupitt sees his position as an
organic development of Christian tradition (see his 1984a). See also David Hart 1993: 5, 14, 134.
[12] See also Cupitt 2001: 9, 27–31.
[13] As this passage illustrates, there is a Gnostic strand in Cupitt's thought; see also 1980: 11 and 1992:
134.
[14] For a survey see Stephen Ross White 1994.

learn to do without ... the belief that we are presented with a ready-made world, a cosmos whose reality and intelligible order are determined from a point that is both outside ourselves, and also outside and beyond the here and now ... No spirit world or transcendent entity mediates the real to us. *We* order the world. (30)

And because we order the world, we need to drop 'the belief in fixed, objective defining essences of things ... things are what we currently take them for' (31). This attack on what he calls essentialism is in keeping with the 'constructivist' vein in much contemporary thought.[15] For Cupitt Christianity is rather like Humpty Dumpty's 'glory' in *Alice in Wonderland*; since it has no essence, Christianity can be whatever Cupitt wants it to be.[16] Thus, although 'people will say that the kingdom religion I describe is "not Christianity" ', he replies that 'we must of course be utterly indifferent to that charge, because it is based on an obsolete assumption' (31).

Realist Christians sometimes ignore the role that culture, language, and institutions play in shaping Christianity and mistakenly identify the faith with one particular cultural or ecclesiastical manifestation of it. They can be far too committed to the view that only one historical or doctrinal expression of the faith expresses it definitively. But if it is true that *ubi Christus, ibi ecclesia*, the kind of essentialism Cupitt attacks in the name of a Kingdom religion based on Jesus' ethical teaching must be false. Cupitt's argument gives the strong impression that he is trying to define out of existence the construal of Christianity accepted by those who disagree with him. Superficially, his anti-essentialism is a neat move against a Bishop wishing to remove turbulent anti-realist priests from his diocese.[17] When a Bishop suggests to anti-realist clergy that what they are preaching and teaching is not Christianity, these priests, armed with Cupitt's argument, can simply reply that the Bishop's view is based on the outmoded notion that there is such a thing as 'Christianity'. But this move is unlikely to persuade. Realist Christians can, for the sake of argument and as a rhetorical strategy, accept Cupitt's denial that there is such a thing and, by Cupitt's own argument, reply that their construction of Christianity, their historical narrative, is

[15] 'Constructivism' is a term widely used in debates about realism. Its precise meaning varies, but in general it suggests the view that the area of reality under consideration is created rather than discovered by us; see Devitt 1991[2]: 157. Versions of constructivism are frequently encountered in postmodern ontologies; for an (ironic) example, see Sokal and Bricmont 1998: 241. A sense of what is at stake theologically is hinted at by the analytic philosopher Hilary Putnam when he argues that on Nelson Goodman's philosophical view 'there is nothing that we did not make to be what it is. (Theologically, one might say that Goodman makes man the creator)' (Putnam 1992: 113).

[16] At one time he regarded his outlook as 'a modest advance on Buddhism' (1992: 50).

[17] The *cause célèbre* here is the Bishop of Chichester's dismissing the Revd Anthony Freeman from his post as a Priest-in-Charge in the mid 1990s.

different: Cupitt is welcome to his, but from a realist perspective, he is recognizably in dialogue with what Christianity is and therefore it is still an open question whether what he describes is 'Christianity'.[18]

It is hardly surprising that the question of whether Christianity is or can be realist has become a matter of increasing and sometimes heated debate amongst Christians – both those who are theologically trained and those who are not. Nevertheless, whilst Cupitt and the Sea of Faith serve to introduce some of the themes of this book, my main purpose is not to reply to or to refute their position, and there are two reasons for this.[19] The first is that Cupitt's main argument for non-realism begins from the same philosophical foundationalism as the objective theism to which he thinks realist Christianity is committed. However, foundationalism suffers major weaknesses and has had as bad an impact on arguments for realism as it has on those against it. It therefore needs to be dealt with in its own right and will be a significant theme of my argument throughout this work, particularly in chapters 4 and 5. The second reason is a development of the first: foundationalism is preoccupied above all with how we secure the foundations of our *epistemological* claims. Again, because this concern has distorted the understanding of Christian faith in both traditional and radical versions, it helps explain why realists and non-realists often seem to argue past each other. What is needed is an attempt to deal with the philosophical and theological issues underlying the dispute in order to get beyond this impasse, and that is what I undertake.

More generally, the Sea of Faith Network and Cupitt's work should be regarded as symptoms of a general philosophical and cultural malaise at the end of modernity rather than as causes of a specific and novel theological problematic. To attempt to deal with this malaise head-on as well as to argue for the realism of the Christian faith would make my project impossibly large since it would require both detailed scholarly diagnosis and

---

[18] Cupitt seems to concede this: see 2001: 39.

  Issues concerning the exercise of power and authority are never far from the surface in Christian non-realists' arguments, and the approach I have sketched could, if undertaken without great pastoral sensitivity, and perhaps inevitably in any case, confirm non-realists' suspicions. Nevertheless, (Archbishop) Rowan Williams is correct when he points out that 'it is not at all clear that non-realism is politically innocent. The implicit claim ... that non-realism represents the irreversible direction of human thinking is a powerfully political one; and the use of "we" by the non-realist (or anyone else, of course), as in "we can no longer believe that . . .", is a claim to power and legitimacy of a kind' (1997: vii). See also (Bishop) Peter Selby's 1997 and Thiselton 1995: 105–17. I have addressed some of the pastoral and ecclesiological dimensions of Christian non-realism in my 1999.

[19] For arguments explicitly directed against Cupitt, in addition to Stephen Ross White 1994, see Keith Ward 1982; Hebblethwaite 1988; Thiselton 1995: 81–117; Rowan Williams 1984; Stephen N. Williams 1995: 110–42.

rigorous constructive argument. Such an attempt would also be likely to be over-burdened by methodological considerations, which, whilst important in their own right, might distract attention from the substantive doctrinal considerations that ought to shape a Christian theologian's diagnosis and treatment of any conceptual problems, particularly those surrounding realism. David Ford has stated 'The question of how or whether one maintains some sort of realism ... is central to much current theological debate' (1992: 209). Nevertheless, perhaps because of the historical and philosophical scope of the problems related to the debate about realism, very few theological works have recently been published focussing on realism as a topic in its own right. The majority approach it in a polemical way (Cupitt is the usual target), or via another problem (such as that of religious language, as in the case of Janet Martin Soskice). Although he is widely regarded as an anti-realist, the very distinguished Catholic philosopher Michael Dummett suggested that 'anti-realism is ultimately incoherent but ... realism is only tenable on a theistic basis'.[20] Substitute 'Christian' for 'theistic' and that could almost be my argument in a nutshell. Dummett has not published the paper in which he argues this, for, as he candidly admits, 'I do not think I know nearly enough about the question of realism to be justified in advancing such an argument' (1978: xxxix).[21] Those who know Dummett's work will disagree; nevertheless, where philosophical angels fear to tread...!

TOWARDS AN ONTOLOGICAL APPROACH

Some terminological clarifications

A major proposal of my argument is that we need to approach the question of realism in Christian faith from an *ontological* perspective. This needs some elaboration. First, I am not concerned to advance an argument for *religious* realism. This is because the doctrinal outlooks of particular religions will require their realism to be defended in ways appropriate to their own particular ontological commitments, and, in any case, not all religions are realist. For example, on the latter point, Francis Cook has written that

The [Zen] Buddhist contribution to the debate [about] language is its discovery that reality does not disclose itself in the form of language but rather reality is obscured by habitual, innate patterns of thought and language which are imposed

[20] The philosopher and practising Jew Hilary Putnam has hinted at a similar view: see 1983: 226.
[21] However, see Dummett's very intriguing 1994.

on a reality that is void of what the language names. In other words, we do not discover the real and then name it, we rather impose or superimpose over reality what it does not possess ... It is a process of *creating* reality rather than *discovering* it. The reality which is so compelling to us that we fight and kill in its name is nothing but mental construction totally lacking in an objective base. (1993: 68)

Most people who debate 'religious realism' are in fact arguing about the Christian religion and/or theism. However, in the light of Cook's words, it might be wiser, more honest, and possibly more respectful to other faiths not to lump all religions together but to seek instead to find out what realism means with respect to particular faiths, and then to examine what degree of overlap – if any – there might be which could justify a general religious realism. Furthermore, it is arguable (one thinks of the Old Testament prophets) that 'religion' can in good measure be a human construct that hides more than it shows of God. Thus, properly speaking, it is not concerning *religion* or *faith* as human phenomena that Christians are or are not realists, but concerning the God who is the object of their faith and the referent of their language.

A second elaboration is that I shall defend a *Christocentric realism*, not *theological realism*. There are several reasons for this. First, although 'theological realism' has become a portmanteau phrase to describe what classical orthodox Christianity upholds and what non-realists such as Cupitt oppose, my own use of the phrase is somewhat narrower and ideal-typical. We shall look at this position in detail in chapter 3, but I have in mind a cluster of methodological moves and philosophical tendencies according to which theology learns how to be (or, how it succeeds in being) realist by drawing from the philosophy of science and philosophical theism. Although no single author demonstrates the position in a pure form, many – for example, Janet Soskice, Arthur Peacocke, John Polkinghorne, and Wentzel van Huyssteen – explicitly claim to be defending 'theological realism', and there is sufficient conceptual overlap and mutual influence between them to identify their common position generically as 'theological realism'. As we shall see shortly, theological realists construe the realism problematic in epistemological and semantic terms, but this has problems which, I believe, can only be tackled from a Christocentrically focussed ontological perspective.

At many points in the argument, I shall refer to 'a Christian realism'. This phrase is intended as a generic term for that which opposes Christian non-realism, but it is also meant to draw into the foreground of the debate the argument that if the triune God reveals his independent reality to humans, it is likely that this will be detected by attending to the practices of individual and corporate Christian discipleship which together make up the Christian faith. As the eminent church historian James Atkinson once said, 'If you want to see God at work, you need to go to the back streets of Sheffield, not the university library.' My argument involves looking in detail at some of these day-to-day 'non-theological' practices of Christian faith, and we shall see that these are at least as important in expressing the reality of God as (academic) theology.[22] Despite the technical nature of the questions discussed, my deep concern is for the witness and well-being of the church.

A further reason for arguing for a Christocentric realism is that whilst the Christian faith is a proper object of philosophical scrutiny, the converse relation also holds. Theology is bound to 'take every thought captive to obey Christ' (2 Cor. 10:5), and that includes philosophical thoughts.[23] So Christianity and philosophy are conversation partners, but if they are to address each other clearly in their own true accents they should not distort or ignore each other. Thus, whilst realism is a problematic that arises when Christian faith is (as it should be) subjected to philosophical scrutiny, I shall give as much attention as possible to Christian faith's own resources for dealing with it. Traditionally, it has been Christianity's focus on Jesus Christ that has distinguished it from other philosophical and religious outlooks. So by using the phrase 'Christocentric realism' I am indicating that I shall endeavour to meet the problematic from an explicitly Christocentric perspective. One of my central points against theological realism will be that it pays insufficient attention to either the distinctively theological issues that give rise to the debate about realism or the distinctively theological resources that can be used to find a way ahead. In this sense, 'theological realism' is not theological enough; if it were more Christocentric it would be a more genuinely *theological* realism.

The third and most important elaboration of my preference for an ontological approach to the question of the realism of Christian faith is that I write from the perspective of one who confesses the living reality of the triune God revealed in Jesus Christ.[24] This means that I write as a Christian theologian who is interested in and loves philosophy, but not as a philosopher of religion.[25] It also has a significant impact on the form of my argument for a Christocentric realism. I shall come back to that shortly, but first I need to deal with an objection to this confession. It might appear that

---

[22] *Mutatis mutandis*, we shall see that this point has been well recognized by Christian non-realists.
[23] For a sustained dogmatic and philosophical meditation on Paul's dictum, see Bruce D. Marshall 2000.
[24] I discuss this in detail in chapter 7.   [25] For an elaboration of this, see my 2001.

in making it my argument fatally begs the most important question by assuming the independent reality of the one whose independence I wish to defend. Against this, it seems to me that some such circularity is unavoidable in any argument for realism, and in this I agree with the philosopher John Searle, who, defending his 'external realism', writes that 'I do not believe there could be a non-question-begging argument' (1995: 184).[26] One is reminded of Barth's famous image of the 'self-enclosed circle' within which theology and its epistemology operate: theology 'realises that all its knowledge, even its knowledge of the correctness of its knowledge, can only be an event' (1975: 42, cf. 1957: 243–54) – that is, a self-originating divine action which can be understood only in terms of itself. Reason is accountable to God and helps us clarify why we believe what we believe, but concerning the things of God, its deliverances fall short of incontrovertible proof.[27] Even regarding the existence of the external world, proof is still wanting. This is not, however, merely a *tu quoque* argument:[28] it is not that among six equally weak and more or less indefensible positions – Christian realism, Christian non-realism, atheist realism, atheist non-realism, agnostic realism and agnostic non-realism – one might just as reasonably opt for a Christian realism until non-question-begging proofs are in. Rather the claim is that the ordering of ontological and epistemological priorities proposed here results in a more theologically coherent understanding of divine and human reality than competing views because it allows us to deal with the problems with which they tried to deal whilst avoiding the pitfalls of those approaches.[29]

The importance of the ontological commitment expressed here can be brought out by considering Eberhard Jüngel's observation in his important essay on (philosophical aspects of) the Christian doctrine of God, *God's Being Is in Becoming* (2001a). Unlike Bultmann, he claims, Karl Barth 'does not ask what it *means* to speak of God, but, rather, in what sense God *must* be spoken of in order that our speaking is about *God*. And Barth asks that question on the presupposition that speech of God is meaningful and possible' because it has to be ' "acknowledged as a fact" ' that human speech about God takes place ' "on the basis of God's own direction" ' (Jüngel 2001a: 1, 2, quoting Barth 1975: 90).[30] The theological realism associated

---

[26] Keith Ward (1982: 5–7, 14) and John Hick (1993: 15) seem to hold somewhat similar views.

[27] On this and on epistemic circularity, see Alston 1993.

[28] On *tu quoque* arguments, see van Huyssteen 1989: 36ff and Helm 1994: 70ff, 209–10.

[29] For a somewhat analogous approach to the philosophical debate, see Devitt 1991².

[30] For Barth's own treatment of these concerns, see 1957: 224–36. The Bultmannian problematic is a bequest of Kant. For a lucid discussion of the influence of Kant on these issues, see Wolterstorff 1998.

with the pioneering work of Janet Soskice – its most philosophically able and influential exponent – reflects Bultmann's concern insofar as it is occupied with the question of 'how we can claim to speak of God at all' (Soskice 1985: ix). To use her preferred terminology, terminology subsequently taken up by many other theological realists, Soskice is concerned with how we gain 'epistemic access' to God and the problem of 'reality depiction', of the referential character of religious language.

Before looking at how theological realists argue for our being able to speak of God, it is worth noticing how epistemological and semantic approaches to realism such as Soskice's can inadvertently lapse into idealism. Michael Devitt has taken as maxims of his defence of realism that we should 'distinguish the metaphysical (ontological) issue of realism before any semantic issue' and 'settle the realism issue before any epistemic or semantic issue' (1991²: 3, 4). The reason for this is that if we make our statements about a putatively mind-independent reality in terms of our epistemic experience or causal relatedness to reality – as theological realists do – then it is quite possible to draw the conclusion that our experience *conditions* reality, and this will mean that we have not succeeded semantically in referring to a mind-independent reality.[31] An illustration of how this argument might run is provided by Richard Wollheim in his exposition of the nineteenth-century idealist F. H. Bradley's 'traditional epistemological argument for Idealism'. He paraphrases Bradley as follows:

Everything that we come across or accept as real, everything that we call a piece of existence or a fact, is always found combined with experience; and if it is always combined with experience, then no meaning can be attached to the assertion that it could exist without experience; and if it could not exist without experience, then it is indivisible from experience; and if it is indivisible from experience, then it is, or is nothing but, experience. (1959: 198)

In addition to the principally theological reasons for beginning with ontology, this provides a prima facie philosophical case for doing so.

The answer theological realists give to the question of how we can claim to speak of God's reality is typically stated in terms of an argument based on analogies between the unobservability of theoretical entities in physics and the unobservability of God. Thus, if we can defend realism in the former case we might be able to transpose the arguments by which we do so into a theological key. However, this way of posing the realism question has a number of theologically undesirable consequences which can be brought to light by considering a series of questions addressed to the theological

---

[31] Another consequence is scepticism: see Moser 1999.

realists' argument. We need to ask whether it is theologically proper to make the success of arguments for the reality of the creator dependent on the success of arguments concerning the reality of the creation. Or we might want to contest the theological realists' premiss that God is unobservable in a way which is sufficiently analogous to unobservability in particle physics for their argument to be run. Or we might want to question the correctness of their apparent assumption that God can be known in broadly similar ways to that in which the physical world can be known. More generally, theological realism takes realism about creation to be less problematic than realism about God; however, should the creation's reality really be more securely grounded in our theological framework than God's? But perhaps we cannot talk successfully about God, or find out how to do so, if we put the question of his reality in abeyance. We shall come back to this in later chapters, but here it should be noted that in our efforts to show how to speak about God, it might be that our methodology has tied our tongues and prevented us from speaking about God at all. To avoid this possibility, I propose that we need to argue from claims about God's reality and show what range of consequences for our views about the ontological, epistemological, and semantic aspects of the realism problematic follows from them.

The most real idol?

An important question to which I shall give more attention later is implicit in Barth's and Jüngel's concern that we should be speaking about *God*, that is, that we should be talking about God and not an idol. This concern is shared by others whose position is far from being realist. For example, Don Cupitt claims that 'Church Christianity eventually turned into the last great form of idolatry' (2001: 10). The most systematic treatment of the theme from an anti-traditional perspective is that of Gordon Kaufman in his radically and self-consciously constructivist approach to theology. The fullest statement of this is his *In Face of Mystery: A Constructive Theology* (1993). His argument is built around the claims that 'theologians should attempt to construct conceptions of God, humanity, and the world appropriate for the orientation of contemporary life' and that 'these notions are (and always have been) human creations, human imaginative constructions' (31). Kaufman has usually been bracketed with nonrealists, but although there are many themes in common this characterization is too crude: his position is both more subtle and developed with more dialectical skill than that of most Christian non-realists.[32] It is also more Kantian ontologically:[33]

One of the most important features of the notion of theology as imaginative construction is that it demands that we clearly distinguish our ideas – especially when we speak of God – from the mysteries to which we intend them to refer. This helps keep us honest in our theological work on the one hand; and it acknowledges, on the other, the full independence of God from what we may think or say. In reminding ourselves of God's mystery we allow God in God's concrete actuality to be whatever God is, quite apart from our symbolizations; in this respect the concept of mystery, just because of its conceptual emptiness and openness, most directly forces upon us what it means to confess God's *reality*; to confess that God is truly *God*, the ultimate reality which is not to be confused with any of our imaginative constructions. (353)[34]

There is much in this with which a more conventional realist about God might agree.[35] However, Kaufman's mistake is similar to that of the early Cupitt: he absolutizes God beyond a Kantian veil of perception as an exclusively noumenal entity.[36] In Kaufman's case, this is combined with the view that because theology is wholly a work of constructive imagination, revelation as traditionally understood is an impossibility.[37]

For much of the Christian tradition – if at times only rather fitfully – God's hiddenness to humans is understood as a function of his holiness, his *moral* otherness, and this is why salvation and revelation are inseparable. By contrast, Kaufman's constructive theology is morally driven, but the moral agenda is written by us. Theology should promote an understanding of God that is 'human-affirming, human-sustaining, and human-enhancing' (424), but here it is a *human* vision of human fulfilment and well-being that fills out these values. '[O]ur construction of the image/concept of God' must be guided by that which 'will most effectively facilitate human flourishing and fulfilment' (42–3). Any understanding of God which obstructs the fulfilment of this vision is idolatrous, and for Kaufman this means most of the Christian tradition.

It is this question of idolatry rather than any knee-jerk supposition that he is a non-realist that should give us pause. Kaufman admits that to worship 'at the shrine of a God, the understanding of which we ourselves

---

[32] Plantinga (2000: 31–42) and Trigg (1998: 187) clearly regard Kaufman as a non-realist; however, cf. Sonderegger 1997: 326ff.

[33] See 1993: 415; cf. 322–40.

[34] For the dialectical subtlety of Kaufman's understanding of the reality of God, see 1993: 320.

[35] Nor should Kantianism be prematurely dismissed by conservative Christians: see Westphal 1993b.

[36] See Cupitt 1985².   [37] See, e.g., 1993: 58.

have imaginatively constructed' will be seen by some as 'the crassest sort of idolatry'. To this, he robustly replies that the charge betrays a 'defensive mentality' and an 'authoritarian mode of theological argument' (50, 43). Faced with rhetoric of this kind, it is probably better not to argue but simply to lay one's cards on the table and repudiate the position. Debate cannot settle which understanding of God – that of Kaufman or the tradition he rejects – truly promotes human flourishing, for that would require us to occupy a position which is not available to us – a God's-eye view of the Gods. However, consideration of the crucifixion of Jesus and the moral, religious, and political debates surrounding and precipitating it might shed some light on both sides of the argument. And that is why, in pursuit of a Christian realism, of a realism that aims to be about *God* and not a humanly constructed idol, I shall orientate my argument around the claim that the living God has revealed himself in the incarnation, crucifixion, resurrection, and glorification of Jesus Christ.

To put this in the terms of my overall argument, I begin from the ontological commitment that the triune God who has revealed himself in Jesus Christ is the Most Real reality there is. By this I do not mean that his reality differs from ours merely as a matter of *degree*; rather, the creator is most real because he gives reality to creation and so is *absolutely* different from creation: its reality is derived, but his is not. I use the tag *ens realissimum* to abbreviate this claim about God. The content of the concept will become clearer in the course of my argument, but it is worth pointing out at this stage that it need not carry the freightage conveyed by Leibniz's and Kant's use of it in relation to what Kant called 'transcendental theology'.[38] As I said, this commitment has a significant impact on the form of my argument, for it means that my exposition of a Christocentric realism has the shape of a transcendental argument.

TRANSCENDENTAL ARGUMENTS FOR REALISM

In modern philosophy, transcendental arguments have their origin in Immanuel Kant's attempt in the *Critique of Pure Reason* to refute David Hume's scepticism. Typically they aim to show that given that a proposition *p* is accepted, certain other conditions must obtain.[39] For example, in his argument against Hume, Kant wanted to show that experience (which for him

---

[38] See Kant 1933: A631/B659ff; cf. A576/B604ff, A592/B620ff, and 1978: 34, 44–81; cf. Dalferth 1999: 127. For more theologically nuanced understandings of God as the *ens realissimum*, see Hilary of Poitiers 1954: 1: 5; Anselm 1979: III.

[39] On transcendental arguments, see Robert Stern 1999, especially 2–8.

includes sensory experience, beliefs, concepts, and judgements) is possible; amongst the several conditions of this is that we cannot know things as they are 'in themselves' (their *noumenal* reality) but only as they 'appear' to us to be (their *phenomenal* reality). Some scientific realists also use a transcendental argument to defend their position. For example, taking a lead from the Marxist philosopher of science Roy Bhaskar (1975: 23), Soskice claims that 'The [scientific] realist ... is committed ... to the intelligibility of what is essentially an ontological question, "What must the world be like for science to be possible?" ' (122). She replies that some kind of realism about the world investigated by science must be presumed. Here, *p* is the proposition that 'science is possible', and we then enquire what must be the case for science to be possible with the answer that realism must be presumed.

Transcendental arguments from truth to God

Transcendental arguments have been used to defend the realism of Christian faith – though without apparent recognition that their form can be construed in this way – by Brian Hebblethwaite in his rebuttal of Cupitt in *The Ocean of Truth* (1988), and, following him, by Ian Markham in *Truth and the Reality of God* (1998).[40] Both versions are different in substance from my own, for they are arguments 'from truth to God' and claim that it is a condition of our being able to make truthful statements that there is a God.[41] As Markham puts it, 'truth is only defensible if one believes in God. Take away God and there is no adequate safeguard against nihilism and scepticism' (1998: 23). Naturalism, these writers think, is an inadequate explanation for this ability of ours, and naturalistic accounts of realism are in any case 'vulnerable, in an atheistic context, to Nietzschean erosion' (Hebblethwaite 1988: 109). If Nietzschean atheism is right,

Nothing remains the same. Not only do traditional moral values crumble. Reality and truth, as well, are evaporated away. Not only God, but an independent, ordered external world, to say nothing of a given human nature, dissolve. In Nietzsche's own words, 'truth is fiction', and nothing remains but sheer Promethean self-assertion and will. (Hebblethwaite 1988: 31)[42]

Thus, for Hebblethwaite even a 'common-sense realism' concerning the world of macroscopic objects is hard to defend against anti-realist

[40] S. R. L. Clark (1998, especially 17–49) has developed a Platonist argument from truth to God.
[41] See Hebblethwaite 1988: 86–7, 102–13; Markham 1998: 69–96.
[42] Cf. Markham 1998: 97–119.

'constructivism',[43] and both writers think that the decline of realism and the rise of constructivism is a consequence of the decline of objective theism. So, in order to underwrite our common-sense convictions about objective reality, we need to invoke a God who is the creator and sustainer of all that is as 'the most plausible hypothesis to account for this objectivity' (Hebblethwaite 1988: 109).

In a nutshell, the argument from truth to God is this: our deep-rooted conviction that truth is a matter of discovery and not invention is best accounted for ... on the supposition of an infinite creative Mind that makes things what they are and preserves them as what they are for us to discover. (Hebblethwaite 1988: 110)

So, the transcendental argument from truth to God claims that God is the necessary condition for our beliefs about truth and objectivity.[44]

Now, there are several problems with this argument, not the least of which are that our culture is increasingly relativist in outlook and that everything from Authorship to Zulu Nationalism via Facts, Quarks, and Reality has been regarded as socially constructed.[45] What is common-sense realism and morally absolute on one side of the street testifies to an old-fashioned 'binary opposition' and moral absolutism on the other. Although Hebblethwaite claims that it is 'very perverse' to argue that we cannot 'get outside our conceptual or linguistic skin and compare the way we see and talk about the world with how the world is in itself' (Hebblethwaite 1988: 112), in one form or another this perversity is very widely accepted (even if only rarely articulated in these terms). Transcendental arguments look for the conditions of possibility of commonly accepted beliefs, but Hebblethwaite's and Markham's starting point in our agreement about truth is by no means sufficiently well grounded in the population to which they appeal to provide a firm basis for such an argument. The question of the social construction of what we take to be real is increasingly open, and the question of whether Christianity is committed to the foundationalist account of truth and objectivity that Hebblethwaite regards as integral to realism and Christian theism is even more so.[46] So the argument from truth to God has to assume a lot before it can begin to be persuasive. By contrast, all or almost all participants in the debate about whether Christianity is realist will agree at least with the proposition that if Christians are realist, then their realism concerns the triune God who is worshipped by the

---

[43] Cf. Hebblethwaite 1988: 109–10.   [44] Cf. Markham 1998: 47–68.
[45] See the list compiled by Hacking 1999: 1.
[46] For a relatively constructivist defence of Christian realism, see Patterson 1999.

church. Indeed, this is often the starting point for repudiations of realism by Christian non-realists.

A more serious objection to Hebblethwaite and Markham emerges from the fact that in order to show that God exists as the creator, orderer, and sustainer of the universe, they rely on arguments of traditional natural theology.[47] This reliance is treacherous, however. The argument from truth to God was set up to show that the concept of truth requires the existence of God. So, if our concept of truth is to be secure we shall need to *know* that God exists. And since our knowing that God exists depends on *arguments*, we shall need to have good reason to suppose not just that our arguments for God's existence are formally valid, but that they are sound, that they are *true*: we can only claim to know that which is true. But this is problematical for Hebblethwaite and Markham: on their argument we need God to exist in order to ground our view of truth, but so far, all we have is (widely contested) arguments for God's putative existence. Without knowing that these are true we cannot know that God exists, but we cannot know that God exists without knowing that the arguments are true. The argument from truth to God requires that we can know that the arguments are true, but this is to beg the question and so render the argument viciously circular because it assumes its conclusion as a premiss.[48]

The argument is treacherous for a further reason. Hebblethwaite holds that we can best account for our conviction that truth is discovered rather than invented by supposing a divine, creative mind. But we need to ask whether a God who is the terminus of an argument can be said to have been discovered rather than invented. Perhaps, to recall *The Hitch-Hiker's Guide to the Galaxy*, God can be made to appear as easily in a puff of logic as he can to disappear. Markham is critical of Swinburne's defence of theism, for he thinks that it produces 'an irreligious view of religion ... Conversion, passion, conviction, and total love of God seem strangely inappropriate on Swinburne's account of faith. It is hardly the faith of Abraham, Isaac and Jacob' (1998: 8, 12). But is Markham's? He writes that 'The cause, the heart, and the hope of the universe are goodness and love. This is what a theist means by God. God is a being that causes all things to be.' And a little later: 'God ... is that in the absence (or presence) of which all beliefs are changed. It is a way of looking at the world' (19, 22, *sic*). I shall leave the puzzles implied by this second definition to one side and concentrate on the first. It is far from clear that the God who appears as the conclusion of Markham's

---

[47] Hebblethwaite 1988: 86–101; Markham 1998: 77–93.
[48] Hebblethwaite anticipates but does not adequately meet a similar objection in his 1982: 230.

cosmological argument is in any fundamental respects different from the God of philosophers such as Swinburne, who also offers a cosmological argument. Nor does Markham provide any argument for the view that the necessary being who is the ultimate explanation of the universe actually is goodness and love; he simply smuggles these characteristics into his definition of what a theist means by 'God'. Again, there is nothing in his cosmological argument from which it follows that the causally necessary being is actively involved in sustaining the universe (i.e. that the necessary being is to be construed on Christian or theistic lines). Thus it is not evident that Markham has avoided arguing for the deist God to which he thinks the argument from design leads.

We are therefore left in doubt as to whether the God of the argument from truth to God is a God who can evoke passion and total love – whether this God is in fact the same as the God of Abraham, Isaac, and Jacob, or whether he/it/she is in fact an idol.[49] As I shall go on to argue, Christians who wish to be realists about the triune God need to ensure that they do not confuse this God with other claimants to divinity. It is far from clear that Hebblethwaite and Markham have succeeded in this. Recall Jüngel's question 'in what sense must God be spoken of?': Hebblethwaite's and Markham's answer seems to be, 'As the ground of truth and objectivity'. But then it is not clear that they give adequate attention to the onto-logical demand that we ensure that 'our speaking is about *God*': this is the main reason to reject their transcendental argument from truth to God.

Outline of the argument of this book

I have suggested that to argue for a realism concerning God we need to begin with God in his self-revelation in Jesus Christ. This is why my argument is transcendental in structure. One can for illustrative purposes regard Jüngel's paraphrase of Barth's question – 'in what sense *must* God be spoken of in order that our speaking is about *God*?' – as setting in train a transcendental enquiry into the conditions which make this speech possible. As Jüngel shows, the most important of these is that God is regarded as 'prevenient': 'God's being *goes before* the theological question about God's being' and therefore before theological questions about the sense in which we must or indeed, can, speak of God (2001a: 9). In the case of the present argument, I

---

[49] Cf. Hebblethwaite 1988: 89; cf. 8, 97–9.

seek to show that, given that God is the prevenient *ens realissimum*, certain semantic, epistemological, and ontological conditions follow if we are to be Christian realists.[50] Because the range of issues needing to be addressed is very broad and because of the primarily linguistic focus of contemporary debate, I give most attention to the semantic rather than epistemological and ontological conditions that follow from accepting God's prevenient reality as the *ens realissimum*.

To demonstrate the importance of God's ontological status for the debate, in the next chapter we look at some problems that can arise from not beginning a defence of realism from a clear ontological commitment to the triune God. Then in chapter 3 I criticize theological realism's epistemological and semantic construal of the problematic. It will emerge that theological realism is inattentive to the distinctive 'grammar' of Christian faith. In chapters 4 and 5 I expound and criticize the arguments of D. Z. Phillips and George Lindbeck, both of whom seek by taking a grammatical approach to stress the particularities of religious forms of life. We shall see that their accounts of Christian faith and its realism are seriously but instructively flawed. Their views help us to see how God shows his independent reality through Christian practices – especially the eucharist – and to offer an account of the relationship between philosophy and theology suitable for defending realism. Taken together these chapters show how Christian faith is distorted if a Christian realism does not begin from an ontological commitment to the triune God.

In chapters 6–9 I present a positive argument for a Christocentric realism. In chapter 6 I discuss, in relation to the reconciling work of Christ, the questions of representation and meaning as they arise in contemporary literary theory and Christian theology. The fruits of my findings are then used to propose a theological account of meaning. In chapter 7 I develop a doctrine of God that is orientated to the realism problematic and suggest the considerations that should orientate theological epistemology and ontology given that God is the *ens realissimum*. With this argument in place I go on to defend in more detail realism's ontological commitment to the prevenient reality of God and argue that realism should be construed as having a regulative role over Christian faith. Chapter 8 draws together the themes of my argument by returning to the question which set it in motion, that is, of Christian speech about God. I examine some parallels between speech act theory and the doctrine of God, especially with respect to

---

[50] Jüngel 2001a and Thiemann 1985 defend God's prevenience.

some philosophical and theological consequences of promising. In the final chapter I put my argument in the context of some contemporary philosophical discussions of realism. We then return to the account of meaning proposed in chapter 6 and see how Christian realism can be fruitfully construed as God's conforming human words to his 'world' and the world to his word.

CHAPTER 2

'Limping with two different opinions'?

ON BEING A REALIST ABOUT THE LIVING GOD

What's in a name?

Our concern in this book is with being realist about God, but this implies that we already know who God is, or, to put it another way, who is God. Many theological realists assume without further examination of the topic that the God whose reality they set about depicting is the God attested in the Bible and that to argue for realism about some deity is *eo ipso* to argue for realism about this particular deity. However, it is not self-evident that these assumptions are sufficient for referential access to the living God.

For example, Soskice combines religious experience with Thomistic arguments for God's existence to support her causal theory of linguistic reference and acknowledges that 'If that which the Christian refers to as the source and cause of all bears no resemblance to God as conceived by Christianity, then he must admit himself to be so deluded as to the nature of the referent that his faith must be lost' (1985: 139; cf. 140, 152). For Soskice, the Christian refers to 'the source and cause of all', but this God might not bear any 'resemblance to God as conceived by Christianity', in which case the Christian is deluded and his faith is lost. To avoid this outcome, 'the source and cause of all' needs to be shown to be identical with 'God as conceived by Christianity', but we are not offered an argument for this. So Christian realists need to be more methodologically self-conscious in ensuring that they are indeed arguing for realism about the God of Christian faith; hence in this chapter we look at the question of the identity of this God and at some of the consequences this has for arguments for realism. In particular, I shall argue that to avoid the outcome Soskice contemplates, we need to distinguish the God of the philosophers from the triune God of Christian faith.

A second reason for being clear about the God to whom Christians intend to refer is that Christians are not the only people who claim to be able to make successful reference to a deity. In our religiously plural culture, many voices are alleged to be the voice of God, and sometimes their adherents' claims imply, in Alasdair MacIntyre's neat phrase, 'mutually exclusive ontologies' (MacIntyre 1955: 260). The demands of responding to the diversity of religions leads some concerned with what they call 'religious realism' to adopt an explicitly pluralist approach. John Hick has worked out a pluralist interpretation of religion over a long period and, by means of an argument heavily influenced by Kant, suggests that all religions finally intend the same reality, what he calls 'the Real'. Thus 'critical realism holds that the realm of religious experience is not *in toto* human projection and illusion but constitutes a range of cognitive responses, varying from culture to culture, to the presence of a transcendent reality or realities' (1989: 175).[1] Hick's views have been subjected to widespread criticism by those who repudiate pluralism,[2] as well as some who accept it. Amongst the latter, the philosopher Peter Byrne argues that 'a realist perspective on human religious thought is best represented by a pluralist view of the religions', and that 'pluralism entails a realist view of religion' (1995: viii, 167), but he attacks Hick (rightly in my view) as an epistemological idealist.[3] As I said earlier, my concern is with how realism concerning the God of the Bible can be stated and defended, and to this end I shall appeal to traditional Christology. Although I do not think that Christians should adopt an imperialist attitude to other faiths, my approach does mean that, against those who claim or assume that all faiths finally intend the same divine reality, Christians need to be clear about the identity of the particular deity whose independent reality they wish to uphold.

At the beginning of this argument it is important to point out that the theological realists we look at are all Christians and they all want to depict God's reality faithfully. Nevertheless, they give regrettably little attention to ensuring that it really is the God of the Bible to whom reference is being made. One way of clarifying the problem here is to look at the question whether 'God' is a (proper) name.[4] Some theological realists treat it as though it is and go on to assume that even if its *connotation* is not completely clear, its *denotation* is adequate to identify the God whose reality they propose to depict. They therefore acknowledge no need for further

---

[1] For a very interesting argument against Hick's Kantianism, see Mavrodes 1995.

[2] Alston (1995a) argues that Hick is a non-realist.

[3] 1995: 170–3, 177.

[4] For influential but opposing philosophical views, see Crombie 1971, e.g., 37, and Rhees 1969, e.g., 127–8. For more recent discussions, see Helm 1988: 195–217, especially 203ff; Durrant 1992; and Geach's reply (1992). Jenson (1992: 98–9) offers a trenchant critique of taking 'God' to be a proper name.

discrimination between putative deities. A typical example can be cited from Arthur Peacocke, who has done major pioneering work on the relationship between science and Christianity.[5] In his book on theological realism, *Intimations of Reality: Critical Realism in Science and Religion* (1984), he writes that 'all religious believers regard themselves as making meaningful assertions about a reality that man can and does encounter, a reality whose name is God in the Judaeo-Christian tradition' (38). Contrast this assertion with that of a Wiccan anthropologist: '[t]he Goddess is very different from the Judaeo-Christian god' (Luhrmann 1989: 46, *sic*). It is obvious from this that 'all religious believers' do not see themselves as referring to the same reality.

This view is well established in biblical tradition. The word *el*, meaning 'God', occurs in all Semitic languages and is of polytheistic derivation; because it functions generically rather than personally it is inadequate to denote personally the unique God of Israel. Similarly, in the New Testament, *theos* needs further qualification if it is to designate the one who reveals himself as 'the Father' of Jesus Christ in contrast to other 'so-called Gods' (1 Cor. 8:5, altered). It might be that there is only one God, but Paul's ontological point is obscured if we ignore the polyvalency of the term and assume that the extension of 'God' is always and exclusively YHWH, and/or 'the Father'. For the Christian who wishes to be a realist, it is not enough to say that we can successfully refer to '*a* reality whose name is God', for this is inadequate to differentiate the particular God of Christians (and Jews).[6] Christians cannot straightforwardly assume that 'God' refers to the triune God attested in Holy Scripture.[7] Furthermore, since one of the jobs a name does is to secure continuity of reference by those who use it, in a pluralist setting with many competing claimants to deity, to say that 'God' is a name – even if in post-biblical Christian tradition it has been used as if it were a proper name with clear connotation and denotation – is now too vague for successful, historically continuous reference to the biblical God. We need to be more precise about *which* God we intend to refer to.

The living God names himself

These issues are neither new nor exclusively philosophical. Moses was not (or at least not obviously) interested in philosophical questions when he

---

[5] For discussions of broader aspects of his work than those I focus on, see Polkinghorne 1996; Knight 2001, especially 7–22.

[6] In my view Christians and Jews worship the same God, but this would be rejected by many Jews (cf. Halbertal and Margalit 1992: 150).

[7] The pervasiveness of this misconception is evident in that it creeps even into the work of the Church of England's Doctrine Commission: see Doctrine Commission 1987: 29, but cf. 66–103.

asked the name of the God who, at the burning bush, promised deliverance
for his people.[8] His interest was more immediate and existential. As Robert
Jenson puts it, 'If Israel was to risk the future of this God, to leave secure
political nonexistence in Egypt and venture on his promises, Israel had
first and fundamentally to know which future this was' (1982: 2). The God
who encounters Moses answers by revealing his name, YHWH (Exod.
3:14f).[9] In order to uphold the holiness of God the tetragrammaton was
not pronounced, so this name appears to have become vocalized in Hebrew
through assimilation to *adonai* meaning 'lord'. Now *adonai*, like *el*, is
not a proper name, though YHWH is, so strictly speaking, 'Lord' is not
God's proper name, but it has become the accepted translation (often
capitalized) of YHWH, so following widespread custom I will treat it as
though it is.[10] The point is that in Hebrew tradition, God renders himself
identifiable by means of his name. Indeed, the continuing existence of the
tradition depends on its use of this name, for, as YHWH says, 'This is my
name forever, this my designation in every generation' (Exod. 3:15, Childs's
translation, 1974: 48, *sic*). However, even though God reveals his name, its
subsequent, punning elaboration in the phrase (which will become very
important in my exposition of a Christocentric realism) *ehyeh asher ehyeh*
('I am who I am', or, 'I will be who I will be') immediately reminds us that
human beings cannot possess this God by his name and that even in his
self-revealing, he remains hidden.

Ancient Israel was aware that there is a class of entities denominated by
the generic term 'God', but the Old Testament claims that the God of Israel
is the God of Gods – that the God named YHWH is pre-eminent amongst
the Gods. It is notable that the New Testament retains the same outlook
concerning the pre-eminence of this God, though its writers modify Jewish
monotheism by confessing it in Christological terms and identifying God
as the one whom the Lord Jesus Christ called 'Father'.[11] As Bauckham says
of Phil. 2:9 and Heb. 1:4, 'the exalted Jesus is given the divine name, the
Tetragrammaton (YHWH), the name which names the unique identity of
the one God, the name which is exclusive to the one God in a way that the
sometimes ambiguous word "god" is not' (1998: 34).

Jews and Christians are not just talking about '*a* reality whose name is
God'; this would be to think, mistakenly, that *el* or *theos* is the name of

---

[8] N. T. Wright (1992: xivf, 471–6) rehearses these concerns suggestively in relation to contemporary
New Testament studies.

[9] The discussions of the exegetical and theological dimensions of the relevant biblical texts by Seitz
(1998: 229–62) and van Beeck (1994: 9–24) are particularly illuminating.

[10] For a clear if slightly dated discussion, see Childs 1974: 50, 60–89.

[11] Note also the 'I am' sayings in John's Gospel. On the New Testament developments of Jewish
monotheism, see Bauckham 1998 *passim*.

the living God. Rather, they are talking about the God who names himself YHWH, the one who, when forbidding his people to have any other Gods before him, introduces himself with the words 'I am YHWH, your *elohim*' (Exod. 20:2). Those who live and think in the stream of this faith and who wish to be realists about its source need to take care to be realists about the biblical God, for, to quote Jenson again, 'That God has some proper name ... means among other things that not all addresses to deity are equally true, that it is possible to be in simple error at the very base of religious life' (1982: 185–6).[12]

Name and narrative

In the biblical tradition, the Lord renders himself identifiable through historical deeds in which he reveals his name and nature, and by which he accomplishes the salvation of his people. Commenting on the story of Moses' call, Christopher Seitz amplifies this theme in the following terms:

God's name is in fact *ehyeh asher ehyeh*. That is, God's name is the most personal revelation of God's own character, and as such is not a proper name in the strict sense (like Jim or Sally), but a name appropriate to God's character as God. In this case, God's 'name' consists of a disclosure of purpose; it 'means' something approaching 'In the manner that I am, or will be, I am who I am.' Yet neither we nor Moses is prepared to understand such a 'name' yet, because what God will be, and is most essentially, has not yet been made manifest. (1998: 239, cf. 243)

Nevertheless, we need to bear in mind that, as Brevard Childs has argued, through God's act of self-identification a genuine knowledge of God is given: 'God's initiative in making himself known tends to encompass all the various times into the one great act of disclosure. To know God's name is to know his purpose for all mankind from the beginning to the end' (1974: 119). However, the name revealed to Moses is not a *definition* of God's nature, that is,

in the sense of a philosophical statement about his being ... a suggestion, for example, of his absoluteness, aseity, etc. Such a thing would be altogether out of keeping with the Old Testament. The whole narrative context leads right away to the expectation that Jahweh intends to impart something – but this is not what he is, but what he will show himself to be to Israel. (von Rad 1975: 180)

In the New Testament's perspective the revelation of God's saving purposes in history is consummated in the coming of God's incarnate Son and Messianic agent with whom he shares his nature. Thus, we find there

---

[12] *Pace* the Preface of the NRSV Bible.

an implicit trinitarianism in which Jesus Christ fully identifies the God whose identity has been unfolded in the historical events to which the biblical narrative bears witness – that is, 'the God and Father of our Lord Jesus Christ' (2 Cor. 1:3; Eph. 1:3; 1 Pet. 1:3).[13] In this regard, notice also the primitive credal formula 'Jesus is Lord' (Rom. 10:9), which is truly pronounced only by the urging of the Spirit (1 Cor. 12:3). Similarly, but more elaborately, the Apocalypse echoes the Old Testament's theology of the divine name: 'the Lord God' declares 'I am the Alpha and Omega ... who is and who was and who is to come, the Almighty [= *pantokrator* (LXX) = *sabaoth* and *shaddai*]' (Rev. 1:8). It is highly significant that a few verses later 'one like a son of man' (who we are to understand is the exalted Jesus) says to John, 'I am the first and the last, the living one', and then at the end of the book 'the Christ claims the title affirmed by the Lord God Almighty in 1:8' (Beasley-Murray 1974: 338–9), and says, 'I am the Alpha and the Omega, the first and the last, the beginning and the end' (22:13). Thus in both Testaments we find the same close relationship between name and nature: the living God is the triune one whose purpose is to save.

About which God should those who name themselves after the Lord Jesus Christ be realists? About the God who led Israel out of Egypt and raised Jesus from the dead. This God is the self-revealing one to whom Jesus referred as 'Father', in internal relation to whom he titled himself 'Son', and from whom the one he identified as Holy Spirit would be sent. Thus, for Christians, the triune name 'Father, Son, and Holy Spirit' is, as Jenson puts it, 'God's true name' (1995: 32).[14] This name identifies the one who created them, reconciled them, and gave them the life of the new creation; that is, the one whose identity is narrated in the Bible. It therefore gives Christians specific and continuing referential access to the living God. As Jenson has pointed out, the triune name compresses into one identity both the name and the identifying descriptions contained in such narrative phrases as 'the Lord is the one who delivered Israel from Egypt' and 'the Lord is the one who raised Jesus from the dead'. Thus it

uniquely identifies the God of the gospel, recounting at once the *personae* and the basic plot of the scriptural story ... Thus the phrase, 'Father, Son, and Holy Spirit' is simultaneously a very compressed telling of the total narrative by which scripture identifies God and a personal name for the God so identified; in it, name and narrative description not only appear together, as at the beginning of the Ten Commandments, but are identical. (1997: 45–6)

---

[13] Cf. Caird 1980: 51; Seitz 1998: 258ff.

[14] In addition to Seitz's fundamentally important paper on 'The Divine Name in Christian Scripture' (1998: 251–62), see also Jenson 1997: 42–74 and Zizioulas 1995: 59f.

Thus, if they are to avoid the 'simple error' of mis-addressing God, Christians who wish to be realists should orientate their arguments for realism around the narrated identity of this self-revealing and self-naming deity.

'Protocols against idolatry'

Jenson has just alluded to the Decalogue. Part of the intention of the first commandment – 'You shall have no other gods before me' (Exod. 20:3) – is clearly to rivet Israel's addresses to deity to the one who identifies himself in these terms: 'I am the Lord your God, who brought you out of the land of Egypt' (Exod. 20:2). Being a realist about the biblical God not only means avoiding erroneously addressing God; it also means avoiding idolatry, as the second commandment makes apparent. The divine name is given to God's people as the surety of his saving presence with them and good will for them. In revealing his name, God calls his people into a covenant relationship with himself, and on the human side this means that God's people should 'hallow' it and protect it from profanation. Christian realists therefore need to be alert to the possibility of idolatry not just for the sake of theological correctness, but for God's sake. YHWH is a 'jealous' God because in creating them and reconciling them to himself he has yoked his name and nature to his people: his repute is implicated in their (un)faithfulness. '[T]he issue at stake turns on guarding the purity of God's self-revelation lest Israel confuse its own image with that of God's': idolatry can become 'a threat to the divine nature' (Childs 1985: 67, 68).

Two episodes from the Old Testament are particularly helpful in bringing out the relevance of idolatry to our theme. The religious consequences of the schism between Jeroboam and Rehoboam (1 Kgs. 11:26–12:33) show that idolatry can arise from a desire to secure YHWH's will for human ends and hence that accusations of idolatry are not principally or exclusively to be located in polemics against other religions. As it turned out, Jeroboam harboured manipulative intentions, and part of the reason is that he had chosen to ignore the association of the name of YHWH with the exodus. In the second case, Ahab, the least of whose mistakes was to follow Jeroboam's example, set up Baal worship in Israel. Now, if the former episode is ambiguous, this one makes it clear that idolatry can arise from a lapsed intention to give exclusive service to YHWH and from a divided loyalty, inspired partly perhaps by a desire to buttress an apparently threatened position (a point of relevance to contemporary Christianity in the West). So granted that idolatry *has* arisen amongst God's people, it needs to be admitted as at least a possibility amongst his people now – as indeed it has been in several contemporary discussions of theological language, though, interestingly enough, more by those opposed to relatively traditional theology.[15]

The preceding discussion suggests that there are three interwoven ways in which idolatry can arise and that to these there correspond three ways of avoiding it, which, following Nicholas Lash, can be termed 'protocols against idolatry'.[16] First, approach God by the triune *name* through which he has granted his people the ability to know and call upon him; second, adhere to the *narrative* of the events through which he has revealed his character and in which he has vindicated his name; and third, uphold the *norm* expressed in the first two commandments.

In the light of these considerations of the name and identity of the biblical God, we come now to criticize theological realism concerning its lack of nuance on the relationship between the God of objective theism and the triune God identified in scripture. In the terms of Elijah's address on Mt Carmel when the 'LORD, God of Abraham, Isaac, and Israel' vindicated himself against the worshippers of Baal (1 Kgs. 18:21, 36), it can be interpreted as inadvertently 'limping with two different opinions' about God.

THE FALSE ASSIMILATION OF CHRISTIAN FAITH TO THEISM

Theological realists tend to assimilate Christian faith to 'objective theism', 'philosophical theism', or 'Christian theism'.[17] Theism is a philosophers' abstraction denoting what they take to be the core beliefs of, usually, the Western religious tradition.[18] Its characteristic features tend to be defined by a concern to articulate in conceptual terms these core beliefs and to defend them against the charge that the beliefs in question are irrational, not justified, or lacking in warrant. The defence of theism that most appeals to theological realists is that which holds that belief in a God is justified by the explanatory power of that belief. Thus, for example, in attacking Cupitt, Hebblethwaite holds that 'Christianity is committed to objective theism' (1993: 210) and adduces explanatory power as a decisive argument in favour

---

[15] In addition to Kaufman 1993, see McFague 1982; and, following her, Barbour 1990: 49ff.

[16] Whilst I agree with the content of Lash's protocols (1988: 210ff), and mine do not contradict his, the content of mine is different.

[17] For a recent articulation of a version of 'Christian theism', see Swinburne 1994. Theologians will note its almost total disregard of the narrative content of Christian faith.

[18] See Swinburne 1977: 1 and Plantinga 2000: vi.

of theological realism.[19] In *The Justification of Science and the Rationality of Religious Belief* (1990), Michael Banner argues for a realist construal of religious belief on the basis of an argument for what he calls 'rational realism' in the philosophy of science.[20] His argument is grounded on two claims: first, that realism in science is justified on the ground that it is the best explanation for the success of its theories (the so-called 'abductive' argument for realism), and second, that realist religious faith can 'be founded upon the explanatory justification of religious belief which the theist is encouraged to advance by reflection on the currently favoured defence of scientific realism' (99).

Theological realists frequently reinforce their appeal to the explanatory power of theism by making the further claim that the explanatory use of models is essential to the case for realism. Barbour clearly implies this when he proposes that 'models of an unobservable God are used to interpret new patterns of experience in human life' (1974: 49, cf. 140ff). Likewise, Soskice insists that 'Christian theism has been undeniably realist about [its] models ... If we wish to maintain that there are structures in theistic reflection which can legitimately be called models, we must take them to be explanatory' (1985: 108, 109; cf. 97–117). In a more muted way, Peacocke bases his panentheistic realism on the view that 'theological models purport to be explanatory' (1984: 44). All these thinkers clearly assimilate realist Christian faith to theism. It is not always evident how deep the assimilation goes, and though most of the theological realists we examine use the language of theism, not all explicitly regard it as a position needing philosophical justification.[21] Nevertheless, their arguments are sufficiently shaped by theism to justify our taking a closer look at the baneful influences of the assimilation and for establishing a methodological cordon sanitaire between philosophical theism and a Christocentric realism.

I shall do this by arguing for two propositions: (A) that one way of avoiding idolatry is to adopt a methodological distinction between the God of philosophical theism and the triune, biblical God, and (B) that central elements of Christian faith resist explanation. Taken together, these propositions undermine the value to Christian realists of assimilating Christianity to theism and suggest that the realism of the Christian faith should be shown in a way that does not involve appealing to theism.

---

[19] See 1988: 7–8, 57, 86ff. Contrast Cupitt 1980: 28.

[20] Banner now writes from a more Barthian perspective: see his 1999.

[21] Barbour is ambivalent: see 1974: 53, 125. Soskice also is ambivalent: see 1985: 138, 141; cf. 148. In her later paper on 'Theological Realism', she seems to attach her causal theory of reference to the cosmological argument (see 1987: 115; cf. Forsman 1990: 123–42).

Proposition A: One way of avoiding idolatry is to adopt
a methodological distinction between the God of philosophical
theism and the triune, biblical God

There is a well-established tradition of thought in which the God of the philosophers is distinguished from the God of Abraham, Isaac, Jacob, and Jesus. In case it is thought that this is a distinction currently favoured only by benighted fideists, note that the philosopher of religion Stephen T. Davis – no advocate of fideism – begins his *Logic and the Nature of God* (1983) by telling us that 'This is a book about the nature of God', and then immediately asks, 'But which God?' (1983: 1). The possibilities he has in mind become clear at the conclusion of his argument when he writes that 'the God who has revealed himself to us [in Jesus Christ] is a profound rejection of the God of philosophy' (150).[22]

It is arguable that the distinction Davis implies made its first appearance on the evening of Monday 23 November 1654 – Pascal's so-called *nuit de feu* when, according to the parchment sewn into his clothing and found after his death, he had written

From about half past ten in the evening until half past midnight.
                                   Fire.
'God of Abraham, God of Isaac, God of Jacob', not of philosophers and scholars.
Certainty, certainty, heartfelt, joy, peace.
God of Jesus Christ.
God of Jesus Christ.
My God and your God. (1995: p. 285)[23]

This is not the place to go into the debate about whether the God of the philosophers is identical with the God of Jesus and the Patriarchs in detail,[24] but it seems to me that a divergence occurs in Christian tradition around this time and that the movement of thought against which Pascal reacted was precipitated in large measure by Descartes's philosophy and provoked by at least the following closely related factors: (1) a reaction against late medieval Nominalist and absolutist views of God and towards

---

[22] For New Testament caution about philosophy, recall Col. 2:8. In the Patristic period, recall Justin's and Origen's defences of Christianity against the charge that it is atheistic. For contemporary estimates of that debate, see Lonergan 1996: 11–32, especially 22–7; Pannenberg 1971: 119–83; Stead 1994: 120–35; and Zizioulas 1995: 52f.

[23] Cf. §§149, 189–92, 588, 781.

[24] The Church of England's Doctrine Commission is ambivalent (if not muddled): whilst it repudiates the God of the philosophers, it also regards Christianity as one of several 'brands of theism' (Doctrine Commission 1987: 56, 104). Historical evidence and argument concerning the distinction can be found in Buckley 1987. See also Tomlin 1999: 207–27, 248–50; van Beeck 1994: 1–8; and Jüngel 1983: ix, xiv, 110f.

human autonomy;[25] (2) a recourse to a 'perfect being theology' where God's principal function is epistemically to reassure the human ego whose imperfection is shown by its capacity for doubt. This is particularly clear in Descartes's work.[26] Although perfect being theology is not accepted by all philosophers of religion, much contemporary theism is indebted to it. Theism is often motivated by challenges from atheists who see God as morally repugnant to an autonomous humanity and who argue that the onus of proof lies on believers to show that God exists and that Christian faith is rationally warranted. And theism continues to function as a support for an epistemological superstructure: to answer the 'why' questions raised at the limit of science but which it is unable to meet.

It is diagnostic of this fateful divergence in Christian tradition that (in Davis's terminology) God begins to be 'used' for philosophical purposes and that this use is regulated by philosophical rather than biblical conceptions.[27] Davis's suggestion that the God of the philosophers and the biblical God 'are two different beings' (148) might be considered by some – especially those smitten by 'rational theology' – to be too extreme.[28] But he seems to me bang on target when he contrasts the personal, providential rule of the Lord with the God of the philosophers who 'is ruled by us: [who] plays a role in a metaphysical system we have devised. [Who] is primarily the object of our theorizing' (148). The demands of rational coherence rather than scripture dominate theistic conceptions of God and his attributes.[29] For example, on Jüngel's reading of Descartes, one of God's attributes or 'perfections' is that he is 'the most intelligent essence. But', Jüngel continues,

intelligence is thought of here primarily according to the model of power. And theologically that is problematic. Highest intelligence here excludes all weakness, vulnerability, powerlessness. That calls forth theological mistrust ... [F]aith in the crucified God forces us to contest the view that God is an absolutely invulnerable essence. (1983: 123)[30]

It is apparent that there are good grounds for a realism which is concerned with the God who revealed himself in Jesus Christ to mistrust

---

[25] See Kasper 1983: 17ff.   [26] See Jüngel 1983: 111–26.   [27] See Davis 1983: 147, 149, 150.
[28] From a theological perspective, Davis's phrase might impugn the view of 'so-called gods' expressed in 1 Cor. 8:5 (cf. Fee 1987: 371–6). In my view, Christians need to recover biblical henotheism – a combination of what the philosopher George Mavrodes has called 'descriptive polytheism' and 'cultic monotheism' (1995, especially 264–5; cf. Seitz 1998: 251–62).
[29] On coherence as a criterion, see Swinburne 1977, especially 149–61.
[30] Cf. Moltmann 1974: 267ff. Understandings of God's omnipotence provide interesting grounds for contrasting the God of the philosophers and the God who revealed himself in Jesus; see here Barth 1966: 46–9, with which compare Swinburne 1994: 151–8 and Mavrodes 1995: 268.

methodologies which depend on philosophical theism. Forgetfulness of the yoke between the triune God's name and nature and therefore also forgetfulness of the historical grounding of God's identity increasingly lead philosophical theism into an understanding of God which puts God to human use and is, as we shall see, tantamount to idolatry.

In contrast to the stream of tradition which tends to 'use' God, Augustine drew a fundamental ontological distinction between those things given to us to 'use' and those that we are to 'enjoy'. Of the latter, the first mentioned is 'the Father, the Son, and the Holy Spirit' (1958: I.III.3–I.V.5). His fundamental philosophical and theological orientation is expressed in a passage composed soon after his conversion: 'I am resolved never to deviate ... from the authority of Christ, for I find none more powerful. But as to what is attainable by acute and accurate reasoning, such is my state of mind that I am impatient to grasp what truth is ... not only by belief, but also by comprehension' (*Contra academicos*, III.20.43, quoted in 1974²: 25). Likewise, although Anselm's philosophical theology was clearly located in a Christian and scripturally authorized context[31] – the ontological argument(s) in the *Proslogion* is (are) addressed to God as prayer[32] – recent versions of it have often been far less so. It is owing to ambivalence about context and authorization and especially about the relationship between philosophy and 'fundamental theology' on the one hand and that between 'fundamental theology' and dogmatic theology on the other that theological realism has been misled by its use of philosophical theism, even when the desire to be faithful to Christian tradition is obvious. In brief, what seems to have happened is that an Enlightenment-inspired and apologetically conceived philosophical agenda has insinuated itself into Christian philosophical reflection. This agenda has co-opted for its own purposes, and in the process distorted, Christian desire to uphold the integrity of speech about the triune God. Lacking confidence in the gospel of the foolishness and weakness of God in the face of the world's strength and wisdom, Christians have sometimes confused the triune God with the God of the philosophers.[33] Theological concern to conserve the integrity of God's *name* and to bear intellectual witness to his *character* has been increasingly eclipsed by preoccupation with defending the logical coherence of an abstract *concept* of

---

[31] Against misleading earlier interpretations, it is now clear that Aquinas belonged to this tradition: see Hibbs 1995; Lash 1996: 140–7; and Rogers 1996.

[32] Anselm 1979, e.g. II. See also van Beeck 1994: 53–68.

[33] The widespread resurgence of interest in the doctrine of the Trinity is a welcome sign that this trend is waning.

God and her/his/its *attributes* from which biblical narrative conceptions have been almost totally eviscerated.[34]

I suggest therefore that there is a good case for adopting a methodology that minimizes the chances of assimilating the triune God to the God of the philosophers, especially when there is a contemporary stream of thought which has denounced it and denied any need for making the assimilation. The Catholic theologian Walter Kasper has argued that modern theism is an ill-begotten child of the Enlightenment and suggested that 'From the theological standpoint we must speak of the heresy of theism ... [It] almost necessarily falls under the suspicion voiced by the critics of religion, that the theistic God is a projection of the human ego and a hypostatized idol, or that theism is ultimately a form of idolatry' (1983: 294–5, cf. 285f, 315). Rowan Williams brings the dangers here into sharp relief when he writes that:

There is a way of talking about God that simply projects on to him what we cannot achieve – a systematic vision of the world as a necessarily inter-related whole. Trust in such a God is merely deferred confidence in the possibility of exhaustive explanation and justification; and deferred confidence of this sort is open to exactly the same moral and logical objection as any other confidence in systemic necessity of this kind in the world. A God whose essential function is to negate the 'otherness' and discontinuity of historical experience, and so to provide for us an ideal *locus standi*, a perspective transcending or reconciling discontinuity into system, is clearly an idol, and an incoherent one at that ... [E]ven if such a form of theism were capable of intelligible statement and defence, it would hardly be compatible with the Christian doctrine of God as loving and active 'in his own right', irrespective of there being a world. (2000: 155–6)

Williams's account of how idolatry can arise *within* traditional ways of 'talking about God' complements the view of the Jewish philosophers Moshe Halbertal and Avishai Margalit. They describe the philosophers' 'abstraction' of God as an 'idolatrous error' *inserted into* biblical tradition: 'the God that appears in the Bible is a living God and not the abstract God of the philosophers ... the concept of an abstract divinity should not be inserted into the Bible' (1992: 135, 134). Either way, if theism is indeed an idolatrous heresy and we accept the protocols against idolatry I proposed above, the issue is, What is the Christian doctrine of God?

The writers we have just heard from suggest that theism is not essential to that doctrine. After asserting that contemporary theism is 'unchristian' and describing the God of the philosophers as a 'most unchristian entity',

[34] Again, the work of Swinburne is typical: see 1994.

Nicholas Lash argues that 'the doctrine of the Trinity simply *is* the Christian doctrine of God. Accordingly, any doctrine of God which has ceased to be trinitarian in character has ceased to be Christian' (1986: 185, 183). Joining the chorus of denunciation, Kenneth Surin suggests that 'theological utterance [will be left] in irreparable disarray' unless we 'abjure ... [t]he divinity of modern theism' and speak of God 'in an irreducibly *trinitarian* way' (1986: 7, 5, 6). This suggests, first, that if they are to avoid 'whoring after false gods' (Lash 1986: 187) or 'limping with two different opinions' (1 Kgs. 18:21), Christians who wish to be realist about the triune God should observe the trinitarian protocols against idolatry I enumerated above and orientate their thinking by those events in which this God has revealed himself. Second, if theism is not essential to but rather detracts from a Christian doctrine of God, it is important that the method we adopt in articulating the realism of the Christian faith maintains a critical distance from it. As I have already pointed out, the theological realists we consider are all Christians and do not exemplify an absolute form of the position that I, following their lead, am calling 'theological realism'. However, their views might be less ambiguous and open to misinterpretation if they were clearer on the fundamental methodological options we are considering.

To introduce my next proposition we consider the relationship between theism and theodicy. Williams's description of the tendency of idolatry to negate otherness is expressed in the context of a discussion of suffering and of explanation as a way of forgetting it *as* suffering. More generally, he suggests that idolatry will seek to 'reconcile discontinuity into system'. This should give theological realists pause. Theological realism is concerned with the question of how theological language can depict reality. They claim to base their models on religious experience, but if theism tends to negate aspects of experience, theological realists' appeals to it in their argument might lead them to obscure the very contexts in which the God whose reality they wish to depict has in fact depicted himself – in the suffering of crucifixion, for example. As we shall see, the Christ-event and the experiences it gives rise to are radically interruptive of and discontinuous with theistic systematizing. On the contrary, they are resistant to explanation in more general terms, and attempts to explain them in alien categories can only be made at the cost of altering their nature.

Proposition B: Central elements of Christian faith resist explanation

To illustrate the point just made and to develop my second proposition I turn to examine a debate between a New Testament scholar and a theological realist about the Christ-event and then look at some abiding aspects of Christian experience which flow from that event.

The Christ-event

In his classic work *The Origin of Christology* (1977), C. F. D. Moule describes the occurrence in the New Testament (and especially the Pauline writings) of 'an understanding and experience of [the risen] Christ as corporate'. Moule goes on to argue that this is 'evidence of [Christ's] special status' (47, 48), but he readily admits that the conception of Christ as corporate is 'extraordinary' (48) and that he himself had viewed it with suspicion. Nevertheless, he insists that 'what causes the puzzlement is a phenomenon that undoubtedly does present itself within the New Testament, explain it how one may; and that it does seem there to be a new phenomenon' (51). 'I am not optimistic enough', he concludes,

to imagine that I can even give a satisfactory account of the Pauline phenomenon – let alone explain it; but I do believe that it is something that throws light, albeit perplexing light, on the meaning of Jesus for Paul and is a Christological datum of great significance. (53)

In Moule's estimation this datum marks a beginning of the description of Jesus in terms appropriate to God himself.

Moule acknowledges that his scholarship has confronted him with an inexplicable 'otherness'. The question is, Shall we negate it so as to bring it into continuity with other views we hold,[35] or shall we attenuate the 'data' so as to make them fit our previously held theories? The second strategy seems to be preferred by Peacocke, a former biochemist. Discussing the meaning of 'incorporation into Christ' he writes that 'the concept of solidarity seems too vacuous in any sense other than the biological, for it to be the foundation of a theory of the work of Christ ...' (1971: 172, quoted by Moule 1977: 49). So, to make sense of Paul's language, Peacocke employs evolutionary theory and writes of the immanent Spirit, present within the evolutionary process, whereby we can speak of the Spirit in us, rather than of our being in Christ.[36]

Now explanation involves 'laying bare the logical structure of a concept' (Ruben 1990: 10). The difference between Peacocke and Moule is that the latter seeks to uphold the integrity of the concept of the corporate Christ found in scripture whilst admitting an opacity in its logical structure and is

[35] This way of handling the apparent unassimilability of the Christ-event appears to have been rejected in New Testament times: see the repudiation of angel Christology in Hebrews 1.
[36] Peacocke still holds this view: see 1993[2]: 320–36.

content to leave the 'data' unexplained; Peacocke admits the 'data' only to dismiss them as 'vacuous' unless their logic is understood within the ambit of biological explanation. But in so doing he has not laid bare the structure of (i.e. explained) the concept at all; he has replaced it with a different concept drawn from biological science. Peacocke is keen to repudiate reductionism, but what we see here is not only methodological reductionism, but a more radical *ontological* reductionism that explains away the corporate Christ into an alien, scientific ontology.[37] Thus, to adopt the kind of scientific explanatory strategy favoured by theism and some theological realists is to risk reducing the 'data' of the Christ-event to the ontological categories of that with which science has already made us familiar. It is to negate the otherness that encounters us in Christ.

Peacocke's approach to the New Testament is also dubious on scientific grounds. The influential philosopher of science Carl Hempel argues that science should not be regarded as 'reduction to the familiar', since sometimes it is the familiar that science is concerned to explain and that therefore 'science will not hesitate to explain ... by means of concepts and principles of novel kinds that may at first be repugnant to our intuition' (1966: 83). Yet this is exactly what Peacocke seems to be doing, and it raises the possibility that his interpretative strategy is flawed on the very scientific terms he claims to value.

It is not as though the difficulties posed by the 'data' we have been examining are those of an isolated erratic in the New Testament. The Christ-event is the New Testament's *raison d'être* and, confronted by its impact upon them, its writers seem often to be at the limits of their conceptual and linguistic resources in their attempts to express its meaning. Peter Baelz has plausibly suggested that 'it was Jesus himself, in his earthly life and risen presence, that compelled his disciples to modify the logic of their theological language, rather than any misconceived attempt to speak about him in a mythological language which already lay to hand' (1972: 30). Granted, this is explanatory language, but by focussing on the puzzles generated by Jesus it leaves intact what Rowan Williams has termed the 'intractable *strangeness*' of that which is '*given*' (1979: 1) in the New Testament witness. So I am not attacking all attempts at explanation in theology; rather I am attacking a tendency of theists and theological realists to explain too much. How much is too much? When the explanations tendered distort rather than

---

[37] On methodological and ontological reductionism, see Peacocke 1984: 35; cf. 1993²: 39–41. For Peacocke's Christology, see 1993²: 288–9, 293–5, 300–11. McGrath seems in danger of making the same mistake as Peacocke when his use of Niels Bohr's principle of complementarity in quantum physics leads him to appear to endorse a functional Christology (1998: 204, but cf. 205).

lay bare the structure of the concept or reality being explained.[38] In the New Testament, explanation is a hermeneutical concept characterized by a desire to lay bare the structure of the Christ-event in such a way that disciples can enter into it more fully.[39] To attempt to explain in the sense required by theological realists would be a *metabasis eis allo genos*, but it is my contention that the foolish acts of God are not consistently explicable in terms of 'Greek' wisdom.[40]

If the Christ-event is inexplicable in terms other than those which respect its intrinsic nature, Christians should be cautious in their deployment of the language of explanation lest in using it they conceal what the Christ-event reveals. The language in which this event is brought to speech by the writers of the New Testament is challenging, difficult, and sometimes deeply culturally alien, but this does not give Christians liberty to dismiss it. Nor does it warrant our attempts to 'explain' it on a Procrustean bed of categories which negate what is difficult and alien, as though the events expressed by that language would be more tractable to understanding if we did. I suggest therefore that scientific explanations, or explanations in terms of scientific methodology, should not be made arbiters of what is credible in theology.

Explanation and suffering in Christian experience

Reflecting on his missionary experiences Paul wrote, 'We are afflicted in every way, but not crushed; perplexed but not driven to despair; persecuted, but not forsaken; struck down, but not destroyed...' (2 Cor. 4:8–9). Atheists often hold that in the face of the evidence of suffering, Christians should give up their faith, especially given the disproportion between the burdens of suffering they are called upon to bear and the apparent fragility of the theistic *hypothesis* they suppose all Christians share. Conversely, many philosophical apologists for theism freely admit that the existence of suffering is the most difficult feature of reality for a theist to explain. These difficulties notwithstanding, on account of the crucifixion of Jesus, suffering is an ineradicable feature of Christian faith. Moreover, attempted explanations and philosophical arguments go back and forth and yet many still find Christian faith a living option. And that not despite but in the face

---

[38] The classic use of explanatory arguments within theology is that by G. F. Woods (1958). He is notably more conservative than Peacocke in the respect he shows to the limits the incarnation imposes on explaining.

[39] Cf. Mark. 4:34 on Jesus explaining 'everything' (*epeluen panta*) to his disciples, where 'everything' refers to the relation between Jesus and 'the secret of the kingdom' (4:11).

[40] Cf. 1 Cor. 1:22–5.

of the frank admission of there being 'a great deal of evidence to suggest that [the natural environment] bears the more the mark of a horrible joke than a vale of soul-making' (MacKinnon 1979: 120). Donald MacKinnon reminds us of Job:

a classical example of a man defeated in the attempt existentially to reconcile experience of personal catastrophe with confession of beneficent and just design; an attempt set in hand because the subject of experience is, by formation, initially predisposed to subsume the hammer blows that rain upon him under some general laws which would enable him to receive each shattering experience as, for example, ultimately remedial. (126)

So MacKinnon concludes, 'No form of the [explanatory] "argument from design" has ever silenced the cry elicited by tragic experience' (127). (Although suffering can and does cause people to lose their faith, this loss is more an existential reaction than a decision based on a revised calculation of the balance of probabilities where suffering is now regarded as making the probability of God's existence smaller than it was once held to be. Indeed, such a cold calculation would in its own way amount to as much of a negation of the experience of suffering as do theoretical theodicies.)

Yet Job and Paul went on believing and trusting. Paul's 'explanation' of his suffering (in 2 Cor. 4:8, 10–12, for example) is not intended to negate it but to direct us to the irreducible, unassimilable, and therefore inexplicable agonies of the cross, and thereby also to the 'God of all consolation' (2 Cor. 1:3) revealed in the resurrection. Paul's sufferings are the credentials, even the *esse*, of his apostolic ministry: they bear witness to and bring to effect the fruits of the death and resurrection of Christ among his churches.[41] So even if Christians see their suffering as part of God's wider purpose, this perception does not constitute an *explanation* of their suffering as required by theistic apologists, for it is always mediated by the cross and chastened by the inscrutable demands of discipleship.

Suffering is of the essence of the faith of those called by Christ to take up their cross and follow him,[42] so to negate it by absorbing it into a theistic teleology would be to cut faith from its vivifying source and goal, the triune God.

All explanation of suffering [i.e. 'into comprehensive explanatory systems'] is an attempt to forget it *as* suffering, and so a quest for untruthfulness; and it is precisely this kind of untruthfulness that is served ... by anti-realism ... The resolution of

---

[41] Cf. Gal. 6:17. On the constitutive role of suffering in Paul's ministry, see A. T. Hanson 1987 and A. E. Harvey 1996.
[42] Matt. 16:24, cf. 10:38.

the sheer resistant particularity of suffering, past and present, into comfortable teleological patterns is bound to blunt the edge of particularity, and so to lie; and this lying resolution contains that kind of failure in attention that is itself a moral deficiency, a fearful self-protection. (Rowan Williams 1989: 78)[43]

The connection Williams suggests between explanatory systems and anti-realism is highly significant, and it prompts the thought that had Paul's faith been an indulgence of self-protection against the evidence resulting in a wilful evasion of suffering, then it is possible that there would have been no Christianity to be assimilated to theism.

In Christian understanding, suffering cannot be explained away or absorbed into some higher metaphysical scheme without concealing its significance as *Christian* suffering – as a consequence of taking up one's cross and following Christ. Moreover, the Gospel tells us that '[i]nstead of explaining our suffering God shares it' (Wolterstorff 1987: 81) and that in the resurrection of Christ, he has conquered it.[44] This is why Christians' beliefs are bonded to their lives with 'a security which seems to be greater than an account of their beliefs as "hypotheses" would warrant' (Banner 1990: 94, cf. 112–16). Unless God had undergone suffering in the man Jesus there would not have been a full divine incarnation or reconciliation between humanity and God. Only because Christ assumed our full humanity, including our suffering, are we able to re-present him in and through our fallen-but-restored humanity, and this, as we shall see in chapter 6, is a significant clue as to how a Christian realism should be articulated.

Much of this chapter has been devoted to arguing the importance of distinguishing between true and false Gods in order to be realists about the living God, but we should remember that none is immune from the temptation to idolatry, especially self-idolatry. So before turning to more detailed criticism of theological realism and lest any become complacent – particularly those prone to over-confidence in their own theological rectitude – it is well to remember the following.

[I]t is as we seek to evade the Exile and the cross that we create idols ... But the real God, even and primally for himself, has the face of the Suffering Servant; so if we want images of immunity or serenity, we have to make them up for ourselves, whether we hew them like second Isaiah's God-carvers or deploy them in the sophisticated mind's eye or practice theology. (Jenson 2000: 10–11)

---

[43] Williams draws here on the profound theological and philosophical insights of MacKinnon 1965, especially 99.

[44] For a theological repudiation of the view that suffering requires philosophical explanation, see Weinandy 2000, especially 32, 261f, 282.

CHAPTER 3

Taking leave of theological realism

I have argued that theological realism is imprecise about the identity of the God whose mind-independent reality its exponents wish to defend and that it underestimates the problems arising from inadequately distinguishing the God of the philosophers from the triune God of Christian faith. In this chapter we explore the ways in which these difficulties ramify into the heart of theological realism.[1] I shall argue that in their use of analogies with the defence of realism in the philosophy of science, theological realists make a 'category mistake'. To adapt Gilbert Ryle's definition, they represent the 'grammar' of God's existence as if it 'belonged to one logical type or category' – in this case, that of science – 'when actually [it] belong[s] to another' (Ryle 1963: 17). Theological realists' methodological outlook is controlled more by the philosophy of science than God's self-revelation in Christ.[2] This category mistake has important epistemological and ontological ramifications and suggests that Christians should take leave of theological realism for a more Christologically nuanced understanding of realism orientated by the triune God.[3]

After an introduction to the debate between realist and empiricist perspectives in science and theology, we examine a number of methodological analogies between science and theology presupposed by theological realists. However, it will emerge that from both philosophical and theological perspectives there are significant disanalogies between the two disciplines. Of these, the most central to the case made by theological realists is the claim

---

[1] Some of this chapter has already been published in my 2000.
[2] On Ian Barbour's typology of ways of relating science and religion, they tend to the 'dialogue/integration' end of the spectrum rather than the 'conflict/independence' end (1990: 3–30). Of the writers we study, Polkinghorne is the most cautious about 'assimilation' (which he thinks Barbour tends towards), seeing himself as a 'revisionist' seeking 'consonance' between the disciplines without compromising the autonomy of theology (1996: 81–6).
[3] It should be noted with regret that the Church of England's Doctrine Commission's report *We Believe in God* is heavily influenced by the line of argument criticized in this chapter (see Doctrine Commission 1987: 25–31, 34–46).

that both they and scientific realists are concerned to defend realism concerning unobservable entities. I argue that this involves a false assimilation and that it misrepresents both (the philosophy of) science and theology. This argument leads to the conclusion that theological realism has not yet successfully defended a realism appropriate to Christian faith and that insofar as theological realism is offered as a defence of realism concerning scripture's God, it is inadequate to that project.

EMPIRICISM AND REALISM IN THEOLOGY AND SCIENCE

Realists in both theology and science are concerned to combat the anti-realist consequences of empiricism. We look first at the religious case.[4] Although advocates of positions taken to be anti-realist or non-realist about religion are keen to deny that they are atheists, they radically revise their understanding of religious language. They typically argue that it is meaningful and continue to use it, but deny that it grants us epistemic access to an independently existing deity. In this sense they can be described as non-cognitivists. They regard religious language as fictional, and maintain that although it is useful for ordering our life and conferring meaning and value, it has no transcendent referent.

Although his work is somewhat dated, theological realists frequently distinguish their position from that of the empiricist R. B. Braithwaite, who wrote whilst Logical Positivism was at full flood. In his famous lecture 'An Empiricist's View of the Nature of Religious Belief' Braithwaite argued that 'the primary use of religious assertions is to announce allegiance to a set of moral principles' (1971: 82). This use does not include belief in the truth or falsity of religious assertions, for, he explains,

A religious assertion ... is the assertion of an intention to carry out a certain behaviour policy ... together with the implicit or explicit statement, but not the assertion, of certain stories ... [A] religious belief is an intention to act in a certain way ... together with the entertainment of certain stories associated with the intention in the mind of the believer. (89)

On Braithwaite's view, religious beliefs express attitudes, emotions, and commitments to act in particular ways: God is a 'useful fiction' invoked to enable Christians to live morally purposeful lives. Against Braithwaite's and similar views,[5] theological realists propose to defend the realism of

[4] I use 'religious' (and cognate terms) to reflect the language in which the debate has been conducted.
[5] See also R. M. Hare's 'The Simple Believer' (1992: 1–36).

Christian faith by means of an argument 'from below' for a realist construal of religious experience.[6]

The best-known exponent of empiricism in contemporary philosophy of science is Bas van Fraassen. To emphasize his view that 'scientific activity is one of construction rather than discovery', van Fraassen designates his position 'constructive empiricism' (1980: 5). Unlike the scientific realist, the empiricist denies that the aim of science is to give us a true story about the unseen world. Van Fraassen defends a more pared-down ontology and defines his anti-realist view of science thus: 'Science aims to give us theories which are empirically adequate; and acceptance of a theory involves as belief only that it is empirically adequate' (12, italics removed). Hypotheses and theoretical constructs enable scientists to make accurate predictions in the realm of the observable – that is, the laboratory and its apparatus. Theoretical terms do not refer: they make no ontological claims beyond the observable realm and the theories in which we encounter them. Constructive empiricism assesses a theory according to its empirical adequacy, that is, whether it 'correctly describes what is observable', rather than whether it discovers 'truth concerning the unobservable' (4, 5). Theories are not candidates for *belief*, but *acceptance*, and a theory is accepted if 'what [it] says *about what is observable* (by us) is true' (18). By contrast, scientific realism typically argues that science gives us 'epistemic access'[7] to the unobservable realm, and that we are therefore warranted in believing that some scientific theories give approximately true accounts of independently existing structures and relations.

Theological realists have been impressed by scientific realists' responses to empiricism and use many of their arguments to defend a realist construal of the unobservable realm in religion. The best-known exponent of such a position is Janet Soskice, who defends theological realism against what she calls religious 'instrumentalism' (an earlier version of empiricist anti-realism in the philosophy of science) on the basis of analogies with the philosophy of science.[8] She summarizes her argument as follows:

The suggestion is ... that, having examined the ways in which metaphorical language can be judged to be reality depicting apart from definitive knowledge in the

[6] For theological realists' discussions of Braithwaite, see Barbour 1974: 56ff, 1990: 45; Peacocke 1984: 40; Soskice (1985: 112f, 147) brackets him with Cupitt.

[7] This concept, taken up by theological realists, is crucial to Boyd's influential account of scientific realism: see 1979: 357–408.

[8] See her 1987: 109ff. *Pace* Soskice and other theological realists, I doubt that there is a genuine theological analogue to instrumentalism. Although van Fraassen is often referred to as an instrumentalist, he himself repudiates this position.

case of science, we might find analogies for the admittedly very different task of reality depiction in theology. (1985: 137)[9]

The core analogy used by theological realists concerns (un)observability in science and theology. However, since this depends on what are in essence putative analogies between scientific and theological method, we look first at the applicability of such analogies to theology.

THE FALSE ASSIMILATION OF DOCTRINAL ACTIVITY TO SCIENTIFIC THEORIZING

The category mistake of interpreting theological method in terms of the philosophy of science can be demonstrated by examining the widespread tendency to understand doctrinal activity in terms akin to scientific theorizing. This, I shall argue, involves a false assimilation of theology to science.

Scientific explanations are not one-off proposals related to discrete phenomena: scientific theories are framed as explanations ranging over a wide array of data so as to be able to discover a covering law.[10] A successful theory is one which makes accurate predictions beyond the range of phenomena it was initially framed to cover and whose explanatory power is more enduring than its competitors'. This link between explanatory power and theory construction is often taken to be the best witness to the rationality of science.[11] The upshot for theological realists who are inclined to a theistic outlook is that they need to show not only that the theistic explanation is good regarding our experience of the world to date, but that it is one which goes on displaying its superior explanatory power in new contexts. Just as the success of science is shown by the smaller-scale successes of individual (clusters of) theories, so the same should apply in theology. Thus it is not just the general explanatory power of the concept of God which shows the plausibility of theistic explanations. The explanatory power of the theories or doctrines which can be developed from this core, along with the data of religious experience, gives even better evidence of this plausibility, for it is from them that we derive novel predictions and learn their applicability in new contexts. So strong is the scientific paradigm that many, though by no

---

[9] Soskice is followed closely in this argument by Peacocke 1984: 40–50, 1993²: 14–16 and van Huyssteen 1989: 125–72.

[10] This, roughly, is Hempel's (1965: 333–496) view of deductive-nomological scientific explanation.

[11] Theologians who defend the rationality of theology sometimes try to do so by rendering theology in a comparable theoretical mode; for example, see van Huyssteen – whom I discuss below – and Clayton 1989 and Murphy 1990.

means all, theologians unselfconsciously refer to doctrines as theories; it is a commonplace amongst theological realists.

One of the reasons theological realists appeal to the metaphorical nature of religious language is that metaphors can suggest new avenues for theorizing in science. Soskice accounts for the reality-depictive possibilities of religious metaphors by appealing to ' "metaphorically constituted theory terms" ' in science, and regards science and theology as members of 'the whole realm of abstract theorising' (1985: 103). The assimilation of doctrines to theories is more explicit in Peacocke, who suggests that 'theories (doctrines) and models in theology' can be interpreted on naive realist, positivist, instrumentalist, or critical realist lines, just as can scientific models and theories (1984: 40). Thus, for a critical realist, theology's 'concepts and the terms in its theories (usually called "doctrines") can refer to realities' (1994: 649). Similarly, theologians 'frame theories', of God's relation to the world, and, in the case of 'atonement theories', of the work of Christ (1984: 41). Peacocke regards the metaphorically expressed deliverances of religious experience as the basis for the conceptually clearer and more rigorous language of systematic theology: 'Both [science and theology] employ metaphorical language and describe reality in terms of models, which may eventually be combined into higher conceptual schemes (theories or doctrines)' (1993[2]: 19).[12] Soskice and Peacocke do not wish to make theology a theoretical activity in precisely the same way that natural science is, but both regard science and religion as engaged in the same general project of theorizing.

In some discussions of these issues, there is an explicit apologetic strategy behind such a perception. This is particularly apparent in the work of Wentzel van Huyssteen, for whom it is culturally imperative to prevent theology becoming a subjective, dogmatic ghetto-activity such as he finds practised by Barth and, 'in its most extreme form' (1989: 22 n.7), by Jüngel.[13] These thinkers' 'positivism' makes it hard for 'the theologian [to] be sure that his statements are in fact about God's Word, and not merely about a human expression of a supposedly divine Word' (84).[14] Thus, van Huyssteen regards establishing the critical realist credentials of theology, and hence also its objectivity, as a way of justifying its inclusion amongst 'the cadre of scientific disciplines' and thereby warranting its epistemic claims and providing it with a 'rationality model' (12). This line of argument will look rather off-beam to those who think that it is above all for the sake of theology's faithfulness to God that they should defend its realism. Nevertheless,

---

[12] Cf. Barbour 1990: 36, 41.   [13] See also van Huyssteen 1989: 14–23, especially 22–3.
[14] Cf. Puddefoot 1994: 139 n. 2.

van Huyssteen argues that theologians 'are first and last theoreticians' (170) who, like scientists, 'construct theories in order to explain, as fully and successfully as possible, the hidden structures of the studied matter' (162).[15]

It is apparent that theological realists make a heavy investment in drawing parallels between theology and science, so we turn now to a critical examination of their stance. First, we consider data and their epistemological significance in science and theology, then the concepts of prediction and progress in science and theology; finally I shall argue that, despite its attempts to rebut the challenges of empiricism and to throw off its influence, theological realism fails to do so.

Data and epistemology in science and theology

An important disanalogy between theology and science arises concerning what each regards as 'data'. Whereas science depends on data whose availability is not in principle spatio-temporally unique and which can therefore be the subject of repeated experimentation, I wish to suggest that theology operates upon the 'data' or 'evidence' which are given by the scriptural witness to God's self-revelation. As we shall see later, in their pursuit of analogies with the philosophy of science theological realists sometimes give God the status of a hypothetical and unobservable entity, this even though some explicitly deny that scripture's God is an entity about whom we can construct experiments and whom we can manipulate in laboratory conditions. The scientist-turned-theologian John Polkinghorne writes of 'the essential ineffability of the infinite God to finite minds and the unavailability of the divine nature to being put to experimentally manipulated testing' and admits that '[t]heology does not enjoy the luxury that experiment grants to science' (1998: 113, 47). Van Huyssteen acknowledges that 'religious experiences [can]not be repeated under controlled circumstances' (1988: 256). Similarly, Alister McGrath argues that theology and science have divergent epistemologies: 'The theologian is unable to appeal to present experimentation, or the results of past experimentation ... Whereas the scientific community takes its ideas from such experimental approaches, the religious community takes them from revelation' (1998:

[15] See also van Huyssteen 1997. The most interesting attempt to put theology on a scientific footing is Nancey Murphy's 1990. Somewhat surprisingly, she finds critical realism 'a questionable philosophical doctrine', and thinks that van Huyssteen's appeal to it is redundant: 'explanatory adequacy' suffices to establish the 'comparable epistemic status' of science and theology (1988: 288, cf. 1990: 197–8). Later (1994) she softens her opposition and appears to think that a version of epistemic realism is important for theology, since it 'aims at *knowledge* of a reality independent of the human subject' (126). Unfortunately she does not develop this point.

206, cf. 87f). Now, since this revelation has been proleptically consummated in Christ and dogmatically articulated in the church's creeds,[16] it seems reasonable to conclude that – this side of eternity – there cannot be any new 'data' or experimental evidence which can claim a higher authority in Christian theology.[17] Thus, it is not surprising that the Catholic philosopher of science (and seriously underestimated contributor to debates about theological realism) Ernan McMullin argues that, 'the notions of evidence in theology are very different from that prevailing in natural science' (1985: 42). To quote Polkinghorne again, the founding 'data' of Christian faith and theological reflection are 'unrepeatably unique' (1996: 18).

This disanalogy has serious consequences for the causal theory of linguistic reference, which, according to Soskice and many other theological realists, is an essential feature of arguments for the reality-depictive (= referential) properties of Christian language. This theory, initially proposed by Saul Kripke,[18] argues that successful reference requires an initial 'dubbing' or naming event which originates a chain of reference in a linguistic community to the dubbed entity. Since this chain passes down to even historically remote members of the linguistic community, continuity of reference to the entity is ensured. In her application of this theory to theology,[19] Soskice maintains that the experience of Moses on Sinai (narrated in Exod. 19) 'truly was of God', and that 'whatever was responsible for the empty tomb of Jesus was God' (1985: 140). These events and experiences function for theology in the same way as 'dubbing' events in science: they initiate a chain of reference (a religious tradition) to the entity which caused them – here, God. Religious language legitimately claims to be referential because reference is, according to Soskice, not restricted to our possessing unrevisable knowledge based on complete descriptions of referents, but is instead established by speakers' usages of terms in particular contexts and traditions.

This is a rather problematic line of argument. Exod. 19 recounts that YHWH 'said' various things to Moses, and that he 'came down upon Mount

---

[16] 'Dogmas are the irreversible communal decisions made ... [in] the church's communal effort to think through her mission of speaking the gospel ... Therefore all theology is subject to the authority of dogma and may in turn contribute to dogma yet to be formulated. The theologian who understands his or her work knows that to proceed in contradiction or indifference to dogma is to turn from theology to another practice' (Jenson 1997: 22, cf. 16–18).

[17] St John's Jesus says to his disciples that 'the Spirit will guide you into all the truth' (John 16:13). This does not mean that there will be later revelations adding to what has been revealed in Christ: see Raymond Brown 1971: 715.

[18] See Kripke 1980[2].

[19] Soskice detects some weaknesses in the theory and supplements it from more traditional perspectives: see 1985: 129ff.

Sinai' and 'called' to Moses. Now, this 'experience' was by its very nature unique and unrepeatable: it was the once and for all giving of the Torah. It was initiated by one who had, at the burning bush, already introduced himself to Moses as unnameable, the one who resists our attempts at naming or dubbing. Similar considerations apply, but with stronger force, to the empty tomb of Jesus. The resurrection of Jesus marked the initiation of the final phase of God's unique, once-for-all work in reconciliation and the renewal of creation as a result of which the eschatological age has dawned. It is also notable that the only attributions of agency regarding the empty tomb in the resurrection narratives are to an angel (Matt. 28:20) and (mistakenly) an unidentified 'they' (John 20:2, 13, cf. 15ff), but not, however, to God as Soskice's argument requires.[20] Soskice candidly admits that her own argument faces difficulties similar to those we mentioned above. She writes that 'the disanalogy with the scientific case is that since such experiences cannot be replicated, fixing reference by means of them demands commitment to the validity of the experiences as reported by the experient' (1985: 138). However, in the face of this disanalogy, Soskice does not attenuate the role of religious experience in her argument, but attempts to bring it into line with theories of reference in the philosophy of science by appealing to a Thomistic view of God's causal relationship with the world.[21] In my view there is a problem with her appeal to natural theology at this point, but I shall discuss this in another chapter; at present, I want to highlight two things about Soskice's theory of reference. First, it lacks the kind of objectivity a scientist would claim on the basis of the replicability of data. Second, it is very anthropocentric: our confidence in the referentiality of religious language depends primarily not on God but on our confidence in other believers and our willingness, as Soskice claims, to 'regard them as authoritative' (1987: 117).

We turn now to consider some of the epistemological aspects of Soskice's analogy with the philosophy of science. These emerge most pointedly when she writes that basing a theory of reference on religious experience in combination with a view of God as causally related to the world 'retains the kind of epistemic agnosticism we want' (1987: 116). She explains her case as follows:

As in the scientific case, to be a realist about reference is to be a 'fallibilist' about knowledge of the referent. Speakers may refer and yet be mistaken, even quite radically mistaken, as to the nature of that to which they refer. So the theist

[20] Of course, God, the Father, and (possibly) the Spirit are named agents in the raising of Jesus (see, e.g., Acts 2:24, 32, 10:40; Rom. 6:4, 1:4).
[21] See 1985: 139ff.

may be mistaken in his beliefs about the source and cause of all and assume it to be something of which one can appropriately predicate personalistic terms when one cannot ... This fallibilism should not trouble the Christian realist if he acknowledges that he may simply be wrong in his various beliefs and that some of them are so central that, if he is wrong concerning them, his whole structure of belief is gravely flawed. If that which the Christian refers to as the source and cause of all bears no resemblance to God as conceived by Christianity, then he must admit himself to be so deluded as to the nature of the referent that his faith must be lost. This possibility of being in error is the risk such a realist takes. (1985: 139; cf. 140, 152)[22]

This fallibilism is a central epistemic component of the *critical* realism advocated by theological realists influenced by the philosophy of science; because we could be wrong about our beliefs, we must be critical of them and ready to revise them. Now, the suspension of commitment this fallibilism implies might be appropriate for a scientist who has the opportunity to repeat the experiments which sustain the chain of reference on which her reality claims are based – and indeed, for the sake of her integrity as a scientist, she ought to do so – but we need to ask how much theological validity it has.

The philosopher Michael Durrant regards Soskice's argument at this point as simply 'unacceptable':

A being of whom (which) it would be inappropriate to predicate personalistic terms would simply not be God; not that, somehow or other, we had got God's nature wrong. After all, Christ himself said: 'He who has seen me has seen the Father.' On Soskice's view presumably Christ himself might have been mistaken as to God's nature; an untenable position for any Christian theist to entertain. (1989: 141)

Soskice's mistake – and she is typical of theological realists here – is that she has put too much emphasis on epistemology and forgotten that Christian faith is motivated by (the God at work in) unique events rather than our beliefs about them.[23] Epistemology has been put before ontology. Roger Trigg summarizes the situation well: 'Critical realism is too ready to start with what we believe rather than what our beliefs are about ... [and] runs the danger, in its eagerness not to be "naive", of becoming sceptical' (1998: 86).

The full consequences of Soskice's theological epistemology and the data with which it deals are most apparent in her account of revelation. Soskice claims that we do not need to believe that models of God were given 'by

---

[22] See also Peacocke 1984: 26 and van Huyssteen 1999: 216.
[23] The same mistake is made by the Church of England's Doctrine Commission: see Doctrine Commission 1987: 25–31.

cosmic disclosure, in a fully elaborated state and immediately embraced by everyone' (1985:153). In her view a theological realism 'from below' whose data are religious experiences is more defensible if we conceive revelation in terms of its being constituted by a range of models developed over time within the religious community.

This accumulation of favoured models, embellished by the glosses of generations, gives the context for Christian reflection and provides the matrix for the descriptive vocabulary which Christians continue to employ in attempts to describe their experience. This accretion of images, all of them hesitant and approximating, yet confirmed by generations of belief, constitutes much of what Christians call revelation. (153)

'Revelation' is not evidently used here principally to denote God's gracious, self-initiated activity towards humanity; it denotes the result of sifting and embellishing human experiences. Against the former view, Soskice insists that religious language cannot describe God. Thus, 'When Christians say that "God is spirit" they are not ... giving a description of God'; rather, their language 'denominates the source of thousands of experiences which Jews and Christians have spoken of' (153, 154). The scriptural deposit of models, images, and metaphors embodies the religious community's understanding of God. Puzzlingly, Soskice adds that it also constitutes 'the source of Christian *descriptive* language' (159, my italics, cf. 160). Quite apart from the apparent inconsistency here, there is a philosophical question which Soskice leaves unanswered: how can we denominate the source of an experience without in some sense describing it? To say that x is the source or cause of y is to describe it. In which case, given her understanding of revelation in terms of our epistemic access to God, it would seem that, by her lights, our ability to describe God must be on the basis of our own experience. And this is a conclusion with which Soskice – who in a later paper describes her account of revelation as 'anthropic' (1988: 174) – agrees: 'experience, customarily regarded as the foundation of natural theology, is also the touchstone of the revealed' (1985: 160).

Sue Patterson pushes the argument a step further when she argues that since Soskice does not mention grace or incarnation, 'the question must be asked: are we in fact only talking of ourselves, and if so, do we need God at all as a reference point?' She concludes that 'Whether or not we regard God as causally connected with world or universe, we are able to form analogies only from the material available to us within our human frame of reference and it is hard to see, on the basis of Dr Soskice's theology ... how this can be done without frank anthropomorphism' (1993: 14). Given Soskice's premisses, this accusation seems to me hard to rebut. Her argument appears to be anthropocentric and empirical rather than kyriocentric and theological: she focusses on believers and their experiences rather than on God in his self-revelation through the work of Jesus Christ.

Prediction and progress in science and theology

Because Christian theology cannot have new 'data', its method will be different from that of natural science. Take the success of science as an example. The best evidence of this is often said to be science's predictive fertility – that is, theoretical development and ontological discovery. As McMullin has written of science,

Fertility is usually equated with the ability to make novel predictions. A good theory is expected to predict novel phenomena, that is, phenomena that were not part of the set to be explained. The further in kind these novel phenomena are from the original set, and thus the more unexpected they are, the better the model is said to be. (1984: 30)

Theology, as classically practised, has no analogue to this. Polkinghorne rightly argues that 'theology does not offer predictions open to straight-forward empirical testing ... because God is not to be put to the test (Dt. 6:16)' (1991: 15).

If Christian doctrines do not make predictions, to suggest that they do is to mistake their role in the Christian faith.[24] Christian revelation is of that which is new, but its ontological novelty is absolute in the sense that it is the advent of the *new creation* which has been uniquely *revealed* in history by Christ.[25] So, combining the main point of the previous section with the foregoing argument, one could say that since revelation is proleptically complete it cannot predict or be confirmed by new facts.[26]

One of the principal arguments for realism in science runs from the appearance science gives of progress to the claim that this appearance is testimony in support of the view that scientists discover underlying structures and processes of reality. But here also it is hard to see a clear analogy between theology and science, at least as the former has been classically conducted. Earlier in the chapter we noted van Huyssteen's claim that establishing theology's critically realist credentials is one criterion justifying its being regarded as a rational, scientific discipline. Another criterion he offers for

---

[24] Eschatology does not *predict* future observations in the way scientific theories do. Scientific theories predict *specific* (novel) phenomena and indicate how we might experimentally confirm their predictions; Jesus' eschatological discourse explicitly forbids this.

[25] See Barth 1962: 712–13.   [26] *Contra* Murphy 1990: see especially 178–83.

theology's being rational is that it, like science, should be 'progressive'. Here, 'theological progress means renewed but also better understanding of the biblical message in each new context or problem situation' (van Huyssteen 1989: 194).[27] But immediately we encounter a problem: what standard have theologians to assess progress? How could we ever decide whether a theological theory is progressive in the required sense? Van Huyssteen offers two main examples of progress: the church's handling of 'the heresy problem' (191), and the replacement of accounts of biblical authority based on mechanical accounts of its inspiration with views more coherent with a science-dominated culture.

Van Huyssteen deals with heresy in a very brief discussion of Patristic Christological controversies, so when in this context he claims that 'the language of theological theories is ... always tentative [and] provisional' (196), one assumes that he has forgotten the credal anathemas. He also alludes to apartheid in South Africa. Although we are thankful for the ending of that evil, it is hard to see it as progress in any theologically weightier sense than that it marks the achievement of a goal. To the extent that apartheid and the theology supporting it were a degeneration from the kind of *koinonia* envisaged in the New Testament, their removal is a restoration of a *status quo ante*, accomplished (in part) by the deployment of the very traditional and unscientific doctrine of the *imago Dei*. For all the horrors perpetrated by the apartheid regime and for all the heroism and statesmanship shown in its abolition, no new 'data' were discovered about God, human nature, or degenerate government which are not already revealed in scripture.

To turn to the second example, van Huyssteen (who is a relatively conservative theologian) tells us that the 'redemptive authority' of scripture is 'a basic criterion' and 'yardstick' (178, 177) of systematic theology. For him 'the Bible, as God's Word, [is] the absolute authority in church doctrine ... [It] has been and remains our only access to the Jesus of Nazareth in whom God finally reveals himself to the Christian' (180, 177). Granted such a theology of revelation, we are led to ask how there could be epistemological or ontological progress beyond what is given in scripture. If scripture has this degree of authority, then other criteria of progress must be relativized to it – including the insights of contemporary scientific thought[28] – and this implies that in practice van Huyssteen's criteria of theological progress are reduced to scripture itself. All of which confirms the hermeneutically

---

[27] See van Huyssteen 1988: 258 for a succinct summary of his criteria, the other of which is 'the ability to critically identify and solve problems' (italics removed); for a full account, see 1989: 143–97.

[28] Cf. van Huyssteen 1989: 176–90.

circular 'progress' of theology and makes us wonder why van Huyssteen gives so much space to attempting to show that theological statements can be put on a sound, scientifically rational basis when he asserts (in an apparently fideistic way) that the Bible is 'the absolute authority' beyond which Christians cannot progress.

In science, progress is achieved through the formulation of hypotheses, postulation of entities, and experimentation. The latter provides new data which, *ex hypothesi*, confirm the hypotheses and (on a realist construal of science) indicate progress in our knowledge of the world. But given van Huyssteen's view of the Bible, there cannot be new 'data' in theology possessing sufficient authority to (dis)confirm a theory and thereby show it to be progressive. On the romantic view of the church held by some of its members, its life is characterized not so much by progress as by degeneracy, a persistent falling away from a biblical or Patristic ideal, for example. Charismatic renewal or high church revivals are – from this perspective – but rare upward blips on the gloomy chart of the church's sad decline. However, one need not hold such views to wonder whether there has ever been any net empirical progress (or degeneracy) in the history of the church. Applying the concept of progress to either the church or its doctrine is a category mistake, especially when the concept's content is specified by the philosophy of science. If progress is an admissible concept it is only so in the sense that the church is, in the mercy of God, granted repentance for past failings and grace for future obedience so that it can tell anew the mighty works of God. As Jean-Luc Marion trenchantly puts it, '*theology cannot aim at any other progress than its own conversion to the Word*' (1991: 158).

Spectatorial empiricism?

Although most theological realists officially reject empiricism (because they use realist philosophy of science in making out their case for theological realism),[29] this is less evident from their arguments than they might suppose. Of course, since a central tenet of Christian faith is that God's word was enfleshed in Jesus Christ, Christians cannot deny that there is an empirical element to their faith. However, my present concern is to point up certain dangers in making experience the priority in one's theological epistemology.[30] Barbour does this when he equates the observational data of science with religious experience, and writes that 'One of the functions

[29] Soskice is the most self-conscious in her efforts: see 1985: 118–26, 142–8.
[30] See here Barth 1986a: 35–42, especially 38–41.

of models in science is to suggest theories which correlate patterns in observational data. One of the functions of models in religion ... is to suggest beliefs which correlate patterns in human experience' (1974: 49). On the basis of just such models, Christians claim to be showing what the God who transcends their experience is like. Similarly, even in her much more sophisticated account of religious language in which she seeks to overcome the legacy of empiricist accounts of meaning, Soskice still develops her argument towards the epistemologically empiricist conclusion that religious 'experiences judged to be of God' are the source of the models which 'the faithful [have selected] as being especially adequate to their experience'[31] and which are therefore taken to 'constitute ... much of what Christians call revelation' (1985: 153). Although they do not rest their epistemic case on *sense* experience as empiricism does, I wish now to argue that the outcome of theological realist epistemology is empiricist in character. In the light of their dependency on arguments from experience, it might therefore be more accurate to say of theological realists that they can at best claim to eschew *reductionist* empiricism.

In a contribution to a conference at which Soskice delivered a paper on realism, Nicholas Lash suggests that theological realists' approach to this problematic leads them into what he calls 'spectatorial empiricism' (1988: 209). According to this perspective,

'observation' is made the paradigm of learning, and accuracy of representation (rather than, for example, soundness of judgement) becomes the standard of knowledge. Knowledge of nature is arrived at by looking carefully at the world. And knowledge of God? This may come either by imagining what might lie 'behind' the world and accounting for its configuration or, according to some people, by the careful study of data which, while constituting items on the list of things that we know, nevertheless do not simply form part of the world in which we come to know them ... The primary task of doctrine or theology is then the construction of conceptual representations of this thing [sc. God] which seek to be, so far as they go, accurate. (205, 210)[32]

The parallels between this spectatorial empiricism and theological realism are striking. Theological realism, construed as 'reality depiction', aims at accurate representation of the divine. (Theological realists may disown attempts to describe God and couch their epistemological claims in suitably agnostic language, but construing reference in terms of the metaphor of 'reality *depiction*' suggests a serious ambiguity or equivocation at this point.)

---

[31] Cf. van Fraassen's definition of constructive empiricism, p. 42 above.
[32] See also Westphal 1993b.

Knowledge of the unobservable entities of science and theology is cast in terms of 'epistemic access'. Religious experience is held to yield cognitive data about an entity which constitutes an item on the list of things we know whilst not being part of the world in which we come to know it. Theism posits a God 'behind' the world as the best explanation of its configuration. Theologians and scientists participate in a differentiated yet common pursuit: they construct models, metaphors, and 'theories in order to explain, as fully and successfully as possible, the hidden structures of the studied matter' (van Huyssteen 1989: 162). In other words, theological realists aim at 'conceptual representations' of God.

So far as this constitutes an empiricist problematic, and if theological realists pursue it in the way outlined by Lash, they have not left empiricism behind.[33] This is evident in a passage from Soskice where, a few pages after admitting the fallibilism of her case, she argues that

it is not surprising that empiricism should lead to religious scepticism – what is surprising is that contemporary theologians and philosophers of religion should cling to an empiricist framework at a time when the same empiricism has been shown to be bankrupt in other areas of philosophy. (1985: 144)

What is strange here is that Soskice does not seem to recognize how hard it is to put even a cigarette paper between her agnosticism and the empiricist's scepticism. Both seem to result from 'spectatorial empiricism'. Polkinghorne is truer to the empiricist temper of theological realism when, after warning against empirical testing on the ground that God is not to be put to the test, he continues, 'Yet if theology is to maintain cognitive claims it must be an empirical discipline to the extent that its assertions are related to an understanding of experience' (1991: 15).

Against theological realists, I contend that their emphasis on theology's *cognitive* claims reflects a post-Enlightenment, foundationalist, and apologetic concern with epistemology. As I said in chapter 1, one of the concerns of this book is to highlight the weaknesses of this and to argue that in defending a Christian realism we should be concerned firstly with ontology, and only secondarily with epistemological and semantic questions. However, the empiricist legacy in theological realism is so strong that it seriously distorts its proponents' understanding of the Christian faith and makes a theologically adequate realism very hard to defend, even on theological realists' own terms. Both the depth of the empiricist influence on theological realism and the importance of properly construing the ontological dimensions

[33] For example, compare Soskice's argument to Ian Ramsey's 'Christian empiricism' (1974: 8–9).

of the debate will become apparent as we turn now to another aspect of the assimilation of theological realism to scientific realism.

IS THEOLOGICAL REALISM ANALOGOUS TO SCIENTIFIC REALISM?

Having criticized theological realism's pursuit of analogies with the philosophy of science on theological grounds, I now examine it from the perspective of the contemporary debate about realism in the philosophy of science. This is important because the plausibility of theological realism depends (logically) on the success of defences of scientific realism. However, since these are made in the teeth of anti-realist objections, for theological realism to be substantively analogous to scientific realism it will be necessary to show that the theological counterparts to these objections can be effectively rebutted. As we shall see, this is far from easy.

The problem of underdetermination

The first objection to scientific realism we consider concerns the problem of the underdetermination of theory by observation. The difficulty here is that 'there may be two or more quite distinct ... accounts of the nature of reality, which have the same empirical consequences' (Redhead 1995: 16–17). In other words, the same set of observations might be explained by several radically different, incompatible theories. Although scientific realists do not regard this as an insuperable objection, it nevertheless has undesirable consequences for theological realism. Since the case for theological realism is made 'from below' by appealing to religious experience (rather than 'from above' by appeal to divine revelation), the question arises as to why experience should be given a theological realist rather than a naturalist account. To recall van Fraassen's constructive empiricism, *ex hypothesi* a naturalist account might be just as empirically adequate as a realist one. This is one of the reasons why not only 'radical' Christians but many thinkers opposed to Christian faith – especially perhaps Darwinian fundamentalists – try to subvert it by offering interpretations contrary to theological realism. Such a naturalism does not deny the existence of the observed phenomena (religious experiences), nor does it deny that they can be interpreted in a realist way. However, their independently existing cause need not be construed in non-naturalist terms. They could be adequately explained as the outcome of a natural occurrence such as a sunset, the sight of a loved one, or a headache.

Naturalist interpretations question whether language used of religious experiences need be given a transcendental reference and whether such experiences give us epistemic access to a transcendental entity.[34] For a religious naturalist such as Willem Drees the problem with religious realism is that it undermines 'the crucial function of a [religious] tradition, namely in providing a guiding vision which shapes our way of life' (1996: 279). Drees's denial of religious realism amounts to a kind of deist naturalist non-cognitivism which in net terms is indistinguishable from Braithwaite's. His account affirms Christian faith as action-guiding and preserves the appearances of religious phenomena but denies that we can have a cognitive relationship with or successfully refer to a transcendent deity.

According to John Hick, the central point of difference between theological realists and non-realists is precisely over whether the universe is to be understood naturalistically or according to religious realism. Although he believes that religious realism can integrate the insights which generate naturalism but not naturalist presuppositions, he thinks, correctly, that 'philosophical discussion cannot ... settle the debate between religious realists and non-realists' (1993: 3). Thus, the problem of underdetermination strikes at the heart of theological realism, for it points up just how far whether or not we are realists about Christian faith depends on the commitments we choose to make to an over-arching theory or meta-narrative by which to interpret the data of experience. At first blush, religious experiences do not *require* a theological realist interpretation: the empirical phenomena of religion do not of themselves offer grounds for postulating a supernatural cause. As Hebblethwaite notes, 'unless supported by rational arguments' for God's existence, reliance on religious experience to defend realism 'is extremely vulnerable to alternative psychological and sociological explanations' (1993: 210). Drees is therefore logically entitled to his approach. Traditional Christians might object, but they cannot deny Drees his claim that the data themselves can be adequately construed in a religiously non-cognitivist way.

Here we encounter a further and very important methodological disanalogy between theological and scientific realism. As McMullin notes,

The scientist *qua* scientist is not called on to take a stand on [scientific realism] one way or the other. Most scientists *do* have views on the issue, sometimes on the basis of much reflection but more often of a spontaneous kind. Indeed, it could be argued that worrying about whether or not their constructs approximate the real is more apt to hinder than to help their work as scientists. (1984: 16)[35]

[34] See Drees 1996: 244–83.
[35] Cf. Polkinghorne 1998: 29–30. For a more detailed discussion of the relationship between the way scientists work and the problem of scientific realism, see Wessels 1993.

Now, if working scientists should avoid making a premature commitment to scientific realism, this is even more important for the integrity of philosophers of science: realism is a philosophical position which has to be established on the basis of a fair consideration of all the relevant data. It follows that if theological realism is mounted on strict methodological analogy with philosophical arguments for scientific realism, its defenders should not make a prior methodological commitment to a realist interpretation of their data. Yet in fact this is just what they do. By operating with a commitment to realism's being true of Christian faith *before* the case for theological realism has been made out, they *over*determine the interpretation of their data by their prior commitment to a particular theory. In effect, they interpret religious experience in a realist way whilst suspending the question whether this, rather than a naturalist, non-cognitivist account is correct.

For example, Soskice admits that theological realism is not 'the only cogent position' but commits herself to it because 'Christian theism has been undeniably realist about [its] models, whether it has a right to be or not.' She further claims that 'if there is to be any valuable comparison of models in science and religion it must be one with realist *assumptions*, and traditional Christian belief has been characterized by these in any case' (1985: 137, 107, my italics).[36] Accordingly, she restricts the range of religious experiences to which she appeals to those in the Christian tradition, preferring 'Pascal's experience to ground my reference' (1987: 116) to that of, say, Gautama Buddha. Were she open to the full range of humanity's religious experience, Soskice's argument might lead her to a religiously pluralist realism of the kind proposed by Richard B. Miller. Miller thinks that naturalistic objections to finding a transcendent reference for 'God' are very hard to rebut, but suggests that a causal theory of reference taking experiences from all religious traditions into account might allow us to 'agree that all men address the same God no matter how differently they conceive him' (1986: 14).[37] As they stand, Soskice's commitments and assumptions and the restricted range of relevant data and hypotheses she considers could be acceptable to a Christian theologian, but to a philosopher of science they will appear arbitrary and partial and, *mutatis mutandis*, likely to lead to bad science.

There is thus a significant difference between the way in which theological realists and philosophers of science approach their data and the question whether they should be construed realistically. For the philosopher of

---

[36] Likewise Peacocke 1984: 12, 38, 44; Polkinghorne 1998: 124; and van Huyssteen 1989: 159–60 and 1997: 41ff.
[37] See also Drees 1998: 620ff; Byrne 1995; Knight 2001, especially 97–105.

science, the ontological component of realism – the question of what exists independently of the scientist and her lab – is up for grabs. Empiricism is a position to be argued against. A philosopher of science cannot presume an ontology of her theoretical terms without begging the question, yet this is precisely what theological realists' commitments lead them to do. They argue as if the ontological component of the realist position had already been settled, yet if the analogy with scientific realism is to hold, this is the central point of contention and so should not be presumed.

The foregoing argument suggests that the fundamental epistemic stance of theological realists who intend to be faithful to Christian tradition is in fact fideistic. Given their prior commitment to a realist construal of Christian faith, theological realists cannot coherently consider the empiricist objection that they have overdetermined their interpretation of their data in the light of a presumed ontology. By talking of God as a hypothetical and unobservable entity, they pay lip-service to an open ontology, but in fact they do not regard his existence as hypothetical, nor do most of them think that all the data of humankind's religious experiences are germane to the project of modelling God. And since they argue for realism by appealing to religious experience, they are deprived of a supervening argument from uniquely authoritative revelation which could warrant such a fideist outlook when, *contra* naturalism, they seek to give religious experience a realist construal. From a theological point of view this puts religious experience at the mercy of a naturalistic empiricism whose interpretative thrall their methodology has no means of resisting. And from the perspective of scientific realism, despite the fact that many exponents of theological realism are explicitly opposed to fideism,[38] theirs will seem to be a groundless and question-begging kind of commitment.

Scientific realists often respond to underdetermination by arguing that experiments can be conducted which will establish which of two competing theories is correct in its predictions concerning the nature of unobservable structures and so more compatible with the data.[39] Although he is a realist about entities rather than theories, the views of the philosopher of science Ian Hacking are relevant. He argues that

> Experimental work provides the strongest evidence for scientific realism. This is . . . because entities that in principle cannot be 'observed' are regularly manipulated to produce new phenomena and to investigate other aspects of nature. They are tools, instruments not for thinking but for doing. (1983: 262, cf. 246–75)

[38] See van Huyssteen 1989; Trigg 1992: 33–43. Polkinghorne (1998: 115, 124) endorses the Anselmian principle of *fides quaerens intellectum*.

[39] See, for example, Devitt 1991[2]: 119–20.

But here the differences between science and theology over data and experimentation have a major impact on attempted defences of theological realism on the basis of analogies with (the philosophy of) science. If we agree that the data with which theologians operate are unique and that experiments cannot be conducted, the appeal – favoured by scientific realists – to experimentation against an anti-realism based on underdetermination is simply not available to theologians.[40] Unless and until some answer to the problems posed by underdetermination is presented by theological realists, theologians might be wise to suspend judgement as to the success of their defence of the realism of Christian faith.[41]

The problem of pessimism

Underdetermination is not the only obstacle that theological realists who wish to draw analogies between theology and realist philosophy of science must overcome. Another reason for favouring anti-realist interpretations of science is that the history of science raises serious difficulties for realism. This is the 'disastrous meta-induction' well known to philosophers of science and succinctly stated by Hilary Putnam: 'just as no term in the science of more than fifty (or whatever) years ago referred, so it will turn out that no term used now (except maybe observation terms ...) refers' (1978: 37, 25, italics removed). Think of the phlogiston theory of chemistry or the crystalline spheres of ancient astronomy: history is littered with the bleached skeletons of abandoned scientific theories and the entities they postulated. Therefore, as Larry Laudan famously argues,[42] since the history of science shows that most theories developed in the past have turned out to be false, it is a reasonable, if pessimistic, induction that present ones will too. So, from these arguments, the anti-realist concludes that it is mistaken to regard science as converging on the one true story about reality. And in any case, she will contend, the result is immaterial for the practice of science: 'non-realist strategies often as not work out' (McMullin 1984: 15), they continue to enable experimental observations and predictions to be made,

---

[40] Nancey Murphy regards 'theology [a]s methodologically indistinguishable from the sciences' (1990: 198), and thinks that the churches are 'laboratories for theological experimentation' (166). Were she to liberalize her view of scriptural data, the problem of underdetermination might be circumvented by reading Hacking alongside her. Theologians who disfavour such a view of theology and the church could rebut underdetermination by arguing fideistically that the givenness of God's self-revelation already determines how 'observations' are to be understood.

[41] Polkinghorne alludes to '[c]oherence and comprehensiveness' as ways of overcoming underdetermination in theology (1998: 114, cf. 106). However, as it stands, this suggestion seems unlikely to lead to a distinctively *theological* response to underdetermination.

[42] See his 1984.

and these are what really matter. So, if scientific realism is to be vindicated, it is necessary to block the pessimistic meta-induction against it.

Scientific realists respond with two related arguments. The first is that the anti-realist argument is partial in its interpretation of history. Realists claim that technological advance is evidence of scientific progress and argue that 'the long-term success of a theory gives reason to believe that something like the entities and structures postulated by the theory actually exist' (McMullin 1984: 26). Thus, scientists construct theories to explain observed features of the world, and they do so by postulating models of unobserved structures and entities which are held to account causally for the observed phenomena. Over time, theories are refined. Some prove fruitless and are dropped, but others go on yielding predictions about hidden structures which are experimentally confirmed, and sometimes, formerly hidden structures are observed. Thus, it is held, realism is vindicated.[43]

The second argument is that unless some such realist account of success in terms of discovery of hidden entities in causal relationship with observations is offered, scientific progress has to be regarded as a 'miracle' or as a series of 'cosmic coincidences' (Putnam 1978: 18; J. J. C. Smart quoted by van Fraassen 1980: 25).[44] That is, anti-realism has more explaining to do than realism. Richard Boyd states the realist position as follows:

> when, in the historical development of any particular science, its theory-dependent methodological practices come to display the sort of intricacy *and* instrumental reliability characteristic, say, of modern physics or chemical practice, only the realistic account of scientific knowledge ... will provide an adequate explanation of that reliability. (1984: 77)

How does theological realism stand in relation to these arguments for its scientific counterpart?

Both arguments present scientific realism as a hypothesis that is in the process of being confirmed. It is not a settled position; it could turn out to be false.[45] Fallibilism is therefore built into scientific realism. Theological realists learn from this and describe their positions variously as 'tentative', 'sceptical', 'qualified', or 'critical'. As we have seen, Soskice is one such, and she has an argument against the pessimistic empiricist objection, but it depends theologically on the appropriateness of her fallibilism and logically on her view that God is necessarily unobservable.[46] I have already argued that Soskice's fallibilism is not appropriate to theology; I argue against the

[43] Against this defence of scientific realism, see Fine 1996²: 112–35.
[44] This argument is frequently used by theological realists: see especially Banner 1990.
[45] See Putnam 1978: 19, 78 n. 1; McMullin 1984: 16.   [46] See 1985: 139, cf. 140, 152, and 1987: 116.

latter in the next section. The most important consideration for the present argument is the fact that the orthodox Christian is and always has been committed to realism about God. The initial 'observations' of the risen Christ which gave rise to Christian faith were unique and unrepeatable, so, unlike hypotheses in the philosophy of science, no falsification of God's self-revelation is possible.[47] Christian faith proceeds on the basis of existential and intellectual commitment to God as he has revealed himself (fully and finally this side of the eschaton) in Jesus Christ, and therefore the Christian is committed to (a version of) realism about the triune God in a way that no scientist could be to a realist construal of a hypothesis.

Disanalogies between Christian doctrines and scientific theories imply that doctrines can neither explain data in a quasi-scientific way nor offer predictions of what will happen in the realm of the observable if certain experiments are conducted. Doctrines might be regarded as explanatory in the sense that they lay bare the inner logic of revelation, but, since no new data are available, they are not open to progressive (dis)confirmation or falsification as scientific theories are. And whereas a scientist holds her hypotheses tentatively and with a willingness to drop them if they are not confirmed experimentally, the security of a Christian's beliefs 'seems to be greater than an account of these beliefs as "hypotheses" would warrant' (Banner 1990: 94). But even ignoring this last point, if doctrines cannot be empirically confirmed in a properly scientific way then the no-miracles argument against anti-realism is not available to theological realists and neither do they have any theoretical success or failure standing in need of explanation. On the other hand, if theological realists wish to pursue their analogy, they must show how and in what sense doctrines can be regarded as making a convergence on truth greater than that given in the initial 'observations' (that is, the religious experiences) which gave rise to them.

The arguments we have examined in this section show that there are powerful anti-realist objections to scientific realism and that the disanalogies between scientific and theological method seriously diminish the initial appeal of arguing for theological realism on the basis of defences of scientific realism. In the next section we examine the core analogy proposed by theological realists and see that even if scientific realism were conclusively proved against all the objections, it would still not be a proper basis for demonstrating a Christian realism.

---

[47] It might be objected that the Big Bang was unique and unrepeatable. But here reference is to a(n) (putative) *event*; my claim concerns unique and unrepeatable *observations* of a unique and unrepeatable event. Furthermore, the Big Bang theory depends on observations which themselves give rise to theories that it was not a unique and unrepeatable event. The objection collapses.

THE FALSE ASSIMILATION OF THE BIBLICAL GOD TO THE
STATUS OF A SCIENTIFICALLY UNOBSERVABLE ENTITY

The most serious disanalogy between theological and scientific realism arises in relation to the question of observation. We have seen that one way of meeting the empiricist challenge is to argue that the success of science (or, more narrowly, of its theories) is best accounted for by the claim that 'at least some of the theoretical terms of a [true] theory denote real theoretical entities which are causally responsible for the observable phenomenon that prompts us to posit their existence' (Newton-Smith 1981: 46, cf. 38). This means that until their existence is experimentally confirmed, unobservable entities have a hypothetical status.

At this point, we should recall that some philosophers of science argue that metaphors play a decisive and indispensable role in establishing scientific realism because it is by means of them that we gain epistemic access to the unobservable realm about which scientists theorize. For example, Richard Boyd contends that metaphors are not merely ornamental adjuncts to scientific theories that we abandon when we have attained a sufficiently abstract level of purely formal theoretical description. Metaphors can propose models, as in the sentence 'The brain is a computer.' Boyd calls such metaphors 'theory-constitutive', by which he means that on the basis of similarities between the 'source' and 'subject' of the metaphor, 'they display what might be called *inductive open-endedness* [and so] suggest strategies for future research' (1979: 363). 'Theory-constitutive metaphors' project 'metaphorically constituted theory terms' – in the case of Boyd's example from cybernetics, such terms as 'programming', 'output', and 'feedback' – which enable us to begin to grasp what would otherwise be beyond our full comprehension. Metaphorical language therefore occupies a place at the leading edge of scientific enquiry where theories make both explanatory and predictive claims that are tested experimentally and thereby, realists claim against empiricists, gives us cognitive access to unobservable reality.

As we have seen, theological realism has to ward off naturalistic empiricism, which denies that religious language refers to a mind-independent God. If it fails, religious metaphors and models should be regarded as noncognitive and merely affective or evaluative redescriptions of human experience. Religious language would then serve a purely functional purpose, as Drees implies.[48] It could still suggest new possibilities for ethical human living, but with the added virtue of ontological parsimony.[49] There would be no need to postulate an unobservable cause for observable phenomena of

---

[48] 1996: 278ff; cf. Clayton 1997: 152.   [49] See Drees 1996: 276–83.

religious experience. Religious metaphors can open up immanent human possibilities without needing an unobservable deity to warrant their use.[50] So why not render theological talk as talk about the observable? Because, in the view of the theological realist, doing so would render religious language 'a topic of philosophical anthropology' (Soskice 1985: 111).[51]

It is therefore understandable that theological realists have been attracted by the scientific realist construal of metaphorical language and have used the putative analogy between unobservability in science and theology to argue for theological realism. Thus, having defended the indispensability of metaphors in gaining access to unobservable entities in science, Soskice applies this argument to theology and builds her case for realism on the claim that an unobservable entity (God) is causally responsible for observable phenomena (religious experiences). She then argues that, like scientists, theologians and philosophers of religion use 'models to describe the unobservable or transcendent' and compliments science by describing its 'necessarily unobservable ... hypothetical entities and relations' as themselves ' "transcendent" ' (1985: 104, 124, 120).

Arguments depending on the view that God is necessarily unobservable are commonly used by theological realists. For example, one of the earliest defenders of theological realism on analogy with science was Ian Barbour. Though he is critical of Soskice's account of reference,[52] he argues that 'As models of an unobservable gas molecule are later used to interpret other patterns of observation in the laboratory, so models of an unobservable God are used to interpret new patterns of experience in human life' (1974: 49). Unlike theological realists influenced by Boyd's and Soskice's arguments for the indispensability of metaphor, the former mathematical physicist John Polkinghorne is reluctant to give a high place to metaphor in science.[53] However, he defends critical realism in science and theology on the basis of the argument

that concepts that have broad explanatory power, making swathes of experience intelligible, should be expected to have ontological reference. They make sense of the world precisely because they bear some relation to the actuality of the world. *They may refer to unseen and unseeable entities (confined quarks and gluons; the invisible God).* (1998: 44, my italics, cf. 24, 122–3)

Van Huyssteen (like Peacocke) follows Soskice's argument quite closely and asserts that

---

[50] Feuerbach and middle-period Cupitt can be interpreted along these lines.
[51] Soskice has, *inter alia*, David Tracy, Sallie Te Selle (McFague), and John Dominic Crossan in her sights (see 1985: 103–12). Cf. Drees 1996: 229–35.
[52] Barbour 1990: 46.   [53] See 1991: 29f, cf. 1996: 19ff.

All our theological models are theoretic constructs ... [T]he object of systematic theology (for example, God, Jesus Christ, the Trinity, Atonement, or Predestination) is *in principle inaccessible to observation* (as are related areas in, for example, microbiology, chemistry, geology, and nuclear physics). (1989: 163, my italics, cf. 136, 152)

It is apparent that theological realists invest heavily in the claim that God is unobservable in principle. Unfortunately, they neither subject the claim to serious theological scrutiny nor engage with the debate about observability in the philosophy of science.[54] This is regrettable because the issues are not as clear cut as their argument requires, and, as we shall see, their arguments have serious theological and philosophical weaknesses which imply that the current scientific realist view of observability prevents theological realists from making their proposed analogy and that even if it did not, it would be incompatible with a biblical view of the (un)observability of God.

Scientific realism on (un)observability

To appreciate why scientific realism prevents the analogy being drawn we need to look at the claims scientific realists make about unobservable entities. In scientific realism an unobservable entity is one whose existence independent of a theory is required for that theory to be (approximately) true. Take genes as an example. In his well-known defence of scientific realism *The Rationality of Science* (1981),[55] Newton-Smith explains that

At one stage genes were posited in order to explain observed phenomena. At that time no one had in any sense observed or detected the existence of genes. However, with the development of sophisticated microscopes scientists came to describe themselves as seeing genes. (25)

With that seeing, the theory of genes came to be held to be true: a theoretical term came to refer to a previously unobservable but now observable entity. As a consequence 'gene' is now taken to be an observation term. McMullin generalizes the point: theoretical expectations concerning hypothetical unobservable entities are frequently made good when 'theoretical entities previously unobserved, or in some cases even thought to be unobservable, are in fact observed' (1984: 33).

The upshot of this is that in scientific realism there is no hard and fast distinction between observation language and theory language.[56] As Grover

---

[54] Michael Banner (1990) is unusual in that he does the latter.
[55] Newton-Smith has modified his view of realism: see his 1989.
[56] Barbour (1974: 44, 96–8) admits the importance of denying the distinction in science but claims that in the religious case models are 'human constructs that help us interpret experience by imagining what *cannot* be observed' (1990: 45, my italics).

Maxwell argued in his classic paper 'The Ontological Status of Theoretical Entities' (1962), in scientific practice the line separating the two is always being shifted 'toward the "unobservable" end of the spectrum' (13).[57] He therefore suggested that we should replace the distinction by the notion of there being a continuum of observability. On this account, as a result of the progressive confirmation of theories, more and more entities are shifted from the unobservable end of the continuum to the observable. As Gary Gutting has argued, 'even electrons and other postulated entities... are in principle observable' (1985: 124). That theoretical terms are in principle cashable by observation is a condition of scientific realism's being true, for it permits philosophers of science to argue that the best explanation of the success of science is the realist one: science gives us access to (presently) unobservable and mind-independent entities, structures, and relations.[58] (Notice that for an empiricist it is important that such a distinction can be made. Only if it can will it be possible to maintain that scientific theories function only with respect to observation sentences by making predictions concerning what scientific instruments will show rather than by referring to and making truth claims about a supposedly unobservable reality.[59])

When theological realists argue for reference to an unobservable God on the basis of an analogy with the referentiality of theory terms in science, they must – as we have seen they do, and if the analogy is to hold – maintain that *both* are *unobservable in principle*. But there seems to me to be no coherent way of following the analogy through. If they wish to uphold the theological side of the analogy (i.e. that God is unobservable in principle), they will have to affirm that scientifically unobservable entities are also unobservable in principle. Yet this denies the principle of scientific realism that the observable/unobservable dichotomy is false, so the analogy collapses on philosophical grounds. On the other hand, if theological realists concede the scientific realist principle and persist in upholding an analogy with reference in the philosophy of science, they will have to contradict their theological principle that God is necessarily unobservable, and so they will be led to affirm that God is in principle observable.[60] The analogy will

---

57 For an empiricist response to Maxwell's argument, see van Fraassen 1980: 13–19, 214–15.
58 Quantum physics poses major difficulties here. For an account of the physics, see Whitaker 1996; for the philosophy, Fine 1996².
59 As to why empiricists argue this way, see Newton-Smith 1981: 19ff.
60 Soskice writes of an eschatologically future perceptual knowledge we *shall* enjoy 'when we see God "face to face"' (1985: 116). McGrath advocates a similar view (1998: 158f) but adds confusion to the debate when he elides the concepts of eschatological verification in theology and confirmation of theories in science. This leads him to the theologically and scientifically dubious claims that 'The key to the relation of theoretical and observable entities [sc. in theology and science] is ... eschatological' (159) and that 'a secularized version of "eschatological confirmation" is found ... in the natural sciences' (137).

then collapse on theological grounds. So, since neither option is faithful to both theological realists' arguments and scientific realism, the proposed analogy is useless as a basis for defending theological realism.

Theological realists might respond to this objection by granting that the unobservables of science are not *in principle* unobservable and by weakening their view that God is similarly unobservable. Thus, they might be able to run a theory of reference by framing a new analogy with scientific realism without committing themselves to a philosophically implausible view of scientific (un)observability.[61] However, even if such a theory were constructed, it would still run into difficulties from a theological point of view because the point at which the analogy between scientific and theological realism fails is not over the question of (un)observability *per se*. Rather, as we shall see shortly, the analogy fails because science understands the relationship between observability and unobservability in a very different way from a theology which gives full weight to the form and nature of God's self-revelation.

I suggest that when they speak of God's unobservability, theological realists make a category mistake by transferring the 'grammar' of observation in the created realm to the creator. In the realm of created reality with which science deals, the 'grammar' of observation implies practices such as prediction, experimental control, and – if we are realists – the ascription of truth to theories; by contrast, the 'grammar' of theology involves believing and obedience. Thus I shall argue that though there is a sense in which it is proper to speak of God's revelation as his making himself observable, this is not a making visible in the same sense in which electron microscopes make, say, genes visible. The revelation of God is conditioned by his sovereign freedom; unlike a gene, God is not subject to human control.

Towards a biblical view of the (un)observability of God

In contrast with theological realism's preoccupation with our achieving epistemic access to an unobservable God and the way in which this enables successful reference to be made to God, Karl Barth writes that

We must not ... base the hiddenness of God on the inapprehensibility of the infinite, the absolute, that which exists in and of itself, etc. For all this in itself ... is the product of human reason in spite of and in its supposed inapprehensibility. It is not ... identical with God and is in no way a constituent part of the divine

---

[61] I am grateful to John Roe for putting this counter-objection to me. I have not come across in the literature any modification of the theological realist position such as I outline here.

hiddenness. What we shall have to say is that God is not a being whom we can spiritually appropriate ... We are not master of God, and for this reason we cannot apprehend him of ourselves ... God is invisible and inexpressible because he is not present as the physical and spiritual world created by him is present, but is present in this world created by him in his revelation, in Jesus Christ, in the proclamation of his name, in his witnesses and sacraments. He is, therefore, visible only to faith and can be attested only by faith. But this means that he is to be seen only as the invisible and expressed only as the inexpressible, not as the substance of the goal or origin of our seeing and speaking, but because he himself has given us permission and command to see and speak, and therefore by his Word, in his free and gracious decision, has given us the capacity to see and speak. (1957: 188, 189, 190; cf. 178–90)

There is much in this passage that is germane to our theme, but for the moment we note in particular Barth's implicit criticism that those who assimilate God's ontological status to that of a scientifically unobservable entity pay insufficient attention to the 'grammar' of divine self-revelation to sinful humanity which governs the (in)visibility and (in)expressibility of God.

Barth says that God is 'visible to faith' and 'is to be seen only as the invisible'. His paradoxical tone is consistent with scripture, particularly the Johannine corpus, where it is affirmed both that 'No one has ever seen [*heoraken*] God' (1:18), and that 'the Word became flesh and lived among us, and we have seen [*etheasametha*] his glory' (1:14). Similarly, in 1 John it is affirmed both that 'No one has ever seen [*tetheatai*] God' (4:12), and that 'what was from the beginning, what we have heard, what we have seen [*heorakamen*] with our eyes, what we have looked at [*etheasametha*] and touched with our hands, concerning the word of life ... was with the Father and was revealed to us' (1:1–2).[62] By attending to the Johannine writers' (or, writer's) understanding of God's (un)observability we shall discover that a biblically informed understanding of God's ontological status and our epistemic relationship with him is very different from that offered by theological realists.

In 1 John 1, the writer tells us that the object of his declaration is 'what we have seen with our eyes, what we have looked at'. As the context makes clear, this is an allusion to the man Jesus Christ. The significance of the different verbs of seeing (and their tenses) is a matter of debate; what is not is that the language of this verse is robustly *sensory*. Howard Marshall comments that 'the qualification "with our eyes" leaves no doubt that *literal seeing* is meant' (1978: 101, my italics).[63] What was seen was 'the eternal life

---

[62] Cf. 1 John 1:1–2 and 4:12; compare also, in the Pauline corpus, 1 Tim. 6:16 and 2 Cor. 3:18, 4:6.
[63] Schnackenburg concurs: 1980: 270 n. 179.

which was with the Father' (i.e. the God whom no one has seen). In other words, just as God's name revealed to Moses reveals him to be unnameable, so the eternally hidden has become seeable in Jesus, yet without ceasing to be eternal or hidden.

Now we need to ask ourselves more precisely: what became observable and was seen? To this we should not answer that it was God's essence, for to assert that it was would be to deny the *oudeis popote* ('no one ever') of John 1:18 and the force of the exchange between Moses and YHWH at Exod. 33:18–23. Nevertheless, we must not deny John 1:14, although as soon as we say this we should also recall that this verse affirms that 'we have seen' the 'glory' of the logos.[64] Thus, since we can no more separate God's glory from God's deity than we can the logos from the Father, we are led to affirm with Barth that '*Etheasametha ten doxan autou* ... means unquestionably that we perceived his *deity*. We saw the Word in the flesh, and the Word was God; it was the divine *doxa* that we perceived' (1986b: 98). The verses we have been looking at do not say *simpliciter* both that God can be seen and that he cannot be seen. We cannot see God's essence, but we can see his glory.[65] There is, nonetheless, a real seeing of God which contradicts theological realists' flat denial that God can be seen because he is unobservable in principle.

A possible line of objection to my argument against theological realism might be that our epistemic access to the unobservable realm in both science and theology is indirect rather than direct. Polkinghorne hints at (but does not develop) such an argument when he writes that 'we habitually speak ... of entities which are not directly observable. No one has ever seen a gene ... or an electron ... No one has ever seen God (though there is the astonishing Christian claim that "the only Son, who is in the bosom of the Father, he has made him known" (John 1:18 [RSV]))' (1991: 20, cf. 1996: 14). Likewise, Peacocke claims that 'In both science and theology ... [models are] representations ... of aspects of reality that are not directly accessible to us' (1984: 41–2). Thus the objector might claim that, just as in the philosophy of science we do not directly see electrons and molecules but only the phenomena they cause, so, similarly, we do not see God's essence, but only his glory.

[64] The 'we' of John 1:14 is to be interpreted restrictively as applying to the first generation of disciples (Barth 1986b: 95f; Raymond Brown 1971: 34–5). However, it can also be regarded as including believers of subsequent generations whose seeing with the eyes of faith is dependent on the eyewitnesses' literal seeing (cf. von Balthasar 1989: 289, 357–68, 470, 521; Käsemann 1969: 160; John; 14:19; 2 Cor. 3:18; Heb. 2:9).

[65] Thiselton goes further: 'Jn. wishes to stress ... that, in Christ the Logos, men can see God in his genuine actuality and reality' (1978: 890).

This argument can be rebutted from two perspectives, that of science and that of theology. To begin with the scientific perspective: first, God's glory is not an effect that he causes and we perceive; to perceive God's glory is to perceive *his* deity, not merely its phenomenal effects on *us* – such as fear in Christ's persecutors or the transformed lives of those to whom he ministered. Second, even if it were correct to speak of indirectly observing God, the indirectness would not be attributable, as it is in science, to contingent limitations of our humanity – here, of our powers of sight – which we can overcome technologically by building, for example, microscopes and cloud chambers. Rather, our inability to see God's essence is 'an essential theological determination of humanity' (Barth 1986b: 128; cf. Exod. 33:20ff). We are (sinful) creatures. Theologically speaking, God's coming to human observability in Christ is a revelatory and saving event initiated by God's grace, not by the projects of our will. As von Balthasar puts it, 'God's self-revelation in the Incarnation of his Word has become visible once and for all historically in space and time, not only as a human form, but as the salvific action that is bound to this historical form' (1989: 289). Unlike the scientist in her laboratory, the theologian cannot act upon (the divine) nature to make God observable. Those who would see God can do so only by adopting an appropriately creaturely attitude towards him.[66] Third, although Christian faith affirms that we can see the divine *doxa*, this is as much of God as we shall ever see; it does not and cannot suggest that what is unobservable of God will ever become observable as we have seen scientific realism does of its presently unobservable entities.

Now to some specifically theological grounds on which the objection can be rebutted. First, the distinction between direct and indirect seeing is theologically inadequate. The mystery of God's visibility goes 'beyond the alternative of "direct" and "indirect" seeing. It is indirect inasmuch as a free person can never be seen other than in his giving of self, and indeed the person will be seen all the more directly as the gaze turns from the "signs" ... to what is signified in them (von Balthasar 1989: 290).' Thus, 'in all this indirectness [of the Johannine signs], the seeing is direct' (290). Second, theological realists stress the unobservability of God in order not only to establish what they regard as a proper agnosticism and tentativeness in their models of God, but also to uphold his incomprehensibility. However, the Johannine literature cuts across this view: whilst preserving God's incomprehensibility to humanity, it achieves this precisely by emphasizing his

---

[66] Cf. Matt. 5:8; Heb. 12:14; von Balthasar 1989: 267.

self-revelation and self-exegesis in the incarnation. The latter is a necessary condition of the former. To quote von Balthasar again:

God is incomprehensible, and the more he offers himself to our understanding mind, the more his incomprehensibility grows ... God's incognito in Jesus was simultaneously his appearing in Jesus' mission and task, and ... this unity of disclosure and concealment was absolutely unique, without any point of comparison in this world. (1989: 318, 321–2)

Furthermore, the Johannine corpus distinguishes between insiders and outsiders in a way that would be totally inappropriate for scientific method: the divine incomprehensibility is only properly recognized by *believers*. Even for 'Doubting' Thomas, but especially for those who come after him, the gift of faith in Christ is indispensable to seeing.[67] Believers see the glory of the Father in Jesus, and yet, in a paradox that is of the essence of Christology, '[Christ] provides the world with so much to see that the miracles ... lead to his death' (Käsemann 1969: 161).

In the light of these dialectics of observability and unobservability and of comprehensibility and incomprehensibility, we must question the appropriateness of the preponderance theological realists give to God's ineffability. Soskice collapses these dialectics when she distinguishes between referring to and defining God and proposes that 'This is the fine edge where negative and positive theology meet, for the apophatic insight that we say nothing of God, but only point towards him, is the basis for the tentative and avowedly inadequate stammerings by which we attempt to speak of God' (1985: 140). Contrast von Balthasar:

[*Doxa*] is the divinity of God as it is freely made known. The fact that it is *made known* means that it has placed itself within an expressive form; but the fact that *it* is made known means that in the same act it bursts through every form. This act of breaking-through such finite bonds makes God, in all religion and mysticism other than those of the Bible, the ineffable, before whom words can only stammer and must in the end (in a finally apophatic theology) be silent. The paradox of the Biblical revelation is that the ineffable *as such* has placed itself in the word: this proclaims its sublime freedom and power, but also the terrifying danger that the word, where it ceases to be a word of prayer, may forget the ineffability of God and absolutise itself as a human *logos*. (1989: 265–6)

From this discussion I conclude that the (un)observability of the God of Jesus Christ is insufficiently analogous either to scientific observability or to scientific unobservability for the theological realist analogy to hold. Moreover, because God brings himself to visibility in Jesus, we must question

---

[67] John 20:29, cf. 5:37ff, 14:8ff.

theological realism's concern with our gaining epistemic access to God and the need to postulate him as unobservable in principle. The biblical texts we have looked at suggest that it is God who has found epistemic access to us in Christ, not we to him. Although the Bible in its constituent parts and as a canonical whole is of no settled mind on the visibility of God,[68] it does permit us to generalize from our survey of the Johannine literature to the conclusions that (1) God grants his observability and his unobservability to be known through his self-revelation and that (2) responsive faith is the indispensable yet divinely granted condition of our seeing God.[69] If these are characteristics of the biblical God and his relationship with humanity, then they should feature in a realist account of him.

As their arguments stand, theological realists assimilate God to the status of a scientifically unobservable entity and so obscure these aspects of the biblical witness. Had they paid more attention to the question we looked at in the previous chapter – About which God should Christians be realists? – or the question posed in the first chapter concerning how God should be spoken of in order that our speaking is about *God*, they might not have confused the ontology of derived, created reality with the underived reality of the creator, the *ens realissimum*. They are left with a dilemma. They can either be fully committed to a scientific outlook, make appropriate changes to their methodology, use the resources of the philosophy of science in the way they do, face the possibility that the balance of the argument concerning the entity they postulate to explain religious experiences will come up favouring naturalist non-cognitivism and then, if it does, drop the realist claim. Or they can drop the proposed analogy, acknowledge that God is not unobservable in the way that the philosophy of science understands such entities, seek an amicable divorce from scientific realism, and find a more theological way of defending the realism of Christian faith.

Clarifying his exposition of the scientific character of theology, Karl Barth complains that

To the question what is the 'science' to which theology must fully adhere, G. Wobbermin ... gives the ingenuous answer: 'Striving after the most exact and complete possible knowledge of the reality accessible to us.' But what good theology will include its object in 'the reality accessible to us'? And will a bad theology which does this really be granted by other sciences the recognition which it seeks? (1975: 8, quoting Wobbermin 1929: 25)

---

[68] See, for example, Exod. 20:21, 24:9, 33:11 and 18–23, 34:29–35 (cf. 2 Cor. 3:7–18), Luke 17:20. Notice that 'hearing (leading to obedience) rather than "seeing" is the vital key to religious experience in Hebrew faith' (Smalley 1984: 246).

[69] Cf. von Balthasar 1989: 277, 291, 358ff, 379f and Käsemann 1969: 159.

With their concern for securing epistemic access to God, theological realists demonstrate that it is still fashionable to construe theology as '[s]triving after ... knowledge of the reality accessible to us'. We have accumulated ample evidence for this not being conducive to 'good theology'. (It is equally open to question whether 'bad theology' finds the recognition it seeks. Writing of the supposed 'interaction' between science and theology, Lash asks, 'Do scientists really expect to have to modify their practices in the light of what they learn from theologians?', and answers, 'Not in my experience' (1988: 204–5).[70]) In the previous chapter, we saw that theological realists pay insufficient attention to ontological questions concerning the identity of the biblical God. To this we can now add that theological realists' concern with epistemological questions, understood in terms of the debate with empiricism in the philosophy of science, ramify into a series of misconstruals or category mistakes concerning theological method and the God whose self-revelation is the proper concern of theology. We have no reason to doubt that the thinkers we have been criticizing wish to be realists about this God, but these category mistakes result in the false assimilations we have examined. I conclude that if Christians wish to be realists about the triune, biblical God, they should take leave of the methods adopted by theological realism.

Nearly half a century ago, Gilbert Ryle argued that

If the seeming feuds between science and theology ... are to be dissolved at all, their dissolution can come not from making the polite compromise that both parties are really artists of a sort working from different points of view and with different sketching materials, but from drawing uncompromising contrasts between their businesses. (1954: 81)

If anything, since Ryle wrote these words, the more threatened by science Christians have felt the more inclined have they been to make polite compromises. The drawing of some such contrasts as Ryle advocates has been my goal in this chapter. I have tried to do this so that Christians can be uncompromisingly *Christian* realists, since, as I take to be the case, Christians can only be realists about the God who identifies himself as *yhwh*, *ehyeh asher ehyeh* if they avoid contaminating the 'grammar' of their faith by dipping their brushes into other people's paint pots. Accordingly, clarifying the 'grammar' of Christian faith will be our concern in the next chapter.

[70] Cf. Gould 2001.

CHAPTER 4

Realism and Christian faith after Wittgenstein

THE GRAMMAR OF FAITH

Ludwig Wittgenstein's place in the philosophical canon is rather less certain at the beginning of the present century than it was in the middle quarters of the last. Though Wittgenstein is a very strong background influence on some major figures in contemporary philosophy, his stock has generally fallen.[1] However, it has risen, albeit modestly, in the philosophy of religion, and arguably these shifts are related. Wittgenstein's work contains many references to theological matters,[2] but his interest in and sympathetic stance towards Christian faith has always been something of an embarrassment to many of the philosophical establishment. Nor did his attitude to philosophical problems flatter them: recall his dictum that 'The philosopher's treatment of a question is like the treatment of an illness' (1978[3]: §255). He thought that the clarity for which philosophers should strive 'means that the philosophical problems should *completely* disappear' (§133). The proper concern of philosophy is the destruction of idols and its aim is, one could almost say, salvific: 'To shew the fly the way out of the fly-bottle' (§309).[3] Though Wittgenstein was not thinking of idols as a theologian would, his approach, especially when cast in language strongly redolent of religion, has understandably alienated some philosophers. Conversely, but for the same reason, theologians seeking conceptual clarity without investing in particular metaphysical theories have often welcomed his work: for him, as for theologians, philosophy is best regarded as an in principle dispensable tool of description and conceptual clarification.

Scientism is an object of fairly widespread concern at present, and its effects are evident in many of the views examined in the last two chapters.

---

[1] Two contrasting opinions are represented by Monk's (1996) and McGinn's (1997) reviews of Hacker's apologia for *Wittgenstein's Place in Twentieth-Century Analytic Philosophy* (1996).

[2] Philip Shields (1993) offers a suggestive but rather tendentious reading of Wittgenstein through the lens of traditional Christian concerns with sin, idolatry, and salvation.

[3] For Wittgenstein's criticisms of idolatry, see Hacker 1996: 84 and Shields 1993: 75–85.

Certainly Wittgenstein foresaw the baleful influence a militant scientific ideology could have on culture in general and philosophy in particular, and by the time he entered his second major period, he thought that the quest for theoretically rigorous, abstract explanation that is proper to science had been allowed to encroach upon and damage philosophy by inclining us to 'search for explanations instead of describing "grammatical" conventions' (Baker and Hacker 1980: 482).[4] 'Philosophers', Wittgenstein wrote,

constantly see the method of science before their eyes, and are irresistibly tempted to ask and answer questions in the way science does. This tendency is the real source of metaphysics, and leads the philosopher into complete darkness. I want to say here that it can never be our job ... to explain anything. Philosophy really *is* 'purely descriptive'. (1969[2]: 18)

Explanations – especially scientific ones – reflect a mistaken 'craving for generality' and a 'contemptuous attitude towards the particular case' (1969[2]: 17, 18). They tend to reductive homogenization of the rich diversity of human culture, but Wittgenstein's emphasis on philosophy's task as the description of 'grammar' is intended to respect this diversity.

'Grammar' has a central role in his later work, and he uses the concept to refer to the way the meaningful use of a concept is governed by a usually unremarked rule or set of rules found by carefully attending to the concept's surroundings in the particular stream of life where it has meaning.[5] A first encounter with Wittgenstein's later work can be baffling: his style is by turns epigrammatic, fragmentary, and conversational; rather than establish positions by sustained argument he makes 'remarks' (1978[3]: vii). But once we realize that he is trying to get us away from philosophical abstractions and back to everyday life, to get us to imagine for ourselves, to 'see' for ourselves, the differences between the way concepts work in different practices, then we can begin to grasp the importance of grammar.[6] For example, the following passage from his 'Lectures on Religious Belief' shows how the grammar of 'belief' differs between empirical and religious contexts.

Suppose someone were a believer and said: 'I believe in a Last Judgement', and I said, 'Well, I'm not so sure. Possibly.' You would say that there is an enormous gulf between us. If he said 'There is a German aeroplane overhead', and I said 'Possibly. I'm not so sure', you'd say we were fairly near. (1966: 53)

That the grammar of belief is different in the two contexts is shown by whether it makes sense to require convincing concerning the object of the

---

[4] Cf. Wittgenstein 1978[3]: §109.   [5] See Baker and Hacker 1985: 41–64.
[6] See Wittgenstein 1978[3]: §§89–133.

beliefs. 'Possibly' implies that we could test the belief – entirely sensible in connection with the perceptual belief (perhaps it's a British plane), but ludicrous of belief in the Last Judgement when we consider that belief in its religious context. So Wittgenstein's later philosophy is concerned to show the conceptual puzzles that arise when we (usually philosophers) ignore the grammar of concepts and come up with what looks like a clearly formulated idea (for example, that belief in the Last Judgement is analogous to perceptual belief), but which, when its grammar is exposed, is clearly nonsense. He thought that theology needed reminding of its grammatical conventions and ridiculed those who make faith 'a question of science' (1966: 57). 'Grammar', he famously said, 'tells what kind of object anything is. (Theology as grammar)' (1978³: §373). In many ways Wittgenstein showed a better understanding of theological method than those – and some of them are theologians – who, confusedly thinking that substantives must correspond to some kind of object, ask 'what kind of object' God is.[7] Now, if theological realists are inattentive to the grammar of Christian faith, it might be thought that Wittgenstein's emphasis on grammar will provide us with an Ariadne's thread through the realism maze. However, this is not so, since, as I shall argue in this and the following chapter, theology is not only a grammatical or regulative activity, but is itself regulated.

To return for a moment to my criticism of theological realism, my point is not just that its exponents downplay the grammar of 'God' but that they ignore the fact that theology has its own grammar which exercises a regulative role over theology.[8] On the one hand, their arguments lead them to construe 'God' in terms drawn from the philosophy of science rather than from its role in Christian activities such as prayer and worship; on the other – and this is a more serious criticism – their arguments do not bring these activities into consideration in such a way as to enable them to make a theologically significant contribution to how we understand the way the term works in Christian language. My own suggestion is that taking account of theology's being a grammatically regulated activity is crucial for defending the realism of the Christian faith.

The *material* question that needs to be raised here is, What regulates theology – what keeps it in good conceptual order? But to ask this presumes an affirmative answer to the *formal* question whether it is even coherent to

---

[7] For contrasting opinions about Wittgenstein's own religious beliefs, see Norman Malcolm 1993: 21 (and *passim*) and McClendon and Kallenberg 1998.

[8] As will become clear shortly, my opinion that theology is 'grammatically' regulated is theological in character rather than philosophical; my use of the term is genetically dependent on, though not a clone of, Wittgenstein's.

speak of theology as grammatically regulated. If it is not, theological realism will have to be regarded as just as valid a way of arguing for realism as any other. Should its methods' tendencies and conclusions provoke conflict with other approaches to the issue, then so much the worse for realism. But so much the worse for theology too. In classical orthodoxy the coherence of theology derived from theologians' shared devotion to a common and universally available (though only by reason of his self-revealing agency) deity – the living God. But now, after the Enlightenment and under the ethos of Romanticism, theological coherence is regarded as being found in a common and more nearly anthropological interest in humanity's religious quest.[9] In this case, theology becomes a means of describing, analysing, or articulating in a more abstract and theoretical mode, religious experience and the quest for meaning.[10]

To speak of theology as a regulated activity is to admit that questions of authority are in play. The great divide between the two styles of theology just outlined is reflected in their attitudes to authority. In very crude terms, the former attempts to give clear priority to the liberating authority of God in Christ; the latter accepts the influence of Kant's moral philosophy, suspects that a theology of a self-revealing God promotes heteronomy, and so places humanity and its experiences at the focus of theological reflection.[11] Theological realism sits uneasily between the two. It appeals to authoritative traditions of realism in the Christian past as a reason for defending realism in the present and uses authority figures to articulate the defence, yet it is the authoritative experience of these figures, rather than the intrinsic authority of a self-revealing God, to which appeal is made. Although the concepts of revelation and religious experience are closely related, it does not follow that they cannot, or should not as a matter of methodological principle, be kept separate. However, the kind of revisionism into which theological realism is led by eliding them makes it hard to identify where the authorization of theology lies (or should in principle be held to lie) – that is, whether it originates in human experience interpreted according to particular religious traditions or whether it is derived from God's unique self-revelation.[12] My claim that theology itself is regulated makes a bid for the latter view, but this needs to be argued for, so we turn now to the formal

[9] A leading example of such an approach is Tracy 1981.   [10] See Schleiermacher 1928: §§15–19.

[11] In his brilliant study *Trinity and Truth*, Bruce Marshall (2000, see especially 50–70, 75–80; cf. 108–40) analyses the issue of authority in terms of whether theological methods grant 'unrestricted epistemic primacy' to the Trinity or whether they display an 'epistemic dependence' on secular philosophical settlements.

[12] This is apparent in Soskice (see above, pp. 48f), but the best recent example from theological realists is Knight 2001, especially 23–44.

question of whether it is coherent to speak of theology as a grammatically regulated activity.

From a strictly Wittgensteinian point of view the answer would have to be 'No', but the reason is instructive and will help bring out why a distinctively Christocentric approach should be taken to the question of realism. In the early 1980s there was a famous debate about Wittgenstein's views concerning what it is to follow a rule – say, for counting in arithmetic. The argument turned on the question of what sustains our rule-following practices – whether it is reality, or our inculturation into a set of practices.[13] The latter option looked vertiginously sceptical and anti-realist, but in fact, though Wittgenstein heavily stresses practices, other of his 'remarks' suggest that the position built on this emphasis was misconceived. In his ruminations on grammar and its rule-like functions, Wittgenstein deliberates with his imaginary interlocutor:

'How am I able to obey a rule?' – if this is not a question about causes, then it is about the justification for my following the rule in the way that I do. If I have exhausted the justifications I have reached bedrock, and my spade is turned. Then I am inclined to say: 'This is simply what I do.' (1978³: §217)

For Wittgenstein there is no meta-practice to which we can appeal that will justify our counting as we do, and neither is there any reason in reality for our counting as we do, nor is there any further justification for our counting as we do. Instead we just have to accept that the bedrock against which the spade turns is 'agreement . . . in form of life' and 'in judgements' (1978³: §§241–2) since these are in place before scepticism or anti-realism can (self-stultifyingly) get going. The essential point here for my own argument is that for Wittgenstein there is nothing apart from our human practices that sustains them: they are self-sustaining, self-subsistent, and self-regulating. Seeking a grammar which keeps our practices in order is a foolish and needless circularity: their grammar is shown through them but is not independent of them.[14]

Thus, when Wittgenstein says that 'Grammar tells us what kind of object anything is. (Theology as grammar)' (1978³: §373), and that 'theology is the grammar of the word "God"' (Wittgenstein quoted by Ambrose 1979: 32), he means that, as Robert Arrington puts it, 'the grammatical statements coming from theology authorize and constrain a particular way of talking – the religious way' and that 'theological statements are grammatical rules

---

[13] Saul Kripke (1982) initiated the debate; it was effectively closed by Baker and Hacker (1984).
[14] See Baker and Hacker 1984: 83–5.

guiding religious action and feeling – as well as guiding occasional descriptive claims about particular persons and events' (Arrington 2001: 173). In other words, theology regulates religious practices; it stands to the practices of Christian faith as the rules of chess stand to the playing of chess.

Now, if correct, this line of argument would seriously weaken my criticism of theological realists, for there would be nothing in virtue of which to distinguish my approach from theirs. They cannot be said to be ignoring the grammar of theological practices, for it is already present simply in virtue of the fact that they are doing theology. To adapt Herbert Morrison's quip about British politics that 'socialism is whatever Labour governments do', theology just is whatever theologians do. In the same way that rules for arithmetic are upheld by nothing other than doing arithmetic, so the grammar of theology is upheld by doing theology. The grammar of theology is given in the practice of theology – it is not something behind, apart from, or in addition to it. In that it regulates religious practices, theology is a second-order, meta-discipline, but there is no meta-meta-discipline regulating theology – indeed, to ask for such a discipline would be to invite an infinite regress. All of which implies that my suggestion that theology itself is a grammatically regulated activity is incoherent.

However, I believe that we must reject the formal objection to my approach represented by Wittgenstein's appeal to a bedrock in practices and his way of understanding theology as a regulative activity. This might appear circular since making a theological objection is itself a theological practice, but the reason for rejecting Wittgenstein's conclusion is that it actually runs against elements of Christian practices. The demonstration of this (and making the required modification of Wittgenstein's account of grammar) will be a major theme of this and the next chapter, but to summarize, I shall argue that whilst theology does have a second-order, regulative function with respect to first-order practices of prayer, worship, preaching, service, and so on, theology is itself a Christian practice which has vitality insofar as it springs from these first-order practices. Just as the former are directed towards, sustained by, and answerable to, God, so is theology, even as a second-order activity. Consequently, I shall argue that Christian practices point to their having authorization from God's radical otherness to and simultaneous 'interruptive' involvement in them by his word and Spirit. Indeed, God's standing in this prevenient relationship to Christian practices is both constitutive and definitive of them; their existence and fruitfulness as Christian practices is dependent on the grace of God. If they are to continue as *Christian* practices (rather than as empty rituals, Christian in name only), they cannot be regarded, as a purely Wittgensteinian approach regards them, as self-sustaining and self-regulating.

There is therefore an interplay and interdependence between these varieties of Christian practice: first-order practices are regulated by second-order practices and the latter are animated by the former, but both stand under the word of God. In this way the approach I am advocating in contrast to Wittgenstein's stands quite close to one Barth expressed in his *Göttingen Dogmatics*, where he explains the function of dogmatic theology – which he construes in a second-order way – in relationship to preaching:

> If I may take a not wholly incongruent parallel from political life, dogma and dogmatics do not represent the legislative branch (which is God's Word) or the executive branch (the church as bearer of kerygma) but the judicial branch, the supreme court. As a critical authority dogma and dogmatics stand above Christian preaching, which may not escape their service (not their lordship) insofar as preaching is a human act that needs a norm. Yet they also stand under it, for they have their origin in it and must yield to it as the moon does to the sun insofar as preaching, proceeding from revelation and scripture, is itself God's Word. (1991: 18)

Thus, to revert to Wittgensteinian idiom and to assert points that will be argued in the course of this and the following chapter: to locate the grammar of Christian practices – that which exercises a regulative function over them – elsewhere than in God himself is to deny to the Christian faith and its concept of God their own particular characteristics.[15] Christian practices are sustained by God, and in virtue of this the terms embedded in them are made fit to convey reality. Thus against the formal objection, I argue that it is not incoherent to suggest that Christian-faith-as-a-whole (i.e. theology included) has a grammar and, as I have already hinted, my argument will be that God himself is this grammar.

This proposal runs against the trend of much recent philosophy of religion and theology done under the tutelage of Wittgenstein's understanding of grammar, notably that of the philosopher D. Z. Phillips and the Yale theologian George Lindbeck. Their work is widely influential, and the position I have just sketched can be developed more fully in dialogue with them. Since both are commonly interpreted as anti-realists, the possibility of finding an argument for a Christian realism that is faithful to the grammar of Christian faith in dialogue with them does not look strong. I shall argue that although this interpretation needs challenging, if we are to be faithful to the grammar of Christian faith, we shall need a more Christologically nuanced conception of realism than either provides.

---

[15] For a more 'Catholic' exposition of theology as second-order discourse see Jenson 1997: 18ff.

PHILLIPS, GRAMMAR, AND REALISM

Phillips contra realism?

D. Z. Phillips is widely regarded as the doyen of Wittgensteinian philosophy of religion. In his view, respecting the grammar of a religious belief means that it is only proper to speak and ask questions about the fact and nature of God's existence from within an appreciation (not necessarily religiously committed) of the ways in which the form of life in which the concept 'God' is used conditions that use. It follows from this that 'Christian beliefs are not answerable to philosophical justification' (1993a: 235). The intelligibility of the claim that God exists should not be defended by philosophical arguments or justified by appeal to a concept of rational justification *external* to the context in which it is used; instead, 'the criteria of intelligibility in religious matters are to be found within religion' (1993a: 8).[16] For Phillips the rationality of belief in God inheres in the practices that exemplify it, but his critics argue that this is fideistic because it seems to make Christian faith independent of a general, neutral conception of rationality and thereby immune to external criticism.[17]

Phillips's analysis of the grammar of God's existence leads him to reject standard understandings of realism in religion and in his important paper 'On Really Believing' (1993a: 33–53) he aims to show that 'realism is not co-herently expressible' (1993a: 34). Taking Roger Trigg and Terence Penelhum as debating partners, he contends that they neglect

> the grammatical issues involved in 'believing' [in God]. They take themselves to be reflecting, philosophically, a straightforward relation between belief and its object. Similarly, theological realism takes itself to be the expression of a truism: we cannot believe in God unless we believe there is a God to believe in. If that were denied it seems belief would be robbed of its object. (1993a: 35)[18]

So, Phillips's attack on realism is two-pronged: first, he addresses the mis-taken idea that God is an object; second, he sets about showing that the realists' view of the relation between belief and its object is mistaken.

Phillips is well known for his denial that the ontologically unique God of religion could be 'an object among objects' (1993a: 12).[19] Despite the

---

[16] Phillips writes of 'religion' as though it were a single phenomenon with a common essence, but there is no such particular practice as 'religion' – there are only practices of particular religions.

[17] See Nielsen 1982; cf. Phillips 1993a: xiff, 30.

[18] The theological realism Phillips attacks is somewhat different from the one we looked at in earlier chapters; the version he attacks typically defends realism by traditional arguments for objective theism but without the use of analogies from philosophy of science. See, for example, Trigg 1998.

[19] Many theologians would agree: see, for example, Barth 1956: 5; Tillich 1953: 191.

tendency of philosophers to do so, the grammar of 'God' should not be interpreted in terms of an alien context – say physics – and then transposed into religion. Again, Phillips is making a grammatical point when he says that the question 'Is God real?' is not to do with matters of fact. Why? Because

To say that *x* is a fact is to say something about the grammar of *x*; it is to indicate what it would and would not be sensible to say or do in connection with it. To say that the concept of divine reality does not share this grammar is to reject the possibility of talking about God in the way in which one talks about matters of fact. (1993a: 2)

By taking God's existence to be a matter of fact concerning an object, realism shows that it neglects the grammar of language about God.

Phillips's emphasis that the grammar of such language is shown in religious practices has led to his being accused of *reducing* God's existence to practices. Although this is a plausible interpretation of his earlier work, Phillips denies that he is a reductionist and would turn the tables on those who allege that he is. He asks,

Is it reductionism to say that what is meant by the reality of God is what is to be found in certain pictures which say themselves? If we mean by reductionism an attempt to reduce the significance of religious belief to something other than it is, then reductionism consists in the attempt, however sophisticated, to say that religious pictures must refer to some object; that they must describe matters of fact. That is the real reductionism which distorts the character of religious belief. (1976: 150)

In other words, realism is the real reductionism because it reduces God to the status of a describable, empirical object. Some would see this as a slightly evasive move, yet whatever we make of it we can see that there is prima facie evidence in his work for treating the reductionist allegation against Phillips with caution. Positively, by emphasizing the role that grammar plays in our understanding of God's reality, he wishes to prevent theologians from making the kind of false assimilations we explored in chapters 2 and 3.

Phillips's attack on those such as Trigg and Penelhum has prompted many to take him to be rejecting realism *tout court*.[20] For example, Penelhum interprets Phillips's opposition to theistic proofs as amounting to 'an understanding of religious thought and practice that shows faith *as it is* to be a

---

[20] Phillips's views have been described as 'expressivist' and interpreted in ways which put him close to Cupitt or Braithwaite (see, for example, Banner 1990: 69). Phillips explicitly rejects Braithwaite's position (1976: 140ff), and although he has sailed close to the expressivist wind, he has recently repudiated it (1993a: 47f).

non-realist phenomenon' (1983: 163).²¹ Although this reading is warranted, there is actually more reason for caution in reading him as a non-realist than there is for seeing his deeper sympathies lying with a form of realism. To appreciate these, we need to look at the second prong of his attack on realism – that is, that realists operate with a mistaken view of the relation between belief and its object. Phillips puts his criticism as follows:

> The theological realist argues, as Trigg does: 'It must be recognised that there are two distinct parts in religious commitment, the acceptance of certain propositions as true, and, as a result, a religious response, expressed in both worship and action' [1973: 42]. The realist argues that the same distinction can be made with respect to all our beliefs. On the one hand we believe certain things are true, and on the other hand we commit ourselves and act accordingly. But what is involved in believing something to be true? The realist can give no intelligible answer to this question. His failure is due to his exclusion of the method of projection within which the relation of belief to its object has its sense. (1993a: 40)

The characteristics of particular beliefs are shown within the practices of which they are *already* a part – this is what Phillips means by his view of 'the method of projection'. The relation between belief and its object is shown by the grammar of the context in which the belief has its sense, but on the view Phillips is criticizing '[b]elieving in God ... is logically independent of any role it plays in the religious life' (1993a: 49). On Phillips's own view, affirmations of religious belief emerge from and are integral to practices. For example, God may have meant nothing to someone until he participates in them; then, suddenly, 'God has become a reality in [that person's] life.' Phillips asks,

> Has this come about by his discovering an object? Hardly. What has happened is that he has found God *in* a praise, a thanksgiving, a confessing and an asking which were not his before. (1976: 181)

In just such contexts do we confess faith in God. The faith is not *prior* to the commitment expressed in the confession: faith is just what is exercised *in making* the confession.²²

---

²¹ Penelhum distinguishes Phillips's alleged non-realism from that of Cupitt, Braithwaite, and Hare who, he suggests, argue that, although theological realism has been 'an integral part of faith as traditionally practised', we should now 'adopt a position which is free from supernatural beliefs' (1983: 162). This is correct: Phillips (1993a: 48) denies that 'religious beliefs are simply the outward forms of attitudes which can survive their demise'. Cupitt (1993: 117–18) suggests that Phillips's treatment of traditional realists is in bad faith. Hick thinks that Phillips is a non-realist 'atheist' (Hick 1993: 8).

²² This point is confirmed by Jesus' practice of summoning people to 'repent and believe'. The order is important, and although it is fiduciary belief to which Jesus calls people, this includes a propositional element.

Realists like Trigg and Penelhum are suspicious of Phillips's insistence on this point.[23] They think that for faith to be realist it must be supported by evidence and/or argument to the effect that God exists independently of believers. Since Phillips denies the need for, and the worth of, such procedures, they regard him as a non-realist fideist. But, Phillips argues, this is because they are foundationalists who think that beliefs and religious commitments must be justified independently of any practices other than those of a 'context-free rationality' (Trigg 1998: 152). The theological realist view is thus opposed to the church's baptismal liturgy, for this has a much more fideistic structure: the Decision to repent and turn to Christ *follows* the Liturgy of the Word and *precedes* the Profession of (credal) Faith.[24]

Against theological realism, Phillips holds that belief is not a mental state we must attain *before* the action of committing ourselves to the object it intends: it is itself an action that takes place in a determinate context. Believing is not a two-stage process in which fulfilment of one's epistemic duties must precede the action of commitment to the content of the belief: we do not come to believe that God exists and only after this engage in the practices of religion. So Phillips is arguing that being an epistemically justified theistic realist is not a necessary condition of being a practising, realist Christian. Theological realism gives a false impression of Christian faith by suggesting that there is such a necessary condition.[25] Conversely, only if it is necessary will the theological realists' critique of Phillips's position as non-realist carry weight. But in any case, Phillips does not think that philosophy can settle whether God exists. Its task is more modest: it can only bring out the grammar of the debate. Philosophy cannot put genuine religious belief on a footing independent of religious practices: such a stance is unattainable in principle. Furthermore, by locating 'the essence of belief' in a foundationalist understanding of the process of coming to believe, theological realism severs belief from its fruits in people's lives and drastically downgrades the latter when really this is the most important aspect of Christian faith.[26] Those who think that Phillips is a non-realist will be surprised by his summary statement of his argument against them: '*realism cannot take seriously the central religious conviction that God is at work in people's lives. The reductionism which the realist finds in non-realism is all too prevalent in the realist's account of believing in God*' (1993a: 47).

---

[23] See Trigg 1998: 134–53; cf. 178–86.
[24] See the Anglican baptism liturgy in *Common Worship*, especially pp. 353–6.
[25] For further discussion, see chapter 7, pp. 187–9.   [26] 1993a: 46ff, 55.

Phillips pro realism?

In the light of the passage just quoted we can see that when Phillips says that 'realism has never been integral to faith', we need to take care not to misunderstand him. He emphasizes this by adding that he 'does not mean that we must embrace non-realism', and goes on to attack Penelhum and Trigg, who, he complains, 'are wrong in thinking that I have done so in my work'. However, before we get too excited and start thinking that Phillips has undergone a philosophical conversion, he pronounces a plague on both houses: 'Theological non-realism is as empty as theological realism. Both terms are battle cries in a confused philosophical and theological debate' (1993a: 35).

Despite his apparently condemning to futility the whole debate over God's reality, Phillips's recent work can be read as a constructive conceptual clarification aiming to show the manner in which God is God.[27] Disarming critics on both sides of the argument, he affirms that 'God's reality is synonymous with his divinity; God is divinely real' (1993a: 17). For Phillips, the rivalry between the essentially empty pictures underlying both realism and non-realism conceals more of God's reality than it reveals. Both make God less than divinely real by putting the reality of divinity on a par with that of any other transient object. Although he gives no clear positive indication of what being divinely real amounts to, it is worth pursuing Phillips's positive affirmations further. Sensitive to being misunderstood as flatly rejecting realism, he claims Kierkegaard and Simone Weil as allies and quotes them as saying, respectively, that 'God does not exist, he is eternal' and that 'in loving God we love something that does not exist' (1995c: 138). And if these recruits will not carry the day against his critics, he concedes:

> by all means say that 'God' functions as a referring expression, that 'God' refers to a sort of object, that God's reality is a matter of fact, and so on. *But please remember that, as yet, no conceptual or grammatical clarification has taken place.* We have all the work still to do since we shall now have to show, in this religious context, what speaking of 'reference', 'object', 'existence', and so on amounts to, how it differs, in obvious ways, from other uses of these terms. (1995c: 138)

In a similar vein, when discussing Lindbeck, Phillips clearly endorses God's 'independent reality' and criticizes Lindbeck for assuming

> that the notion of an independent reality *only* has application where talk of physical objects is concerned. [For], when a believer strays from the ways of God, he clearly thinks of himself as departing from a reality which is independent of himself. (1988a: 203)

---

[27] Thus he returns to a position he proposed in his 1993a: 1–9, originally published in 1963.

Contrary to his position at an earlier period, in the more recent passages just quoted Phillips is implicitly conceding that traditional realist language does not *entail* conceiving God as an object amongst other objects or that God's independent reality *must* be construed on the same lines as that of a *physical* object. Thus insofar as he once held that such moves were an inescapable feature of realism and that criticizing them in the way he did was constitutive of non-realism, it is now mistaken exegesis to regard Phillips as a non-realist.[28] Indeed, the way seems open to take him to be a realist. This is shown by his condemning Lindbeck for, he thinks, jettisoning 'talk of "ontological truth" where religion is concerned. Instead of doing so, he should have explored the grammar of "the independently real" in a religious context' (1988a: 206). Unfortunately for his expositor, Phillips does not offer such an exploration.

Any hopes that Phillips has now seen that it is possible to be a realist without getting involved in the kind of mistakes he has exposed in theological realism are dashed when, just a little later in the same book as that in which he criticizes Lindbeck, he takes away with one hand what he has seemed to offer with the other. Discussing another Yale theologian, Paul Holmer – to whom he is generally sympathetic, and who, like Lindbeck, is influenced by Wittgenstein, Phillips criticizes him for using such words as 'real', 'rational', 'objective', and 'true' even though Holmer emphasizes that these words must be understood in a grammatically appropriate way. Such criteriological words are members of the realist family, so on the basis of what he has just said of other members of the family – 'ontological truth' and 'independently real' – we reasonably expect Phillips to agree with Holmer's desire to see them understood grammatically. But Phillips doesn't: instead he seems to demur at his incipient realism. He writes that 'insisting that [such terms] be applied to religion and other forms of discourse may do more harm than good' (1988a: 227). But Phillips seems inconsistent here: why might Holmer's grammatically sensitive use of 'real' do more harm than Lindbeck's less grammatically sensitive use of 'independently real', especially since affirming the latter is to make a stronger claim than the former? (Consider: sense perception is real regarding the sensation, but it does not follow that what is sensed is independently real.) We are not told.

In large measure, Phillips's ambivalence towards realism originates in his Wittgensteinian perception that 'philosophical terms take on a life of their own'. Words such as 'real' and 'objective' are introduced to clarify

---

[28] Mistaken on *exegetical* grounds; see Davis 1995: 90. Paul Helm (1997: 53–76) and William Alston (1995b: 21–4) debate sympathetically with Phillips but regard him as anti-realist because he epistemizes truth. See also Scott and Moore 1997.

conceptual puzzles, but then 'the primary language which occasioned the original puzzlement is soon forgotten' (1988a: 225). The puzzles get assimilated to 'traditional metaphysics' and 'philosophical conceptions of ontology' (1993b: 205), and what was intended to be philosophical clarification becomes autonomous from the practices and forms of life it was introduced to explicate. We have seen the results of this in the version of theological realism Phillips opposes and in that which is influenced by the philosophy of science: the ontological status of God as the *ens realissimum* is in danger of being lost from a specifically Christian theology, and theology is at risk of becoming a meta-explanatory project in essential continuity with science. I have suggested that a grammatical approach might help us to avoid these problems but that whilst Lindbeck and Phillips have much to teach us, theirs are paths we cannot follow because they ignore the way in which Christian practices are themselves regulated. This is the topic of the next chapter, but to prepare the ground for it, I shall now show, first, that on Phillips's argument Christian practices are not an infallible guide to the grammar of realist language, and second that his understanding of that language is insufficiently informed by theological considerations.

The Sea of Faith and the fallibility of practices

To see that practices are not an infallible guide to the grammar of Christian language we can begin by considering Phillips's view of a person's relationship with God. He highlights 'the emergence of spiritual awareness [in] "coming to God" ' and the importance of making a 'worshipful response' (1995b: 6, 12). This language appears realist: 'to be aware' could imply an object, and 'to respond' does; the language implies awareness of some 'object' and response to 'something'. But not necessarily: *spiritual* awareness need not have an object (as Phillips's scare quotes are perhaps intended to indicate); responding worshipfully does not entail an object to be worshipped. Similarly, Phillips says that it 'should not be a surprise to find that God's reality is a spiritual reality. To find God is to enter into some kind of affective relationship with the divine' (1995a: 5). This looks like realist language too: to speak of a relationship with the divine implies some 'other' with which one enters into relationship. However, to say that the relationship is affective raises the question of whether it is *only* affective. Phillips is very reticent about how the grammar of the language here is to be interpreted, so the questions arise: are Christians of all people the most deluded? Is their spiritual affect merely an effect of their practices, a solipsistic projection; or is it the result of an encounter with the Divine Other?

If he really means it when he says that a believer thinks that God has 'a reality which is independent of himself' (1988a: 203), Phillips cannot dismiss such questions as the confused result of language's idling and doing no work because the grammar of 'God' has been ignored.[29] Unfortunately, he does not offer much help in answering them either. So those who want to understand what realism amounts to in this Wittgensteinian perspective are left in the midst of practices, with permission to understand them realistically, but without any idea of how God's independence is to be understood. Until this is clarified, Phillips must face the question of how, if God's independent reality is to be understood by looking at practices, this reality is nevertheless not a projection of them or otherwise constructed. In other words, how is his tentative affirmation of realism to avoid collapsing into another version of Cupittian expressivism or, more radically, a version of Christianity that mimics the practices, language, and theology of realist Christianity – including its concepts of knowledge and truth – but which begins from the denial that God exists?[30] This is an urgent question, yet Phillips thinks that the dispute between realists and non-realists is a result of idle talk and hence impossible to resolve.

The Anglican priest Anthony Freeman shot to public prominence in Britain when he published his *apologia* for renouncing realist faith *God in Us: A Case for Christian Humanism* (1993). We get a flavour of his non-realist Christianity when he writes that, 'Christian prayer ... is about stillness and recollection and aligning one's will and one's actions with one's highest values' (1993: 57). The echo of Cupitt is not accidental. Freeman is associated with the Sea of Faith Network, of which Cupitt is a guiding figure. Freeman was a Priest-in-Charge of a parish in Chichester diocese until, having published his book and not changed his mind after being given time for reflection by his Bishop, he was removed from his post. It is not surprising that the Church of England has wondered how it should meet the challenge represented by the Network,[31] but more pertinently for our present discussion, the dispute about the reality of God and what constitutes a legitimate development of a religious tradition has in this instance clearly occurred within a (set of) religious practice(s). Non-realists perform many of the same liturgical (and non-liturgical) practices as their realist counterparts and the changes they introduce are claimed to be an organic

---

[29] Cf. Wittgenstein 1978[3]: §132.
[30] For a technical philosophical presentation of these problems, consider the 'quasi-realism' advocated by Simon Blackburn (1993) and explored in relation to Wittgensteinian philosophy of religion by Michael Scott (2000).
[31] The Bishop of Oxford, Richard Harries (1994), has replied to Freeman.

development of earlier ones,[32] so it cannot be enough to appeal to practices as though they can show the grammar of 'God' (unless, as we shall see, we modify our understanding of 'grammar'). *Ex hypothesi*, the grammar of 'God is *not* independently real' will be shown by the same practices as will the grammar of what it means to say that 'God *is* independently real.' Although Phillips might have much to say about the reductionism implicit in Freeman's Christianity, his emphasis on context, practices, and grammar does not give sufficient resources to deal with the questions raised by the debate, and thus he cannot cogently rebut the challenge presented by avowedly non-realist positions.

Indeed, it appears that he does not even think that the problems presented by the Sea of Faith Network could arise. He writes that '[t]he possibility of the unreality of God does not occur *within* any religion, but it might well arise in disputes *between* religions', and then explains that a 'common religious tradition' suffices to ensure that we worship the same God, even though the content of 'God' might change (1993a: 3). But clearly, in the case we are considering, the possibility of God's non-reality has arisen *within* the tradition and practices of a religion: *a fortiori* a common tradition has not ensured that the same God is being worshipped.[33] Phillips might be moved to suggest that realist and non-realist Christians are, unknown to them, actually worshipping the same God since their practices are those of a 'common religious tradition'. But this will no more satisfy the Bishop who dismissed Freeman than it will Cupitt and his allies, who accept that they share a common tradition with their realist opponents but are at pains to emphasize that they do not worship the same God as realists. They argue that the God of realism produces a smothering heteronomy, and hence that if faith is to become autonomous and promote human well-being we must take leave of the realist God for another, constructed out of traditional Christian ethical, liturgical, and scriptural practices.[34]

Construed in terms of Phillips's philosophical argument, the debate about realism and non-realism may be a result of idle philosophical talk, but our illustration shows that at the level of contemporary Christian practices it certainly isn't. Idle talk may not now cost lives, but it cost Freeman his job. Christian practices themselves directly raise the very questions that Phillips thinks are confused. 'Well, then, perhaps Christians just are confused', he might reply. But this will not do: it was attention to practices

[32] See Cupitt 1984a and David Hart 1993: 10–14.
[33] The best example of the debate within the Anglican church remains that between Rowan Williams (1984) and Don Cupitt (1984b), and this bears out my argument.
[34] See chapter 1, pp. 5f above.

that was supposed to help us see the grammar which could deliver us from confusion, but now, in the example we are looking at, it is the practices themselves that seem confused and incapable of providing a path out of the problems (non-)realism raises for the church. We can imagine the following conversation taking place: 'You want to know what God's independent reality amounts to? Well, look at the practices in which the expression "God" has its sense.' 'But some of the practitioners I talk to say that God is not and never was independent.' 'Well, they are worshipping a different God from the one who is independently real.' 'But both groups say the same creeds and use the same liturgy and some of their leaders are ordained by the same Bishops to whom they make the same vows.' 'Oh, well then', the Nonconformist might reply, 'you must be thinking about the Anglican church, in which case I can't help you.'

Reductionism, autonomous practices, and the grammar of 'God'

I have argued that Phillips is too confident in what he thinks we can deduce about the nature of God's reality from Christian practices. I wish now to suggest that he himself is the victim of a very similar tendency to the one we have seen him criticize in others: he allows a philosophical agenda about realism to generate a picture of Christian practices as possessing an autonomy which they do not. Consequently, he fails to see that we need to talk about theology and other Christian practices as themselves being regulated.

Phillips is so keen to get Christianity out of the grip of the distorting metaphysical picture presented by theological realism that he does not see that his own picture of Christian practices misleadingly assumes that they are autonomous. Not only does this affect his view of the debate about realism, but it also distorts his appreciation of substantive doctrinal points within it. In his discussion of Paul Holmer he raises the question whether 'the primary language of faith' could ever be in jeopardy and die. Here, Phillips tells us, '[t]he philosophical issue is whether the grammar of theology allows for its own demise' (1988b: 31). Responding in the spirit of 1 Cor. 13:8–13 (where Paul acknowledges the transitoriness and relativity of our temporal knowledge of God), a Christian realist will freely admit that theology's grammar does indeed allow for its own demise. It does so, first, in the weak sense that theology subserves our earthly pilgrimage and that therefore there will be no need for it hereafter when it will have done its allotted job and can cease to exist. But, second, theology also bears witness to the reality of the eternal God who is the terminus of our pilgrimage, and this means that theology can allow for its own demise in a strong sense as well: the church and all its theological works could become extinct and yet the eternal it had known and witnessed to could abide. Such a conception is part of the substance of Christian belief and it points to an important aspect of what it means to say that God's existence is independent: the existence of the church and its practices is contingent; it is not necessary to God's existence that anything else exists. All Christian practices could cease to exist but God would still be God; God's divine reality is his aseity.

Phillips seems to have a clear grasp of this when he writes that

> there is no contradiction ... in the supposition that all people could turn their backs on an eternal truth. A religious truth is not less eternal, for those who believe it, if it can be said to disappear from the face of the earth. (1988b: 31)

The Christian realist can agree that there is no contradiction here, but she will enter a note of reserve because part of Christian belief about the church is that it is indefectible: its *esse* is the risen Christ and it has a role in God's unbreakable purposes which means that it will not cease to exist. All people *could* (logically) turn their backs on the eternal truth of God, and God is at liberty to annihilate the church, but as a matter of contingent fact these things will not happen because God's word of election in Christ is 'Yes' and not 'No'.[35]

So far, decent theological sense can be made of Phillips's argument about the demise of the language of faith. However, immediately following the passage just quoted, he continues,

> To think otherwise is to think that religious faith is dependent on [a] kind of external conception of necessity ... To say that God will see to it that a religious epistemic practice persists, is to abstract it from its natural sense without that epistemic context. (1988b: 31–2, cf. 1988a: 246–50)

Phillips thinks that God's seeing to it that a religious epistemic practice will persist raises a dilemma: either God is subject to an external constraint or else he will not see to it at all. Given these alternatives, Phillips thinks that theology should be prepared to conceive its own demise; God cannot be subject to a metaphysical, and therefore alien, conception of necessity. But to preserve this essentially sound point about God, such reasoning is not required and the dilemma as Phillips puts it is false. He criticizes Holmer for not being prepared to allow that religious language could be in jeopardy, but perhaps Holmer thinks this because he has a better grasp of the grammar we have just been looking at. The church is contingent, and

---

[35] 2 Cor. 1:18ff.

its perdurance hangs on the providential care which is internal to God's nature: we do not need to introduce philosophy to explain this any more than we need it to explain why a parent acts in character when she leaps to stop her infant putting his hand in the fire. It seems as though for all his emphasis on understanding religions as distinct forms of life to be described and understood in the context of their own practices, Phillips has disregarded an internal, theological perspective on the Christian faith. The reason for this seems to be that he is so keen to rid theology of bad metaphysics that he can only conceive of God's acting in our practices in terms of such views. This is why he treats practices as autonomous from God and fails to see that Christianity cannot avoid having metaphysical conceptions (such as 'providence' and 'contingency') embedded within it.

The reason why Phillips can all too readily conceive the demise of faith seems to be that his method precludes him from understanding the reality of God in such a way as to allow him to see why God would prevent it. Joseph Incandela has examined Phillips's interpretation of Wittgenstein in the context of the legacy of Logical Positivism (which had of course influenced Wittgenstein) and concludes that the 'notion of form of life permitted the defenders of the meaningfulness of religious language to sail boldly into port and drop anchor in the positivists' own harbour of "reality" (viz. observable events)' (1985: 464). In other words, in Phillips's account religious practices have the status of an empiricist's observable events, and thus, as Soskice rightly judges, his work is 'very much in the spirit of twentieth-century linguistic empiricism' (1985: 145).[36]

It is hard to know how far it is the influence of empiricism on Phillips's work that results in his having nothing to say about (the grammar of) revelation in his work, but it would be interesting to know what he would make of the Christian conception of God's revealing himself in and through practices. I suspect that this would lead him to modify his description of Christianity in a way that would make it far easier for him to show what God's independent reality amounts to. As his work stands, Phillips never manages to make clear that Christian practices intend anything other than themselves or their practitioners. He rightly criticizes others for abstracting religious concepts 'from the human phenomena that lie behind them' (1970: 143), but what if behind them there is a divine phenomenon? Phillips's method prevents him from considering the grammar of this – which is why, in the end, he must be judged to be a kind of reductionist who, despite his more recent writings, never quite succeeds in being a realist.

---

[36] See also Trigg 1998: 139, 144ff.

Because of this, Phillips sets practices free from the very conception – that is, of God's independent reality – which could save them falling into a damaging autonomy.

We move on now to examine another figure, a theologian rather than a philosopher, who has advocated a Wittgensteinian grammatical approach to Christian faith. In the same way that Phillips has tried to move the philosophy of religion out of some well-established ruts, George Lindbeck has been profoundly influential in reshaping debate about theological method. Like Phillips, Lindbeck has been regarded as promoting anti-realism, and this is particularly surprising given his theological conservatism. By examining his position we shall see the kind of impact Wittgenstein has had in theology, and from its weaknesses learn more of what it means to say that Christian faith is grammatically regulated.

LINDBECK, GRAMMAR, AND REALISM

The cultural-linguistic approach and realism

Lindbeck's *The Nature of Doctrine* is a brief, difficult, and exegetically perplexing book, but in terms of the number of words written in response to it, it must count as one of the most provocative theological books to have been published in recent decades. In it Lindbeck argues for what he calls a 'cultural-linguistic' view of religion (and of Christianity in particular) in contrast to 'cognitive-propositional' and 'experiential-expressive' views of Christianity and its doctrine. The latter are characteristic, respectively, of the conservative and liberal theologies he rejects.[37] Influenced by the anthropologist Clifford Geertz, he construes doctrinal activity as the task of communal self-description whereby the church's identity and well-being are upheld.[38] Doctrines 'resemble grammatical rules' (1984: 84) and hence '[t]he function of church doctrines that becomes most prominent in this perspective is their use, not as expressive symbols or as truth claims, but as communally authoritative rules of discourse, attitude and action' (18). Lindbeck has been criticized by many theologians for down-playing the cognitive and propositional aspects of doctrine, and one can readily understand why given his apparent denial that doctrines make truth claims. Many have also been led to believe that Lindbeck is for this reason an anti-realist, but we should be cautious not to dismiss his position without

[37] For a personal statement of his theological stance, see Lindbeck 1996: 246–9.
[38] See 1984: 74.

examining his argument in detail, and doing so will help us see further why we need a Christocentric realism.

Lindbeck developed his cultural-linguistic approach in order to uphold the cognitivity of religious truth claims whilst attenuating the absolutism with which they are sometimes held, and he hoped thereby to open up a way in ecumenical discussion which would permit 'doctrinal reconciliation without capitulation' (16). Philosophy knows a similar phenomenon in the attempts of post-Kuhnian philosophers of science to reconcile realism with theory change. On this analogy, a cognitive-propositional theory of doctrine is similar to a naive realist understanding of scientific theories: neither can cope with the problem of how doctrines/theories can refer to the same reality in drastically different cultural or conceptual contexts. Lindbeck states the problem in a way that could, at first glance, be interpreted as a capitulation to non-realism. He says that,

The first-order truth claims of a religion change insofar as these arise from the application of the interpretive scheme to the shifting worlds that human beings inhabit. What is taken to be reality is in large part socially constructed and consequently alters in the course of time. (82)

Before dismissing this as non-realist constructivism, notice two things: first, he does not say that reality itself is socially constructed. Only in the absence of serious reflection would anyone think that acknowledging that our (linguistic) outlook on the world makes the world seem a different place from the one our forebears knew entails admitting that the world itself is a linguistic creation.[39] Second, it is such acknowledgements as these which initiate rather than conclude the realism debate. This is why a philosopher (of science) would be far less willing to dub the passage quoted an example of non-realism, especially given its position in Lindbeck's overall argument as a problematic to be discussed rather than as a conclusion that has been deduced.

Another important thing to bear in mind is that, against the backdrop of philosophical modernity, Lindbeck wishes to call into question and to rethink theological understandings of truth.

Both the Protestant who insists on scriptural inerrancy and the Roman Catholic traditionalist counterpart are likely to be suffering from vulgarized forms of rationalism ... but in the early centuries of the church, ontological truth by correspondence had not yet been limited to propositionalism. Fundamentalist literalism, like experiential-expressivism, is a product of modernity. (51)

[39] Cf. Hensley 1996: 76–9.

In the light of this historical perspective it is reasonable to hesitate before thinking – as, for example, does Francis Watson[40] – that Lindbeck must oppose realism simply because he questions correspondence theories of truth; indeed, many now question whether truth as correspondence is essential to realism. Nevertheless, Lindbeck's approach is inadequate on grammatical grounds for building a case for a Christian realism; to see why, we need to look in more detail at his account of religious language.

Lindbeck on language and truth

Lindbeck's understanding of religious language can best be understood by examining the three interweaving and mutually dependent levels at which he can be interpreted as regarding it as operating. First-order discourse is the relatively concrete language of Christian life (prayer, praise, preaching, and so on), and of this he explicitly affirms the possibility of the 'ontological truth of religious utterances' and their 'correspondence to reality' (64). Possibility needs emphasis here, for it is important to bear in mind that these affirmations are made in the context of his overall theory. First-order, propositional truth claims can only be made successfully if they are doctrinally regulated in the setting of religious practices. Lifted out of these contexts they can be distorted and opened to grave misunderstanding[41] – which is why he thinks that the cultural-linguistic approach is so important to the recovery of a proper understanding of the nature of Christian truth claims. Thus, in a passage which includes one of his few explicit references to realism, Lindbeck concludes that

a religion can be interpreted as possibly containing ontologically true affirmations, not only in cognitivist theories but also in cultural-linguistic ones. There is nothing in the cultural-linguistic approach that requires the rejection (or the acceptance) of the epistemological realism and correspondence theory of truth, which, according to most of the theological tradition, is implicit in the conviction of believers that when they rightly use a sentence such as 'Christ is Lord' they are uttering a true first-order proposition. (68–9)

Here Lindbeck carefully maintains his guard against those who would be too quick to identify him as either a realist or a non-realist along the lines of modernist presuppositions. All the same, at this first-order level, Lindbeck clearly thinks that religious language is to be construed referentially and

---

[40] See 1994: 133ff.
[41] This is one of the points he wants to make in his much-disputed claims about the blood-soaked Crusader's cry 'Christus est Dominus' (see Lindbeck: 1984: 64ff; I discuss this in chapter 6).

therefore realistically: 'it is propositionally true that Christ is Lord: i.e., the particular individual of which the stories are told is, was, and will be definitively and unsurpassably the Lord' (63).

The second level at which Lindbeck understands religious language is that of second-order, doctrinal language, and it is here that Lindbeck seems to espouse non-realism, for he denies that doctrinal language makes ontological claims. Doctrine regulates referential language; it is not itself referential: 'theology and doctrine, to the extent that they are second-order activities, assert nothing either true or false about God and his relation to creatures, but only speak about such assertions' (69). The normative function of doctrine is to elaborate 'the categories (or "grammar" or "rules of the game")' which, if 'adequate' (48), make possible the first-order language in which propositional truth claims are made. Doctrinal truth is solely 'intrasystematic' and is thus a matter of internal *coherence* amongst propositions rather than *correspondence* to facts.[42] Thus, while his repudiation of modernity should be borne in mind, regarding truth (competition between theories of which has been a defining point of difference between idealists and realists) Lindbeck appears to stand in the non-realist camp when it comes to Christian doctrine.[43]

In his 1990 Bampton Lectures, Alister McGrath argues that Lindbeck's view of doctrine is similar to the instrumentalist's in the philosophy of science: doctrinal/theoretical terms have 'no referent outside the theoretical system itself' (1990: 32). This, McGrath suggests, 'entails the abandonment of any talk about God as an independent reality and any suggestion that it is possible to make truth claims ... concerning him' (29). However, whilst McGrath's charge could be levelled fairly against Lindbeck's account of doctrinal language, it would not be enough to establish that Lindbeck is an anti-realist across the board. To do this McGrath would have to show that in a realist Christianity doctrinal terms must refer, that Lindbeck's distinction between first- and second-order doctrinal discourse is unsound, and that Lindbeck is an instrumentalist concerning first-order Christian language. Yet, as we saw, Lindbeck does understand first-order language in a realist way, and this makes McGrath's claim rather implausible: for Lindbeck 'Christ is Lord' is referentially true. The problem is that McGrath fails to consider the question of realism in relation to the conceptual shift Lindbeck

---

[42] See 1984: 63–9, especially 64. Pannenberg has advocated a similar position: see 1991: 19–22; cf. 24–5, 52ff.

[43] Coherence theories of truth are a defining characteristic of nineteenth-century idealism; whether contemporary coherence theories are anti-realist is disputed; see Bruce Marshall 2000 and Alston 1996.

is commending; he over-simplifies Lindbeck's position by flattening out the complex contours of his thought; and he does not consider Lindbeck's explicitly stated view that it is at (what I am calling) the first and third levels of language use that reference occurs. Realism is not ruled out by Lindbeck's claim that the task of second-order, doctrinal language is to mediate the categories which make reference and the 'ontological truth of religious utterances possible' (64).

Lindbeck's understanding of the categorial function of doctrine gives a Kantian twist to his broadly Wittgensteinian position. In Kant's philosophy, what he calls 'The Categories' 'form the grammar of thinking ... and the conditions for objectively valid judgements of experience' (Caygill 1995: 104, 106). Similarly, for Lindbeck, 'the linguistic categories and grammar provided by the religion are necessary *conditions* for both cognition and experience' (Murphy and McClendon 1989: 206). Categories are described by Lindbeck as adequate if they can 'be made to apply to what is taken to be real' – to God, for example. Categorial adequacy 'makes meaningful statements possible', which in turn 'makes possible propositional falsehood as well as truth' (Lindbeck 1984: 48). Thus on Lindbeck's view, intrasystematically true doctrine is a necessary condition of the referential truth of first-order propositions. However, the notion of categorial adequacy mediates not only between first-order and doctrinal language but also between doctrinal language and the whole religion. A religion having adequate categories 'can be said to be "categorially true"' where 'a categorially true religion would be one in which it is possible to speak meaningfully of that which is, e.g., most important ... (i.e., "God")' (48–9).

Internal coherence is the touchstone of truth in doctrinal matters, but it is not only a matter of internal *conceptual* coherence: utterances must cohere not only amongst themselves

but also [with] the correlative forms of life. Thus for a Christian 'God is Three and One', or 'Christ is Lord' are true only as parts of a total pattern of speaking, thinking, feeling, and acting. They are false when their use in any given instance is inconsistent with what the pattern as a whole affirms of God's being and will. (64)

'[T]he pattern as a whole', the whole religious form of life as it is lived by the members of a religious community: this is the third level at which Lindbeck regards religious language as operating. The quotation illustrates just how closely interwoven are the levels of Lindbeck's theory of language. We have already noticed that first-order propositions need second-order doctrinal language; it now becomes evident that for Lindbeck doctrinal language has truth not only intrasystematically but also insofar as it subserves the lived faith of the church. Thus, at this third level, a religion as a whole can be regarded as making affirmations about God.

As actually lived, a religion may be pictured as a single gigantic proposition. It is a true proposition to the extent that its objectivities are interiorized and exercised by individuals and groups in such a way as to conform them ... to ... ultimate reality ... It is a false proposition to the extent that this does not happen. (51)[44]

It is not just first-order propositions used in a religion that may refer;[45] the religion itself is, in Lindbeck's view, a semiotic system that should be regarded as a proposition whose successful conformity to reality depends on the lives of its practitioners.[46] But the relationship here is reciprocal, for the first-order assertions of a religion 'cannot be made except when speaking religiously, i.e., when seeking to align oneself and others performatively with what one takes to be most important in the universe by worshipping, promising, obeying, exhorting, preaching' (69). Lindbeck seems to imply that being religious is a necessary condition of one's truthfully uttering, for example, 'Christ is Lord.' This is highly controversial and seems to be anti-realist, for it appears to make the truth of an assertion dependent on some subjective condition of the utterer; however, as we shall see in chapter 6, there is an important theological point here.

In its stress on the relationship between utterances and utterers in accounting for truth in religious language, Lindbeck's position is strongly holistic. So too is his understanding of the interaction between the kinds of truth claims made at each of the levels of religious discourse. Where first-order language is in a relationship of *correspondence* to reality, and doctrinal language aims at the truth of internal *coherence*, at the third level, Lindbeck's understanding of truth is closer to a *pragmatic* theory.[47] Even if (owing to his imprecise use of his own semi-technical vocabulary) it is very hard to see clearly and in detail how Lindbeck's overall argument works, it is strongly in favour of his avowedly 'nontheological' (46) method that his view of religion enables him to hold together all these theoretical

---

[44] Cf. 65ff. Lindbeck can be hard to exegete: compare his earlier statement that 'languages and cultures do not make truth claims' (23). I infer from his overall argument that Lindbeck intends more weight to be given to the passage quoted in the text.

[45] Although Lindbeck himself only identifies two levels of religious language (first- and second-order), we can see from this quotation that it is helpful to identify a third: construing a religion as a gigantic proposition is essential to understanding the other two levels.

[46] Lindbeck mentions religious 'epistemological realists' (1984: 64) only in passing and in the context of this third level of discourse.

[47] Many contributors to the debate about Lindbeck's work see him as a pragmatist. See, for example, O'Neill 1985: 429; Tracy 1985: 470; Michalson 1988: 118 n. 7; Wainwright 1988: 124f; Zorn 1995: 514.

aspects of truth.[48] Lindbeck neither hypostatizes religion as though it had a reality independent of its practitioners nor atomizes it into the particular assertions of individual believers: a religion is a gestalt of believers, their assertions, the doctrines which regulate assertions, and practices of ritual and story-telling, all of which together (and only together) can conform to reality. Even if individual first-order utterances can be true (or false) only in a context where this gestalt constitutes 'a form of life, a way of being in the world, which itself corresponds to the Most Important, the Ultimately Real' (65), that they, or the religion of which they are particular expressions, can be true (or false) in relation to an independent divine reality is not in question for Lindbeck and this is why, all things considered, it is incorrect exegesis to suggest that he intentionally promotes anti-realism.

Some difficulties with Lindbeck's approach

Despite my argument against those who too quickly dismiss him as a non-realist, Lindbeck's position is not without problems, particularly in his account of doctrine's grammatical functions, and these seriously weaken any claim that he is a robust defender of realism. The first area of weakness to consider is Lindbeck's division of Christian language into first- and second-order discourse. On Lindbeck's account creeds are archetypically second-order, regulative forms of discourse. Although many clearly have (or had) this function, we should note that they also have clear first-order use in Christian worship, for example, in baptism and as a response of faith to the liturgical Ministry of the Word. As Geoffrey Wainwright observes, Lindbeck fails 'to appreciate the significance of the fact that the Nicene bishops chose to insert their *dogmatic* definition in a creed, a genre whose primary use is that of *confessing* the faith at baptism' (1988: 127). Lindbeck is similarly mistaken when he refers to '[t]he *doctrine* that Jesus is the Messiah' (1984: 81, my italics). Certainly, 'Jesus is the Messiah' can be a doctrinal statement: it can be and often is a statement of Christian teaching and belief, and, as Lindbeck indicates, as such provides a rule for the interpretation of scripture.[49] But the Messiahship of Jesus is also the matter of excited confessional cries in the New Testament and these would, in Lindbeck's terminology, have to be classified as first-order statements. Thus, while the distinction between first- and second-order discourse might be helpful heuristically, if it is intended to denote a rigid distinction between two

---

[48] In this he is reminiscent of Donald MacKinnon, who argues for a similarly holistic view of 'The Christian Understanding of Truth' (1948).

[49] Cf. Childs's (1992: 21–2) views of Lindbeck.

separate, discretely identifiable kinds of Christian statement it might obscure more than it discloses.

The significance of this for our theme can be seen by noticing a circularity implied by Lindbeck's claim about 'Jesus is Messiah.' In his view, second-order statements regulate first-order ones, but here Lindbeck is elevating a first-order expression ('Jesus is Messiah') to the status of a second-order, doctrinal expression which, on Lindbeck's account, must regulate itself *qua* first-order (confessional) expression in scripture. Whilst Wittgenstein avoids this circularity by making it clear that expressions cannot, at one and the same time, be used both to express and to apply a rule,[50] it is not clear that Lindbeck does. Furthermore, if we accept Lindbeck's position, we need to ask what rule governs thought as it translates first- into second-order statements. How do we decide that the first-order statement is true and warranted for elevation to second-order status? Do we need another order of statement after that? Or perhaps we need a divinely appointed office in the church to make the rules, but then who makes their rules? And so on ... Lindbeck does not consider these questions, but they are central if his theory is to succeed – as he hopes it will – in breaking the ecumenical log-jam on the question of authority in the church. Instead, he leaves us with what looks like an infinite regress, which will, in my view, only be stopped if we acknowledge what I outlined in my introduction to this chapter and will argue in more detail subsequently, namely, that God himself, by his word and Spirit, is the grammar of Christian practices. In illustration of this, notice that although Luke 24 and 2 Cor. 3–4 use or imply 'Jesus is the Messiah' as an interpretative rule, it is emphatically not a rule alone that enables the correct interpretation of scripture in these passages; rather it is the direct presence of God in the persons of Christ and the Holy Spirit.

In fact, Lindbeck seems not to think that doctrinal activity is a practice which itself need regulating. The reason is that 'Rules, unlike propositions or expressive symbols, retain an invariant meaning under changing conditions of compatibility and conflict' (18). He thinks that grammatical rules subsist in the church in the same way a genetic code remains identical over time without its bearer having to undertake its maintenance.[51] (We should notice in passing that Lindbeck is mistaken here. First, the illustration is seriously misleading, for the truth of the biological matter is precisely the opposite of what Lindbeck thinks. By means of natural selection genetic codes *do* change over time, which is how species diversity arises, and this

<hr />

[50] See Baker and Hacker 1985: 46f.   [51] See 1984: 83.

suggests a very different understanding of ecclesiology and doctrinal development from Lindbeck's. Second, Lindbeck's view of rules departs from Wittgenstein's – he did not regard grammatical rules as invariant.[52]) Hence Lindbeck sees no need to invoke God's sustaining activity to enable him to argue for his account of doctrinal continuity, for 'There is nothing uniquely Christian about this [sc. theological] constancy: supernatural explanations are quite unnecessary.' Simply telling the Christian story ensures that 'the basic rules for its use remain the same' (83).[53]

By seeing the rules of the Christian semiotic system as self-sustaining and self-regulating, Lindbeck effectively denies God's sustaining activity within its practices and thereby risks implying that Christian faith is autonomous from God. But here we must ask Lindbeck the same question we have already discussed in relation to D. Z. Phillips: if Christianity is self-sustaining and self-regulating, what resources has Lindbeck's position to enable him to say that the church's being co-opted by non-realists is a distortion of Christian faith – this especially in view of the fact that his general position seems to warrant the judgement that he would thus regard it?[54] How would he argue that non-realists promote an invalid continuation of Christian faith – after all, they tell the same story, use the same creeds, and use the same liturgy?[55]

Lindbeck excludes God from his account here because he wants to develop a universal theory of religion within which to appreciate particular religions and enable dialogue between them. Because his theory of religious doctrines must embrace all religions, he is unwilling to stress the particular grammar of doctrinal continuity in the Christian faith.[56] However, his argument seems to involve him surrendering even the modest knowledge of God available to Christians he implies elsewhere in his theory. He claims that 'it is the framework and the medium within which Christians know and experience, rather than what they experience or think they know, that retains continuity and unity down through the centuries' (84). Is Lindbeck being fair to Christian faith here? Have not Christians claimed that it is *God* whom they know and experience, and who is invariant through time? Lindbeck's claim could invite the charge that he is a non-realist who (in Donald MacKinnon's mordant phrase apropos nobody in particular) thinks that '[t]he proper study of the theologian is ecclesiastical man' (1972: 299),

---

[52] See 1978[3]: §83, p. 147 (b).
[53] Hans Frei is correct in suggesting that Lindbeck's overall argument 'is a modest transcendental inquiry' into how rules can retain invariant meaning (1990: 277).
[54] See Lindbeck 1996.   [55] See David Hart 1993: 68–95.   [56] See 1984: 46–63.

and effectively reduces the continuing content of Christian faith – namely, the God who revealed himself in Jesus Christ and who continues to bear witness to himself in the power of the Holy Spirit – to grammatical rules. Such allegations would be partial and unfair, but that they *could* be made indicates the serious weaknesses of a grammatical approach to realism whose starting point is, as Lindbeck himself admits, philosophical and social scientific rather than theological.[57]

Further weaknesses of his approach can be brought out by examining Lindbeck's understanding of categorial adequacy. Recall that for him a religious form of life may succeed (or fail) in corresponding to 'the Ultimately Real' and that it is in virtue of success at this level that first-order utterances can refer. The latter can be true only if the former is. But this is sufficiently counter-intuitive to cause suspicion as to its correctness. Consider: if I assert that 'The cat is on the mat', we know that we could find out if my utterance is true because we have established procedures by which we settle empirical truth claims. More generally, we have different procedures for settling various kinds of truth claims in particular domains of reality, but what would it be to check whether a whole language(-game) is true, to check the truth of our understanding of how we show that 'The cat is on the mat' is true? Wittgenstein's appeal to a bedrock of practices was introduced to stop this kind of difficulty arising, but Lindbeck's theory raises it in an acute form. His argument requires that we should be able to have a God's-eye view of God so that we can compare the Christian semiotic system with God and on this basis establish that a first-order utterance can refer. But no such *locus standi* is, or could be, available to mortals: we are creatures; he is the creator.

A parallel drawn from discussions of truth in contemporary analytic philosophy will help draw out more of the difficulties here.[58] Lindbeck believes that a categorially adequate system should be 'unsurpassable'.[59] This implies the ontological claim that there is nothing that is real but which falls outside the purview of the system: it must be comprehensive, true of the whole of reality. Hence if there were anything in reality to which the system's categories could not be applied it would fail to be adequate and would fail to be 'categorially true' because there would be something real but to which the system's categories would not enable reference to be made. There is a

[57] 1984: 7.
[58] See especially Alston (1996: 225–6), who deploys a line of reasoning similar to my own against some of the British idealists.
[59] See 47ff.

crucial weakness in Lindbeck's argument at this point. Let us suppose that Lindbeck's categories *had* omitted something, namely, the God 'Widget'. Lindbeck would then be in the position of claiming unsurpassability for Christianity and its God when (*ex hypothesi*) the Christian God is only rather puny alongside Widget. In this case, not only would Christian doctrine not be categorially adequate, but first-order assertions (for example, that the name of Jesus 'is above every name') made on its basis would be false and the lives the religion promoted would not conform to 'the Ultimately Real' (65), that is, to the reality that is Widget. On Lindbeck's cultural-linguistic outlook, we need to be able to establish the categorial adequacy of a religion's grammar and thus its unsurpassability, but without a God's-eye view of the Gods, we cannot do this: we cannot establish whether the God of Christian faith or Widget is the Ultimately Real.

Furthermore, in the light of religious pluralism, unsurpassability cannot – on Lindbeck's argument – simply be assumed without a faith claim about the religion itself. However, although Christian religion is a *faith*, the object of this faith is the God who gives it, not the faith of the religion. Thus, from a Christian point of view, the unsurpassability of *Christianity* should not be assumed. Rather, Christian faith assumes the unsurpassability of God's self-revelation in Christ. If the creator is unsurpassable, this is something which by definition creatures cannot prove: God's vindication will come from God; if Christians have spoken truly of God, their vindication will come from him. Against Lindbeck, I therefore suggest that the truth of Christian assertions depends on God, not on the categorial adequacy or unsurpassability of the Christian faith.

These rather abstract objections can be brought down to earth by recollecting that the conflict between Jesus and the official representatives of first-century Judaism revolved partly around the question of who speaks for God, who is an impostor, and how to settle which is which. In Lindbeck's terms, was the religion unsurpassable, and did it conform individuals to the Ultimately Real? Were its categories adequate, and did they enable true first-order assertions to be made? Regarding the question whether Judaism's categories were adequate, we have to say both that they were (they produced Jesus) and that they were not (they produced those who put his crucifixion in train). In a sense, both parties thought that they had a *locus standi* from which to decide the issue, but they could not both be right. However, Jesus' resurrection can be seen both as God's self-vindication and as the vindication of a single, reforming religious language-user against a corrupted religion which was 'surpassed' by this one individual who explicitly thought that the truth of his utterances lay in the hands of God, not (*pace* Lindbeck) in the unsurpassability of the religion or the adequacy of its categories.[60]

Intratextuality, extratextuality, and realism

It is a curious and major inconsistency that Lindbeck underplays Christology at this point in his argument, for he famously holds an 'intratextual' view of religions which emphasizes their particularities and seeks to allow them to be appreciated in their integrity without supervening generic concepts. Christianity is a self-contained semiotic system 'paradigmatically encoded in holy writ' (1984: 116). Scriptural narrative provides the normative interpretation of the whole of reality 'outside' the text. 'Intratextual theology redescribes reality within the scriptural framework rather than translating Scripture into extrascriptural categories. It is the text, so to speak, which absorbs the world, rather than the world the text' (118). Lindbeck's point here is indebted to Wittgenstein: the reference and truth of religious terms should be determined within their native context; they should not be treated as examples of more general and more ultimate trans-religious phenomena. Contrary to cognitive-propositionalism and experiential-expressivism, 'the proper way to determine what "God" signifies, for example, is by examining how the word operates within a religion and thereby shapes reality and experience rather than by first establishing its propositional or experiential meaning' (114).

For all his emphasis on the normativity of scripture, Lindbeck unfortunately compromises his intratextual stance by setting his account of Christianity within the context of a general theory of religion. His proposals are, he says, 'meant to be ... religiously neutral' (9). The consequences of this can be seen by noting that the notion of correspondence Lindbeck depends on in his understanding of categorial adequacy is, as Phillips observes,

entirely unmediated ... No use of capitals in talking of the 'Most Important' and the 'Ultimately Real' can hide the fact that he is trying to place these concepts, whatever they are, in a logical space which transcends the language-games and forms of life in which concepts have their life. The notion of such a logical space is an illusion. (1988a: 206)

A general, context-neutral conceptual space is in principle unavailable;[61] what it means for a proposition to be true must be determined from within

---

[60] In fairness to Lindbeck it is important to note that for him, two of the regulative principles present in the creeds are 'historical specificity' and 'Christological maximalism' (1984: 94).

[61] See Phillips 1988a: 195–224.

the religion in question. Lindbeck's argument therefore lacks conceptual integrity, for, despite advocating an intratextual, grammatical approach to doctrine, he is insufficiently particularist on the question of truth and reality. In short, his approach is insufficiently informed and disciplined by that which makes Christianity unique – Christology. Had it been, he might have been able to avoid the charges of those who believe that his intratextuality leads him away from realism into denying the possibility of reference to extratextual reality, and even to docetism and idolatry.[62] Yet on the other hand his intratextualism is judged by Bruce Marshall to be 'modestly realist' (1990b: 71).

Beneath these conflicting assessments of Lindbeck's intratextualism is the question whether it is possible to have reality without its being narrated or textually encoded, or, to put it more philosophically, under some conceptual scheme, theory, or description. Can we have it 'raw', as it really is in itself; is it possible in principle for us to give *the* true description of reality? Can we 'have' reality unmediated by any textual or conceptual framework, by any interpretative grid? It is widely believed that we can and that science provides the technique and the metaphysic to obtain such an 'absolute conception of the world'.[63] This position is called 'metaphysical realism'. Typically it involves commitment to the correspondence theory of truth, to the view that there is in principle one true and complete description of reality, and, its detractors claim, to the possibility of having a God's-eye view of reality. Many of those who oppose Lindbeck think that if Christians are to be realists, they must be metaphysical realists.[64] Amongst other versions of realism is the view that we cannot (knowingly) have a true and complete description of reality but only an account of what there is from within some theory or description. Hilary Putnam, its major contemporary exponent, calls this position 'internal realism'.[65]

However, we need not look to philosophy for the origins of intratextual views in theology. It is arguable that the idea that those whose lives are shaped by the biblical narrative only ever have reality under a (narrative) description goes back to the earliest tellers of the Patriarchal narratives, to the composers of the Bible's creation 'myths', and, perhaps most significantly for the Christian, to the narrated drama of the Christ-event.[66]

---

[62] Watson 1994: 152, 224.   [63] For an exposition and critique, see Putnam 1992: 80–107.

[64] See Barbour 1990: 15; McGrath 1996: 150. Mark Wallace (1990: 108, cf. 104–10) finds Lindbeck a realist *malgré lui*.

[65] See Putnam 1981: 48ff; cf. 1978: 123–40. Putnam changed his outlook in 1994; he now affirms that 'the world is as it is independently of the interests of describers' (1994: 448), but continues to uphold the view that we have it through the medium of language. Haldane (1996) has argued that Putnam's views do not now exclude and may require metaphysical realism.

[66] An important study here is Hays 1983.

Until the modern period, the believing reader of the Bible so inhabited its narratives that they constituted the reader's symbolic universe. (In a similar way but to a lesser degree soap operas constitute the symbolic universe of many of our contemporaries.) It was only as empirical science replaced that universe with one of dark matter, quarks, black holes, red giants, white dwarfs, quantum vacuums, and so on that this pattern of thought broke down.[67]

Contemporary intratextual theology and the view of realism associated with it had its birth in Yale in the 1970s and 1980s under the presiding genius of Karl Barth. Beside Lindbeck, another leading figure there was Hans Frei. He suggested that Barth wished

to indicate two things simultaneously: (1) that this world [sc. 'the temporal world of eternal grace'] is a world with its own linguistic integrity, much as a literary art work is a consistent world in its own right, one that we can have only under a description, under its own particular depiction and not any other, and certainly not in pre-linguistic immediacy or in experience without depiction; but (2) that unlike any other depicted world it is the one common world in which we all live and move and have our being. (1992: 161, cf. 139)

Lindbeck takes his lead from such an interpretation of Barth and states that 'A scriptural world is . . . able to absorb the universe' (1984: 117). Lindbeck is not denying an independent ontological status to extratextual reality; rather, he means that an authoritative religious text 'supplies the interpretative framework within which believers seek to live their lives and understand reality' (117). 'Intratextual theology redescribes reality within the scriptural framework rather than translating Scripture into extrascriptural categories' (118).

Notice how these quotations can quite easily be 'translated' into a scientific idiom: 'The scientific world-view is able to absorb the universe'; authoritative scientific theories 'supply the framework within which believers [in science] seek to live their lives and understand reality'. The third quotation might be paraphrased as: 'The scientific world-view redescribes reality within the scientific framework rather than translating the scientific framework into extrascientific categories.' That these translations cause little intellectual offence makes us wonder whether it is only Lindbeck's proposed abolition of the hegemony of the scientific imagination that makes his intratextualism seem odd. As van Fraassen notes,

Myth is explanatory; it explains both the natural order and the development of the social order. *So does science.* Myth has a strong grip on the human imagination; it

---

[67] See Frei (1974) for the story of the breaking down of the biblical narrative universe.

supplies the classification and the categories, the pigeon-holes and the concepts, the *categorial framework* within which every subject is placed and understood. *So does science.* (1994a: 129)[68]

So we can understand Lindbeck to be saying that, since there is no such thing as uninterpreted reality, Christians need to be clear about which interpretative framework they use to understand and refer to reality. As the analytic philosopher Nicholas Wolterstorff observes, 'we all live story-shaped lives. The issue is not *whether* we will do so; the issue is rather, which are the stories that will shape our lives?' (2001: 212). We can change the myths, the texts, the conceptual schemes, by which we live. Lindbeck thinks that the Enlightenment 'text' absorbs only to spew out the Christian 'world', and wishes to show how by absorbing the universe, the scriptural world discloses universal redemption.

However, once again, Lindbeck's thought is weakened by being insufficiently orientated by substantive doctrinal considerations. John Webster rightly criticizes the reception of Barth by the so-called 'Yale School' on the ground that it regards scripture as *text* rather than as 'normative *testimony* to the absolute act of God's self-manifestation in free grace' (1995: 31). Furthermore, he argues, intratextual theology drastically downplays the importance of Jesus Christ for Christianity's catholicity. Thus, he claims against Lindbeck that

[r]ather than retaining the identity of Christianity by envisaging it as a tightly structured [and highly 'local'] territory of meaning, it is imperative to locate Christianity's centre outside itself, in the history of Jesus Christ. That history, because of its identity with the being and action of God, cannot in principle be assimilated to any one scheme ... No conceptual or narrative scheme can render such a reality in a wholly adequate way. (1992: 10)

Webster's argument echoes my own criticisms of Lindbeck on the invariancy of rules, categorial adequacy, and the unsurpassability of a religion. Despite his modestly realist intentions, Lindbeck's intratextuality does seem to confuse the manner in which we know reality with reality itself. It may be true that we can only make Christian affirmations about reality so far as scripture mediates our knowledge, but this is not the same as saying that reality itself is textual. We might not be able to have reality other than mediated by some conceptual scheme, but for a Christian realism there is more to reality than the scheme. Scripture (the scheme) witnesses to the reality (the triune God).

[68] See also Hesse 1998.

So in the end the problem with Lindbeck and Phillips is that in different ways they fail to take into account central features of Christian faith – Lindbeck, Christology; Phillips, the fallibility of practices. As a result neither offers an account of realism that is theologically satisfying. The bulk of the rest of my argument is devoted to arguing for a Christian realism which seeks to hold together the particularity of Christian faith with the view that whilst we do indeed only have reality under a description, our account of it must uphold the ontological priority of God's action in Christ. It is to aspects of this in relation to Christian practices that we now turn.

CHAPTER 5

The grammar of Christian faith and the relationship between philosophy and theology

THE GRAMMAR OF FAITH REVISITED

Neither Phillips's nor Lindbeck's grammatical arguments seem able to yield a theologically coherent account of Christian realism. If these approaches do not work, but, as I argued at the end of chapter 3, we need one which respects the grammar of Christian faith, how are we to argue a case for a realism that does respect this grammar? In the previous chapter I suggested that the grammar of Christian faith is God himself; this is where my proposal parts ways with Wittgenstein and his followers. We saw that for Wittgenstein it is 'agreement ... in form of life' and 'in judgements' (1978³: §§241–2) that keeps our practices and our use of particular expressions in order. Hence, when he makes the parenthetical remark 'Theology as grammar' (§373), what he means is that theology articulates or uncovers the rules governing language about God as it is used in our practices: it is a clarification of what it makes sense to say about God, how the term 'God' is to be used. 'What is ridiculous or blasphemous also shows the grammar of the word' (Wittgenstein quoted by Ambrose 1979: 32). Now, so long as we are confident that we can distinguish blasphemous from reverent Christian language, this might seem to be acceptable.

The problem is that Christians' powers of discrimination are being tested by non-realism and the Sea of Faith Network. Here is a dispute concerning what is ridiculous or blasphemous to say about God. The problem for Christian speech is that conceptually speaking we do not know how to find our way about: the same practices and forms of life support different agreements in judgement about how words are to be used. To think that theology can function in a direct, regulative way is to assume that our language about God is in order as it is – for example, that it is self-sustaining as Lindbeck thinks. It isn't. We may think that the creeds function regulatively, but they will do so effectively only if we are in broad agreement about the meaning of, say, *homoousios*, the nature of doctrinal development, and so of the relevance of the term to contemporary church life. Christian faith differs from other forms of life in that the agreements in judgement that undergird our language use need continually and consciously to be re-formed. As we shall see, Phillips cannot really make sense of the realism debate because he thinks that Christian speech and practices are in order as they stand; Lindbeck acknowledges that they are not, but gets into a muddle trying to sort out the issue regulatively without allowing God's agency into his account.

Our puzzle is whether it makes sense to say of God that he does or does not exist independently of our minds. The Wittgensteinian view is that we cannot get outside our practices to have a 'view from nowhere' – an Archimedean point from which to survey the relationship between language and that which is presumed to be independent of it. (For theological reasons to do with the creaturely perspective which is a mortal's lot, I agree with Wittgenstein, and this is a major reason why I think that we need to mount a transcendental argument from an ontological perspective to defend realism.) Although Wittgenstein thought that we cannot prove realism, he saw no need to do so, but he did not deny that reality impinges on our practices.[1] The grammatical conventions that inform our practices have natural limitations imposed by their running up against reality, and this shows up in linguistic absurdity and nonsense.[2] We do not need an Archimedean point.

In the theological case it is less obvious when we run up against (God's) reality. The crucifixion of Jesus is the supreme instance of this: all the parties involved thought that they knew their way around conceptually, except perhaps the one who spoke least. As events turned out, the theologians and custodians of religious practices were of all the parties the most mistaken over whether and how their (linguistic) practices were running up against divine reality. So this episode implies that, owing to God's moral hiddenness and the freedom he grants to his creatures, it is possible for humans to act as if his independent reality did not impinge on their practices. If the grammar of an expression is shown through the practices in which it is used, Jesus' crucifixion suggests that the grammar of 'God' is far from pellucid. If it were, then the fact that Jesus' teaching about God and his claims about himself were not blasphemous would have been obvious.

---

[1] The literature on the question whether Wittgenstein was a realist is considerable. Diamond 1991: 39–72, 1996 and Hacker 1997: 322–35 can be recommended; see also Kerr 1986: 101–41 and 1989. The best philosophical discussion of Wittgenstein and religious realism is Scott 2000.

[2] See Baker and Hacker 1985: 329–38.

As we shall see more fully later, religious practices tend to mislead, and the language embedded in them to be deceptive, when the humans engaging in them disobey God and allow the practices to become ends in themselves or means to humanly devised ends (such as shoring up human prestige and power relations). Jesus revealed the Father because to do his will was his meat and drink; the Father and the empowering Spirit were the grammar, the warp and woof of Jesus' practices, and that was why he could say, 'Whoever has seen me has seen the Father' (John 14:9, cf. 4:34). However, he could not step outside his skin or his cultural context to prove this; it was a matter of trusting and obeying for him then just as it is for us now. The importance of remembering that practices of faith are governed by God's direct presence lies principally in that they thus honour him but also in the fact that they can turn against their practitioners in much the same way as did the practices of Jesus' day. So when I say that God himself is the grammar of faith I mean that it is he who regulates our practices (including theological ones), teaches us their point, and thereby keeps our language in good order: God enables us to show his independent reality because he shows himself through the practices of faith.

The proposal that God is the grammar of faith might strike some readers as a (possibly unwarranted) novelty, so it is worth noticing that essays in the same direction have been made by several other theologians. For example, in a very striking passage, Barth argues that where humans appropriate God's promise,

In this use our words then possess the entire veracity which they have in God himself, in which God the creator, who places them at our disposal, knows about himself, and with which he describes himself. In this use, God himself lives and speaks in them. In this use human words become God's own word. (1957: 231)[3]

In his critical examination of Barth's doctrine of God (*Persons in Communion* (1996)) Alan Torrance uses Wittgenstein to describe the way in which human language becomes a fit vehicle for expressing God's character. Preparing the ground for his argument for our 'semantic participation' in the life of God, he writes that 'the trinitarian event of communion ... constitutes the very grammar of ... worship ... and epistemic communion' (324). Jenson has a similar view of God's direct involvement in the life of the church: 'The Christian God *is* his own word, and all churchly words are either the actuality of God's word and so the presence of God himself,

---

[3] Thus Barth says of the Old Testament's anthropomorphic terms for God: 'all these human, all too human concepts are not just that, are not just descriptions and representations of the reality of Yahweh; *they are themselves the reality of Yahweh*' (1975: 36, my italics).

or the means by which we combat his presence' (1992: 97). Thus, regarding
the regulative function of dogmatic theology, he argues that 'the chief thing
to be done about the integrity of the church across time is to pray that *God*
will indeed use the church's structures of historical continuity to establish
and preserve it, and to believe that he answers this prayer' (1997: 41, cf.
16–20).

So in arguing that God is the grammar of faith, I do not deny that theology has a regulative role: dogmatic theology can helpfully be regarded
as offering rules for thought about God. However, according to my argument it should not be given a privileged, quasi-legislative stance of the
kind Wittgenstein's followers suggest. Theology is a practice as much at risk
of falling into disrepair as any other; its language is as likely to idle as any
other. Ultimately, it is God who engages the running-gear and grants idling
tongues to become vehicles of praise. Theology also is under God. This is
why there is a material need to speak of theology as being regulated, and
why, although practices can be adequately maintained by God, nevertheless,
theology needs to incorporate the concept of realism as a supplementary
meta-rule to preserve its distinctive and traditional character. The burden
of the first half of this chapter concerns the demonstration of the need
for such a conception of realism. (I discuss it in more detail in chapter 7.)

This can be brought out in a preliminary way by examining some aspects of Christian non-realism. Non-realists set out to make Christian faith
autonomous from the God of theological realism and from the minions of
his 'cosmic Toryism', but they want to remain in historical continuity with
the church. Adopting traditional practices helps them achieve this – despite
any embarrassments arising from its realist language. Unsurprisingly, this
involves attenuating the content of Christian faith so that it will tell a story
acceptable to the spiritual aspirations of humanity in the twilight of modernity. In making this move, non-realists acknowledge that Christian faith
involves regulative structures and therefore find it acceptable to introduce
their own regulative structure, but they do this by means of a new meta-rule
for understanding Christianity. Where regulative structures encroach upon
their determination to autonomy, they repudiate them; they are permis-
sible so long as they have been freely chosen. David Hart exemplifies the
use of this meta-rule when he writes that, because Christian liturgical and
scriptural resources are couched in realist language, 'we shall need to make a
shift in our interpretation of the texts' (1993: 70).[4] Similarly, Cupitt's taking

---

[4] Notice how the prescriptive tone fits the regulative purpose. David Hart (1993: 76–93) gives an
impression of how the non-realist meta-rule is applied in practice. Freeman (1993) offers a more
personal statement. See also Cupitt's (1993) critique of Phillips.

leave of God can be understood as his embarking on a project of systematically reinterpreting Christianity according to the ruling conception that the realist God does not exist and that Christian practices are the bedrock of the Christian reality.

The general effect is as though non-realist Christians were like a group of chess players. One day they announce that they have decided upon a new rule of chess that revises all the other rules of the game and in virtue of which in future all players of *authentic* chess will be those who incorporate this meta-rule. But against the plausibility of this as an argument for the continuity of non-realist with realist Christianity, notice Wittgenstein's remark that without rules a 'word has as yet no meaning; and if we change the rules, it now has another meaning (or none), and in that case we might just as well change the word too' (1978³: 147n.). It is false and misleading of those who introduce a new rule to say that theirs is the authentic game; they have invented a new game, just as picking up a football and running with it invented rugby.

If this analysis is correct, despite having roots in Christianity, in its substance non-realist faith is not *Christian* faith at all. In fact, it seems to illustrate in a particularly clear way what Barth called 'the paradoxical fact ... of heresy'.

Faith does not stand only, or even in the first and most important sense, in conflict with unbelief. It stands in conflict with itself, i.e., with a form or forms of faith in which it recognises itself in respect of form but not of content ... [Faith] can only understand this faith as another faith so far as concerns content ... By heresy we understand a form of Christian faith which we cannot deny to be a form of Christian faith from the formal standpoint, i.e., in so far as it, too, relates to Jesus Christ, to his Church, to baptism, Holy Scripture and the common Christian creeds, but in respect of which we cannot really understand what we are about when we recognise it as such, since we can understand its content, its interpretation of these common presuppositions, only as a contradiction of faith. (1975: 31–2)

Cupitt aims to show 'how the profession and practice of a thoroughly reformed version of Christianity could again come to look attractive to a thinking person, *after* dogma, and *after* the Church' (2001: 2) and thinks that 'perhaps Sea of Faith is itself the first church of the future' (1998: 163). To the extent that this language denotes a conscious taking leave of the historic church and its faith, Cupitt and fellow Anglican members of the Sea of Faith who subscribe to these views should have the courage of their convictions, leave the Church of England, and establish a new 'church'. If instead they think that they are reforming the church by jettisoning the content of the faith whilst retaining its form, those Bishops who refuse to ordain or to license members of Sea of Faith must be judged to have upheld the discipline and guarded the faith of the church.

PRACTISING THE PRESENCE?

The difference between Wittgensteinians and non-realist Christians is that whereas the former do not regard it as ruled overall, the latter recognize that Christian faith is a regulated whole and that to make it autonomous they need to introduce a meta-rule. In this respect, non-realists are closer to scripture and realist Christianity than Wittgensteinians. We turn now to look at some scriptural practices which will make apparent that the Wittgensteinian approach to grammar ignores this overall ruling and that non-realists change it in such a way as to confirm the judgement that theirs should not be regarded as an authentic development of Christianity.

We look firstly at Moses' sermon in Deut. 6:20ff, which commands the recitation of a credal salvation-history as part of the wider context of the *shema*,[5] and then at Paul's writing on the celebration of the Lord's Supper in 1 Cor. 11:17–34. These practices assume a grammar of faith and see themselves as open to the authority of God because he reveals himself through them. They show that Christians need to guard against thinking that the only agents in their practices are human and/or that their practices can be pursued autonomously: practices do not have their rationale in themselves but in the God who gave them as a means of sustaining divine–human fellowship.

This becomes apparent, for example, from Moses' sermon where he explicates God's covenant with Israel and the commandments which enshrine its ratification. He says,

When your children ask you in time to come, 'What is the meaning of the decrees and the statutes and ordinances that the LORD our God has commanded you?' then you shall say to your children, 'We were Pharaoh's slaves in Egypt, but the LORD brought us out of Egypt with a mighty hand. The LORD displayed before our eyes great and awesome signs and wonders against Egypt, against Pharaoh and all his household. He brought us out from there in order that he may bring us in, to give us the land that he promised on oath to our ancestors. Then the LORD commanded us to observe all these statutes, to fear the LORD our God, for our lasting good, so as to keep us alive, as is now the case. If we diligently observe this entire commandment before the LORD our God, as he has commanded us, we will be in the right.' (Deut. 6:20–5)

---

[5] I take Moses to be the canonical speaker without prejudice to questions of historical criticism.

'What is the meaning?';[6] the answer implies a warning: the practices enjoined upon God's people can become meaningless and can become ends in themselves, but if so, they can lose their originating purpose. Moses' instruction implies that what gives them meaning is the recital of the story of those events in her life which taught Israel to recognize the hand of YHWH and in which his purpose had been shown and his promise given. The law was given as an expression of the will and character of YHWH. God's will expresses his person, and therefore his character and his will are inseparable: 'Knowledge of [God's] person and character are identical, and both are grounded in his self-revelation. To lack knowledge of God is described as disobeying his will and therefore it evokes his anger' (Childs 1985: 51). As the expression of obedience to his will, Israel's socio-religious practices live out the presence of God and thus, where God's will is performed, there his character is displayed.

In terms of our current interest, Moses' point is that the link between practice and presence is contingent; there is no *necessity* by which the practices automatically convey the character of God. The two could become detached: to forget God's self-revealed character by not reciting the story has the same effects as failing to keep up the practices, as disobeying his will. Because the relationship is contingent, the practices can be performed whilst the living God is forgotten. Properly understood, religious practices and the recital of God's saving deeds are an integrity, though neither can be reduced to the other. As Paul argues in 2 Cor. 3, reading scripture can occur in a *religious* way and yet be *spiritually* worthless. Just as YHWH's character cannot be known or conceived other than as he has shown himself to be in history, so upholding the testimonies, statutes, and ordinances is fruitless unless they are recollected as the expression of the will of Israel's saviour. God called Israel into being and gave her particular practices: his reality cannot be reduced to practices, nor can the practices themselves suffice to show God. Thus, the practices that express YHWH's will receive their meaning from his character as it is recited in the narrative which accompanies the practices. In other words, the Exodus narrative stands in a regulative relationship to the practices, the decrees, the statutes, and the ordinances: it sustains their meaning.[7]

In its canonical setting Moses' sermon contemplates the possibility of practices losing their meaning. We turn now to examine the way in which

---

[6] There is no word in the Hebrew text corresponding to 'meaning'; inserting the term is faithful to the original, however, and is accepted by many commentators.

[7] Notice that here story – usually taken to be first-order discourse – stands in regulative, second-order relationship to practices.

Paul confronts the near actuality of this happening in the woefully divided Corinthian church. In his commentary on Paul's teaching concerning the Lord's Supper at 1 Cor. 11:17–34 Gordon Fee emphasizes the importance of understanding the 'abuses' at Corinth in the light of the twin realities of consuming the eucharistic food within the setting of a (cultic) meal, and suggests that, 'the Corinthians ... were in grave danger of losing altogether the meaning of the food, and thus of the meal as well' (1987: 532). According to Fee, the abuse involved a double failure to 'discern the body'. First, by humiliating its poorer members at the Lord's Supper, the Corinthian church failed to discern the body in the sense that they divided Christ's body, the church; second, Paul regards the humiliating 'abuse of the "body" ... as an abuse of Christ himself' (533). Fee's comments are worth quoting in full:

The bread represents [Christ's] crucified body, which, along with his poured out blood, effected the death which ratified the New Covenant. By their abuse of one another, they were also abusing the One through whose death and resurrection they had been brought to life and formed into his new eschatological fellowship, his body the church. Thus Paul's need to take them all the way back – to the actual words of institution – so that they will restore the meaning of the food to its rightful place in their meal. 'Do this', those words remind them, 'in remembrance of *me*'. To which Paul adds, 'for as often as we celebrate this meal we proclaim the Lord's death until he comes'. Believers eat in the present in fellowship with one another, focusing on Christ's death which brought them life; and they do so as eschatological people, awaiting his return. In that context they must 'discern the body'; otherwise they put themselves under the same condemnation as those who crucified him in the first place. At his return he will execute judgement on those who do not believe; by their actions the Corinthians are already incurring that judgement. They must change so as not to come under that final judgement as well. (533)

Paul assumes that the crucified and risen Lord will make this food and meal a (the?) primary locus of his activity in the church, and that that activity brings to present effect the reality of judgement and grace enacted in Christ's reconciling death. Thus, the Lord's Supper is celebrated in grateful obedience to the one whose death is memorialized in it, and who is now alive as transforming presence giving meaning to Christian practices in the present.[8]

Eucharistic practices tend to autonomy when they seem to humanity to have meaning only to the extent that they construct it and impose it on them. Paul reminds the Corinthians that the Lord's Supper was not invented by them: these practices have been given to the church; they were

---

[8] For a helpful theological description of this, see Ford 1995, especially 366ff.

not invented by them.[9] Forgetting these things God's people lose their sense of being one body loved, redeemed, and reconciled to God in Christ. In their abuse of the poor and marginalized of their church, they forget that, in Emily Dickinson's words, "Tis beggars banquets best define / 'Tis thirsting vitalizes wine' (1959: 28). They then construct (albeit unconsciously) a meaning of their own for the meal which, in its divisiveness, denies the meaning given to it by Jesus.

This forgetfulness and constructivism can be caused and made evident in various ways, but how it happens and how it is evident is less important than that it does, for the result is the same: knowledge of God is lost and God allows these practices to be turned against their practitioners. Failure to eat and drink the eucharistic food anamnetically profanes the body of the one who gave himself for all humanity on the cross. Nevertheless, even when they do not 'discern the body', the Corinthians participate in the events the institution narrative recollects: just as those who initially enacted those events brought unintended consequences upon themselves by a failure of discernment, so also Paul believes that one can eat and drink one's own judgement and reap physical consequences.[10] It is possible to try to construct a counter-meaning for the ritual, but this does not eradicate the meaning the Lord gave it. As Ernst Käsemann puts it,

The Corinthians have to be reminded of this particular content of the Supper [sc. Christ's atoning death] because in their enthusiasm they fondly imagine that they have been withdrawn from the jurisdiction of this justice and the tribunal which administers it. The self-manifestation of Christ calls men to obedience and this means that, at the same time, it calls them to account before the final Judge who is already today acting within his community as he will act toward the world on the Last Day – he bestows salvation by setting men within his lordship and, if they spurn his lordship, they then experience this act of rejection as a self-incurred sentence of death. (Käsemann 1964: 126, quoted by Barrett 1971[2]: 272)[11]

So, since the Supper is an occasion of the Lord's presence with his people in judgement and grace, the eucharistic meal and food retain the character Christ gave them as (in some sense[12]) a medium of his presence, and this even when they are part of forgetful practices which implicitly or explicitly

---

[9] See Thiselton 2000: 867f.
[10] See verses 29–30. It is unlikely that Paul meant this to be taken metaphorically: see Thiselton 2000: 894ff.
[11] Cf. the 25th Article of Religion of the Church of England.
[12] Precisely what sense is, of course, a matter of controversy in sacramental theology that does not need to be decided for my argument. However, the Zwinglian views current in some parts of the church seem to me to exclude important aspects of Paul's thought. For a Catholic perspective, sensitive to the issues we are considering, see Loughlin 1996: 223–45.

declare autonomy from the act of God which they memorialize. The eucharist should therefore be regarded as ineradicably the sacramental enactment of God's judgement and grace and as incapable of losing its meaning because God grants it through his gracious presence. Thus, rather than saying that practices commanded by God can lose their meaning, it would be more accurate to say that in spurning the divinely granted meaning the abusers turn the practices against themselves, and thereby perhaps reinforce their sense that they are meaningless, worthless, and even corrupting unless and until they give them some other meaning of their own devising.

Such a constructivism is explicit in the work of non-realists. David Hart (who at the time of his writing was a member of the Sea of Faith steering committee) claims of the sacraments that 'much of what occurs ... occurs in the perception of the participants and is not something that happens irrespective of these perceptions' (1993: 86). The epistemic idealism here is directly related to linguistic idealism, for, as Hart goes on to elaborate, 'all human meaning is infinitely adaptable and relative to the insights of the individual(s) involved in a particular nexus of signifiers' (87). This anthropocentric construal of the sacrament's meaning combines conveniently with post-Structuralism so that Hart can elide 'discerning the body' into 'the importance of "discerning the signifiers"' (79). In other words, eucharistic significance or meaning is a human creation: there is no transcendental signified, no signified body, only an endless chain of naturalistically interpreted signifiers.[13] If Paul mistakenly thought that 'discerning the body' involved moving from signifier to signified, too bad he hadn't read Derrida.[14]

The gravity of the debate between realists and non-realists seems to me to be captured well in the following words:

Jesus is active in the corporate life of the Church; what he gives to human beings, he gives in significant part through the mediation of the common life, which is itself his 'body', his material presence in the world, though it does not exhaust his identity or activity ... [The] ritual of the 'Lord's Supper' dramatizes all this; the concrete food and drink of the meal is interpreted as the material presence of Jesus, and the conduct, the 'style', of the meal, so Paul argues, is supposed to display the character of the community as itself the body, the material thereness, of Jesus (and when it fails to do this, the community comes under severe, even annihilating, judgement). (Rowan Williams 2000: 189 cf. 192–3)[15]

---

[13] Compare Marion's (1991: 165ff) powerful statement of a eucharistic realism against transignification.
[14] Unlike Derrida (whom Hart seems to have in mind here), and in common with analytic philosophy, I use the term 'signified' for the object, not the concept: cf. Derrida 1976: 63.
[15] Williams writes of *interpreting* the meal: this is not constructivist because his interpretation aims at elucidating Paul's words rather than *re*interpreting them. It goes without saying that Williams's note of warning bears heeding as much by realists as non-realists.

THE GRAMMAR OF FAITH AND THE REALITY OF GOD

Paul Holmer has done much to bring Wittgenstein's concept of grammar to the attention of theologians, especially that of his Yale colleague George Lindbeck (though his use of that concept is rather different from Lindbeck's), and a brief examination of his understanding of the concept will help us appreciate what it means to say that God is the grammar of Christian faith. Theology is not just 'a kind of grammar that passes into the "how" of a human life' – it is not just regulative of that life, as other Wittgensteinians think – for, Holmer continues, through the manifold that St Luke witnessed, it was as if 'he could also plot, like a grammarian, God's ordering of human affairs. He learned, in congress with Jesus, what *God* meant, what *love* required, what *hope* was justified, where *peace* was given' (1988: 9). The meaning of Christian language is learned from God's involvement with human life, but since the practice of theology is not separable from this, it is not enough to say that theology is the grammar of faith. It is not from theology that we learn how to use Christian discourse correctly; it is from God's action amongst his people by the Spirit of Jesus. God is the grammar of faith. Practices help us discover the meaning of Christian discourse, but unless they are pursued in obedience and acknowledgement of God's involvement in them, they are an inadequate guide to meaning. Thus Holmer sees what Lindbeck and Phillips do not: it is God-in-Christ who teaches what they had thought could be learned from practices or from rules. Without God's incarnate involvement there would be no Christian discourse.

We can now see that a conception of Christian faith's having a grammar is formally required, not just to prevent practices from becoming autonomous – that might only be to invoke God as a pious gloss on a decision we had already made – but to express the fact that God has made things to be this way. He has given Christian faith a grammar simply in virtue of his giving an order to human affairs and his bringing that order to fulfilment in Jesus' proclamation of the Kingdom. The practices of Christian faith should express the rule of God, but that they fail to do so to the degree they ought is due to sin; that they do so at all is owing to God's grace. This is why human rules and practices, even those of theology, are never an infallible guide to the meaning of theological terms: God's rule is not reducible to human rules and practices.

It will be helpful at this point to distinguish between *intended* and *apparent* grammar when speaking of God as the grammar of Christian practices. God intends particular practices to mediate his presence; when they are performed according to his will, God is known through them as their *intended* grammar. However, owing to sin and disobedience, practices fall short of their intended purpose, and in this case the grammar they make *apparent* is apt to mislead as to the nature of the reality God gives it to them to intend. The Corinthian's participation in the Lord's Supper gives a false impression of the grammar of 'body' in Pauline discourse. It shows not the intended grammar but only an apparent grammar of 'body'. The selfish behaviour of some members of the church might lead an outsider to imagine that 'body' meant an agglomeration of individuals in a Hobbesian state of nature – a body whose members perpetually compete with and threaten each other. God's judgement upon those who abuse the body of Christ is intended to bring them to repentance and to restore the intended grammar of 'the body', so that 'body' now stands in a proper relationship to Christ and what had become 'apparent' grammar will be once again 'intended' grammar.

Thinking that rules and practices can, by themselves, show the meaning of theological terms is analogous to thinking that law (= Torah) is the substance of the Kingdom. We need to recall that 'Christ is the end (*telos*) of the law' (Rom. 10:4). The law is not an end in itself, nor are Christian practices. Christ is the one whom Christian practices intend in a similar way to that in which he is that to which the law points. This is why *the material content of the grammar of faith is the presence of God-in-Christ*.

Think again of Moses' instruction and Paul's exhortation. For present purposes their most notable feature is that they present the recital of a story of the Lord's saving deeds as necessary to maintaining the integrity of the practices.[16] This integrity consists in their continuing to sustain the relationship between God and his people. Moses anticipates the possibility of practices losing meaning and inserts the story of God's deeds as the factor which will prevent this. Paul confronts a situation in which the meaning of eucharistic practices is being subverted and corrupted. To reform things, he tells his readers that the meaning of their action is not self-subsistent: their action is in a tradition, linked to its source by reciting the story of Christ's reconciling death, though it is only by God's gracious presence amongst them that the narrative of this past event can give the meaning he intends to their action. We should not restrict the sovereignty of God (for example, by asserting that particular conditions must obtain for him to act), but our illustrations permit us to say that, where obedient practice is accompanied

---

[16] Of the *practices*, note: it is not my argument that recital is a necessary condition of God's presence to his people.

by recital of story, belief is warranted that God will make these actions meaningful to those who participate in them, that he will be their intended grammar. Recital is not a sufficient condition of God's self-presence to the people who tell the story. God is not identical with the story (as Lindbeck's mistaken emphasis on scripture as text rather than normative testimony could suggest);[17] it narrates his character, and he comes to his people's practices as he does in the story – freely, in judgement and grace.

A closer look at 1 Cor. 11:26 sheds more light on God's being the grammar of faith and how this relates to realism. Here Paul writes, 'For as often as you eat this bread and drink this cup, you proclaim the Lord's death until he comes.' This is the hinge about which Paul's thought turns here, and it provides the rationale for the rest of his argument. The institution narrative governs eucharistic practices, but things had gone wrong even though Paul had delivered it to the church as from the Lord. We cannot determine exactly why Paul reminds the Corinthians of the narrative,[18] but, as we saw above, it appears that intended grammar was becoming merely apparent. Paul thinks that to obviate this the narrative needs to be supplemented by a further reminder that the church's eucharistic practices amount to a proclamation of the Lord's death and that this act of proclamation makes present what happened between God and humanity on the cross of Christ. In effect, Paul's reminder adds what we might call a *realist meta-rule* to his instructions to the Corinthian church.

It should be borne in mind that Paul's theology of the eucharist is to be understood in the light of his theology of God's word, through which, he believes – to put it in legitimately anachronistic terms[19] – God's independent reality is established. On the preaching of the word, witness the early chapters of 1 Cor. and Rom. 10:5–17. In the latter text (especially verses 12–17), Paul makes a structurally similar point to that which we have noted in his theology of the Lord's Supper: God gives salvation to his people when they call upon the one named in 'the preaching of Christ' (verse 17). (If this genitive is subjective,[20] the case for locating an argument for realism in Paul's theology of God's word – including the word of the institution narrative – is reinforced.) Conversely, those who hear but do not heed the preaching of Christ experience judgement (cf. verses 18ff).

So, where word and sacrament are duly administered, God is their self-presencing grammar. These practices are means of God's presence to those

---

[17] See p. 106 above.   [18] Cf. Barrett 1971[2]: 26.   [19] *Contra* Kerr 1989: 29–30.
[20] See Cranfield 1979: 537.

who participate in them whether or not the realist meta-rule is explicitly admitted. Paul adds his realist meta-rule to bring out what is happening amongst the Corinthians and so that, 'when we are judged by the Lord . . . [and] chastened, we may not be condemned along with the world' (1 Cor. 11:32). He does not insert it in a legalistic way: it is not added in heteronomous competition with the liberating work of the Spirit,[21] it does not add anything to the Corinthians' practices which they could not have worked out from what had already been delivered to them, nor does it contribute a new chapter to the story of God's work – this is proleptically complete. Paul's purpose can be brought out by comparing him with Wittgenstein:[22] he issues reminders about what lies before our eyes, reminders of what we were in danger of forgetting because of confusions about grammar, reminders, in this case, that turn remembering into anamnesis. Anamnesis is eschatological: it looks forward by looking back to Christ's death and resurrection as the proleptic consummation of God's purposes. Anamnesis expects the Lord to make the eucharist the holy place where he meets his people in judgement and grace, and equips them to bear witness to him. In short, in judging and giving grace God acts in such a way that our lives are *interrupted* and brought into *correspondence* with him.[23]

Some, such as the kind of theological realists Phillips attacks, will ask for proof that God acts in this way. However, it seems to me that it is not possible to provide such proof. Consider Paul's account of his conversion.[24] The source of his faith lies in the Lord who met him on the Damascus road and 'interrupted' his resolve to defend Judaism by persecuting followers of the Way. Paul writes as he does to draw his readers' attention to these matters on the presumption that God does so act. Not only does he assume this in relation to the eucharist, but he regards it as the basis of his apostolic credentials: there is no indisputable proof that God acts in this way in the eucharist any more than there is of Paul's appointment to apostleship. We cannot revisit the Damascus road in a time machine, and it is doubtful whether if we could the Lord would deign to glorify our technological marvels or grace our wilful scepticism by his presence. Such proof is unavailable in principle: to attempt to find it would be to seek an 'authenticating' element over and above the supremely authoritative calling word of Christ.[25] The only credentials on offer are those Paul incurred

---

[21] See 2 Cor. 3:17.   [22] 1978[3]: §127, cf. §89.
[23] My terminology here is borrowed from Jüngel 1976. On correspondence, see also Bruce Marshall 2000: 266–73.
[24] Acts 22: 6–16; cf. Gal. 1:15f.   [25] Cf. Barth 1933: 69f.

for the sake of the Gospel of Jesus and which he bore in his body.[26] His suffering reproduces the suffering of Jesus and brings to his converts the effects of Christ's atoning work: Christ's death is at work in Paul; through him his risen life is at work in them.[27] The suffering which Paul endured in the course of his ministry is itself proof of the interruptive calling of God in Christ and of his being brought into 'correspondence' (or, in Pauline language, conformity) with Christ.[28] Just as the Lord's act in calling Paul to apostleship cannot be proved by external means, so neither can the Lord's acting as Paul teaches he does in the eucharist.

Paul does not attempt to prove that God acts as he does any more than he seeks to prove philosophically that God is independently real, and the reason is that, in the light of his earlier attack on the pretensions of 'human wisdom' at 1:18–2:5, it would be evangelistically irresponsible, theologically inconsistent, culturally foolish, and even sinful to attempt to do so. It would be to reinforce a central problem of the Corinthians, that 'they believe, not in God, but in their own belief in God' (Barth 1933: 17). The reality of God's saving power is manifest in the word of the cross – that interruptive folly which has intrinsic probative wisdom. God shows himself existentially through the gift of his Holy Spirit, or (to paraphrase 1 Cor. 1:30), through the wisdom, righteousness, sanctification, and redemption which believers share with Christ. Ultimately, Paul believes, God will vindicate himself and his people's trust in him at the *eschaton*. To offer proof as demanded by 'human wisdom' would only be to underline the apparent folly of God's ways and to subvert God's own way of proving himself. To put the point in more contemporary philosophical terms, we can say that God's verification of himself is eschatological.[29] It has taken place proleptically in Christ's resurrection; its final consummation is anticipated in the eucharist.[30]

In discussing proof, we have moved into territory traditionally occupied by philosophers, so it is appropriate at this stage in the argument to sketch out how I regard the relationship between philosophy and theology. Owing to limitations of space, the discussion must be restricted to the topic so far as it pertains to our subject matter and main debating partners.

[26] On these issues see 1 Cor. 9:1f, 15:1–19; 2 Cor. *passim*, particularly 1–6 and 10–13. Paul summarizes his arguments in 2 Cor. 4:7–12.
[27] See A. T. Hanson 1987: 39–78.
[28] This illustrates why apologetic theodicies that tend to mitigate or negate suffering can actually reduce the Christian's ability to show the reality of God; cf. pp. 37–9 above.
[29] The concept of eschatological verification in relation to religious language was introduced by Hick 1966[2]: 176–99; cf. Pannenberg 1968: 53–114.
[30] The epistemological circularity in my argument is, it seems to me, unavoidable. For argument and references, see my 2001, especially 324ff.

THE RELATIONSHIP BETWEEN PHILOSOPHY AND THEOLOGY

Philosophy's gift to theology

Richard Rorty declares that 'The notion that there is an autonomous discipline called "philosophy", distinct from and sitting in judgement upon both religion and science, is of quite recent origin' (1980: 131). Despite challenging many aspects of modern philosophy, Rorty does not question whether it *should* be autonomous; I want to argue that it is not because, like every region of human life, it comes within the ambit of the redeeming work of God.

In a predominantly secular and plural culture, theology is aware that its voice is only one in a sometimes cacophonous human conversation. However, it need accept neither that its own truth is simply to be relativized by the equal and competing claims of its interlocutors nor that only philosophy can arbitrate truth. Lessing's 'ugly ditch' between 'the accidental truths of history' and the 'necessary truths of reason' neatly encapsulates the apparent choice here: *either* a form of relativism according to which truth and falsehood are decided by conformity or disconformity with a particular, contingent historical incident *or* the certainty of truths arrived at by universally applicable canons of reason and evidence.

However, the task facing theology, particularly in the twilight of modernity, is to uphold the universality of God's truth revealed uniquely and with scandalous particularity in Jesus Christ whilst simultaneously avoiding the hollow triumphalism of ignoring conceptual difficulties or the faithless defeatism of giving up on the task of articulating a position which has a *theological* integrity derived from its not conceding methodologically or substantively to unbelief. To take either of these options would be for theology to forsake its vocation as a witness to God's redeeming word. Many a thoroughbred has fallen at Beecher's daunting brook; theologians should not quiver at the sight of Lessing's ugly ditch but remember that the one in whom dwelt the fullness of God and who is now the glorified Lord of all entered the Holy City on an ass. From a theological perspective, Christ's universal lordship should determine our account of the relationship between philosophy and theology. Although each has its distinctive methods and subject matter, both should be related to the truth of God revealed in Christ; neither should be seen as autonomous or as independent of the other.

For the last two hundred years, theology has sought an accommodation with the necessary truths of reason, and it has done so under the tutelage of

the position now known as foundationalism. The edifice of human knowledge must have secure foundations: all other ground – opinion, belief,
superstition – is sinking sand. So, granted that knowledge is justified true
belief, then according to foundationalism for a belief to count as knowledge it must either (1) be self-evident, or (2) be evident to the senses (or
'incorrigible', as this criterion is sometimes put), or (3) have been validly
inferred from what is evident in one or both of these ways.[31] Though foundationalism barely survives in this form in contemporary philosophy, it
has had a decisive, and some would say disastrous, impact on theology.
Enlightenment thought threatened the very existence of theology as a discipline principally answerable to God, for it seemed to rule out any appeal
to revelation. The claims of revelation were judged to fall outside the criteria of knowledge and therefore to be epistemically below par (at least,
until they could be shown not to 'be contradictory to our clear intuitive
knowledge'). In the words of Immanuel Kant, who was the most influential philosopher of the Enlightenment and who wanted to provide a secure
basis for religion, theology is to be practised 'within the limits of reason
alone' (1960: 8). The best way to secure the intellectual prestige of theology
therefore seemed to be to show that it could conform to foundationalist criteria. Thus, Christian beliefs have been mediated by philosophical beliefs or
rendered 'epistemically dependent' on them in the sense that 'the primary
criteria for deciding about the truth of Christian beliefs, at least in part and
perhaps as a whole, must not themselves be distinctively Christian' (Bruce
Marshall 2000: 50).[32] The upshot has been that on this model, theology
has been regarded as subordinate to philosophy – both methodologically
and, implicitly if not always explicitly, substantively.

   However, as Bruce Marshall has shown with particular power and rigour,
this accommodation to a supposedly neutral, foundational rationality has
had a far-reaching and damaging impact on the way Christian doctrine
is articulated.[33] The doctrinal core of Christian faith has tended to be expressed in an apologetic key and there has been a corresponding weakening
of theology's confidence in its own intellectual integrity. We saw something of this in the version of theological realism I criticized in chapter 3
where we encountered theologians – notably, though in different ways, van

---

[31] Definition adapted from Plantinga 1983; note now his 2000. For a good survey, see Alston 1992;
   for philosophical polemic, see Rorty 1980; for genealogy, Stout 1981; for a theological introduction,
   Thiel 1994; see also Westphal 1990: 207–20.
[32] On the problems that epistemic dependence creates for articulating a Christian realism, see Bruce
   Marshall 2000: 106f. On philosophical mediation, see Michalson (1999).
[33] See Marshall's discussion of the doctrine of the resurrection, 2000: 50–80, 127–37.

Huyssteen and Peacocke – who seek to render theology credible according to scientific canons of rationality and to construe doctrinal affirmations on analogy with scientific theories. Ronald Thiemann clearly articulates the baleful effects of foundationalism:[34]

> When theology is conceived as a theoretical activity seeking the ultimate ground of church practice, it naturally seeks those goods associated with theoretical activities. Theology takes its place beside other theoretical inquiries ruled by general principles of rationality. Whenever a theoretical inquiry diverges from those general principles, it must justify that divergence by special apologetic argument ... If a foundationalist theologian is concerned at all to guard the distinctiveness of the theological subject matter, apologetics inevitably emerges as the *primary* theological task. The two most important theological activities – the development of a universal justificatory argument and the defence of Christian claims before the bar of rationality – are carried on independently of the internal logic of Christian belief and practice and with little reference to criteria of judgement internal to the Christian tradition. As a consequence the foundational view tends to subordinate the characteristic patterns of Christian speech to the patterns of philosophical and apologetic argument. This position has grave difficulty affirming the irreducible integrity of Christian language. This is especially the case if the primal religious experience which grounds the language of church practice is capable of expression in a universal philosophical language, for then the characteristic patterns of Christian speech are reducible to the structures of the more ultimate basic language. (1985: 74)

'The irreducible integrity of Christian language' – that, precisely, is what we found to be put into question by theological realism. At root the problem here is that the Enlightenment elevated to supremacy a single, idealized understanding of what it is to be rational and how truth is to be attained. A foundational and universally normative conception of rationality has obscured from full view the fact that reasoning is carried out in diverse ways few of which conform to the prescribed ideal yet many, if not all, of which count in their own terms as rational. As Martha Nussbaum suggests,

> [t]here is a mistake made, or at least a carelessness, when one takes a method and style that have proven fruitful for the investigation and description of certain truths – say those of natural science – and applies them without further reflection or argument to a very different sphere of life that may have a different geography and demand a different sort of precision, a different norm of rationality. (1990: 19–20, quoted by John Webster 1998a: 14)[35]

---

[34] Strictly speaking, the version of foundationalism discussed in the text is what Plantinga refers to as *classical* foundationalism. As an epistemological model, foundationalism need not be rejected. For example, Plantinga's criticism of classical foundationalism is consistent with the Reidian foundationalism he proposes (1993: 183ff).

[35] Note that in his critique of foundationalism, Plantinga (1983: 90) seems to concede that atheists and believers 'have different conceptions of reason'.

Rationality is exemplified in particular practices of human conduct; there are family resemblances between them but no universal core feature that can be abstracted from those diverse practices and used as a neutral canon of rationality across all disciplines of art, skill, and intellect. As we shall see, philosophy has much to offer theology, but it is mistaken to think that it is foundational to it.

Thiemann's reference to 'criteria of judgement internal to the Christian tradition' could lead us to suppose that a Wittgensteinian approach might offer a more fruitful way of understanding the relationship between philosophy and theology. After all, Wittgenstein wrote that 'Philosophy may in no way interfere with the actual use of language; it can in the end only describe it. For it cannot give it any foundation either. It leaves everything as it is' (1978: §124). According to Phillips, Wittgenstein 'shows the possibility of a common [philosophical] method, a common engagement in disinterested enquiry which Christians and non-Christians alike can participate in' (1993a: 232). This method does not blunt the particularities of language-games for it does not prescribe universally applicable criteria of truth, rationality and meaning:

disinterested enquiry reveals a variety of meanings and conceptions of truth which cannot be reduced to any single paradigm ... this variety *can* only be shown by clarifying the grammar of the various concepts involved in the language-games we play. (1993a: 232)

On Phillips's account the task of philosophy is descriptive;[36] it does not have any normative relation to theology. The two are distinct forms of life comprising discrete, independent language-games lacking any means of mutual critique and interaction.

Phillips thinks that philosophy does not and cannot prescribe how any (non-philosophical) practices should be undertaken, but this, as Frei rightly judges, is to make philosophy 'wholly external' to theology (1992: 51). This is the ideal of Phillips's approach, but in practice he finds it impossible to maintain a sharp demarcation between the two disciplines. For example, examining the relationship between God and Christian belief in theological realism, he is content to say that '[w]e cannot appreciate the relation between belief and its *object* while ignoring the appropriate context of application' (1993a: 42, my italics). Phillips applies the word 'object' to God in a philosophically self-conscious way, so even for the purposes of his own analysis of *theological* realism he needs to import *philosophical* language. In

---

[36] Phillips has in fact misunderstood or reinterpreted Wittgenstein's view of the descriptive role of philosophy: see Baker and Hacker 1980: 548; cf. Hacker 1996: 123.

general, Phillips wants to warn us off ontological talk until we have done the grammatical work, but in fact, as this passage shows, he is hard-pressed to keep the boundaries impermeable. The implication of his use of 'object' seems to be that once we have got the method of projection right, then we can properly appreciate what the relation amounts to, but in order to show this, he cannot avoid using ontological language and he does so to show how philosophy can help clarify conceptual puzzles. Thus, in practice, Phillips's approach is not as philosophically disinterested as his official view professes: he wants us to reconceive a relationship that he thinks is internal to Christian practice and this is fine, except that by suggesting a philosophical means of doing so he contradicts his own methodological prescription and gives theology a considerable investment in philosophy.

If pursued rigorously, Phillips's official approach to the relationship between philosophy and theology would effectively prevent the two from having any interaction at all. Philosophical ideas and concepts (such as 'object' in epistemological or ontological contexts) could not be used, even in a theologically disciplined way, to elucidate the content of Christian faith. Yet Phillips sees that there has been interaction and, arguing against theism, acknowledges 'that abstract concepts have found their way, by various routes, into creeds and declarations of Faith. Even so', he continues, 'to the extent that they have any life there, it will not be by forming the abstract foundations of Faith, but by having a lively application within it' (1988a: 228). What Phillips seems really to object to is the contamination of devotional practices by reflective ones, for he thinks that conceptual grammar is shown in the former and that the latter are not natively part of them. But in fact, the two cannot be so easily separated. For example, one might ask of Phillips whether he thinks that preaching is an exclusively devotional practice. Paul's sermon at the Areopagus (Acts 17:16ff) uses pagan philosophy to make a Christian conceptual and devotional point (against pagan philosophy, notice) – that the God who made the world and is worthy of worship is revealed in Jesus Christ. The sermon also illustrates the fact that since its earliest days, Christianity has used philosophy internally and that the line between devotional and reflective practices is very blurred.[37] Fortunately for those who enjoy such things, philosophical argument can itself be an expression of love for God. As Alfred Louch puts it with only slight irony, '[s]ome worship through song or prayer, others through argument' (1993: 114).

---

[37] See Moule's (1982) study of the use of ontology in the New Testament.

As we have seen, a Christian realism will be focally concerned with the God who became incarnate in Jesus Christ, but Phillips's method has serious difficulties dealing with this, for it means that interactions between philosophy and theology are unavoidable. Christians cannot insulate themselves from the influence of the cultural and philosophical climate they inhabit any more than the incarnate Son of God could seal himself off in a specious philosophical aseity from those he came to save. To anticipate, Jesus is the ground of God's speakability: not only can we not avoid using ordinary human language in referring to Jesus and to God through him, but to refuse to use all the resources of human language in speaking of this person would be to deny the incarnation and make God himself unspeakable. Apophatic theology needs cataphatic if it is to be Christian. To name Jesus 'Lord' is to affirm that, as Robert Jenson puts it, 'Jesus is the *object* we have in knowing God' (1982: 145, my italics). Just as the church has felt compelled to yoke the name of Jesus with God, so it cannot avoid speaking of Jesus as an object since it is a person in space and time of whom we are talking, but not only of *a* person in space and time but of this particular person in relation to the one he addressed as Father. As MacKinnon observed in defending 'substance' language in Christology,

> while initially Christian theological practice might be innocent of any self-conscious involvement with ontology, the simplest affirmation, for instance, concerning Christ's relation to the Father, must include the use of the sort of notions of which ontology seeks to give an account. (1972: 288)

An extreme (but not implausible) result of adopting Phillips's wholly external view of the relationship of philosophy and theology would be that had he followed Phillips to the letter, John could not have used the logos concept in writing his Gospel.[38] Conversely, if contemporary theology does not use, or is prohibited from using, philosophy, or, as Frei puts it in the conclusion of his discussion of Phillips, if 'theology [is made] purely internal to the religion, its result is a theology of total silence when one cannot simply and uncritically parrot biblical and traditional formulae' (1992: 55).

Philosophy can have two equally disastrous effects on theology. On a Wittgensteinian approach it can make it impossible to contextualize the logos outside a very narrow spectrum of cultural experience – that of the first-century Middle East. On a foundationalist approach, it can reduce its content to that which passes muster at the bar of Enlightenment reason.

---

[38] Cf. Moule 1982: 2–3, 5.

Christian theology then becomes either an ossified relic of interest only to anthropologists and experts in religious studies or an extension of the hard sciences which, by becoming part of a more general explanatory project, loses its defining uniqueness.

This, however, is a rather one-eyed way of describing the potential impact of philosophy on theology, for although it can be a threat, a proper response is to see it as a gift. On this view, philosophy bequeaths theology an opportunity to refine its confidence in, and a means of extending, its own distinctive idioms. Such a confidence neither defensively parrots scripture and tradition nor reduces Christian speech to a supposedly more basic language, whether philosophical, ethical, psychological, or sociological. Philosophy can help us discover (or recover) confidence in an accidental truth of history within which is unfolded the meaning of history and the purpose of our practices of reasoning.

Philosophy in theological perspective

If we are to make proper theological sense of philosophy's *gift* to theology, we need to consider the relationship between the two in more detail. Christian theology proceeds in dependency on the grace of God and on the basis of God's self-revelation in the Christ-event through which he fulfilled the promise he had made to Israel on behalf of all humanity. It follows that the Christ-event is unsurpassable and that any other witness he has given to himself will conform with this person. I take these to be primary and organizing principles of Christian theology and its method. Theology is rational because it follows the rationality of God's work, not because it conforms to either its own intrinsic, self-subsistent rationality (Wittgensteinian approaches) or an alien extrinsic rationality (as theological realism learns from Enlightenment foundationalism). Christians are enabled and authorized to believe what they do on the warrant of and in conformity to revelation and they have a corresponding responsibility to bear faithful witness to it.

I take it therefore that, as a matter of theological principle, God's self-revelation in Jesus Christ should be regarded as epistemologically and ontologically prior to all other (secular) determinations of the nature of reality and our cognitive relations with it – as 'epistemic trump', as Bruce Marshall describes the Gospels (2000: 116). The Christian is as entitled to work on the basis of this principle as the agnostic who inverts it and argues that the determination of God must be suspended until mundane reality has been determined.[39] Of course, we cannot totally suspend all other determinations of reality – we cannot completely unlearn what we have learned from philosophy, but we can attempt to proceed on the basis of the methodological principle I have stated and hope that it might yield more theologically fruitful results concerning the realism of the Christian faith than other approaches. What we can attempt to do is to allow a primary theological datum to shape our account of how we are able to write and speak meaningfully of God.

So my account of realism does not and cannot proceed a priori, either presuming that we know nothing of God or suspending what we do know in an attempt to appease secular rationalism. Rather, it attempts to bring out the conditions and assumptions which make this realism possible and in this way amounts to a transcendental argument for a Christocentric realism. No neutral position is available to the theologian, not simply and tritely because every thinker is ineluctably (if unwittingly) committed to some position, but rather because the theologian is one who already participates in God's new creation even whilst living in the midst of the old. This means that the motifs of eschatology and redemption need to be brought into the consideration of the relationship between philosophy and theology.

Phillips thinks that Christian practices are in good conceptual order as they stand, and for this reason his work implies an overly realized eschatology. His argument against the use of philosophical conceptions in theology suggests that he thinks theology operates with a language that is perfect and never needs to internalize the positive lessons which philosophy can teach it. He assumes that we already speak a pure language of Zion, that our practices cannot be corrupted, that they are transparent vehicles of the reality he holds that they show. He relaxes the tension between the 'already' and the 'not yet' too much when he implies that our practices are pellucid reflections of the divine glory. But this is a mistake: Christians are sinful creatures who look forward to seeing face to face, but for the present they see and show God's glory as in a mirror, dimly. The opposing, foundationalist tendency can also be interpreted as operating with an overly realized eschatology where the Christian vision of universality is naturalized. By the canon of secular reason, theological language is reckoned not to be in working order as it stands. An ideal and representationally perspicuous language is sought, founded on the new universal: abstract, theoretical rationality. Science is seen as the supreme

---

[39] As I said in chapter 1, I do not hold this simply on the grounds of a *tu quoque* argument.

exemplar of this and the end to which theological speech should strive.[40] However, as we have seen, the loss to theology is its own distinctive internal logic.

The two views of the relation between philosophy and theology we have been looking at not only operate with a mistaken eschatology, but also presume a mistaken understanding of God's having reconciled all things to himself.[41] The Wittgensteinian methodological perspective would make it unnecessary to conceive of philosophy being reconciled to God, for theology and philosophy are entirely discrete and externally related to each other; the foundationalist, on the other hand, has absorbed the universalizing motif in Christian eschatology only to secularize it into a totalizing discourse abstracted from any particular context. But if God has reconciled all things to himself, every discourse, however modest or grand its claims, needs to be drawn into the compass of theological thought. Philosophy can and should be an object of Christian reflection. It is not just a tool to be used by theologians: as a human practice it needs to be drawn into the light of divine grace, renewed and brought to its proper fulfilment in the service of the good news of its own redemption. Philosophy is neither an irredeemable surd nor a unique, redeeming axiom. To hold it external to theology is to sell it short of its own – not immanent, but divinely granted – possibilities; to treat it as a foundational, totalizing discourse is idolatry: *ta panta en Christo sunesteken* (Col. 1:17).

Because the end has not yet come and the dialect of the tribe awaits its final redemption, philosophical tools have to be used to articulate and clarify Christian faith. A perennial danger here is to think that philosophy can help it attain a knowledge of God which is greater or more ultimate than that given in Christ and the biblical witness to him. Insofar as it seeks to go behind rather than to elucidate the Christ-event, this 'knowledge' is better regarded as speculation. Donald MacKinnon's words are programmatic here:

It is not through the mediation of Christ's revelation of the Father that we are enabled to plumb the structure of being; but rather it is through the use of ontological categories that we are enabled to see precisely what it is that it may be confronts us in the person of Jesus. (1972: 294)

---

[40] Cf. Schleiermacher 1928: 78ff, especially 84–5. Sometimes philosophers see the issues more clearly than theologians: van Fraassen's opposition to scientific realism is connected with his rejection of scientism and his view that philosophy is 'at most . . . a voice in the wilderness, clearing the way for the Lord' (1999: 179, see also 1994a, especially 133 and 1993).
[41] Col. 1:19–20.

Theologians are not debarred from using philosophical concepts and insights, but they should do so in such a way that they are brought under the discipline of the Christ-event. If on the one hand we risk speculation, we need also to avoid a woodenly literal approach to scripture which forgets that it is testimony to divine reality. This is what Calvin accused the Arians of doing: they also thought of theology as an unreflective parroting of scripture.[42] Against them, Calvin advocated a regulative approach to dogmatics,[43] according to which, to elucidate and defend the credal affirmations implied by scripture, 'we ought to seek from Scripture a sure rule for both thinking and speaking, to which both the thoughts of our minds and the words of our mouths should be conformed' (1960: 1.13.3).[44] Finding such a rule allows novel words to be brought into Christian faith, 'renders the truth plain and clear' (1.13.3), and serves to confute the 'impious' who 'hate and curse the word *homoousios*' (1.13.4).[45]

So, non-scriptural terminology imported into Christian speech is provisional and subservient to the truth it is introduced to clarify. It is generally used neither univocally nor equivocally, but taken up and given distinctive meaning by its place in the overall 'ecology of faith' (David Ford's phrase) whilst retaining analogical relations with its original context. As I argued earlier, because the incarnate Jesus inhabited space and time, use of physical object language is unavoidable in reference to him. Moreover, on the basis of his relation to the Father we refer to God through him. Before we get burdened with questions about the 'how' of our referring, the key point for a Christian realist is that this relationship both warrants engaging with and (re)defines the ontology of the divine.[46] Although the grammar (in Wittgenstein's sense) of non-theological uses of ontological vocabulary will need modification if we are to talk in a Christian way of the godhead, nevertheless, the incarnation commits us to use human, and therefore ontological, language to express the 'what' and 'who' of Christ. Thus, 'if it is a mistake to suppose that the use of ... [ontological] notions can be avoided, it is also a mistake to forget that their employment must include the enlargement of their sense by reason of the totally novel use to which they are bent' (MacKinnon 1972: 289). Theology cannot avoid using the full range of human vocabulary available to it, for it seeks to guard and

---

[42] 1960: 1.13.1ff. R. P. C. Hanson suggests that 'the Arians failed ... because they were so inflexible, too conservative, not ready enough to look at new ideas' (1988: 873).

[43] See Serene Jones 1995: 112ff, 148, 195ff.

[44] This rule works reflexively in that it also guides our reading of scripture: see Calvin 1960: pp. 6–8.

[45] Hilary of Poitiers emphasizes God's ineffability more than does Calvin but argues for a similar position: see 1954: 2.1–5.

[46] See Jenson 1982.

express the truth of the word who became fully human and redeemed the whole human condition.

Towards a 'dialectical fideism'

In the small amount of space available I can only sketch out the relationship between theology and philosophy presupposed by my argument for a Christocentric realism. I call the approach 'dialectical fideism' and shall use it as an explicit methodological principle at several points later on.

A key point in orientating our view of the relationship between philosophy and theology is that of the relationship between the universal and the particular. As Wittgenstein saw, there is a danger that philosophy will assume a mistaken universality and dominate and then transform those particular fields of enquiry which fall within its purview. (For example, he scorned Fr O'Hara, who, he thought, made religious belief 'a matter of science' (1966: 56f).) Theology can attempt to do the same thing when, influenced by this philosophical model, it sees itself as a meta-explanatory framework – as 'just a superscientific theory' (as Swinburne regards it (1993: 186)). But neither philosophy nor theology should be regarded as a universal method rendering the particular fully perspicuous. The reason for this is not just that the Enlightenment ideal of pure, abstract reason as exemplified by mathematical sciences flattens out the diversity of human discourses. It is rather that God has identified human beings in their uniquenesses with the crucified, risen, and ascended Christ, and that all the diverse particularities of human life finally find their intelligibility only in the light of God's proleptically consummated work in this particular person. Though they are incomplete apart from him, particularities of human life are not annihilated in their particularity by being brought within Christ's universal lordship: each aspect of creation has its own particular *telos*, and its fulfilment is only achieved by being brought into relation to Christ. God has given human beings a priestly responsibility towards all creation which, under God, is to further its restoration.[47] Philosophy, just as much as anything else, falls within the ambit of those called to exercise this responsibility.

Created reality has autonomy relative to God's grant and permission, but when humans grasp at an absolute autonomy they grasp at equality with God and so witness to creation's being fallen and disordered. In Adam and Eve humanity succumbed to the illusions of an absolute autonomy and sin was brought into the world. Theology and philosophy can be done

---

[47] On this, see T. F. Torrance 1981: 128–42.

under the same illusion. Both types of philosophy we examined above illustrate this: foundationalism achieves an empty universality at the cost of suppressing and flattening out features of life which do not readily fit it, notably religion; the Wittgensteinian approach respects the diversity of human life but at the cost of losing the possibility of commensurating this diversity. In contrast to philosophy, the task of theology is to think and bear witness to the unity-in-diversity of particularities under the universal lordship of Jesus Christ.

Note that theology itself is only a witness and that it is engaged in by fallen human beings. Where Christianity and its theology forget either of these they risk a hubristic autonomy; however, so far as their arms are wide open, they show the breadth of the embrace of God's love in reconciling the world to himself. The church is not co-extensive with the Kingdom; it too is fallen, under judgement, and in need of grace. Moreover, God's work is neither restricted by nor confined to the life of the church: the whole creation is the object of his redeeming love – even if this is visible only to the eye of faith and in Christological perspective. So the church cannot ignore what is happening beyond its walls, for God is at work there too, witnessing to himself. Sometimes this witness reproaches the church and its theology; at others it confirms and builds them up. Therefore, whilst Christian theology witnesses to the universal particularity of the ascended Christ attested in scripture, it also listens for God's word of judgement and grace in the 'secular' realm.[48] By these means the church remains faithful to its Lord and bears effective witness to God's work of reconciliation in Christ.[49]

Three elucidations of my position follow. First, my understanding of the relationship between theology and philosophy might broadly be described as *fideistic*. That is, my claim is that knowledge of God is given by him in the gift of faith; neither is it a product of a priori reasoning nor is it deduced from what is evident to the senses. Faith does have an empirical component, but it is the history of God's involvement with his people, consummated in Jesus Christ. Peter's confession of Jesus' Messiahship and divine commission is central here: the knowledge of God given through Christ is a matter of God's own revealing rather than natural human ability.[50] The *fons et origo* of theology is God in his self-revealing and to say this is, in philosophical terms, fideism, for here Christian belief is based not on reason but on revelation. However, a significant caveat needs to be entered at this point, for contrary

---

[48] This has been helpfully articulated by Rowan Williams (2000: 29–43, especially 31, 39).
[49] For good discussions of these themes, see Berkhof 1989: 303ff and Hunsinger 1991: 234–80.
[50] Cf. Matt. 16:16.

to certain construals of fideism, this version is not irrational in the sense that it wilfully and gratuitously believes what is absurd and/or repudiates the use of reason. This fideism is of a second-order, reason-giving, rather than reason-less variety: theology exercises reason as it does because it believes that in virtue of God's action in Christ, the knowledge of God given in faith is a supervening reason in favour of subordinating and disciplining the use of reason according to God's rationality in his revelation.[51]

Second, this reason-giving fideism is *dialectical*: it does not isolate itself from, but engages in and converses with the life and thought of its surrounding culture. The work of God in judgement and grace is known in and by the church, but God's work and self-witness are not restricted to this community. The church needs to be open to the wider world if it is to recognize God's contemporary work and to learn to be a more effective witness to him. The church knows God principally through scripture's testimony and the work of the Holy Spirit, but it needs also to learn from the world's critique of the church to hear God's word of judgement on its failings so that by God's grace it can be a more effective herald of that grace.[52] The church should never so retreat from the world as to allow itself to be regarded as 'fiddling around in "Bible land" as the world burns' as Tilley accuses fideists of doing (1989: 95). Theology is concerned for the world precisely because it is the object of God's love and the forum in which it is called to bear witness to him. Dialectical fideism is confident in the God who judged, graced and gave new life to the world in Jesus Christ. It is fideistic because it is a 'mode of thought in which knowledge is based upon a fundamental act of faith'[53] – that act of faith towards humanity in which God gave himself to be known in the gift of faith; it is dialectical because, while the church awaits the return of Christ, there is a reciprocity and interdependence between church and world as *loci* of God's work in judgement and grace.

The Church which does not ask itself whether it is not threatened by apostasy, and therefore in need of renewal, should beware lest it become a sleeping and a sick Church, even sick unto death. But where the Church understands the question it will listen with constant attention to the warnings which come to it, explicitly, or possibly only indirectly through a great silence. It may be that the Lord has bidden those outside the Church to say something important to the Church. The Church

---

[51] On the distinction between first- and second-order fideism, see Helm 1994: 189–216, especially 192ff; on fideism in general see Stephen Evans's sympathetic treatment (1998). See also Alston 1993 and Bruce Marshall 2000: 141–7.

[52] For a fine example of what I have in mind, see Westphal 1993a.

[53] So *Shorter Oxford English Dictionary*.

therefore has every reason not to ignore the questions and warnings of the outside world ... The Church must enter into the questions and movements of the age, but in order, by doing so, to understand better what the true Church is. (Barth 1954: 228–9)

Hence, third, church theology cannot pretend to be an autonomous language-game isolated from and conceptually incommensurable with the world. Kai Nielsen famously criticized 'Wittgensteinian fideism' for denying that the concept of God is graspable by someone who does not have faith and for making religious language-games distinct and autonomous from all others.[54] On the view proposed, such an option is not available to theology: the church served by theology is inescapably involved in the world because God witnesses to himself in his involvement with it. For the church to try to operate with autonomous language-games would be a Unilateral Declaration of Independence from the world and from the one in whom all humanity live, move, and have their being. To do so would be to deny that it is part of the meaning of the miracle of Pentecost that 'there is no language in which the mighty works of God may not be proclaimed' (Watson 1994: 9).

A dialectical fideism cannot refuse 'to participate in the human conversation': Christians should not 'isolate their own views from any serious questioning by those who don't share their commitments', nor should they 'deny a voice to those who disagree with them', as Tilley suggests fideists do (1989: 87, 88, 89). Any of these would involve closing one ear to God's witness to himself. However, while theology learns from being questioned by others and takes up some of their language and concepts, it should not seek to make itself coherent with the views of the 'epistemically hostile' by adopting a mediating natural theology.[55] Theology loses touch with its *esse* when it attempts to make itself coherent with a view of life which fundamentally rejects that which gives it its rationality or when it allows itself to be syncretistically absorbed in a scheme of 'transreligiosity' (James Barr's term, 1993). Church theology mediates between God and the world when it faithfully performs its dialectical role of bearing witness to the anterior mediating work of Christ.[56]

Likewise, theology should not assume a correlating stance between 'the Christian message' and the world, as Tillich famously suggested and to whose work my own approach might superficially appear to be indebted.

---

[54] See Nielsen 1982 and Phillips's reply 1993a: 56–78; cf. Bell 1995; Kerr 1986: 28–31.
[55] As John Greco suggests it should (1993: 171, 186–92). Graham White (1984: 54–70) proposes a mediating narrative theology in his critique of Barth's theological realism.
[56] On the inadequacy of 'mediating' theologies, see Michalson 1999: 128–38.

Neither theology nor the Christian message is primarily concerned to provide 'answers to the questions implied in human existence' (1953: 70): to conceive them in such terms is to sell dogmatics short to an abstract philosophical apologetics. Worldly forms might structure the content of theology, but to reduce its content to a human need (i.e. answers to questions) – as Tillich appears to do – is to restrict the cosmic significance of the Christ-event to what is capable of human telling. God is not really the sovereign and gracious Lord if the content of his gift can be encompassed by but never extends beyond all that we can think or grasp. Tillich's method of correlation correlates with neither the grace of God nor the sinfulness of humanity. On the other hand, a dialectical fideism might. As Paul Holmer puts it, 'theology is always polemically poised; and it, too, like God, has to wound before it heals' (1988: 17). In our quest for a Christian realism it is time to attempt a bit of healing, so in the next chapter we look at the realism problematic in the context of the source of our healing – the reconciling work of God on the cross of Christ.

CHAPTER 6

Representation, reconciliation, and the problem of meaning

Introducing this work, I said that it has the form of a transcendental argument. Such arguments typically aim to show that given that *p* is accepted, certain other conditions must obtain. In the present case this comes out as follows: granted the view that the triune God is the *ens realissimum*, we need to propose accounts of epistemology, ontology, and language that are coherent with it. By contrast, although it is not usually defended by transcendental arguments, theological realism tries to work up to God from semantic and epistemological problematics, but, as we have seen, this leads to serious problems. Paradoxically, theological realism is insufficiently theological. An alternative account of the realism of Christian faith therefore needs to be more theological and integrated with a different approach to epistemology, ontology, and semantics. Because of the current concern with semantic issues this will be the main focus of my positive account, and developing it will take up the remainder of the book. In the next chapter we look at some ontological and epistemological issues so as to locate realism's conceptual place in Christian faith, then in the final two chapters I draw the threads together by describing how we can be said to speak the reality of God. In this chapter, some of the ground for this approach is laid by giving theological shape to the realism problematic, for, as we shall see, the issue is not principally about our gaining cognitive access to God or how we can succeed in representing him linguistically; rather, it concerns our moral and ontological standing as creatures before our creator. This will take us into an examination of the reconciliation God has brought about with humanity and then to a discussion of the problem of meaning. To get the issues in proper perspective, we begin with idolatry and the crisis of representation.

IDOLATRY AND THE CRISIS OF REPRESENTATION

The question of realism can be understood as concerning representation, and the problem about realism in contemporary Christianity is inseparable from, though only partly accounted for by, what has been called 'the crisis of representation' pervading our culture.[1] For example, contemporary philosophical discussion of realism in the analytic tradition is strongly influenced by empiricist conceptions with their emphasis on designative, representational uses of language.[2] Consequently, making the case for scientific realism involves rebutting the legacy of Lockian empiricism in its contemporary guise as instrumentalism and showing that we can refer to or represent what lies beyond appearances.[3] Richard Boyd exemplifies these influences when he writes that 'the accommodation of linguistic categories to the causal structure of the world is essential to the very possibility of the epistemic success characteristic of reference' (1979: 397).

Theological realism is similarly concerned with accommodating language to God where God is conceived as the cause of experiences the cognitivity of which is expressed through referential success. Language which does refer is said to 'depict' reality. When Soskice argues that 'we must claim to *point to God via some effect*' (1985: 139, my italics), she implies that warrant for the realist case about an unobservable God is provided by observable effects, but, as we saw,[4] this can lead theological realists to construe the question of representing God along empiricist lines. This was not their intention, but it is arguable that their mistake arises from being misled by the designative view of language – that is, by a desire to be able to point to God so as to secure the referentiality of religious language. It is this concern with *our* attaining linguistic access to unobservable reality that leads to the 'crisis of representation' – or, in theological realists' terms, the question of 'reality depiction' – in theology.

Some light is cast on the nature of the problem by Jacques Derrida. Writing on the relationship between sign and thing signified in Rousseau, Derrida suggests that

Representation mingles with what it represents, to the point where one speaks as one writes, *one thinks as if the represented were nothing more than the shadow or reflection of the representer* ... In this play of representation, the point of origin becomes ungraspable. (1976: 36, my italics)

---

[1] Jean-Luc Marion (1991) offers a very good analysis from a post-Structuralist, phenomenological perspective. In analytic philosophy, the view has been widely canvassed that, as Putnam puts it, we need 'to distinguish carefully between the activity of "representation" (as something in which we engage) and the idea of a representation as an *interface* between ourselves and what we think about' (1994: 505).

[2] Against this influence, see Charles Taylor's important contrast between 'designative' and 'expressive' views of language (1985: 215–92; cf. Kerr 1989: 27–31).

[3] See Boyd 1979: 364–72.   [4] See pp. 52–4 above.

The modern form of the question of representation was opened by Locke's and Hume's empiricist questioning of the nature of reality and of the way language related to it. Kant attempted to resolve the question but with famously disastrous consequences for the possibility of knowledge of God.[5] In Derrida we see the process taken a step further: the problem concerns not just the knowability of reality, or the relation between language and reality; rather, if the idea of there being a gap between sign and thing signified is unintelligible, then so is the conception of our representing the point of origin in reality of our supposed representations of it. The question of how language 'hooks onto' reality has vanished, and with it the idea of there being anything for it to hook onto. If representation is not possible, then realism is a pseudo-problem. But if it is true that Christ is the *eikon* of God,[6] then he stands in some kind of representative relationship to God, and Derrida's is a theologically unacceptable conclusion.[7]

Derrida can, however, help us to clear away some unhelpful aspects of the way theological realism deals with the problem of representation. Soskice defines the realist problematic as that of 'reality depiction' and believes that for Christian usage of models to be fully cognitive 'a critical realist theologian must take' a position such that he 'can reasonably take his talk of God, bound as it is within the wheel of images, as being reality depicting, while at the same time acknowledging its inadequacy as description' (1985: 141). At a key point in her argument she makes explicit her dependency on Aquinas's view that humans are causally related to God.[8] From this we can infer that her thought contains an implicit appeal to an analogy of being. Now, there need be nothing intrinsically wrong with such an approach so long as it is orientated by Christology. However, to see the dangers presented to theological realism by an analogy of being lacking such an orientation,[9] note the words of Aronson et al., who, writing of building models of unobservable reality in science, stress that the 'role of [a] common ontology ... is essential to this cognitive activity' (1995: 64, cf. 62).[10] In science, unobservable reality is taken to be of the same ontological kind as observable, and hence scientists are able to cause observations from which they build models of that which is not observable. Soskice believes that because theologians have cognitive access to God on the basis of models and metaphors drawn

---

[5] As he wrote, 'I have found ... it necessary to deny knowledge, in order to make room for faith' (1933: B xxx; cf. A698/B726).
[6] Col. 1:15; cf. 2 Cor. 4:4; Phil. 2:6.   [7] See chapter 8, pp. 209–13 below.   [8] 1985: 139–40.
[9] Discussions of Christology are noticeably absent from the work of theological realists.
[10] Cf. Newton-Smith 1989: 185.

from human experience, they are able to depict God's unobservable reality. Of course, as Aquinas argued, it does not follow from our sharing some ontological characteristics (such as 'being') with God that God is of the same ontological kind as we are.[11] However, if we claim to have cognition of God on the basis of our experience of being causally related to him and then propose to use arguments from model building in the philosophy of science to explicate the referentiality of Christian language, then, if Aronson et al. are right, the suspicion arises that a common ontology is in play. To put it more bluntly, theological realism's use of the concept of a causal relation between God and humanity suggests appeal to an analogy of being according to which God is regarded as a member of the same ontological kind as his creation. This suspicion is compounded when we recall that for Soskice, revelation consists in the church's 'accretion of images' (1985: 153) born of religious experiences and drawn from the created order, rather than in God's gaining access to us and thereby giving us a relational knowledge of himself which we could not otherwise have. If Soskice's view does depend on a common ontology and she understands revelation primarily in terms of human experience, then it is hard to see how she can avoid confusing representer and represented in her account of religious language, and creator and created in her theology.

Using Derrida's terminology, we might suggest that in their pursuit of a theory of reference based on epistemic access, theological realists mingle their representations with what they were intended to represent to such an extent that they have become inseparable, and because of this, unrepresentative. Theological realists depict the represented in a way which makes it very hard to take it as anything 'more than the shadow or reflection of the representer'. Although this is undoubtedly alien to their intentions, it is hard to avoid wondering whether theological realists' view of revelation and their use of analogies with scientific realism lead them inadvertently to an argument for making God in our likeness – that is, to an idolatrous misrepresentation of the divine. This is remote methodologically and in spiritual tenor from the crass and wilful anthropocentricity of Kaufman's understanding of idolatry.[12] Nevertheless, our concern is reinforced when we recall theological realism's lack of clarity about the identity of the God whose reality it seeks to depict and its claim not to be describing God, but only denominating the source of experiences. Theological realism's account of Christian models and metaphors is very close to Edward Curtis's

---

[11] 1964: 1a.13, 3, resp.   [12] See Kaufman 1993: 79–80.

account of images of ancient Egyptian Gods: these 'were not intended to *describe* the appearance of the god. Rather, they *depict* various ways in which the deity was thought to manifest himself or herself' (1992: 377, my italics).

These mistakes might have been avoided had God's status as the *ens realissimum* been held firmly in view, for then the argument for realism would have been circumscribed by the need to avoid confusing representer and represented. That said, the risks here are sufficient to deter anyone. In the Decalogue God has forbidden making images of him, so the question naturally arises whether it is possible or right to offer *any* representation of God. This is the central problem any Christian would-be realist faces. 'Yet', says Augustine, 'woe to them that speak not of Thee at all, since they who say most are but dumb' (1978: 1.iv). It was this dilemma that Barth addressed when he spoke to fellow ministers at Elgersburg in 1922, still devastated by the First World War and beginning to feel the first draughts of the twentieth-century crisis of representation:

As ministers we ought to speak of God. We are human, however, and so cannot speak of God. We ought therefore to recognize both our obligation and our inability and by that very recognition give God the glory. This is our perplexity.

Then, with a flourish of reassurance, he adds, 'The rest of our task fades into insignificance in comparison' (1935: 186). This *theological* crisis of representation touches all language. 'There is not ... a pure conceptual language which leaves the inadequate language of images behind ... Even the language of ecclesiastical dogma and the Bible is not immune from this crisis.' There is nothing that does not 'stand under the crisis of the hiddenness of God' (Barth 1957: 195). In other words, the crisis of theological representation is a crisis about revelation and the sinfulness of humanity.

REPRESENTATION AND REVELATION

Christ the representative

Given their Christian commitments, it is surprising that theological realists do not pay more attention to the theological character of the realism problematic. This is especially the case when, in the context of the question of 'reality depiction', we recall that Gen. 1:26–7 tells of God's making humanity in his 'image' and 'likeness'. The exact meaning of this language is unclear, but its general meaning is that 'The Creator created a creature that corresponds to him, to whom he can speak, and who can hear him' (Westermann 1974: 56). Without either entirely suppressing the echoes of Barth or inferring too much philosophically from the use of 'corresponds', we can say that the *imago* speaks of God's grace in creation whereby humanity is enabled both to receive God's self-representation and faithfully to represent God.

That God has already taken the initiative by creating humanity in his image and granted us to show his reality through our humanity suggests a major recasting of theological realism's preoccupation with how we can depict God's reality linguistically. In writing as he did, the author(s) of Genesis 1 shows an astonishing daring, for, in a culture that banned all images of the divine, to teach that men and women are created in the image of God is to attribute to them 'the power of divine disclosure which, in pagan culture, was attached to the image of the god' (Sherry 1989: 35). This power is God's gift, but by grasping at equality with God humanity has so marred that image that the power of disclosure has been distorted to the point of being lost. Instead of finding our end and fulfilment in God, we seek it in autonomy, for, as John Zizioulas says, the conditions for an 'ontology of personhood exist only in God', but fallen '[m]an wishes to be God' (1991: 42). It is the condition of fallen humanity to be discontent with being the representer and to want to be the represented. With the loss of our ability to show God's reality comes a general dislocation between human cognitive and linguistic powers and reality. This is expressed in epistemic alienation. To seek 'epistemic access' to God for purposes of depicting his reality is, we can now recognize, a problematic whose principal origins do not lie in the Enlightenment, in philosophical foundationalism, the crisis of representation, or empiricist views of language. They lie at the heart of what it is to be a fallen human: in the desire to be like God and to usurp his divinity instead of to re-present it in a properly creaturely way.

Were the Fall the end of the story our plight would be great, but the New Testament tells of its reversal and of the redemption of the lost image by Jesus Christ, the 'image of God' (2 Cor. 4:4). Just as Adam represents fallen humanity, so, according to Paul, Jesus Christ is 'the last Adam' (1 Cor. 15:45) who died for the old humanity, represents the new, and by his Spirit gives human beings the 'new birth' through which they 'are being transformed into the same image' (sc. of Christ) (2 Cor. 3:18). Through the grace of God and in our (redeemed) creaturely nature we are able to represent God the creator.

Christ the revealer

Karl Barth summarizes these Christological points when he writes that

Jesus Christ, as [the] Mediator and Reconciler between God and man, is also the *Revealer* of them both. We do not need to engage in a free-ranging investigation to seek out and construct who and what God truly is, and who and what man truly is, but only to read the truth about both where it resides, namely, in the fullness of their togetherness, their covenant which proclaims itself in Jesus Christ. (1961a: 44)

Jesus Christ is the word of God made flesh (John 1), whom to have seen is to have 'seen the Father' (John 14:9). But it is not only in virtue of his divinity that Jesus is the revealer; he is so also in virtue of his humanity. For it is the one, undivided person in, through, and by whom God is revealed. To put this in terms of our current enquiry, we could say that in and through the particular human being Jesus of Nazareth, God depicts his own reality. In the person and work of Christ, creator and creature are in the closest possible 'correspondence'. Thus, it is not only *God's* reality that is depicted in Christ; it is also real, 'proper', iconic *humanity*. Acute ontological problems are raised by these assertions, but they are not made speculatively or arbitrarily;[13] rather, we are impelled to make them as we reflect upon the realities attested in the Gospels – the realities of Jesus' living, ministering, dying, and rising. This means that to conceptualize revelation in exclusively propositional terms is misleading: it puts a strait-jacket on both its mode and its manner, for Jesus' deeds as well as his words enact and reveal God and his Kingdom. The advent of God and his 'proper man' within creation heals, reorders, transfigures, and redeems it from death and futility. Hence Paul exults that at last, 'the old has passed away and the new has come' (2 Cor. 5:17). God's work in Christ reveals the true nature of things, even if, from the standpoint of those who live between the times, it is only manifest proleptically.

IDOLATRY, REPRESENTATION, AND RECONCILIATION

In chapter 4 we considered Phillips's argument with Holmer over the demise of the language of faith and I argued that in a fundamental sense the language will not vanish because God's unbreakable purposes have been climactically established in the crucifixion and resurrection of Jesus. Phillips considers the possibility of all people turning their backs on God, and in

---

[13] See MacKinnon 1972; 1979: 70–89; and 1987: 145–88.

the passion drama its reality is demonstrated by those who stand for all Adam's children. Any discussion of the meaning of God's independent reality must take account of these events.

The crucifixion not only illustrates the dangers of religious practices becoming autonomous but also points up the way in which fallen humanity wishes to play the role of God. Reading the Gospel accounts of Jesus' death with theological hindsight we can see how we arrogate to ourselves God's right to judge who represents him. The charge of blasphemy against Jesus encapsulates our desire to judge, for, as N. T. Wright puts it in his retelling of the trial narrative,

The prisoner, in agreeing to the charge of being a would-be Messiah, 'prophesied' his own vindication in such a way that a plausible charge of 'blasphemy' could be added to the list. He had now not only spoken false prophecy against the Temple, [and] confessed to messianic aspirations ... He had done these two things in such a way as to prophesy that he, as Messiah, would sit on the throne beside the god of Israel. (1996: 550–1 *sic*; cf. 643–4)

Doing these things was not just blasphemous, but tantamount to setting oneself up as an idol, for in Jewish thought whoever sits beside God is worthy of the same worship.[14] Indeed, Bauckham argues that Matthew's 'consistent use of the word *proskynein* and his emphasis on the point show that he intends a kind of reverence which, paid to any other human being, he would have regarded as idolatrous' (1992: 813). Thus the question implied by and never far from the surface of the narrative of Jesus' trial and death was whether he was an idolater or God's faithful representative.

In the minds of his antagonists, the possibility that Jesus might have spoken and acted truly was too threatening. Religious (and political) practices must not be subverted; the one who threatened them had to be exterminated. So the crucifixion illustrates the nadir of the tendency throughout Israel's history for religious practices to be pursued as though they were self-sustaining and autonomous. Through the prophets, God had sought to reform practices by reminding his people that they were sustainable in their original intent only insofar as they acknowledged his lordship over them. At Jesus' trial and crucifixion the double-faceted vocation of Israel to represent God to humanity and humanity before God is transferred onto Jesus, the unique representative of God and faithful remnant of Israel. Humanity's desire for God-like autonomy engages all the actors on this stage.

The events by which God reconciled humanity to himself are the *locus* of the deepest crisis of representation. It is not just that there is a dislocation

---

[14] See N. T. Wright 1996: 624–9.

between humanity and the world which leads to the crisis of (linguistic) representation highlighted by deconstruction. Through the passion the crisis of representation is seen to be precipitated by humanity's alienation from God. The deepest crisis of representation concerns the *moral* hiddenness of God. Both crises are in play as we approach the cross. The focus narrows and gathers on the increasingly solitary figure of Jesus. First, the garden: 'Did God really say …?' Was Jesus of all people the most deluded? Was the sense of divine vocation – of divine sonship[15] – he had received at his baptism and heard confirmed on the Mount of Transfiguration merely the yowling of empty voices in his own head? Were his deeds and words faithful to reality, or were they a trickster's deception? Perhaps it really had been by Beelzebub's power that he had worked; perhaps *he* was the idolater and *his* the unforgivable sin. Then on the cross: 'My God, my God, why have you forsaken me?' (Matt. 27:46). Lost now the intimacy of Jesus' 'Abba'. Was the intimate, material proximity of sign and thing signified expressed by that address cancelled out by the apparently final *différance* of the derelict cry? Was the reality depicted by that man nothing but the final absence of presence? Was the death of Jesus the death of God, and with it, the death of meaning?

The Christian Gospel is of Christ's resurrection from the dead, but his being raised is not merely the reversal of the cross, a restoration of the *status quo ante*: it is also the vindication of Christ,[16] of his words *qua* human being and of his being *qua* divine word. Jesus' perceptions of the Father and his deeds are declared veridical; his life and ministry are declared by this act of God to have been faithful to him – representative. So here, in the climactic events of Jesus' life, God's independent reality is vindicated too. It is demonstrated by his direct, immanent, interruptive engagement with human practices: *independent* because humans can neither get the conceptual measure of him[17] nor annihilate him; *real* because Jesus is risen with all the reality of the creator God, the *ens realissimum*.

In the death of Jesus the one true *imago* was crucified, but precisely as the obedient one, God's last Adam cannot be held by death: in raising Christ, God has undone the consequences of the Fall, redeemed humanity, and restored its representative capacity. As the early Christian community discovered, Jesus' death and resurrection are potentially universal in scope; his

---

[15] On God's Son as God's *representative*, see Keck 2000: 96–103, especially 99.

[16] For discussion, see Keck 2000: 110.

[17] The question of Jesus' identity is a recurrent theme in John's Gospel. See, e.g., 8:21–30, where Jesus responds to the question 'Who are you?' by indicating that his identity will be revealed 'When you have lifted up the son of Man' (verse 28), and this despite his having told it *ten archen*.

humanity is vicarious. So by incorporation into him, the reality depiction effected by Jesus can also be made by those who, empowered by the Holy Spirit, share his risen life. Yet the old Adam of self-idolatry wars within us. God's self-representation is veiled, hidden and concealed in ambiguity. God continues to be present to his creation in the freedom of his word and Spirit, though not in any way that we can master. Always the pattern seems to be that he grants us to represent him only where the will to autonomy is being set free. As the Australian poet James McAuley put it: 'We know, where Christ has set his hand/Only the real remains' (1981: 294). It is not given to us to represent the independent reality of the Risen One other than by taking up our cross, following him, yielding our humanity – our representative, iconic capacities – to his healing gift and acknowledging that we are 'earthen vessels' (2 Cor. 4:7).

Before we move on, another side to this discussion needs to be borne in mind because the argument so far indicates that our moral standing before God – our being reconciled creatures – has a crucial role in our capacity to represent him by the words and deeds which constitute our humanity. George Lindbeck is notorious for denying that the meaning and truth of first-order propositions is independent of 'the subjective dispositions of those who utter them', and that therefore, in his famous example, 'The crusader's battle cry *"Christus est Dominus"* ... is false when used to authorize cleaving the skull of the infidel (even though the same words in other contexts may be a true utterance)' (1984: 66, 64). This sentence has been widely attacked as a clear example of Lindbeck's supposed non-realism.[18] Realists typically claim of realism that if p is true, it is so because p states how things are independently of the presence or absence of any subjective condition in the utterer of p. Therefore it is held that in the theological case, what is said about God is true or false independently of the moral standing of the utterer. Lindbeck seems to infringe this realist claim. Without doubt his argument leads him into deep water, but his argument deserves reconsideration.

Recall that Jesus saw the 'objective' truth of his assertions about God as dependent on the 'subjective' truth of his own relationship with God, and that it was precisely because of this that he was tried as a blasphemer.[19] Others could have said much the same as Jesus said about God but without total obedience to the will of the Father; it is this latter which made Jesus' representation in word and deed unique and true. It follows that the truth

---

[18] Against Lindbeck, see Wallace 1990: 105ff; for sympathetic interpretations, see Hunsinger 1991: 165–73 and Marshall 2000: 191–4.

[19] E.g., John 7:16f; 8:12–59.

of Jesus' statements about God was not independent of the subjective condition of his stating them. Hence, if Lindbeck's claim is applied to Jesus, it is correct. To speak truly of God is not just a matter of what is said; it is also a matter of the manner of life, the obedience or disobedience to the will of God, of the one who says it.

Furthermore, since it is only on the ground of Christ's reconciling work that humanity can speak truthfully of God, we can see that Lindbeck's denial implicates all of us; apart from God's work in Christ, no human being's assertion about God is in principle any different from the crusader's. There is no occasion for semantic self-congratulation or self-righteousness. The ontological disruption caused by sin is perhaps simply more egregious in the crusader's case than we can perceive in ourselves. In the perspective of the Fall, no human being's life is intrinsically anything less than a falling short and thereby also a failure to honour the one whose perfect speech in the person of Jesus Christ is the measure of the imperfection of our own. Nevertheless, in virtue of Jesus' obedience 'God has made him ... Lord' (Acts 2:36). It is because God raised Christ that it is true that he is Lord; no condition on our part could make this true. So, if in reconciling us to himself God has identified all humanity with Jesus and enabled us to speak of him, then that we are not condemned by our own mouths is sheer grace.[20] And this is why, only in God's mercy, the crusader can be said to have made a true utterance, even if as with the rest of us, his deeds gave the lie to his words.[21]

RECONCILIATION AND THE PROBLEM OF MEANING

A transcendental argument for meaning?

At the heart of the late modern crisis of representation lies the question of meaning, and one of the most eloquent contributors to discussions about this has been George Steiner.[22] He earned the nickname 'Pfarrer George' for the theological, even hieratic, tenor of *Real Presences* (1989). In this he argues passionately against deconstruction (and implicitly against the position advocated by religious non-realists) and claims that 'the wager on the meaning of meaning ... is a wager on transcendence' (4).[23] Steiner observes that for Derrida 'the origin of the axiom of meaning and of the

---

[20] Though cf. Matt. 7:21ff.
[21] Cf. the reflections on the use of the tongue in the letter of James. Paul's puzzling claims at 1 Cor. 12:3 should also be borne in mind; cf. Fee 1987: 581f.
[22] See also Taylor 1985: 222–7.   [23] See also 1989: 214–16.

God-concept is a shared one' but that deconstruction effects a 'break with the postulate of the sacred' which amounts to a 'break with any stable, potentially ascertainable meaning of meaning' (119, 132).[24] Similarly, he pronounces that the *'break of the covenant between word and the world ... constitutes one of the very few genuine revolutions of spirit in Western history and ... defines modernity itself'* (93). Positively, Steiner's essay 'proposes that any coherent understanding of what language is and how it performs, that any coherent account of the capacity of human speech to communicate meaning and feeling is, in the final analysis, underwritten by the assumption of God's presence' for 'the meaning of meaning is a transcendent postulate' (3, 216).[25]

The importance of Steiner's book for my argument lies in his attempts to account for our capacity to 'communicate meaning' (and to establish a kind of realism against the idealism of much post-Structuralism) apart from an understanding of the theological crisis of representation so far as this is defined by the moral hiddenness of God revealed in Christ. It is also of interest that his line of reasoning resembles that found in transcendental arguments.[26] Clearly, if his held up it would undermine my own Christocentric argument. Steiner's argument can be reconstructed on the following lines:

1 Linguistic meaning, artistic creativity, and communication are possible, as witnessed both by his own work and that of those he opposes.
2 A necessary condition of these possibilities is the wager on God's presence.
3 Thus, if God's presence is not wagered (1) is false.
4 But, denying (1) leads to absurdity, therefore (2).

The central factor here is Steiner's understanding of God's ontological status. Transcendental arguments sometimes require modifications to the conditions under which what is commonly accepted to be the case really is the case. The modification here is that Steiner's God is only a 'supposition', an 'assumption', an 'absence', wagered upon. (As we shall see later, the thrust of his argument is that God does not actually exist.) For Steiner, God's existence appears to amount to no more than that of a regulative ideal whose purpose is to keep the linguistic show on the road.[27]

---

[24] Derrida succinctly states his views (which would not comfort Steiner) on stability of meaning in his 1988: 150ff.

[25] Pessimism concerning the ability of linguistics and the philosophy of language to account for our linguistic successes can be found in a range of distinguished twentieth-century figures in, or associated with, the analytic philosophical tradition. These include Bertrand Russell (on Wittgenstein, in Wittgenstein 1961: xxi), Roy Harris (1996: 179), and Stephen Shiffer (1987: xv, 271).

[26] See Steiner 1989: 212–14.

[27] Cf. Cupitt's use of 'God' as a condition of 'religious seriousness'.

Now the question to be asked of Steiner's riposte to deconstruction is whether it offers anything that is any more secure from deconstruction's appetite than what is already grist to its mill. Steiner traces the origins of deconstruction to Mallarmé's 'repudiation of the covenant of reference' (96) and the 'deconstruction of the first person singular' (94) in Rimbaud's cerebral pun 'Je est un autre.' Steiner comments:

The provocation is deliberately, necessarily, anti-theological. As invariably in Rimbaud, the target is God ... Any consequent deconstruction of the individuation of the human speaker or *persona* is, in the context of Western consciousness, a denial of the theological possibility and of the *Logos* concept which is pivotal to that possibility. '*Je est un autre*' is an uncompromising negation of the supreme tautology, of the grammatical act of grammatical self-definition in God's 'I am who I am.' (99)

Steiner thinks that Rimbaud is fundamentally at fault for being anti-theological. Ironically, however, something similar is also true of Steiner's counter-proposal concerning language and creativity. Both he and Rimbaud (on Steiner's reading) enact a Promethean 'rivalry with the "jealous God"' (207).[28] Thus, on the one hand, Steiner's official view seems to be that it 'may be the case that nothing more is available to us than the absence of God' (1996: 39). Nevertheless, if God does have any existence more substantial than that of a postulate we must ask how the 'agonistic' counter-creativity he proposes can recover for the sake of creativity that 'necessary possibility of "real presence"' (1989: 3) which its rivalrous aim is in the end to uncreate. Creativity and meaning would then require the deconstruction of their own conditions of possibility. On the other hand, James Wood has argued that 'Nowhere does Steiner appear to believe in this final presence [of God]. His wager is not a wager on a final presence that might mean enough to guarantee meaning' (1999: 163).[29] If God exists only a postulate, we must ask what difference a postulated entity can make to the world of actual entities wherein the 'covenant between word and world' has, supposedly, been broken. If God does not exist as postulated, then any linguistic thing is just as possible as impossible. Derrida has merely exposed what was the case all along. The onto-theology he unmasks as the presence upholding the covenant between word and world is indeed a sham, and with its collapse goes Steiner's wager on his God's existence.[30] Whichever

---

[28] For the Promethean aspects of *Real Presences*, see 1989: 203f, 207.
[29] Peter Phillips (1998) offers a more positive, Thomistic reading of Steiner.
[30] That Steiner's God (real or not) is not the living God is made clear from his secular demythologization of the passion and resurrection of Christ (1989: 231–2).

way we interpret Steiner, the result is the same: he paves no royal road to the palace of meaning that would be adequate for a Christian account of realism.

Dialectical fideism and the problem of meaning

Steiner's response to deconstruction shows that something deeply para-doxical is going on in contemporary critical theory. If the more extreme readings of Derrida are correct, then literature, philosophy, and science are all threatened.[31] The meaning of meaning, the very possibility of meaning-ful discourse, the possibility of there being 'anything *in* what we say'[32] seem to have disappeared. As Terry Eagleton puts it, 'critical theory is out to liquidate meaning'.[33] Yet deconstruction's exponents attempt to persuade us of this in language that is not always wholly opaque. We can understand them. Deconstruction meaningfully asserts meaninglessness. Here is the paradox: meaninglessness expressed meaningfully. Kevin Hart summarizes the problem:

Even though deconstruction may launch its critique from the 'other' of meta-physics, the critique of metaphysics seems unable to free itself from a complicity with metaphysics. Deconstruction's problem, it seems, is a problem about vocab-ulary or, at any rate, about the relation between vocabulary and argument. For even though Derrida provides us with a persuasive argument against metaphysical totalisation, the stating of the argument requires a vocabulary which would seem to call into question the efficacy of the argument. (1989: 135)

How can this be, this paradox? Can it be accounted for theologically rather than metaphysically, and can we thereby both appreciate and go beyond deconstruction?

From the perspective of what I am calling a dialectical fideism, I be-lieve that we can. My contention is that apart from a clearly formu-lated acknowledgement of Christ – the vindicated word of God – in our thinking about it, language will always be threatened by the possibility of unmeaning which Steiner strives to rebut. As a human phenomenon, lan-guage is a created reality; the meanings we express by using it have no more autonomous self-subsistence than anything else. Just as those of our

---

[31] There are left- and right-wing readings of Derrida, but even if his argument is not as radical as the former reading proposes, that the reading is proposed and taken seriously is enough for my argument.
[32] Steiner 1989, from the sub-title.
[33] Inaugural Lecture in the University of Oxford, 27 November 1992.

deeds that strive for autonomy from God stand under annihilating judgement, so also do speech and thought that agonistically strive for autonomy and, thereby, exclude Christ from their reckoning, stand under the negating sign of the cross. In the same way that deeds testify to the disorderedness of creation, so too can our thoughts and words. Unreason and unmeaning are the threatening possibilities under which fallen humanity lives.[34]

As I shall argue a bit later, meaning in the sense of purposiveness, and hence meaning as connected to 'the meaning of life', is related to linguistic meaning. For example, the philosopher of language Stephen Shiffer writes with studied ambiguity of his 'no-theory theory of meaning' that even if it 'is not a defeatist program[,] I am less certain if it is not despairing' (1987: xx). D. Z. Phillips writes that 'the crisis religion faces ... is not lack of sufficient evidence, but a crisis of meaninglessness' (1985: 95). Similarly, Cupitt, revelling in bourgeois postmodern *jouissance*, seeks to persuade us that, 'There is a certain decency about ... meaninglessness and the pathos of transience. We are all of us nihilists nowadays – at least, when we are thinking clearly' (1990: 67). Alongside this, Ian Barbour's declaration that 'Meaninglessness is overcome when people view human existence in a wider context of meaning, beyond the life of the individual' (1990: 37) seems both untheological and complacently banal. If unmeaning and unreason are paradoxical signs of our intellectual fallenness,[35] nihilism is its symptom. Some of the importance of deconstruction for theology lies in its power to alert us to this.

Consider again Jesus' crucifixion. Here the meaning of his words and deeds is held over the abyss. In the cry of dereliction we hear the Godforsakenness of the incarnate word of God and witness the rupture of the covenant between word and world. The one to whom the gift of speech was archetypically given – and therefore by whom it was most faithfully and realistically used – now stands for all those other children of God in their (albeit often unwitting) tendency to blasphemy and idolatry. His speech had been the efficacious sign of God's Kingdom, ours the would-be undoing of it.

A dialectical fideism will try to hold together the fact that the Christ-event reveals the world to be the object of God's judgement along with the fact that it is simultaneously the object of his grace. Thus, from the point of view of judgement – and lest they become over-confident, Christians

---

[34] On postmodern interrogations of the claims of rationality, see Gasché 1994: 105–28.
[35] On the fallenness of rationality, see Westphal 1990.

should remember Peter's words of betrayal – none of the linguistic aspects of the crucifixion signify, save in the ironic and pathetic designation of the woe-begone man hanging there, 'poor, bare, forked', and dead. On the other hand, from a faith perspective graced by the *pneuma* poured forth from the cross, the crucifixion was the accomplishment of that for which God's word goes into the world and returns to him.[36] It was God's taking into himself the loss of meaning that faces a world that marginalizes and finally abandons him. It was God reconciling his children to himself in the body of his Son and restoring to them the gift of speech. The word of the cross does not end in absolute negation – as Cupitt would have us believe when he writes that 'The crucifixion is an awesomely nihilistic image of the absolute nothingness from which we sprang, over which we dance, and into which we return' (1997: 23).[37] God's 'no' in Christ's death is the occasion of an absolute affirmation: precisely because the one who died was obedient and faithful to his author, he was vindicated by God. In him, as we shall see more fully in subsequent chapters, the linguistic nexus between God and humanity and amongst human creatures is restored. Thus,

[I]t was the mark of love within Christ's Lordship that, so far from overthrowing the given order of things, he rescued it from the 'emptiness' into which it had fallen (Rom. 8:20–21). His redemptive love fulfilled the creative task of Adam, to call things by their proper names. (Oliver O'Donovan 1986: 26)[38]

With this in mind we can now make sense of and overcome the paradox we discovered in deconstruction. God's love in Christ shows that the created order – and with it, meaning – is itself sustained by God. We should not be surprised when we find ourselves understood, when we find meaningful communication to be a human possibility. That is the way it is with the graced world, the world renewed in the resurrection of Christ. Equally, however, we should not be surprised to find that we are threatened by apparent unmeaning in an apparently unintelligible world. That, *per impossibile*, is the way the world can appear to thought which does not take into consideration the actuality of its redemption in Christ – which is why there is

---

[36] Isa. 55:11.

[37] Contrast Barth's opinion that with respect to the word of God 'there is only one possibility, the possibility of obedience. Man's genuine freedom does not consist in the ability to evade this Word. If he does not submit to it he chooses the impossible possibility, he chooses *nihil*' (1954: 215). Compare also Derrida's claim that the risk of a failure of performative meaning is 'a necessary possibility' (1988: 15). See further the discussion in chapter 8, pp. 209ff below.

[38] By contrast, Derrida's project is 'the demonstration that Babel *precedes* Adam's naming day in Eden' (Kevin Hart 1989: 129).

truth, but not the whole truth, in Cupitt's celebration of meaninglessness and nihilism.[39] To quote O'Donovan again:

> The meaning of the world, the 'Logos', came down at Christmas; the man without Christmas is a man without meaning. The bestowal of meaning is part of God's saving work in history, for in nature man can discern no meaning. (Oliver O'Donovan 1978: 25)[40]

Deconstruction and the meaningfulness of Christian language

The pessimism pervading many secular attempts to account for the meaningfulness of language has not deterred those contemporary writers on Christian language who have argued that it is possible and/or necessary to mount a case for realism on the basis of a general, non-theological account of language. Christian Barrigar's claim is typical:

> The search for language by which to talk about God is one of the pre-eminent occupations of theology today. An important component of this search must be the attempt to understand how human language in general has meaning and reference, in order to understand more precisely how theological language can have meaning and reference. (1991: 299)

Barrigar therefore goes on to examine 'how linguistic reference is successfully made in language in general, and then ... appl[ies] the results to trinitarian language' (299). This argument and others like it amount to a kind of natural theology of language. We will by now reserve judgement about the success of such a project. This not because it is a natural theology, but because the possibility of establishing philosophically the meaningfulness and reference of language in general is questionable on inductive grounds (there is not even a single generally accepted approach amongst philosophers about how we might begin to develop such a theory) and because, *ex hypothesi*, even if it is possible, we shall have to wait until it has been established before we can find out how we refer to God. However, the argument needs to be considered because if it can be run, my claim for the necessity of a Christocentric argument will again be weakened.

---

[39] The same dialectic is found in Ecclesiastes (see, e.g., 3:11). James Barr comments that the Preacher 'has examined everything that is, as we would say, "in our world", but he cannot find signs of God in it, he cannot find theological meaning' (1993: 93). That, of course, is why, anticipating what we know as *différance*, the Preacher exclaims 'vanity of vanities! All is vanity' (1:2). One finds it also in Barth's account of the 'inherent contradiction', the 'impossible possibility' of sin (1960b: 351).

[40] O'Donovan is less dialectical here than in later work (see 1986: 13, 26, 156–9). It is not that humankind is without meaning, or that there is no meaning in nature. God is not absent. Rather, in our condition as fallen creatures, unless Christ is included in our conceptualization of meaning, accounting for it can lead to nihilism.

In some writers there is a clear appeal to natural theology in their arguments for the meaningfulness of Christian language;[41] others assume that human language in general is more readily intelligible than Christian and that insights from the former need to be used to clarify and defend the latter.[42] We saw the kind of difficulties this second approach can lead to in our examinations of theological realism. We note now that from the perspective of deconstruction, the language in which either kind of argument is couched will always be subject to 'erasure', for, as Kevin Hart puts it, 'crossing *over* from the phenomenal to the transcendental involves a provisional crossing *out* of a word's metaphysical commitment' (1989: 136). Attempts to argue for the meaningfulness of Christian language before considering its redemption – its being brought back from the abyss of unmeaning – are bound to be unsatisfactory because such arguments will negate the metaphysical commitments which are required if they are to be made successfully. Against such views, I have suggested that it is only the resurrection and glorification of the incarnate word that enables us to see how – in virtue of God's goodness in creation – *any* language is sustained above the abyss of unmeaning. This is especially the case when it comes to metaphysical language such as that used in natural theology,[43] but we must also include Christian language, for – quite apart from deconstructive arguments – as Paul admits, if Christ is not raised from the dead then preaching and faith are 'vain' (1 Cor. 15:14).

Such is the slender thread on which a Christian view of language hangs. Steiner admits that

On its own terms and planes of argument, terms by no means trivial if only in respect of their bracing acceptance of ephemerality and self-dissolution, the challenge of deconstruction does seem to me irrefutable. (1989: 132)

I have already argued that Steiner's own 'terms and planes of argument' are incapable of meeting deconstruction's challenge. Now if, on the basis of God's judgement against sinful humanity, we are willing to entertain Steiner's conclusions against deconstruction but, on the basis of God's grace in Christ, reject his positive proposal, it follows that arguments for the meaningfulness of Christian language mounted *remoto Christo* will be unable to function as they are intended. The terms in which they are set will always be liable to fall short of allowing the relationship between sign and signified that would be required if they were to be able to offer to us

---

[41] See, for example, Crombie 1971; Ernst 1979: 57–75; Graham White 1984; Markham 1998.
[42] The most notable example remains Soskice 1985.
[43] For a survey of the difficulties here, see Ingraffia 1995.

the reality to which they are intended to lead. This is the case simply in virtue of their being another part of fallen, human, and therefore, *ex hypothesi*, unredeemed discourse; it is quite independent of any question of the arguments' logical validity and soundness.

Notice also that since canons of logic are part of deconstructible human discourse they are as liable to nihilistic corrosion as the terms of the arguments which observe those canons.[44] Terry Eagleton states that 'The tactic of deconstructive criticism ... is to show how texts come to embarrass their own ruling systems of logic' (1983: 133), and Hart concurs:

Différance is not merely the name of a particular concept but also the condition of possibility for conceptuality as such. Thus *the scope of deconstruction is unlimited*: it operates in all texts – philosophical, theological, literary or whatever – as well as in all the various positions in any given dispute. (1989: 138, my italics)[45]

It therefore does not matter what kind of reasoning natural theology uses: when subjected to deconstruction its semantics will fail and be of little value in giving an account of Christian language. Unless the restoration of creation and human language about it in Christ are taken into the reckoning, there is little of positive theological value to be gained from natural theology. Deconstruction therefore serves to confirm an aspect of Paul's diagnosis of the human condition: human beings 'did not honour... God or give thanks to him, but their arguments became futile and their uncomprehending minds were darkened' (Rom. 1:21, New Jerusalem Bible). Furthermore, from a Christocentric perspective, arguments from natural theology for the meaningfulness of Christian language are otiose: what we had searched for apart from Christ, but had been unable to find, is given to us in the word made flesh, in the Signified made sign.

THE LANGUAGE OF SOTERIOLOGY AS A TEST CASE

The Rahnerian alternative

My argument proposes a view of the theology of language diametrically opposed to the one underlying Karl Rahner's account of the *Foundations of Christian Faith* (1978).[46] Because this difference is methodological his

---

[44] See Westphal 1990. [45] See also Derrida's critique of onto-theology, for example, 1992: 79.

[46] Paul Ricoeur's account of language is another alternative to my own and represents a similar challenge to it. However, Rahner's is closely interwoven with his soteriology, which is why it is of particular interest at this stage in my argument. (Vanhoozer's criticism of Ricoeur is pertinent, however: 'By attributing to the poetic word the sacramental function of manifesting transcendence, Ricoeur erases the ... distinction between nature and grace' (1990: 180).)

argument presents a good example of an alternative to, and therefore a test-case against, my own. In his work on soteriology and Christology, Rahner is concerned to show how Jesus can be 'ultimately meaningful' and so 'significant for salvation' (*heilsbedeutsam*). As Bruce Marshall explains, Rahner 'supposes that in order to believe in Jesus Christ as the unique redeemer it is necessary to show how the belief is possible and credible, and to do so by an appeal to general criteria of religious and moral meaningfulness' (1987: 15). Rahner argues that

man always and inescapably has ... experiences which cannot satisfy the claim to absoluteness or to absolute fulfilment and salvation in the immediate 'objects' which are in the foreground of the experience and through which the experiences are mediated, a claim nevertheless which man inevitably makes in view of these experiences ... The fact that the claim of this inescapable experience is not satisfied is also the point at which we experience what is meant by the word 'God'. (1978: 208–9)

Rahner believes that the relationship between God, the human capacity for self-transcendence, and theological language is a given and unproblematical point of departure in theology. Notice also that he appears to understand the meaning of 'God' on the basis of a perceived need for transcendence rather than from the standpoint of the transcendent God's taking up and redeeming human language in his work of reconciliation in Christ.

In Rahner's view, what he calls a 'transcendental Christology' is necessary for two inter-related reasons.[47] First, what in his technical vocabulary he calls an 'absolute Saviour' is a conceptual requirement of theological anthropology. According to his 'transcendental anthropology' human beings are always transcending themselves towards 'the mystery which we call God' (209). Such self-transcendence finds its goal in humanity's acceptance of God's self-communication. For these two 'moments' to be 'irreversible' and 'irrevocable' each requires an absolute saviour as its *telos* and climax.[48] Second, human beings need an absolute saviour in order to be saved. However, for Rahner, exposition of this is made difficult by the historical particularity of the saviour. Christology must overcome a contemporary version of Lessing's ugly ditch because the Christian message does not make sense to modern humanity.[49]

Now, the underlying question here concerns the relationship between the universal and the particular in Christian faith, and in his critique of Rahner

---

[47] Rahner's thought shares many of the characteristics of Kantian transcendental arguments in that he argues for God as a condition of the possibility of our experience of knowing, feeling, and willing. For commentary, see Vass 1985a: 23–9.

[48] See 193–5.   [49] See 138–9.

Marshall contrasts theological methods which approach the universality of redemption through close attention to the particularity of Christ with those which ground it in the mediating role of the 'logically general and implicitly universal' (Marshall 1987: 8). The latter strategy – which is Rahner's – faces two tasks:

One task is to show how the kinds of significance Christians ascribe to Jesus Christ can be universally meaningful and accessible on the strength of their coherence with logically general criteria, which indicate what kind of thing can count as 'ultimately meaningful' ... The complementary task is to explicate ... the basic conviction that Jesus Christ is the particular person to whom alone these various kinds of significance actually belong. This is often done by indicating some way in which dominant features of Jesus' particular life seem to fit with the material significance, presumed to be meaningful on other grounds, which Christians ascribe to him. (Marshall 1987: 9)

Notice therefore that for this soteriology to be viable, meaningfulness must be cogently available to thought *prior to the attempt explicitly to relate Christ to thought*.

Marshall now shows how Rahner's theology develops these methodological motifs in his attempt to present Christ as the absolute saviour. These involve 'a basic distinction between the credibility or meaningfulness of salvation and the enormous variety of things Christians say about it on the one hand, and the credibility of Jesus Christ as the saviour on the other' (23). And this in turn means that the concept of an absolute saviour who is 'ultimately meaningful' for all humanity must be a semantically meaningful conception *before* we can say that it is instantiated. We need to understand what it is for someone to be *a* saviour before we can recognize *the* saviour, and if we can do this then it is logically possible that we might find the meaning of the concept instantiated as the *telos* of our self-transcendence.

The failure of Rahner's approach

After detailed and rigorous testing of Rahner's argument, Marshall concludes that Rahner's methodological decision to argue from general criteria of human meaningfulness to an identification of Jesus as the 'ultimately meaningful' saviour 'is radically inconsistent with his own most basic commitments about the place of Jesus Christ as a particular person in the Christian belief in redemption and a redeemer' (Marshall 1987: 106). There are two of these commitments. First, Rahner wishes to uphold the church's teaching that it is the particular humanity of Jesus that makes him significant for salvation. That is, in the statement 'Jesus is *heilsbedeutsam*', the subject has priority over the predicate. Jesus is 'logically indispensable' to speech about salvation since it '*requires*' identifying reference to be made to Jesus, and the actions and events that make up Jesus' life are 'materially decisive' for the language of salvation in such a way that that language '*depends*' on him (Marshall 1987: 55). Second, Rahner is committed to his transcendental anthropology and transcendental Christology. However, as a result of his trying to hold these two commitments together serious inconsistencies arise.

Rahner believes that only by falling within the scope of the general categories of the transcendental orientation expounded in his anthropology 'can any reality affect us as a whole and so be genuinely saving' (Marshall 1987: 56). However, Marshall shows that given Rahner's first commitment,

we are not, and cannot be, oriented in this way toward Jesus Christ; he himself can in no way be derived or deduced from our transcendental orientation and its content. Therefore Jesus Christ is not, and cannot be, *heilsbedeutsam*, significant for salvation.

The same kind of argument applies when Rahner ascribes a specific characterization of that which is *heilsbedeutsam*, namely the status of the 'absolute saviour' (or whatever cognates he might want to employ), to Jesus Christ. An absolute saviour is *heilsbedeutsam* in that he or she is the object of an *a priori* orientation towards, or *Ausschau* for, supreme fulfilment. But Jesus Christ himself, and thus the actions and events which make up his life, is not a part of, or included in, the universal orientation in virtue of which alone an absolute saviour is *heilsbedeutsam*. Therefore, as Jesus Christ in his particularity is not, and cannot be, *heilsbedeutsam*, so also he is not, and cannot be, the absolute saviour. (56)

Thus Marshall argues that Rahner can have either Jesus or his saving significance, but not both; he cannot consistently retain the church's teaching about the saving significance of Jesus and his theological method. Moreover, if he wishes to retain his method, he must sacrifice the determinant historical characteristics of Jesus – that is, lose Jesus' particularity – and face the obverse result that

'Socrates' or 'Martin Luther King' could be the 'absolute saviour' in just this sense and on just this basis. That is, another subject could conceivably be *heilsbedeutsam* in the very way in which, Rahner assumes, Jesus is in fact so, namely, by being the actualization of that for which all persons are necessarily on the lookout. (59)

Rahner's soteriology is plainly unsatisfactory, but it is not that so much that concerns us but rather the relation between it and his account of human language. Rahner deploys his transcendental anthropology to show that meaning is possible, that the conception of an absolute saviour at the generic level of the 'logically general and implicitly universal' *is* possible, and that it is instantiated in Jesus. He reaches this conclusion by means of claims about the nature of language very different from my own. On my account, we can only speak of Christ as saviour on the basis of his achieved work of reconciliation made available by grace and appropriated by the faith that grace miraculously creates. Until this work is received into theology, the language by which we try to express it will (in the last analysis) hang with the crucified Christ over the abyss of unmeaning illustrated by deconstruction. By leaving open the question of the ultimate meaningfulness of theological language, Rahner's argument therefore also leaves open and unresolved the impossible possibility of meaninglessness meaningfully expressed, which is why, in the end, his argument should be rejected.[50]

TOWARDS A THEOLOGICAL ACCOUNT OF MEANING

It is now time to begin the task of developing a positive theological account of meaning. The following argument is an initial theological approach to the subject; it is developed further in chapter 8, when more of the philosophical machinery required for a fuller discussion will be in place. I suggest that we can usefully distinguish three different senses of 'meaning': the first three are 'semantic meaning', 'teleological meaning', and 'narrative meaning'. These three contribute together to a fourth, 'full meaning'. The inter-relations of these three in theological language can be brought out most helpfully by looking specifically at promises.[51]

Writing of the relationship between the Old and New Testaments in his essay on 'Redemptive Event and History' (1970: 15–80), Pannenberg observes that 'the promises of God were fulfilled in a different way from that in which they were understood by those who first received them, but in such a way that the promises themselves hold good in the change of their content' (1970: 31).[52] Pannenberg's language is not as clear as we could wish, but he seems to think that God sustains the meaningfulness of his promises and that they hold good despite the change of 'content' which occurs between their first reception and their subsequent fulfilment. Nor does Pannenberg adequately clarify the concept of 'content', but I

---

[50] For counter-arguments to Marshall's reading of Rahner, see Fiddes 1989 and Endean 1996.
[51] For a good if rather too historicist discussion of the relative significance of promises and assertions as fundamental modes of theological discourse, see Pannenberg's (1970: 96–136) debate with Gadamer.
[52] This still seems to be Pannenberg's view; see 1991: 245 n. 146.

offer the following reflection: in the perspective of the New Testament one of the most significant of the Old Testament promises concerned the advent of a saviour who would reveal (the meaning of) God's being his people's salvation.[53] We noticed earlier the way in which the crucifixion of Jesus was in part the result of a conflict of interpretations of Old Testament promises. By Pannenberg's lights, this conflict is attributable to a *change* of their content; however, I suggest that the conflict arose because the 'content' of the promises had not been fully revealed. If this gloss is correct, it raises the question, In respect of what can content be said (in Pannenberg's terms) to have changed between the promises being issued and being fulfilled or (in my terms) not to have been fully revealed? In different terms, considered empirically and historically, what is it in the promise that undergirds its continuing appropriation in the various historical contexts in which it is received? By virtue of what can we say that the promise received in the eighth century BC is the same as the promise received in the first century AD? I want to suggest that it is (initially and in part) the semantic construction – the form of words – by which the promise is transmitted.

However, we must not forget that the promise was issued by God. So, to bring out the need to distinguish between semantic and teleological meaning, we should bear in mind that God's promise has a meaning which is being unfolded through his purposive work with his people: this purposiveness of God grants teleological meaning to his promise. His promise's semantic meaning is the form of words in which it was couched when issued and subsequently transmitted. Teleological meaning is its meaning with reference to the purposive work of God in history. Semantic and teleological meaning are necessary conditions for 'the promises themselves hold[ing] good'. Those who initially received and transmitted the promise understood both what the words meant semantically and that they had a teleological meaning so far as God expressed an intention in uttering them; however, they did not understand what the promise would mean in its (eschatological) fulfilment.

To have understood a promise is not just to understand the words and trust the intention backing it up; it is also, and perhaps most importantly, to understand what it means when it has been fulfilled. The full meaning of a promise depends on the fulfilment of the intention expressed in the issuing of the promise. So inability to understand what God's promise *will* mean is not attributable to any defect on God's part or his people's; rather

[53] Cf. 2 Sam. 7:8–16; Isa. 11:1–12:6.

it arises naturally from language use. My point here can be illustrated from marriage.[54] When at their wedding the parties promise 'to have and to hold' and 'to love and to cherish' each other until they are parted by death, they can (in normal circumstances) be taken to understand the semantic meaning of the words by which they make their promises. However, each act of promising *ipso facto* expresses an intention to give meaning to these words 'for better, for worse, for richer, for poorer'. That is, the words which express the promise have a teleological meaning which is expressed in the whole course – through all the ups and downs – of the couple's married life. The promise works as a kind of 'glue' in the marriage precisely because it extends into the future and engages the intentions of the couple continually to bring to expression in their present circumstances the semantic meaning of the promises made on their wedding day.

The partners can be taken to have understood the semantic meaning of their promises (if they do not, they can look up the meaning of the words used in a dictionary; if they are fortunate, they will have been well prepared by the minister conducting their marriage), and we can reasonably hold that they have understood them to require certain intentions to be brought into effect and thus for them to have a teleological meaning. However, what the promise to cherish amounts to in particular circumstances – for example, where one partner becomes addicted to alcohol – depends on the teleological meaning of the promise being fulfilled, and this can be done in a variety of ways according to the temperaments and circumstances of the partners. There is therefore a sense in which what we are to understand by 'cherish' is only apparent through the fulfilling of the promise. Thus, if we ask for the full meaning of the promises the couple made, we have to say that it is only known when they reach the end of their life together, when there is no more fulfilling of their wedding promises to be done. This meaning will be unfolded as a story: 'When I was swamped in alcohol, I needed something to help me to cope with the financial pressures and the constant demands of the children. You were never at home. You were a workaholic, but when you saw what that was doing to me, you changed your job and spent more time at home and that helped bring me to my senses. I felt I could share the load with you and depend on you. Then I could acknowledge that I needed help.' In other words, understanding the meaning of a fulfilled

---

[54] We can distinguish between promises whose meaning is 'open' and those whose meaning is 'closed'. In the latter (for example, 'I promise to buy you a ring of five diamonds set in platinum by 5.00 p.m. on 30 October 2001') there is far less interpretative leeway in fulfilling the promise than in 'open' promises such as those examined in the text. A similar analysis could be made of closed promises to the one I offer of open ones.

promise involves reference to a sequence of intentions and actions expressed over time, and, as many contemporary theologians have stressed, such a sequence is best expressed in narrative form. I therefore propose that to understand the full meaning of a promise we need to consider not just the semantic meaning of the words which express it and the intentions and actions to which its speaker is committed (its teleological meaning) but also its narrative meaning.

Thus, in the theological case, that the words by which God's promise is expressed to his people will have some fullness of meaning depends on God's purposively bringing the promise to fulfilment,[55] and this has been accomplished in the incarnation and resurrection of the word as testified to in the Gospel narrative. As Robert Jenson puts it, 'The biblical promise has a narrative content; it is "about Christ"' (in Braaten and Jenson 1984: 131, quoted by Thiemann 1985: 98). The risen Christ – the vindicated incarnate *logos* – is the full meaning of God's promise: he is the resultant of its semantic, teleological, and narrative meanings. However, this was not known to the people of Israel who received and transmitted the promise, and so there is a lacuna in the logic of promising between the issuing of the promise and the revelation of its full meaning. Nevertheless, because the promise is sustained by its teleological meaning expressed in God's purposive action, this lacuna can be referred to as the 'teleological suspension of full meaning'.[56]

We can now gloss Rahner's Christology in the terms just developed and recognize that the semantic meaning of 'saviour' is unavoidably connected to teleological conceptions of 'meaningfulness'. The problem with Rahner's approach is as Marshall indicates: the dominant teleological orientation is human (that which is *heilsbedeutsam*) rather than divine (for example, God's desire for fellowship with his lost creature) and semantically involves 'the logically general and implicitly universal' rather than the particular person Jesus Christ. For Rahner we can identify Jesus as *heilsbedeutsam* and subsume him under the concept of 'saviour' because of *our* sense of the teleologically meaningful. But this is to assume what is by no means obvious unless we already know Christ as saviour: that our sense of teleological meaningfulness is in fact warranted by some *telos* – which is to beg the question.[57] However, as Jüngel argues, meaningfulness is only established by God's justification of sinners: 'Our justification is in response to an

[55] Cf. Isa. 55:9, 11.   [56] Further explanation of this concept follows in chapter 8.
[57] Vass rehearses a similar criticism of Rahner when he asks 'if God's self-revelation is discovered in reflecting upon one's own subjectivity, then "to what purpose is history, the finite world, the cross and the resurrection?"' (Vass 1985b: 147, quoting Eicher 1977: 368).

all-pervasive *loss of meaning*' (2001b: 262). Any *telos* we establish or think we have found apart from Christ is illusory.[58] Thus Rahner's approach seriously underplays the fact that the church's teaching about salvation depends on God's fulfilling his promise in Christ: the words and deeds of this particular human being are materially decisive for 'saviour' to be meaningful in a theological context.[59] A drowning person might greet his rescuer with the spluttered words, 'My saviour!', but this experience would not enable him to establish Jesus as saviour in the theological sense of the term because only through Jesus are our plight and our need to be saved from it revealed.[60]

So the semantic meaning of God's promise in the Old Testament must await the fulfilment of the teleological meaning it had for God as an expression of his own purposes when he uttered it. Until the fulfilment of God's purpose in Christ, the full meaning of God's promise was teleologically suspended. God's word goes forth to accomplish something and to prosper in that accomplishing through a particular temporal sequence which reaches its climax in the incarnation of the word. To understand God's promise of a saviour we need to attend to the identity of this particular human being in the full range of his interactions with his contemporaries since it is through these that the meaning of 'saviour' is given.[61] The full meaning of 'saviour' is instantiated in Jesus and is the resultant of the semantic meaning of the word 'saviour', the teleological meaning of God's bringing his promise to fulfilment in Christ, and the narrative meaning expressed by the Gospels' testimony to him.[62]

CONCLUSION

In this chapter we have seen how close the relationship is between the crisis of representation and humanity's relationship with God and the way in which this relationship ramifies into considerations of meaningfulness. In a sense, by pointing to Jesus Christ – the word of God incarnate among fallen speakers, the one into whose death and resurrection we are baptized and to whose community of speakers we thereby belong – we have said

---

[58] For the full argument, see Jüngel 2001b: 262ff.

[59] Had Old Testament usage been enough to establish this, Jesus would not have been crucified.

[60] The significance of this for preaching should not be overlooked.

[61] Notice that the New Testament identifies Jesus as saviour in virtue of his having been raised: see, for example, Acts 5:31; Eph.1:15–2:7; 2 Tim. 1:8–10.

[62] In broader theological context, my argument could be seen as an attempt to apply a 'progressive' doctrine of revelation to the question of how theological language works. There is a hint of such a possibility in Seitz's account of the revelation of the divine name in Exod. 3; see 1998: 244–5.

all that needs to be said (and probably in the end all that can be said) about human linguistic representation of God. Humanity does not need to 'search for a language by which to talk about God' (*contra* Barrigar 1991: 299). Jesus spoke the language of his contemporaries and God vindicated him; his followers two millennia later can have confidence that in him, their language also is acceptable to God and that he will not confound that confidence.

CHAPTER 7

God, reality, and realism

It is time to move out from our focus on Christ and soteriology to wider questions concerning the doctrine of God and God's relationship with humanity. I have already stated that transcendental arguments typically show what other conditions must obtain granted the starting point of the argument, and in the previous chapter I tried to show that we need to approach questions about language and representation through the Christ-event. In this chapter, by taking covenant as a focal concept I want to retrieve some biblical resources so as to argue for an approach to questions of epistemology and ontology which follow from taking the triune God to be the *ens realissimum*. These are vast issues, and for reasons of space only pointers for future research and a brief outline of the issues sufficient to undergird the defence of realism can be given. To round off the discussion, and because this is the source of a number of problems with non-Christocentric defences of realism, we then look at the conceptual role realism has played and should play in Christian theology.

GOD AND HUMANITY

We have seen that theological realism confuses the creator with the creature by not taking sufficient account of the fact that God is the *ens realissimum*. Speaking of God in this quasi-technical way is to use language drawn from and partially shaped by a (theological and) philosophical tradition, but there need be nothing intrinsically mistaken in doing this provided that the usage is theologically disciplined.[1] Granted that God is the *ens realissimum*, I begin by providing internal, theological warrant for the use of the phrase, and I shall do so initially by exploring further the theological and philosophical implications of Exodus 3 – a passage which, as I argued in my critique of theological realism, has particular importance for the identification of scripture's God.

[1] See chapter 1, p. 14 and chapter 5, p. 132.

As we saw in chapter 2, the name revealed to Moses, YHWH, *ehyeh asher ehyeh*, and the narrative context in which it is given – that of the promise of the liberation of God's people from slavery in Egypt – imply that God reveals himself, but that his self-revealing is a simultaneous self-veiling. God's name reveals that he is unnameable, ungraspable, unencompassable. We may see God's glory but not his essence. God remains veiled even in his self-unveiling: as Barth puts it, 'this revelation of the name . . . is in fact, in content, the refusal to give a name' (1975: 317).[2] The enigma here is deepened by the fact that the phrase *ehyeh asher ehyeh* can be translated as both 'I am who I am' and 'I will be who I will be.' The phrase's ambivalent tensing implies that it is mistaken to understand this God as an Aristotelian Unmoved Mover, or, with Hegel, as self-realizing historical *Geist*.[3] Against views which would identify God with temporal processes or altogether re-move him from them, the narrative presents YHWH as involved in and moving with time. This God has a distinct character – he is who he is – to which he will be faithful and which he reveals in his historical actions. Not only does God name his presence as active being, but his name also dis-closes his essentially relational nature. The Baptist scholar Gwynne Henton Davies explains that the Hebrew words 'have the quite practical meaning I AM *who and what, and where and when, and how and even why you will discover* I AM. I am what you will discover me to be' (1967: 72).

God's self-naming in this narrative context also implies that he posits himself as simultaneously a perfect harmony of being and act without either implying a privation of the other. God already is in himself what he intends and promises to be in his deeds through and among his people. The text implies that this is and will be the case and that it is and will be manifest historically; hence we can expect to be able to 'read' his acts as an assertion of his character and as leading to the fulfilment of his promise.[4] Using language from speech act theory (which I shall use extensively in the next chapter), we can say that God's revelation of his name is *assertive* of his being, and a *commissive* promise to act in faithfulness to his being. God's nature is expressed in his unbreakable word: that he means to be his word is implied by his promise, and that he will keep it is implied in his self-assertion.

Beyond what we have already said concerning his character, scripture does not permit us to say what *motivated* God to reveal himself to Israel. 'However', as Childs puts it in language which shows how integral are

---

[2] Cf. Ricoeur 1981: 93–5.
[3] See Noth 1962: 45; Childs 1974: 74ff, 1985: 39. For an opposing view, see Mettinger 1988: 34.
[4] Cf. Exod. 3:16–21, 6:2–8.

teleological conceptions to scripture, 'if one asks what was his purpose, that is, his *goal* toward which his self-disclosure pointed, then the Old Testament is eloquent in its response. God revealed himself that all may see and know who God is' (1985: 45). God will be what he is and is what he will be. However, and this is the important point for my argument, because God's purpose is disclosed in history, God's character is revealed to his people through the sequence of promise and fulfilment which is attested in scripture.

And this (unsurprisingly) is just what we see in Exodus 3. God reveals his name not as a proposition for Moses to contemplate in its crystalline, metaphysical sublimity. God's name reveals his character and he will cause his name to be glorified throughout time and eternity – in this instance, by bringing his people out of Egypt, into a land flowing with milk and honey. We can put it this way: the God who asserts his being and promises that he will be faithful to his being stakes his character on effecting the fulfilment of his promise in the future of his relationship with his people; they in turn are to be a people of praise who glorify God and make his character known through participation in and worshipful recitation of his mighty acts – paradigmatically, for Jews in the *shema* and for Christians in the eucharist. God's relationship with his people can be understood as a reciprocal purposiveness in which God is the initiating agent: he freely purposes to be faithful to himself and thereby elicits the free, responsive desire of his faithful covenant partners to glorify him.

Because God is both act and being, he is grace: since he *is* in himself, it is gratuity that he also *will be* for his creature, but because he will be himself, what he is cannot not be grace: there can be nothing which restricts God's freedom to be who he will be. None of God's acts result from a need to express his Godhead because he lacks fulfilment or could not be God without humanity. Such thought is foreign to scripture.[5] God means to be who he is, and he does so freely. He cannot be threatened or thwarted by his creation, even in death. Freedom and grace are at the heart of God's self-expression to his people, not, say, retributive justice, or his being subject to an external, metaphysical necessity such as worries D. Z. Phillips. As God reminded Israel after the exodus, he chose his people simply because he loves them.[6] In the harmony of being and act and in the liberty of this love, YHWH, the God and Father of our Lord Jesus Christ, is the *ens realissimum*, for he is 'incomparably more real than anything that can be called real in the sphere of human thought and knowledge' (Barth 1954: 211).

5 Cf. Childs 1985: 43.   6 Deut. 7:6–8.

That God acts out of love to liberate us to love and glorify him suggests a view of God's authority which is at variance with that found in the work of non-realists. God commands his people to worship him alone not because he is a moody tyrant or because he is a Cupittian 'cosmic Tory'.[7] So far as his covenant partner is concerned, God's authority rests upon his faithfulness to his promise in his action towards her: '*I am* the Lord your God, who brought you out of the land of Egypt, out of the house of slavery. *You shall* have no other gods before me' (Exod. 20:2, my italics). A human 'ought' can be derived from the divine 'is'.[8] We can now see that the autonomy advocated by Christian non-realists is doubly dangerous. First, because humankind's flourishing and destiny are dependent on God. Second, because, as we saw in our discussion of non-realists' eucharistic practices, if persistently pursued, autonomy could lead to God's people losing touch with the saving events by which God sets them free to be fully human and in which the divine 'is' is revealed as promise and fulfilment for the benefit of all humanity. In this context, Hans Walter Wolff's pithy summary of aspects of Old Testament anthropology bears noting: 'In praise [consists] the destiny of man ... Otherwise man, becoming his own idol, turns into a tyrant; either that or, falling dumb, he loses his freedom' (1974: 229).

Human beings can be free because they have been made in the image and likeness of God. They are therefore capable of participating freely in the drama of the divine promise and fulfilment whereby God's glory is made known. However, as we have seen, this relationship of likeness cannot be presumed upon; Adam's children have defaced and even lost the *imago* as God intended it to be. Indeed, in Paul's view, the glory of God which humanity was made to reflect has been given up to idolatrous purposes so that by ourselves we cannot be what God intended: we have preferred to 'suppress the truth' (sc. of God) (Rom. 1:18–23).[9] Only through Christ's true humanity is the reality of our fallenness revealed and overcome. As Paul argues in 2 Corinthians 3, God's purpose has been accomplished in Christ so that those who turn to the Lord behold his glory and have the *imago* restored, for 'we all ... seeing the glory of the Lord ... are being changed into the same image from one degree of glory to another' (3:18). Paul's climactic affirmation is very important for our argument, for (as was noted in the previous chapter of a similar Pauline claim) it meets the quest of theological realists for a means of representing or depicting God's reality.[10] God has so acted as to elicit from us the offering of lives of praise, but we

---

[7] Cupitt 1990: 54.   [8] I owe this point to Oliver O'Donovan.   [9] See Cranfield 1975: 112ff.
[10] Bruce Marshall has reached a similar conclusion by a different route: see 2000: 265–71.

do not thereby so much represent or depict God's unobservable reality; it would be more correct to speak with Paul of our reflecting God's glory.

For this reason, if a Christian realism were to be defended on the basis of an *analogia entis*, it would have to be borne in mind first of all that if there is an ontological relationship between God and humanity, it can only be known in the perspective of God's self-revelation in the ontological rupture of the cross. If theology speaks of analogy to express the means by which God is represented in human lives, it should speak firstly of an *analogia fidei*: his faithfulness is the ground and substance of our faith in him and our reflection of his glory.[11] 'It is the God who said, "Let light shine out of darkness" who has shone in our hearts to give the light of the knowledge of the glory of God in the face of Jesus Christ' (2 Cor. 4:6).

GOD, COVENANT, ONTOLOGY, AND EPISTEMOLOGY

The covenanting God

Underlying the realities of promise and fulfilment and of freedom and obligation we have been exploring is that of God's covenant. This is the overarching context of human life before God, and in it God's faithfulness towards himself is expressed in and for the world. God binds himself to his people and they to him in a relationship of mutual obligation.[12] It is arguable that the thematic unity underlying the biblical understanding of covenant is a theological and moral consequence of God's nature as it is revealed in the tetragrammaton. Thus the Old Testament knows God's covenant love as 'steadfast love';[13] God will not be to his people other than he is in himself. Likewise, a theologically rich and philologically persuasive translation of God's 'righteousness' speaks of his 'covenant faithfulness'.[14] These characteristics of God's relationship with his people find climactic expression in the coming of Jesus: in his incarnation as the Messianic agent of God's faithfulness to his promissory word; in his ministry of salvation to sinners, the lost, and the marginalized; in his vicarious self-offering as the sacrifice of praise acceptable to God; and in his resurrection, whereby the promise of God by and for which Jesus had lived is fulfilled in triumph. As Mendenhall and Herion point out, 'Covenant is not an "idea" to be embraced in the mind ... [it] is an "enacted reality" that is either manifested in the concrete

---

[11] Cf. Alan Torrance (1996: 162–7; cf. 180–9) and Jüngel (1983: 281–98).
[12] I follow Childs (1992: 413–51), who finds in scripture a basic unity underlying the various expressions of God's covenant with his elect.
[13] E.g. Isa. 55:3. [14] See N. T. Wright 1991: 231–57.

choices individuals make, or not' (1992: 1201). In the incarnation we see this reality fully enacted. God binds himself to the human being Jesus of Nazareth, who in turn binds himself to God and lives out the obligations towards God which his people had freely taken upon themselves.

We turn now to examine the consequences of this in the realms of ontology and epistemology. The object here is not so much to develop full-dress accounts of these topics as to indicate the implications of taking the covenanting God as the *ens realissimum* specifically in the realm of human living, that is, of nature and history.

The concepts of nature and history in the light of the covenant

So far as Christian concepts of an ordered nature and meaningful history are traceable in the Old Testament, they are predicated of God's covenant with the world. This is important for the overall argument of this book. I have contended that God is the *ens realissimum*, the Author and Sustainer of creation, but this claim would be seriously weakened if these concepts could be secured on another basis – say that of the philosophy of science or an immanent historical teleology. If they could, it might be possible to argue from knowledge of created reality to the reality of the creator without the need for God's first revealing himself – which, in other words, would amount to a rather static view of the *analogia entis* inadequately grounded in Christology. Such a line of argument would seriously weaken my own, for it would open up the possibility of an alternative, non-Christocentric defence of realism and render my transcendental argument superfluous. It might also suggest that knowledge of the reality of the creator is to be grounded in the logical achievements of the creature, but this would make calling God the *ens realissimum* more than somewhat paradoxical. I therefore argue against the possibility of such arguments by showing how – from a Christian point of view at least – the concepts of an ordered nature and meaningful history are themselves grounded in God's self-vindication in Christ. Later on I justify the stronger claim (which is necessary to block mistaken forms of argument from an *analogia entis*) that for an adequate Christian faith these concepts *must* be so grounded.

Take firstly the Old Testament's view of the dependency of the natural order on God's covenant. This is expressed as an absurd counterfactual in YHWH's word to Jeremiah:

If any of you could break my covenant with the day and my covenant with the night, so that day and night would not come at their appointed time, only then could my covenant with my servant David be broken. (Jer. 33:20–1)

The reliability of God's covenant with David is expressed in terms of the supposition – ridiculous to Jeremiah – that the covenant whereby God orders day and night could be broken by a human being. The Isaianic writer makes the same point more positively:

> For the mountains may depart and the hills be removed,
> but my steadfast love shall not depart from you,
> and my covenant of peace shall not be removed,
> says [YHWH], who has compassion on you.   (Isa. 54:10)

The claim here is that God's covenant is more secure than the world, so, given the stability of the world he has created, it is ridiculous to imagine his relationship with the world being changed. As Brueggemann puts it: 'Israel's testimony about Yahweh as Creator is fully embedded in Israel's larger covenant testimony. As Israel believes its own life is covenantally ordered; so Israel believes that creation is covenantally ordered' (1997: 157).[15] The cosmos is the arena in which God expresses his character and causes his name to be glorified. It is therefore under his lordship. Nature is teleologically ordered, not a formless chaotic happenstance, and scripture knows this on the basis of God's covenant faithfulness to himself and his prophetic word.[16]

Israel also understood her own identity as 'covenantally ordered' and as having been brought into existence and sustained by God's faithfulness to his word of promise to Abraham, to the slaves in Egypt, and the exiles in Babylon. Her identity is therefore to be found through a narratable history of God's involvement with the world. God chose his people to be a people of his praise and thereby made them *a* people; without his faithfulness to them in their sojournings they would not have *a* unifying story, and they would not have *a* history in which *meaning* could be found. Recitation of the *shema* makes the individuals who ask why these testimonies and statutes are performed into members of the family of Judah, participants in a history made meaningful by the saving events and the obligation to glorify YHWH.[17]

The implications of this are important, so to clarify them consider an argument proposed by the moral theologian Paul Ramsey. He suggests that we should not imagine that we

first learn what history means and then know better the God whose field of action history is. The Hebrews did not know first what an 'event' was, a genuine and

---

[15] Cf. Dalferth 1999: 131.
[16] Cf. Gen. 9:8–15; Ps. 104. For dogmatic exposition, see Barth (1958: 94–329) on 'creation as the external basis of the covenant' and 'covenant as the internal basis of creation'.
[17] See Deut. 6.

meaningful part of their history, and then learn to know God. They first knew God through the covenant and learned to sense the eventful. (1950: 372)

The point is that for the Hebrew mind, and, derivatively for the Christian also, the concept of meaningful history derives from God, not the reverse: without God there would be no such thing as history.

Though we can agree with Ramsey's conclusion, there appears to be a flaw in his argument for it. The revelation of the divine name to Moses before the exodus might be construed as suggesting that Moses first had to sense the eventful (i.e. the possibility that God would indeed be faithful in leading his people out of Egypt and so give them a history) and that only on this basis could he know God as the covenanting God. If this were the case, then Ramsey's assertion that knowledge of God through the covenant precedes knowledge of the eventful would clearly be false. But Ramsey anticipates this difficulty and says that the events which led up to the exodus 'were eventful only to those who proleptically responded to and obeyed their covenant with God', whilst to those who chose to stay in Egypt and serve other Gods, these 'were not *significant* events, not parts of *meaningful* history' (372 n. 14, my italics). Moses' encounter with God could only come to have significance as a history-making event because of his readiness to obey and trust this God's faithfulness to his promise. Thus the dependency of the concept of meaningful history on God's covenant is preserved.

However, there is a further problem with Ramsey's argument, and this concerns the identity of the true, history-making God. Up to the consummation of the covenant in which God's being and intention are fully revealed, it remains ambiguous to the Israelites whose 'history' is genuinely 'meaningful' – the Hebrews' or their slavemasters'. The answer depends on whether YHWH's promises are reliable. The exiles pondered a similar question in Babylon, and the exilic Isaiah sought a concrete answer to it. This is why he looked forward to God's proving that he, not the Babylonian deities, was the promise-keeping God who makes meaningful history for his people. Commenting on the outlook of the exilic prophets, Jenson explains that

all history is understood as a judgement in which it is the identity of God that is at stake. That the sequences of time embody the significance of *some* deity is taken as tautologous; the matter to be settled by the actual content of the sequences is *which* deity. And this decision is still future. Yahweh promises, by the word of his prophets, what he will do; and if it happens, all will know that the hidden meaning of the events is his will, that 'I am [Yahweh]' is true revelation. (1982: 38)

In the light of the way in which 'eventfulness' itself awaits resolution (for Moses), I suggest that we should say that it was not only Moses' response which was proleptic but also the eventfulness itself. However, as a result of God's redemptive action in history (in the exodus and the return from Babylon), Israel's knowledge that YHWH is her creator is firmly established.[18]

Only by God's having adopted them into Israel can Gentile Christians recognize that God has consummated his covenant in Christ's resurrection. His promises and his deity are revealed as genuine in the light of their fulfilment in him, for by his death and resurrection he has overcome the powers of chaos and darkness. On this basis, the New Testament testifies that God's action in Christ has brought into being that 'new thing' which God had promised through the exilic prophets – the new creation and the calling into being of God's own people.[19] The New Testament reformulates and confirms the truth of the Old.[20] God has proved that he is the creator who gives meaningful pattern to sequences of time, that he makes meaningful history for his people, and that he is the true God. This is the necessary basis for our agreeing with Ramsey that

In the Bible, neither 'history' nor 'nature' has a nature or an order of its own. Each has a source and an ordering. Both have meaning which stems from covenant. The idea of nature and the idea of history may neither of them be derived from the other; rightly grasped they may both be reduced to simple corollaries of the idea of covenant without which the Hebrew mind would have known little of either. (1950: 372–3)

This perspective is decisively confirmed by the New Testament witness. As the fulfilment of God's covenantal promise, the Risen Christ is the one in and through whom ordered creation is known and meaningful history is established and perfected. It follows that our understanding of both is eschatological in character.[21] And because what God promised would happen has been fulfilled proleptically in Christ, he grants all to 'know that the hidden meaning of the events is [God's] will'. To express this in the terminology developed in the previous chapter: the semantic, teleological, and narrative senses of meaning are now fully revealed as coinherent. Furthermore, since Jesus is both representative of all humanity and the redemptive

---

[18] On the other hand, note that 'From a theological perspective ... the present canonical shape [of Israel's testimony] has subordinated the noetic sequence of Israel's experience of God in her redemptive history to the ontic reality of God as creator' (Childs 1992: 385).

[19] On the new creation, see Isa. 65:17ff; 2 Cor. 5:17; on God's people, see Hos. 1:6ff, 2:16–23; 1 Pet. 2:4–10. Note that the latter pericope echoes Isa. 43:21 and 42:6f, both of which are pronounced in the name of YHWH, the creator, and bring into view the 'new thing' he is going to do (42:9, 43:19).

[20] See Childs 1992: 396ff.   [20] See Col. 2:15ff; Rev. 5.

being-in-act of God, God's work has a prospective nature looking forward to the creation of 'a new heaven and a new earth' (Rev. 21:1). The risen Christ is therefore the one in whom the true nature of reality, both divine and created, is revealed.

Ontology and epistemology in the light of the consummation of the covenant

Ontology

That only a few decades after his crucifixion, the one who had been humiliated at the feet of a Roman princeling should be worshipped as the one at whose name 'every knee should bend' (Phil. 2:10); that the one who met his end hanging helpless upon a cross limb nigh-torn from limb should be acclaimed as the cosmic *telos* in whom 'all things hold together' (Col. 1:17); and that of the one whose last words had been of God-forsakenness it should be asserted that 'he sustains all things by his powerful word' (Heb. 1:3) – all these are signs of the rapidity with which the conceptual revolution brought about by Christ's resurrection took hold in the church.

The New Testament writers were no purblind 'volunteers' for this revolution. Paul had been in the vanguard of the counter-revolution until the scales were removed from his eyes. The persecution did not end when he became a follower of the Way, and neither did the church's struggle to find conceptual resources with which, as Luke puts it, 'to set down an orderly account of the events that have been fulfilled among us' (Luke 1:1). Indeed, such was the struggle that Luke and Paul sometimes seem at odds with each other as they try to express the resurrection reality. No doubt factors of personal history and theological outlook were influential, but we cannot ignore the strikingly different vocabularies the two writers use and the ontologies they suggest. As J. D. G. Dunn points out,

> In Luke's account Jesus' resurrection body is very 'physical': Jesus himself says, 'Handle me and see; for a spirit has not flesh and bones as you see that I have' (Lk. 24:39). Paul however makes a clear distinction between the body of this life (= 'physical or natural body') and the resurrection body (= 'spiritual body') (1 Cor. 15: 42–6). And he concludes his discussion on the point with the ringing declaration: 'I tell you this: flesh and blood cannot inherit the kingdom of God...' (1 Cor. 15:50). What Luke affirms (Jesus' resurrection body was flesh and bones) Paul denies (the resurrection body is *not* composed of flesh and blood). (1985: 74)

Yet despite the differences between New Testament writers, they are united in expressing the conviction that God's raising Jesus from the dead has radically altered the way about which not only Jesus but the whole of reality is to be thought.

A Christian realism should not ignore the ontological implications of this. We have already seen that the concepts of history and nature are only properly thinkable by the Christian mind on the basis of God's eschatological accomplishment of his covenant promises in Christ. In the New Testament, this is undergirded negatively by the vision of the day of judgement when God's sovereignty over his creation will be fully manifest and all things will be 'dissolved ... and the elements will melt with fire' (2 Pet. 3:12).[22] Paul is led in a similar direction, negatively expressed in his view of the creation as having been 'subjected [in hope] to futility' (Rom. 8:20), and positively in his new creation theology (in 2 Cor. 5:17, for example). Behind all this, and in addition to Jesus' resurrection, perhaps we can trace a teasing out of implications of his healing and nature miracles. If so, this ontological grounding will diminish our embarrassment at the highly figurative language used by the New Testament writers: they are using the language and conceptual resources available to them. Our surprise and puzzlement is perhaps little different in kind from that which they would feel towards our metaphysics-influenced conceptual reworkings of their more 'mythological' ontologies, for it is arguable that the theology of each generation is expressed under the same compulsion to testify to God's work in Christ in the terms available to it – and, of course, to refashion and extend those terms in faithfulness to Christ.[23]

Certainly, suggestive connections can be made between the New Testament thinking we have just been examining and features of the intellectual life of our own day. Postmodern philosophies of history and science challenge the ontologies underlying the modern pursuit of these disciplines, which themselves arguably depend on a Judaeo-Christian outlook on the world. Thus, writing about postmodern historiography, Gertrude Himmelfarb quotes Hayden White's statement that 'We require a history that will educate us to discontinuity more than ever before; for discontinuity, disruption, and chaos is our lot' (1997: 170, no reference given). The consequence of such a view is, she contends, 'to trivialize history by so fragmenting it that it lacks all coherence and focus, all sense of continuity, indeed, all meaning' (170). Though he is no postmodernist, Niall Ferguson embraces a 'chaotic' approach to historiography in the introduction to his *Virtual History* (1997). In this, he sets out to write 'chaostory', or 'virtual

---

[22] Notice that the scoffers (against whom the author writes) ground their ridicule of the Christian hope in God's promise on an appeal to 'the stability of the natural order' (Kelly 1969: 356). But in 3:5–7, the author opposes their forgetfulness of God's authority over his creation by asserting the basis of this stability in God's word.

[23] Cf. 2 Cor. 10:5b.

history' on the basis of an explicit repudiation of teleology – either of a (theologically construed) historical determinist or idealist kind (of which, he asserts, postmodern views are merely a rehash). Instead, he wishes to base historiography on an ontology drawn from contemporary science, namely, that reality is chaotic (by which he means stochastic rather than anarchic).[24] In a revealing sentence, he says of the past – which, remember, has been a present: 'There is no author, divine or otherwise; only characters, and ... a great deal too many of them. There is no plot, no inevitable "perfect order"; only endings ... [History] unfolds in a fundamentally chaotic way' (1997: 68, 69).

If Himmelfarb and Ferguson are correct, the notion of meaningful history which we found secured by Christ's resurrection is fundamentally threatened. By finding the meaning and possibility of history to consist in one individual and his relationship to God, Christians not only reintroduce the forbidden notion of teleology, but also privilege one (set of) narrative(s) over all the others which exist in 'virtual history' – for example, those in which the crowd cried for Jesus rather than Barabbas, or in which there was no resurrection – and which are just as good a clue to 'what really happened' as those we do possess. Against these views, I suggest that Christian theologians refrain from taking history (either as an intellectual discipline or as an aspect of reality) as unproblematically secure unless it is moored on Christology, for, as Pannenberg has argued,

Biblical faith is not only the temporary, accidental presupposition of the Western consciousness of historical reality, but the origin to which this consciousness remains essentially bound ... Historical experience of reality is preserved only in the biblical understanding of history, in the biblical faith in promise. (1970: 33)

Similar observations can be made about the philosophy of science. Its practitioners have recently been exercised by the 'Sokal hoax' in which 'ingeniously contrived gibberish' (Boghossian 1996: 13) was passed off as postmodern, constructivist anti-realism.[25] As Sokal and Bricmont explain in their 'Comments on the Parody',

[t]he first two paragraphs [of the article] set forth an extraordinarily radical version of social constructivism, culminating in the claim that physical reality (and not merely our ideas about it) is 'at bottom a social and linguistic construct'. The goal

---

[24] Baudrillard's nihilistic outlook on 'history' is similarly shaped by a rejection of Christian teleology: see 1997, especially 44f.

[25] The article, 'Transgressing the Boundaries: Towards a Transformative Hermeneutics of Quantum Gravity', is readily accessible as an appendix to Sokal and Bricmont 1998: 199–240. The relationship between constructivism and voluntarism should be noted: see Searle 1995: 158.

in these paragraphs was . . . to test whether the bald assertion (without evidence or argument) of such an extreme thesis would raise any eyebrows among the editors [of *Social Text*, the journal in which the hoax originally appeared]. If it did, they never bothered to communicate their misgivings to Sokal, despite his repeated requests for comments, criticisms and suggestions. (Sokal and Bricmont 1998: 241–2, cf. 199ff)

Constructivism is a serious position in the philosophy of science, but it usually concerns the construction by scientific practices of science's 'products and representations' rather than physical reality itself.[26] Yet this very radical latter position is what Sokal was arguing. From a theological point of view, what is interesting about this is the fact that the article was taken seriously and published in the first place, for it underlines the readiness of some thinkers to suspend the broadly realist conception of an ordered nature upon which science seems to depend.[27]

In the light of our earlier discussion of the concepts of 'history' and 'nature', atheistic postmodernism's nihilism and anti-realism should neither surprise nor disturb us. Indeed, these phenomena underscore my earlier suggestion concerning the perspective I called dialectical fideism according to which we should expect to find signs of God's judgement and grace in the world with which he has made covenant. More particularly, unease and dispute over the question as to what is real is perhaps an occasion for discerning the work of the Holy Spirit in calling theologians and Christian philosophers to a renewed engagement in ontology.[28] So the suggestion is that, as a matter of first principle, a realist ontology appropriate to Christian faith needs to be guided by the conviction that the risen Christ is the one in whom 'all things hold together' (Col. 1:17), rather than the secondary and derived conceptions of 'history' or 'nature'.[29] Only then will it be possible for theology to function as it should – 'as the warden of realism in a world of illusionists' (Dalferth 1992: 101).

The present argument reinforces that in chapter 3 against theological realism. What has now emerged is that from a theological point of view, since the concept and existence of an ordered nature are dependent on God's

[26] For a balanced discussion, see Fine 1996[2]: 185–8.

[27] In somewhat more conventional philosophy of science, see Feyerabend 1994. The postmodern critique of science has a very eminent genealogy within twentieth-century physics; see Beller 1998. The importance of biblical conceptions in the rise of modern science has been argued by Foster (1934). Peacocke sees science as 'the independent offspring of a Christian culture', and regards its 'autonomy' as a boon which secures it against 'interference by religious bodies' (1994: 657, 655).

[28] Particularly notable here are Jenson (e.g., 1982) and Jüngel (e.g., 1989: 95–123). See also Milbank 1990, especially pp. 259–438, and Lash 2001.

[29] Cf. Plantinga's argument that 'naturalistic epistemology flourishes best in the garden of supernaturalistic metaphysics' (1993: 237).

covenant in creation, some fundamental conceptions in scientific realism seem only to be supportable on a theological basis. Holding confidence about the viability of a realism appropriate to Christian faith in abeyance until arguments for it based on analogies with scientific realism can be found involves presupposing that the reality of 'nature' as investigated by science is as theological realism will require it to be. But this cannot be taken for granted. Far from conclusive though it is as an argument, the snapshot of postmodern constructivism in the philosophy of science we have looked at strongly suggests that the ontological status of 'nature' is in fact not secure enough for theological realism. 'Nature' is, on the post-modern reading, a social construct.[30] Hence, to the extent that theological realism is based on a contested view of nature and does not provide independent theological reasons for accepting the concept of nature it depends on, it will beg the question of the ontological status of 'nature'. (The same will apply, *mutatis mutandis*, to arguments for the realism of the Christian faith based on a 'natural theology' conceived independently of revelation in Christ.)

It is not only theological realism that has been misled by a question-begging ontology: so too has Christian non-realism. In his early non-realist ontology, Don Cupitt assumes a conception of fact that is so tied to a scientific understanding of 'nature' that it is unsurprising to find him inferring that New Testament faith was not realist and that fact language is therefore best dropped from theological contexts and replaced by expressive language.[31] These themes can be seen in the following argument:

The crucial objection to religious realism is that insofar as it succeeds in being realistic it necessarily ceases to be religious. The modern notions of fact, truth and so on are religiously neutral, so that insofar as an apologist manages to establish a realist interpretation of some major doctrine he necessarily destroys it as religion. Today the factual is non-religious. What are the implications of the converse, that religion is non-factual? The New Testament is a religious book, and hermeneutics is an attempt to appropriate its religious meaning. So the resurrection is a religious reality – that is, a state of the self and a form of salvation. (1980: 45)

Influenced by Bultmann, Cupitt thinks that religious reality cannot be factual. But against this, it does not follow from our understanding factuality or events in a different way from that in which the Gospel writers did that we must deny legitimacy to talk of events or happenings when we read them.

---

[30] Recall that it is partly to rebut arguments such as this that Hebblethwaite and Markham run their transcendental arguments from truth to God (see chapter 1, pp. 15–18).

[31] See 1980: 44–55.

Although we need to treat their words with more historical sensitivity than Christian evidentialists typically do, both Paul (for example, 1 Cor. 15:3–8) and Luke (for example, Luke 1:1–4) operate in a thought-world in which such conceptions are not as alien as Cupitt's argument requires. Nevertheless, the Christian tendency to canonize 'Doubting' Thomas as patron saint of sceptical empiricists is risky when it leads to ignoring Jesus' blessing on those 'who have not seen and yet believe' (John 20:29). As I shall argue in the next section, neither our objectivity nor our subjectivity is as the world's is: a theological fog-horn needs sounding, but it is mistaken to hear it as a cry to abandon ship. Cupitt is right to indicate the hermeneutical difficulties presented by the New Testament, but he does not solve any problems by suggesting that even though the New Testament is (in his view) non-factual, it possesses an expressive religious meaning which we can appropriate. This is merely to beg the question by shifting the source of the hermeneutical problem from ontology to semantics, from conceptual content to the concept itself.

Objectivity and subjectivity in epistemology

I turn now to consider some questions of theological epistemology in the light of the resurrection. Realists often insist that if talk of God is to be understood realistically, our reference must be to what is *objectively* knowable.[32] But the problem with stressing epistemological objectivity in this way is that it inverts the ordering of general and particular.[33] It puts the metaphysical cart before the theological horse and assumes that the right metaphysical conceptions are sufficient (if not necessary) to ensure the integrity of the language of faith. However, on my argument, what God has done in Christ (the particular) is central in our thought and we regulate our (general) metaphysical conceptions by that, rather than the converse. In other words, theological epistemology needs to be orientated by God in his self-revelation rather than by general metaphysical or epistemological considerations.

New Testament talk about God proceeds on the basis of the resurrection of Christ, for had he not been raised, there would have been no New Testament. Hence, if our knowledge of God and our being able to reflect his glory depend on what he has done for us, we should recognize that although emphasizing objectivity and subjectivity might (just) complement

[32] See, for example, Trigg (1992: 41ff; cf. 1989²), who regards the distinction between subject and object as a touchstone of realism.
[33] On this, see p. 133.

a reading of Luke–Acts,[34] the concepts would unnecessarily restrict our ability to appreciate Paul's distinctively participatory and 'mystical' language. John's Gospel also illustrates the difficulties facing us if we would impose a rigid subjective/objective distinction: an empiricist might say that a person's walking through closed doors belongs to the world of subjective appearance, whereas placing hands on wounds does not. Likewise, where on the polarity of objective and subjective knowing should we place Peter's knowing by revelation that Jesus is the Messiah (Matt. 16:16ff)? On a classical foundationalist understanding of objectivity it would have to be dismissed as sheer subjectivity: it is neither evident to the senses nor self-evident, nor validly deduced from either. Against such Procrustean views, this very brief survey of the New Testament suggests that more epistemological flexibility is called for where the things of God are concerned than a rigid contrast between 'objectivity' and 'subjectivity' allows. This is emphatically not to deny that theologians should talk in the kind of way usually indicated by objectivity language, that is, of God's deeds, and in terms of events or something's having happened, but it is to make a plea for allowing the epistemology by which we settle questions about such things to be determined by the nature of the putative reality rather than to confine it in the straitjacket of an inappropriate ontology and epistemology.

Yet even if we are reluctant to jettison the terminology of 'subjectivity' and 'objectivity' from theological discourse regulated by theological rather than metaphysical conceptions, we should note that the issues under consideration are connected with the crisis of representation and therefore need situating in a wider cultural context. Thus, we may ask, do we strive for objective knowledge because we think that it is the only way we shall be able to arrive at a (perceptually) correct representation of reality? Perhaps if we do, our striving reflects our not being at home in the world, our desire to master it, and our denigration of that which does not cohere with our prejudices about who is qualified to offer and assess claims to know. If so, we should heed Jonathan Culler's observation that 'Objectivity is constituted by excluding the views of those who do not count as sane and rational men: women, children, poets, prophets, madmen' (Culler 1982: 153, quoted by Rorty 1992: 236). If Culler is right – and it is hard to give an account of the Gospel story without referring to women, children, prophets, and accusations of madness – then the theological conclusion is obvious: where objectivity is concerned with representational mastery, the resurrection of

[34] Note however, the conclusion reached by the New Testament scholar Markus Bockmuehl: 'even the most apologetic of [NT] texts never really accommodate an objectivist epistemology' (1998: 300, citing Acts 10:41, cf. 283).

Christ is likely to be excluded from consideration – as, of course, it was by the disciples to whom the women announced the resurrection.[35] However, just as the risen Christ burst forth from the tomb, so he does from conceptual straitjackets and blind prejudice.

Should we not rather regard our knowledge of God as the fruit of his self-giving love, which knowledge, like the risen Jesus in his encounter with Mary Magdalene, is never to be clung on to or possessed (John 20:17) – a knowledge shared at God's costly initiative, entrusted to his covenant partners, and quickened in worship, prayer, and service? The resurrection of Christ shows us that God is not an object amongst objects, knowledge of which/whom can be brought within the masterful purview of human techniques, but that he nevertheless makes himself known as he really is.[36] As Barth puts it in his important lectures of 1929 on 'Fate and Idea in Theology' (which are remarkable for their bold blend of idealism and realism):

theology has God as its object only to the extent that it strives to have absolutely no other origin than the communication which God actually gives of himself. No step, not even the smallest, can be dared by theology except on the ground that God allows himself to be found before we have ever sought him. (1986a: 27)

Two years later, in his study of Anselm's *Proslogion*, Barth gives an extended analysis of the relationship between the divine and human poles of theological epistemology and concludes that 'God gave himself to be known and [Anselm] was able to know God ... God gave himself as the object of his knowledge and God illumined him that he might know him as object' (1960a: 171).

Concerning theological epistemology and ontology, I suggest that we say something like the following: God's reality is not one to which we must achieve 'epistemic access' through religious language, the resultant deposit of which we call 'revelation'.[37] Rather, in Christ and by his Spirit, God has found ontological access to humanity, revealed himself, and given himself to be known in his objectivity by the responding faith he creates. In so doing, he has restored to creation its own nature and to human beings their history, and thereby enabled them to reflect his transcendent glory. In the wake of this, one of the theologian's tasks is to continue the Anselmian

---

[35] Luke 24:11.
[36] God gives himself to be known in his objectivity and puts himself at risk of what Bultmann called 'objectification', but it does not follow that thinking about God in a way which is responsive to his gift necessarily involves our objectifying God. See Bultmann 1985: 45–50 and cf. Fergusson 1990.
[37] So Soskice 1985: 153ff.

vocation, summarized in the maxim, *Credo ut intelligam*: 'It is my very faith itself that summons me to knowledge' (Barth 1960a: 18).

THE ROLE OF REALISM IN CHRISTIAN FAITH

I have suggested that to develop a Christian realism we need a view of ontology and epistemology shaped in the context of the covenant consummated in Christ. My argument is conveniently summarized in a passage from Ingolf Dalferth's exposition of 'Karl Barth's eschatological realism'.

Barth calls the eschatological reality of God's saving action in his revelation the 'real reality', the Word of God the 'concrete reality' (*concretum*), and Jesus Christ, the incarnate Word of God, the 'most concrete reality' (*concretissimum*). This is to be taken literally. Compared to this most concrete reality everything else is at best abstract reality, that is, reality abstracted from this most concrete reality. It is held, as Barth puts it, by God and 'by him alone above the abyss of non-existence ... It is real so far as He wills and posits it as real.' Precisely as concentrating on this concrete reality of God's eschatological coming in Christ and expounding it as the basis and frame of all reality is theology realist. (1989: 27, quoting Barth 1975: 389)[38]

Barth is emphatic that just as the reality of God ontologically precedes the reality of what he has created, so 'God's being *goes before* the theological question of God's being' (Jüngel 2001a:19). Because God is *prevenient* he should not be regarded as a *presupposition* of Christian faith. To think in this way would be to put created reality before the creator's reality and make the Lord of all creation a postulate of human thought. (This is precisely where theists and Christian non-realists embrace and hence why they seem to argue past each other.) But if God is the *ens realissimum* (the consequences of which view the previous sections of this chapter have tried to outline), it would seem to be obvious that in defending realism his reality should be taken to be prevenient. Looking at some of the ways in which the conceptual role of realism has been misconceived by realism's defenders will help us clarify the issues here.

Some misconceptions

Realism as a research programme
Arthur Peacocke articulates the concerns of many caught off-balance in the back-wash of postmodernity and states the need for defending realism in

---

[38] Cf. Augustine 1978: 7.11. We await a full account in English of Barth's realism.

broad cultural terms. He conceives the project in response to 'an unprece-
dented and frenetic search for "reality"' (1984: 12) or as 'the darker stream
of the search for meaning' (1988: 45). Defending realism, especially in religion, is made more difficult by the fact that science confronts religion with
a 'crisis of authority' which means that religious texts and traditions cannot
be 'self-authenticating' (1988: 47). Peacocke sees the drawing of analogies
with questions of realism in science as a means of assessing the authenticity
of religious language and thus of putting religious claims on a properly
warranted footing. To correlate his scientific and theological concerns, he
proposes that critical realism has the conceptual role of a 'heuristic' or
'program for the natural sciences' (1988: 49, italics removed).[39]

In other words, realism's role is that of a policy guiding research. However, this conception is liable to distort both science and theology. As I
shall argue later, although realism *is* a kind of guiding policy or regulative principle in theology, theology is unlike science in the way that the
latter may be said to carry out research programmes guided by particular
hypotheses. To think that theology is analogous to science in this respect
is to risk being seriously misled.[40] The danger of distortion is particularly
evident when we apply Peacocke's view to science. Although he admits his
indebtedness to Ernan McMullin's 'formidable case for scientific realism'
(Peacocke 1988: 49), Peacocke ignores McMullin's careful defence of scientific realism (in the same paper from which he derives his own argument)
against its philosophical critics who

assume that defenders of realism are prescribing a strategy for scientists, a kind
of regulative principle that will separate the good from the bad among proposed
explanatory models ... The realism/antirealism debate has to do with the assessment of the existential implications of successful theories *already in place*. It is not
directed to strategies for *further* development ... the defender of realism must not
be saddled with a normative doctrine of the kind attributed here. (1984: 15–6)[41]

Following realism as a policy or programme for research (as Peacocke
suggests) could result in scientists prematurely rejecting theories which,

---

[39] 'Heuristic' is a technical term in Lakatosian philosophy of science. Heuristics 'are plans for future
   development of the [scientific research] program' (Murphy 1990: 60); Peacocke seems to have
   something like Murphy's definition in mind.

[40] *Pace* Murphy 1990, 1994.

[41] McMullin's view is quite close to that of Richard Boyd (1979) and middle-period Putnam, who
   regard scientific realism as an empirical hypothesis (see Putnam 1978: 4, 19ff, and compare Hacking
   1983: 21f, 26f, 262ff). Van Huyssteen (who is cautious about applying defences of scientific realism
   to theology) seems to want to have it both ways: whilst realism in theology is 'not yet quite an
   established theory of explanation but rather a very promising and suggestive hypothesis' (1988: 251),
   Christians also make 'basic realist assumptions' (1997: 41, cf. 1989: 159, 162).

whilst apparently implying non-realism, nevertheless have considerable promise for future enquiry.[42] Plainly, such a rejection would be bad scientific practice.

As we saw in chapter 3, non-realism is advocated by some philosophers of science because 'non-realist strategies often as not work out' (McMullin 1984: 15). Peacocke, however, cannot genuinely allow the possibility of non-realist interpretations being true in science because he is committed to defending both theological and global realism (his 'search for reality') on the basis of scientific realism *qua* research programme. The problem with this for his argument is that if scientific realism is rejected, so must global realism and theological realism. But in fact, Peacocke's attachment of global realism to scientific realism is unnecessary. Michael Dummett has shown that one can be a realist concerning one class of entity (macroscopic objects in the physical world, for example) and an anti-realist concerning others (say those of mathematics) without presuming 'that opting for an anti-realist view in one instance will demand the adoption of such a view in others' (1991: 16). Thus (quite apart from the question of whether scientific realism can meet a cultural demand for 'reality'), even if it is decided that realism is inappropriate to, say, quantum physics, and that it should not have the role of a research programme, realism in the Christian faith is not thereby disqualified.[43] This means that the case for the truth of realism in Christian faith is separable in principle from that of scientific realism and goes some way towards confirming my argument for the dependence of concepts of an ordered nature on Christology. McMullin reaches conclusions similar to my own. He states of Peacocke: 'I am not nearly as sanguine as Dr. Peacocke is about there being a doctrine of "critical realism" that applies in similar ways to both' science and theology, and wonders 'Why ... does he stress the commonality between science and theology when the methodological differences are so profound?' (1985: 39, 45).[44]

Realism as a practical postulate

Pragmatic arguments for realism as a practical postulate of Christian faith have been advocated explicitly by van Huyssteen and implicitly by Janet Martin Soskice. In defending his account of critical realism in theology, van

---

[42] A classic example here is the dispute between Albert Einstein (who was a kind of policy realist) and Niels Bohr over the now generally accepted (but from a realist point of view still deeply problematical) Copenhagen interpretation of quantum mechanics.

[43] Van Fraassen, though a non-realist in the philosophy of science, is a Catholic who seems to hold realist views of Christian faith: see 1993: 323f and cf. 1994b: 292.

[44] For a similar argument, but from a naturalistic outlook, see Drees 1996: 139–42, 144–8.

Huyssteen argues that 'Within the context of the epistemic claims and purposes of rational inquiry, realism ... is a practical postulate justified by its utility, and as such ultimately rests on a pragmatic basis' (1999: 216). However, this claim is open to attack on the ground that we have not been shown that utility requires us to accept realism as a postulate. Christian non-realists do not think that it is. In fact, they argue on pragmatic grounds that it is not. It may indeed be that theological realism has pragmatic utility, but the position under examination needs two further arguments if it is to be satisfactory: one that will show that utility is an argument for realism and another to outflank the pragmatic sceptic inclined towards a Christian non-realism or an atheistic naturalism. After all, many human beings manage to get by with a far more parsimonious ontology than realist Christianity implies.

Soskice begs the question in a similar way when she argues that 'realism is advocated for theology ... because so much of the Christian tradition has been undeniably realist in sensibility' (1985: 137). True though this is, if this really is why realism has to be defended, it is hard to see how Soskice could rebut Cupitt's pragmatic argument that although Christian faith has traditionally been realist, our autonomous sensibility now requires that we become non-realists. Perhaps Soskice and van Huyssteen are just behind the *Zeitgeist*. Perhaps a postmodern sensibility does favour the utility of non-realism. If so, the balance of the pragmatic argument could come down disfavouring realism. As Soskice herself admits, a Cupitt-type reinterpretation of Christian language 'would be perfectly consistent' (1985: 106).[45]

A further problem with arguing from practical utility is that Christians who are realists typically do not just want a spiritual path that enables them to negotiate life; they want a faith which offers a personal, noetic relationship with God as he really is. And such is Christian faith. God saved humanity from sin and death not merely because they have a low utility rating and promote dysfunctional life-styles but because he loves us and wants us to enjoy him for ever. To regard God's reality as a postulate of practical utility looks suspiciously like a realist version of an autonomous non-realism, as though what is theologically important is 'using God practically', as Anthony Freeman puts it (1993: 23).

Realism as an assumption of Christianity
Why not make a Cupittian reinterpretation of Christian faith? Soskice offers another reason for defending realism: 'traditional Christian belief has

---

[45] Cf. Barth's agreement with Feuerbach, 1957: 6.

been characterized by ... realist assumptions' (1985: 107). Echoing her, van Huyssteen suggests that 'a pragmatic form of critical realism ... purports to explain why it makes sense not to abandon some of the Christian faith's most basic realist assumptions' (1999: 217). These statements are incontestable insofar as they describe the traditional faith of the church. However, if the conceptual role of realism is that of an assumption of the church's faith, it is bound to seem that an argument from tradition is being used to beg the question in favour of realism. The question needs to be asked, Why should Christians be realists in any case? It is not obvious that saying that realism has been assumed in the past offers anything like a satisfactory answer to the sceptic.[46]

Realism as a necessary condition of rational faith
Theological realists sometimes structure their arguments in such a way as to give the impression that a successful defence of theological realism is a logically necessary warrant for Christian intellectual integrity.[47] However, given this general structure, it follows that if their arguments turned out to be invalid, the rational standing of central tracts of the Christian faith would be so defective that we should have to conclude first that religion does not 'tell us about a world that is real to *us*' (Peacocke 1984: 14), and second that if we chose to continue to use religious language, it might be wiser to reinterpret it on non-realist or naturalist lines.

The position advocated by the theological realists we have looked at so far is close to that advocated by Roger Trigg.[48] He argues for a kind of 'bootstrap' view according to which rationality and objective knowledge are only ultimately defensible on the basis of theism, though this position must itself be rationally grounded in metaphysical realism. As he says,

The nature of faith depends above all on the possible independent existence of what we have faith in. Faith cannot be a mere decision to live a certain kind of life, nor is it an arbitrary commitment. It must involve a specific belief about its object. Whether our faith is justified or not depends on whether that belief is true. It certainly may not be. The object of faith may not be as we conceive it to be, to the extent even of not existing. (1992: 35)

---

[46] It should be noted that my argument is not that all appeals to tradition as a reason for defending realism are mistaken. In a related context of debate Colin Gunton (1991: 18–19, cf. 28) implicitly appeals to tradition against Cupitt, but instead of assuming or presupposing God, he begins with God's prevenience.

[47] See, for example, Peacocke 1988: 47; Soskice 1985: 139; and Hebblethwaite 1988 *passim*, especially 37f.

[48] See Trigg 1992, 1998: 112–33, 175–95, 205–9.

For Trigg, 'the concept of a reality that is independent of thought [is] ... the foundation of human thought' (1989²: 220). In his *Reality at Risk: A Defence of Realism in Philosophy and the Sciences* (1989²), Trigg defends realism by showing the philosophical incoherences and cultural malaise which follow from banishing realism from this foundational role and seems to argue that realism has a kind of regulative function within our conceptual scheme. As will emerge shortly, some of this argument is quite close to my own view. However, there is a crucial difference in that Trigg thinks that in theological exposition of Christian faith, God's reality should not be taken as prevenient. To think that it is would be to allow the possibility of being deluded or of falling into the clutches of the fideist bogey-man. God's existence must be argued for: only if the object of faith is demonstrably as faith believes it to be can theism be true and belief be rational. This means that even though Trigg willingly admits the need for revelation, it cannot be self-authenticating but must always be tested at the bar of neutral reason.[49] Hence 'natural theology should not be regarded as a substitute for any particular revelation but as the necessary rational underpinning for the acceptance of any' (1998: 182).

The upshot appears to be that not just rational faith but also the reality of God and the truth of Christian belief are logically dependent on our proving them. From a theological perspective this seems mistaken for the simple reason that one can obey Christ's call to faith and know God's reality without *knowingly* being a realist, let alone being able to prove that realism is true. God's prevenient reality is the basis of Jesus' words to his disciples: 'Truly, I say to you, unless you turn and become like children, you will never enter the kingdom of heaven. Whoever humbles himself like [a] child, he is the greatest in the kingdom of heaven' (Matt. 18:3–4). This life of child-like trust certainly has noetic content, but the disposition of the heart and will is more important in securing it than having proficiency in the rules of inference or the right metaphysic.[50] Or would we disqualify the little ones from enjoying the saviour's embrace? At the end of his work on *Rationality and Religion* (1998: 214), Trigg writes that 'Without an ability to reason, we could never prepare ourselves for the possibility of a God who is revealed.' Such words, however well intended, cannot but appear profoundly offensive to any (relative of a) mentally handicapped person.[51]

Christian faith is given by God through Christ's call to discipleship, the manner of which call we cannot predict or predetermine: this is (part of)

---

[49] 1998: 178ff.   [50] Cf. John 7:16ff.   [51] On this question, see J. O'Donovan 1986.

what we mean when we say that God 'goes before' faith.[52] *A fortiori*, God's reality 'goes before' exposition or defence of a Christian realism. Although Christians should not be wilfully irrational, a Christian's (intellectual) integrity lies in Christ, not in the strength of her arguments.[53] The church offers conceptual elucidations and credal definitions of its faith without defending realism, as for centuries Patristic theology did. The Fathers could presuppose God's reality because they knew that God's reality precedes the faith they sought to commend and elucidate.[54]

The principal mistake in theological realism's understanding of the conceptual role of realism is that God is not allowed to 'go before' theology. His reality is secured as the conclusion of an argument set in motion by a desire to prop up a tradition and its sensibility. If Christian faith is realist in its sensibility, if it has been pervaded by realist assumptions, if Western culture has been realist, and if a realist metaphysic is possible, this is because God, the *ens realissimum*, is prevenient.

Realism and Christian faith

Realism expresses an ontological commitment to God's prevenience
Realism plays two roles in Christian faith. The first is that it gives conceptual expression to an ontological commitment to the prevenience of the God who calls humanity to faith in Christ. We have already seen something of what this amounts to in our observations in chapters 4 and 5 concerning Christian practices. God's action whereby he reveals himself as the intended grammar of human practices enables and therefore 'goes before' the corresponding human response, and these responses are *ipso facto* ontological commitments to the prevenient reality of God.

We can begin to see what this means by differentiating between scientists and theologians in the following way. When scientists theorize about unobservable entities, they tender *hypothetical* ontological commitments which are made good only if subsequent experimentation produces data which confirm their theories. Yet even this way of putting it risks prematurely conceding too much to the truth of scientific realism. In the philosophy of science, realism is widely regarded as an empirical hypothesis to the effect that the best explanation of the success of science's seeming to make good

---

[52] *Contra* Trigg, this is why Christian faith as God's gift cannot be either an 'arbitrary commitment' or a 'mere decision'.
[53] I take this to be implied by Col. 3:1–10. Cf. Augustine 1978: 6.5.
[54] See, for example, Origen 1965: 1.2. I use the word 'presuppose' advisedly; the reason will become clear shortly.

its hypothetical commitments is that reality really is constituted by enti- ties, and relations between entities, as these are modelled in its theories.[55] Thus, whatever scientists' practices, philosophically speaking their onto- logical commitments are best regarded as seeking progressively stronger confirmation.[56]

By contrast, from a theological point of view, God's proleptically com- plete revelation in Christ means that a Christian's ontological commitments are much firmer than a scientist's. As we saw in chapter 3, theology cannot have new data surpassing what has already been revealed in Jesus Christ, transmitted by the Holy Spirit, and given to the church in scripture.[57] It follows that when Christians formulate doctrine, their work should not be construed as akin to scientific theorizing. Christian faith's ontological com- mitments concerning the prevenience of the triune God are closed in a way that science's ontological commitments to the entities postulated by its the- ories cannot be. Physicists may anticipate that, having developed a theory that unites electromagnetism with gravity, they will have a Grand Unified Theory, but they would cease to be scientists if they seriously thought that there could in principle be no new data which might require the theory to be modified or even replaced. Theologians seek to elucidate the truth given in revelation, they do so in the context of the church's contemporary debates, and they use whatever fitting conceptual resources lie at hand, but revelation in Christ rules out, for example, the expectation that trinitarian doctrine be replaced by 'quadritarian' doctrine.[58]

So, we should not construe a Christian's ontological commitments on analogy with (the philosophy of) science. If doctrines really are akin to scientific theories, then Christian discipleship and theology are debarred from operating with their particular kinds of ontological commitment to God's prevenient reality. They must make their commitment in a merely hypothetical rather than unqualified way and wait and see if it will be made good.[59] Moreover, since theology cannot admit the possibility of there be- ing new data in the sense required by science, a scientifically construed account of theological realism will never be able to argue for realism on the terms in which it is argued in science, i.e. that realism is the best expla- nation of the continuing success of science in predicting and discovering new data.[60] As McMullin concludes in his survey of four types of theology,

---

[55] See, for example, Boyd 1985: 3; Putnam 1978: 123; and van Huyssteen's astonishing concession to empiricism: 1997: 101–2.

[56] Cf. McMullin 1984: 11 and Drees 1996: 138.   [57] See pp. 45–6 above.

[58] Some evangelicals seem seriously to entertain that it could be: see Stackhouse 2000: 45f.

[59] Cf. Luke. 9:57–62.   [60] See pp. 28–9.

'none ... sustains the "best explanation" form of argument for realism that works in science' (1985: 43). Theologians who imply an assimilation of the role of realism in Christian faith to its role in (the philosophy of) science seem to face two possibilities. Their work will either be self-subverting because their methodology involves changing a firm ontological commitment into a merely hypothetical one, or it will go the whole scientific hog, deny its essential nature as a revealed faith, put itself on the same standing as science, and wait patiently for the results to come in.

Don Cupitt implicitly recognizes this dilemma in the passage quoted earlier in the section on ontology.[61] His resolution of it in favour of non-realism is instructive. Cupitt's outlook, like that of theological realists, is shaped by empiricism, but he sees what they do not: if we wish to uphold a realist account of Christianity which accepts the empiricist terms in which the debate is usually set, theology must surrender to a scientific conception of fact, and with it to the destruction of traditional orthodoxy. However, since realism leads to heteronomy it is not worth salvaging, so, for the sake of preserving Christianity as religion, Cupitt opts for autonomous expressivism. It is arguable that philosophical scepticism is parasitic upon an epistemic realism which is reactive against the legacy of empiricism.[62] In a similar way, Cupitt's non-realism is parasitic on an epistemically construed theological realism.[63] This dependency can be illustrated from his reinterpretation of 'the will of God'. Unless he had already encountered the phrase in its realist context, he would not have been able to revise it to mean the 'unconditional religious requirement' and 'an autonomous inner imperative that urges us to fulfil our highest possible destiny as spiritual, self-conscious beings emerging from nature' (1980: 94–5). Cupitt's non-realism and his understanding of autonomy are logically and conceptually dependent upon realist Christianity.[64] Non-realism relies on a covert admission of God's prevenience and an ontological commitment which is as coherent as that of the psalmist's 'fool'.[65]

The distinguished philosopher John Searle calls the kind of ontologically committed outlook I am favouring 'external realism' (which he abbreviates to ER). He defines it as the view that 'The world (or alternatively, reality or the universe) exists independently of our representations of it' (1995: 150). He then explains that

---

[61] See p. 179. [62] See M. Williams 1993 and Craig 1993. [63] See Cupitt 1997: 17.
[64] Cupitt is in a line of modern thinkers who systematically reinterpret and subvert the rules of Christian discourse about divine sovereignty and human agency in order to circumvent problems supposed to derive from it: for a detailed analysis see Tanner 1988.
[65] Pss. 14:1, 53:1.

ER is a purely formal constraint. It does not say how things are but only that there is a way that they are that is independent of our representations ... [O]ur ordinary linguistic practices presuppose external realism ... Pretheoretically we take external realism for granted, and for that reason it need not be a belief, but is prior to having beliefs. (1995: 188, 194, 195)

In asserting that ER 'does not say how things are', Searle is taking care not to allow any epistemic content into his argument, for this would open the door to idealism or scepticism. His claim 'is about conditions of *intelligibility*, not about conditions of *knowledge*' (195).

Although it might not be the last word against critics of realism in philosophy, Searle's position is worth discussing at this point, for it can help us to refine our understanding of the relationship between realism and epistemology in Christian faith. Whereas Searle carefully separates the two, it seems to me unlikely that a Christian can.[66] When God reveals himself in the call to follow Christ, he not only reveals *that* he is, but also reveals *who* he is, that he is *Lord*. Therefore, in responding to this call, Christian faith is created and enabled to make an ontological commitment which unavoidably has an epistemic component. However, since this component is a gift and its reliability is underwritten by God's covenant faithfulness in Jesus, the veracity of realism is not dependent on the success or failure of our attempts to prove it, for example, by arguments for epistemic access to God. This means that, when properly understood (i.e. on the basis of God's prevenient reality), realist Christian faith can be regarded as conveying epistemic content prior to our articulating that content and without the attendant risk of radical scepticism. In his ontological precedence, God is a perfect integrity of act and being; so, when he reveals himself, the epistemic content he gives to faith will stand for all eternity, for this content is that he is *YHWH*, *ehyeh asher ehyeh*, Emmanuel, the God who by his Spirit abides in, with, through, and alongside us.

In calling us to be redeemed *imagines Dei*, God creates and provides the ontological and epistemic conditions for our representing his independent reality. This does not mean that whatever knowledge of God faith professes is always true. Human beings are fallen; a shadow falls between their finite cognitive claims and the infinite divine reality. But so long as disciples are available to God, he will separate their wheat from their chaff and make of their representations that which will glorify him forever.

Thus, the crucial difference between Searle's external realism and my Christocentric realism lies in the fact that revelation is a necessary condition

---

[66] This is not to deny that the orders of being and knowing need to be carefully distinguished and priority given to the former.

of Christians having the ontological commitments they do. This can be clarified by developing the distinction between the role of realism as a philosophical outlook in our conceptual scheme and the reality of God as something which is shown in Christian practices. Searle writes of realism being 'presupposed' and 'taken for granted' but does not distinguish between them. However, this distinction needs to be drawn if we are to avoid the confusions made by theological realism about the role of realism in Christian faith and theology. I have suggested that being a Christian does not *entail* defending realism, which is to say (in Searle's terms), that taking realism for granted 'is prior to having beliefs'. Theologically speaking this taking for granted amounts to an ontological commitment to God's reality preceding Christian faith. This is not the same as *presupposing* God's reality, since such a presupposition would play the role of a self-referring postulate of theology.

However, there is a sense in which it is correct to speak of realism as a presupposition. Doctrinal and philosophical expressions of Christian faith are acts of thought which reflect conceptually on God's self-giving in Christ and the church's witness to that event. Thus, when Christians do theology, it *is* appropriate to talk of realism as a presupposition of that conceptual and reflective activity. It upholds Christianity's ontological commitment to God's prevenient reality; it prevents that commitment becoming essentially self-referring.

Realism is regulative
Another way of describing Cupitt's understanding of 'the will of God' is to say that he uses non-realism as a meta-rule governing the 'first-order' language of Christian faith. This finding is entirely to be expected in the light of my discussion of Christian non-realist practices in chapter 5, where I introduced the idea of realism as a regulative concept or meta-rule on analogy with Paul's teaching about the Lord's Supper. Thus my second suggestion concerning the role of realism in Christian faith reiterates the claim that we should regard it as just such a regulative concept or meta-rule operating over Christian faith.

In the terminology I introduced in chapter 5, we can say that the role of realism in Christian faith is to ensure that Christians give proper expression (conceptual and other) to God's ontological and epistemic prevenience as the intended grammar of those practices through which he shows his independent reality. The concept of 'realism' cannot express God's independent reality by itself, for, as Dalferth puts it, 'Regulative ideas are not concepts of things, but instructions on how to relate to and use that which we conceive and do not conceive in particular ways' (1999: 128). Concepts which function regulatively facilitate those practices in which the phenomena they serve can show themselves. As a regulative concept operative over all Christian practices, realism reminds us of the ontological commitment to the triune God implied by discipleship and it instructs us so to interpret doctrine as not to deny God's independent reality. Realism is, in Searle's terms, 'a purely formal constraint': it does not add to the concept of God or to the practices of Christianity.[67]

To understand more fully what I have in mind when I suggest that realism has these two conceptual roles in Christian faith, remember that unless we are philosophers or eccentrics, the 'prevenience' of reality over our engagement with it is unproblematical.[68] We operate with ontological commitments to there being a reality independent of ourselves, and more often than not, our commitments are borne out by experience. When we go rock climbing, we know that we had better not take risks on the basis of a gamble that gravity might be weaker than usual today. There is 'that to which we cannot avoid relating' (Peacocke 1988: 47), and our appreciation of this prevents us from doing crazy things. A rock climber makes an ontological commitment to 'prevenient' reality before embarking on a pitch. She estimates the quality and texture of the rock, the size and reliability of holds, the shape of cracks in which she hopes to place protection, and the trustworthiness of her belayer. If she is inclined to reflect on such technicalities of the physics of climbing as 'fall factors' and 'impact forces', then her explanations of these things can be said to *presuppose* realism, but this presupposing will only amount to giving conceptual expression to the realism which showed itself in her climbing. Here, realism is not a further factor which needs explaining alongside or before reflection on 'impact forces'; still less is it a necessary condition of her going climbing. In this sense, realism is a 'purely formal constraint' which is regulative over the conceptual expression of the physics of climbing; it is a meta-rule which reminds us when we theorize not to forget the ontological commitments we made when we set foot on rock and before we asked about physics.

Realism becomes problematical as soon as we forget its roles as expressive of an ontological commitment and as a regulative presupposition of conceptual expressions of our commitments. As we have seen, Cupitt and the Sea of Faith Movement recognize that realism is a regulative conception in Christianity, but when they make non-realism a meta-rule regulative over the whole of Christian faith, their position becomes incoherent, for

[67] Non-realism's parasitic nature is shown in that it applies non-realism as a meta-rule that is a materially substantive constraint: it alters the Christian concept of God along with its practices.
[68] Recall Searle's statement that '[p]retheoretically we take external realism for granted' (1995: 194).

it involves them in denying what they must already have assumed. If they were climbers, it would be as though they were to say, not just that realism does not constrain their explanation of the physics of climbing, but that climbers can and should ignore the constraints reality imposes.[69] But reality will not be insulted; gravity will have its way.

CONCLUSION

Reality shows itself in our practices. God's reality 'goes before' faith, and it is shown through the lives of those who exercise faith. The life and ministry of Jesus is the defining instance of this, but we should not forget that down through the centuries the same ontological commitments that Jesus made have been shown in the life of his disciples. The church has learned that sometimes Christians are called to bear witness to their master by taking up their own cross and dying a martyr's death. The pattern of self-sacrificial offering learned in eucharistic anamnesis is then repeated most profoundly and its intended grammar most fully evident. In the hour of their death, martyrs have found a ground of unquenchable hope in God's future and given testimony of his reality to others.

The killing of Dietrich Bonhoeffer illustrates this. As he went down to be executed, he is recorded as saying, 'This is the end – for me the beginning of life' (Bethge 1970: 830). The doctor who witnessed his death did not know who Bonhoeffer was, but evidently his manner and bearing made a lasting impression on him. Ten years later he wrote the following words:

Through the half open door in one room of the huts I saw Pastor Bonhoeffer, before taking off his prison garb, kneeling on the floor praying fervently to his God. I was most deeply moved by the way this lovable man prayed, so devout and so certain that God heard his prayer. At the place of execution, he again said a short prayer and then climbed the steps to the gallows, brave and composed. His death ensued after a few seconds. In almost fifty years that I worked as a doctor, I have hardly ever seen a man die so entirely submissive to the will of God. (H. Fischer-Hüllstrung, in Zimmermann and Gregor Smith 1966: 232, quoted by Bethge 1970: 830–1)

We cannot prove whether Bonhoeffer really died in submission to the will of God or was just expressing 'an autonomous inner imperative'. Nor can we verify whether his death was vain and futile. Yet faith testifies that it was

---

[69] The former climber Paul Pritchard testifies ironically to the absurdity of ignoring reality's constraints when, writing of a very hard and dangerous climb, he describes how, by 'Using [the] meditation . . . "I am weightless. I have no mass", even the most dreadful R[ealized] U[ltimate] R[eality] P[iton] placement could be forced into offering some support' (1997: 82).

not, and that through it God's mysterious ways in judgement and grace were shown. He died not just because he was a disciple who had accepted the cost of discipleship; he was killed because sinful men could not bear to have their actions exposed to the light of God shining in the lives of Christians. He was 'killed to cover up the reality of the world'.[70]

The survival of the church in the face of persecution testifies to the grace God offers the world. But it is not only the world that needs grace. The church's practices can become corrupt and its own arguments and divisions can become the means whereby God testifies to himself.[71] Remember Hugh Latimer's words to Nicholas Ridley in Oxford on 16 October 1555: 'We shall this day light such a candle, by God's grace, in England, as I trust shall never be put out.' His dying testimony flares with hope. It still has power to move the heart of a theologian working a stone's throw from where Latimer and Ridley were burned and makes him wonder, Is theology written today as a witness only to quirks of chance and blind necessity, to the waning power of an ancient myth, or is something other shown through it?

[70] Thus the Jesuit Jon Sobrino of the death of six of his companion priests in El Salvador as reported by Jim Wallis during a conference at the Oxford Centre for Mission Studies, 25 April 1991.

[71] Consider Donald MacKinnon's comparison of the Austrian sacristan and martyr Franz Jägerstätter and Bishop Defregger: the latter carried on 'the business of living only at the cost of a cultivated neglect of its ultimate demands ... The Jägerstätters of this world sit in judgement upon the Defreggers, though the former earn a martyr's death and the latter episcopal dignity' (1979: 107, 111).

CHAPTER 8

Speaking the reality of God

MARTYRDOM AND THE END OF CHRISTIAN LIFE

A martyr's death is an act of worship offered to God in praise of the one by whose stripes we are healed; it is also a prophetic act which, by virtue of its being responsive to Christ's call to bear witness to him, is directed towards the church and the world. From both perspectives it is an eloquent act speaking of the fallenness of created reality and of its teleological ordering towards God as its ultimate fulfilment.

Germain Grisez observes in his discussion of martyrdom that 'In a world fallen and redeemed, human fulfilment is only possible by sharing in the fulfilment of the risen Lord Jesus' (1983: 652). It is precisely because the integrity of human personhood is ontologically dependent on Jesus' willingness to undergo disintegrating death for his loved ones that the consciousness of the disciple is shaped by a radical decentring and disintegration which finds integration in the crucified and risen Jesus.[1] As a practice consequent upon Jesus' invitation to take up one's cross and follow him, Christian witness and the martyr's death to which it sometimes leads is as absolute a repudiation of autonomy as one could imagine. The martyr's last act draws to a culmination the setting of mind and desires on 'things that are above': the martyr has learned to know Christ and to be confident that one's life is 'hidden with Christ in God' (Col. 3:2f). Imprisoned in Rome, Paul contemplates the very real possibility that he might be called to a martyr's death and writes that 'to me, living is Christ and dying is gain' (Phil. 1:21). So, because martyrdom speaks of the end of human life as being found in the God who, even when we were dead in sin, raised us with Christ,[2] it is not a Manichaean rejection of the goodness of created life. In expressing the orientation of the martyr's life it is also a means whereby God addresses the world. He acts 'interruptively' into it, calling it to repentance and new life in him. Just as Jesus' death brought the church to life, so too have

---

[1] Col. 3:1ff; cf. Jenson 1982: 178f; Westphal 1992.   [2] Cf. Rom. 5–6, 8.

martyrs' deaths sustained and renewed the church's witness to and hope in the independent reality of a God who is simultaneously profoundly engaged with it.[3]

The faith expressed by word and deed throughout a Christian's life is extended to vanishing point in martyrdom, for such is the *telos* of all Christian witness: all Christians, not just martyrs, stake their all on God's vindication. The whole meaning of a Christian's, and *a fortiori* a martyr's, life as a redeemed *imago Dei* is focussed in hope on God's eschatologically verifying his trust by raising him to be with Christ. If that verification should not be forthcoming, then, whilst a martyr's death might be consistent with the myth that shaped it, it is a vain act shaped by a futile faith. Of course, this is something which we cannot ascertain: we cannot peek behind the veil separating time and eternity to see whether God will vindicate our faith; we can only trust to the measure that the Holy Spirit gives us faith to act. This is why Christian ontological commitments are most urgently expressed in a martyrdom: it is an act of integrity only if it expresses the sovereign rule of the independently real God.[4]

A martyr's death is an act of worship in praise and prophecy which, because they are orientated to the glory of God, are paradigmatic forms of Christian speech.[5] I have written of martyrdom as a deed which *speaks* with the intention of hinting at the way in which *acts* can be regarded as speaking and, in this particular context, at the way in which God can be regarded as speaking in and through a martyr by reorientating the church and the world to himself. God shows his reality by speaking, partly but not exclusively, through Christian acts. How this comes about is the subject of this chapter.

SPEECH ACT THEORY

Speech act theory, developed by the post-war Oxford philosopher J. L. Austin, has had less impact on discussions of Christian language than might be expected.[6] This is surprising, principally because its root idea – that

---

[3] See Kreider 1995: 13.

[4] See here Gooch's *Reflections on Jesus and Socrates* (1996), from which it emerges that Socrates' belief in the immortality of the soul makes him, in Plato's rendering, '*less human* than the Jesus of the Gospels', who faces death as 'the loss of the self' (272, 298).

[5] And, so far as it is redeemed, of all human speech too: cf. Ps. 138:4–6; Isa. 45:23; Rom. 14:11.

[6] Notable exceptions are Donald Evans 1963; McClendon and Smith 1994; Vanhoozer 1998 and Watson 1994: 140–51. Other theological uses of the theory include Lindbeck 1984; Thiemann 1985: 99–111; Wolterstorff 1995; Patrick 1999. Anthony Thiselton has used it in theological hermeneutics: see his 1992.

speech is a kind of action – appears to lend itself readily to articulating a Christian doctrine of God which understands him as one whose actions (in creation, for example) are often performed by speaking.

We get a hint of the potential usefulness of the theory for a Christocentric realism in the contrast Donald Evans draws (in his pioneering theological work on speech act theory) between designative (or 'propositional') accounts of language and his own. The latter is based on the Bible's

account of divine revelation (God's 'word' to man) and ... its account of human religious language (man's word to God). In each case the language or 'word' is not (or is not merely) propositional; it is primarily a *self-involving activity*, divine or human. God does not (or does not merely) provide supernatural information concerning himself, expressed in flat statements of fact; he 'addresses' man in an 'event' or 'deed' which commits him to man and which expresses his inner self. Similarly man does not (or does not merely) assert certain facts about God; he addresses God in the activity of worship, committing himself to God and expressing his attitude to God. (1963: 14)

The relationship of which Evans writes is the covenant between God and humanity. As I have already argued, this is the context in which to understand that it is as redeemed *imagines Dei* that humans are able to represent God. This has happened proleptically in Christ, so, since humanity's fulfilment lies in worshipping its maker, it is natural to try to locate a realist account of Christian language in this mutually self-involving relationship between God and humanity.

First, we need to look more closely at speech act theory. In everyday life, language is used not only to refer, describe, designate, report, inform, and so on, but also to bring about new circumstances. We *perform* deeds by means of language as well as *state* things in it: priests marry a couple by presiding over their mutual consent and covenant promises and by *declaring* them to be husband and wife; judges *pronounce* sentence in the very act of so doing. We speak in order thereby to perform actions: we warn, request, promise, confess, order, proclaim, worship, command, direct, criticize, forgive, request, and so on. Austin calls an utterance involving such actions an 'illocutionary' act, and he defines it as the 'performance of an act in saying something' (1975^2: 99).

Not only do we act by speaking, but we are also the subjects of others' speech acts: we are convinced, persuaded, married, edified, inspired, worshipped, and so on. Austin calls speech that achieves such effects 'perlocutionary' acts, and he defines them as 'what we bring about or achieve by saying something' (109). Austin does not forget that speech acts also involve 'the utterance of [certain words] with a certain "meaning" in the favourite philosophical sense of that word, i.e. with a certain sense and a certain reference', and this he calls 'the performance of a locutionary act' (94). For reasons argued by Austin's pupil John Searle, I shall call the meaning of a speech act its 'propositional content'.[7]

Now, illocutionary acts are very diverse, but they can be broken down into a small number of categories, and both Austin and Searle offer taxonomies of them. In my argument I shall use Searle's, which, along with their corresponding illocutionary points and some verbs denoting typical examples, is as follows:[8]

'*Assertives* ... commit the speaker to something's being the case, to the truth of the expressed proposition' (1979: 12). For example, to assert, conclude, deduce, judge, praise, preach, state, testify, witness.

'*Directives* ... are attempts ... by the speaker to get the hearer to do something' (1979: 13). For example, to adopt, appoint, beg, bless, choose, consecrate, convict, curse, decree, defy, exhort, forgive, hallow, intercede, inspire, invite, justify, ordain, order, pardon, plead, pray, preach, rebuke, reproach, request, send, urge.

'*Commissives* ... commit the speaker ... to some future course of action' (1979: 14). For example, to acknowledge, adopt, bless, give, intercede, love, magnify, obey, pledge, preach, promise, repent, swear, testify, trust, witness, worship.

'*Expressives* ... express our feelings and attitudes' (1979: viii, cf. 15). For example, to appeal, confess, cry, complain, comfort, encourage, entrust, intercede, love, magnify, mourn, praise, pray, preach, repent, thank, worship.

'*Declarations*'. 'It is the defining characteristic of this class that the successful performance of one of its members brings about the correspondence between the propositional content and reality, successful performance guarantees that the propositional content corresponds to the world' (1979: 16–17). For example, to acquit, correct, declare, judge, justify, love, pardon, preach, proclaim, reckon. Note that Searle adds to this class that of 'assertive declarations' where assertives are 'issued with the force of declarations' (1979: 20, 19). For example, when the referee calls a player 'off side', an assertion is made which, even if false, carries the force of incurring a penalty.

Some of the examples occur in more than one category (and one in all); this is because the same speech act can have more than one illocutionary force. Thus, interceding for someone has the force of *expressing* one's feelings about the object or person of concern (expressive act) as well as of *asking*

---

[7] See Searle 1969: 23 n. 1, 29f.   [8] Many of the examples are from Thiselton 1992: 299.

God to bring about what we ask (directive act); it is also self-involving in the sense that, for example, in praying for missionary work, God might call the intercessor to work as a mission partner (commissive act). Overlap can also occur in the case of declarations: for example, for a judge to pronounce a person guilty, she must have ascertained the facts, and therefore the judgement combines the illocutionary force of an assertive and a declaration.

A further reason for overlap is that contextual, extra-linguistic, and institutional factors significantly affect an expression's illocutionary force. This is a particularly important feature of declarations, the successful performance of which usually requires that

there must exist an extra-linguistic institution and the speaker and hearer must occupy special places within this institution. It is only given such institutions as the church, the law, private property, the state and a special position of the speaker and hearer within these institutions that one can excommunicate, appoint, give and bequeath one's possessions or declare war. (Searle 1979: 18)

Extra-linguistic institutions are constituted by rules which confer a status on speakers in virtue of which they can bring about what Searle calls 'institutional facts' (1983: 172). Thus, in our society, not just anyone can declare a couple husband and wife; for a marriage to have legal and social recognition it must have been solemnized by a properly authorized person. Declarations are therefore only effective in particular contexts. Status need not be conferred by institutions, however, though it can still be relevant to a speaker's successfully bringing about a perlocutionary effect. For example, an armed robber can steal a car by ordering its owner to hand over the keys whilst holding a gun to his head.[9] God's declarations are exceptional in not requiring an institutional context, and Searle refers to these as 'supernatural declarations' (1983: 172, cf. 167; 1979: 18): for example, in virtue of his status, God can declare 'Let there be light', and thereby bring about a non-institutional fact in the absence of external institutional conditions.[10]

We come now to the topic of 'direction of fit' between words and world in speech acts. This will be important later. Searle, who introduced the idea, explains that '[s]ome illocutions have as part of their illocutionary point to get the words (more strictly, their propositional content) to match the world, others to get the world to match the words' (1979: 3). When a judge pronounces a person guilty, her words – for example, 'Jimmy James, I pronounce you guilty of armed robbery' – are an assertive the propositional

---

[9] Searle 1979: 7.
[10] Theologically speaking there is an *internal* institutional condition, and this is God's eternal resolve to be faithful to himself.

content of which (Jimmy James is guilty of armed robbery) states how things are in the world. Her words are conformed to the world: they have what Searle calls *word-to-world* direction of fit. When she says 'I sentence you to five years' imprisonment' her words are a declaration with the illocutionary point of bringing the world into conformity with her words: they have *world-to-word* direction of fit, so Jimmy is sent to prison. Achieving a desired direction of fit is usually part of the point of an illocution.

From a consideration of the different types of illocution, we get the following pattern of conformity between word and world: assertives have word-to-world direction of fit. Directives are world-to-word: they are, for example, attempts to get our hearer to obey us and thereby conform himself to the desire expressed in our words. Commissives are world-to-word: we promise to bring something about, to conform the world to our words. Expressives have no direction of fit: 'the speaker is neither trying to get the world to match the words nor the words to match the world; rather the truth of the expressed proposition is presupposed ... the utterance can't get off the ground unless there already is a fit' (1979: 15, 18). Declarations are unusual in possessing both directions of fit, though if there is no assertive element (as when declaring a couple husband and wife), they function by bringing a direction of fit into being: the world is brought into conformity with the words.

Speech act theory is more concerned with the pragmatics of language than with semantics; that is, with how speakers *use* words rather than with how words have meaning *qua* lexical entities. Such a view is naturally congenial to my stress on the practices and grammar of Christian faith. The linguistic questions the realism debate throws up become relatively less important and much more tractable if the burden of the argument is shifted away from concerns with our linguistic representation of God and onto his making us capable of representing him in virtue of his act of redeeming us. My argument is therefore more concerned to elucidate the theological and spiritual context in which questions of representation, meaning, and reference have their vitality than to attempt to deal with the latter issues in a directly philosophical way. The introduction of speech act theory is intended to promote the modest theological task of *describing what* we do when we use Christian language rather than *explaining how* we can or should do it. Many accounts of theological language appear to try to arrive at a theory, the successful implementation of which will enable us to speak of God. This seems to me to be fundamentally flawed (and not just because of its theological elitism). That we can speak of God is owing to his grace in incorporating us into Christ; it is not because we have discovered or invented and then applied the correct theory. So if my argument has any prescriptive force, it should arise only from the fact that understanding what we *are* doing sometimes help us see what we *should* be doing.

SPEECH ACTS AND THE PROMISES OF GOD

We can begin to connect speech act theory with Christocentric realism by noticing the importance of speaker's intention in making illocutionary acts. In his work on *Intentionality* (1983), Searle develops an account of meaning according to which 'certain fundamental semantic notions such as meaning are analysable in terms of even more fundamental psychological notions such as belief, desire and intention' (1983: 161).[11] Thus, to perform an illocutionary act, the utterer must have the intention of bringing about what she wishes, desires, hopes etc. Searle indicates the basic or conceptually primitive role of intentions in speech acts by pointing out that whilst we can ask what a sentence means, it makes no sense to ask the meaning of, say, a belief or a desire: the answer will simply direct us back to the intention.[12] We can develop this line of thought a bit further: when we want to ask for the meaning of an intention, this is because we have not understood the speech act by which it was expressed. Thus, considering God's choosing his people, we have fully understood the reason why when we are told that he called them because he loved them and is faithful to his covenant. We cannot usefully go on asking for further, occult reasons behind God's election; his intention to be himself in his relationship with his people – that is, to be love – is fully expressed in the speech act of making an everlasting covenant with Abraham to bless all the nations of the earth.[13] Since intentions are expressed in actions, it is a mistake 'to construe "intention" as a matter of "having certain mental processes" which can usually be observed only by introspection' (Thiselton 1992: 558). God's intentions are expressed in his actions, and their meaning is expressed in them too.

God's purpose/intention is revealed in the commissive speech act of promising to be Abraham's and his descendants' God, and this act is performed in the extra-linguistic and institutional context of covenant making. Thus the making of the covenant should be regarded as a declarative speech act in which the relationship between God and humanity expressed in it is thereby brought about. This declaration is 'supernatural' in the sense that before God made it in the primordial speech act of creation there existed no divine–human institutional context in which it could be lived out; it is based solely on God's own covenant faithfulness.

[11] For discussion of the relation between psychological concepts and language about God, see Alston 1989: 64–80.
[12] Searle 1983: 27–8.   [13] Gen. 12:3, 17:1–8.

In declaring his covenant, God purposes to be himself in his relationship with his people by making a promise to them. The speech act of promising is crucially important in theology, for it is at the heart of God's nature as well as his relationship with humanity and our faithful response to him. As Paul puts it, 'all God's promises find their Yes in' Adam's antitype, Jesus Christ (2 Cor. 1:20). Paul's assertion is based upon the logical and material prevenience of God's self-utterance. We can therefore paraphrase *ehyeh asher ehyeh* in terms drawn from speech act theory: in his self-expression as 'I am who I am', God can be understood as the paradigmatic assertive speech act: he is who he asserts he is; he corresponds with himself. God's self-expression is in conformity with who he is: he is the perfection of word-to-world direction of fit. As 'I will be who I will be', God can be understood as the paradigmatic commissive speech act: he commits himself to be who he will be in his own future so that he will be the perfection of world-to-word direction of fit.

Part of God's being who he is/will be is his yoking himself to his covenant partner, but exactly what this means for his people is opaque to them. God has to be taken at his word. For the great ones of salvation history – Abraham, Moses, Zechariah and Mary,[14] Jesus, Paul and Peter, for example – faith and self-abandonment to God's purposes are the indispensable conditions of participating in the fulfilment of the promise. Consider the example of Moses. In his exegesis of the revelation of the divine name at Exod. 3, Seitz argues that

Though God tells Moses ... that this is his name ... we must wait until the second divine encounter to learn just what the name means – or will mean. In this sense, even Ex. 6:2–9 does not report the revelation of God as YHWH so much as anticipate it. In the events of the exodus God will be fully known as YHWH. (1998: 244–5)

Thus, only on the basis of the exodus event can 'the final [*asher ehyeh*] of "I am who I will be" [find] its proper content: "I am YHWH your God who brought you out of the land of Egypt" (Ex. 20:2)' (245).

In the technical terms I introduced at the end of chapter 6, we can see that the revelation of the divine name to Moses at the burning bush has assertive and promissory elements whose semantic meaning is apparent to Moses (he can understand the words), but whose teleological meaning is carried by God's intention to fulfil his promise – to be who he will be.

---

[14] Remember that Zechariah could (for good reason) not believe and so became mute. Later, when with the gift of a son, he responded obediently and named his son John, '[i]mmediately his mouth was opened and his tongue freed, and he began to speak, praising God' (Luke 1:64, cf. verses 8–20). Mary, on the other hand, believed the word and became *theotokos* (Luke 1:26ff, cf. 11:27–8).

Moses cannot understand the full meaning of the promise: it is teleologically suspended. God *asserts* his name and nature, but the *promissory* aspect of God's disclosure is simultaneously suggestive of his hiddenness. Moses has to trust God when he tells Pharaoh and the Hebrews of God's promise of deliverance. As Seitz says earlier in his discussion, 'neither we nor Moses is prepared to understand such a "name" ... because what God will be, and is most essentially, has not yet been made manifest' (239, *sic*). However, through the exodus God makes good the intention expressed in the promise, and thus its full meaning is given only in these events. As he says to Moses before the exodus, 'I will take you as my people and I will be your God. You shall know that I am the LORD your God, who has freed you from the burdens of the Egyptians' (Exod. 6:7). Thus, when God meets Moses at Sinai after the exodus, his words of introduction – 'I am YHWH your God who brought you out of the land of Egypt' – convey the narrative meaning of the promise which had been teleologically suspended until God fulfilled his word. Moses can now be said to understand fully the promise given him at the burning bush. God's identity as YHWH is given through the events in which he is who he will be in making good his promise. He shows his independent reality by his sovereignty over history in setting his people free to love and worship him. The paradigmatic instance of this for Christians is the Christ-event.

CALVARY AND THE TELEOLOGICAL SUSPENSION OF MEANING

Jesus as hearer and fulfiller of the promise

Whilst the distinctions between semantic, teleological, narrative, and full meaning are proposed as a contribution to theological rather than philosophical discussions of language, there are some interesting parallels between my theological account and that offered by some recent works in the philosophy of language. The most important point informing my account is that established by Wittgenstein: linguistic meaning is to be understood, not principally as a 'private', mental phenomenon but as a public, communal, and activity-focussed one.[15] Second, some developments in speech act theory point in a similar direction to my theological argument. For example, François Recanati defends separating semantic and pragmatic aspects of language use in developing a theory of meaning, distinguishes utterance meaning from sentence meaning, and argues that 'the meaning of an utterance

---

[15] See Hacker 1997: 245–75, especially 250f. Craig 1997 offers a view opposed to Wittgenstein's which is relevant to the question of realism.

[is] the state of affairs it represents or the conditions that must hold in order for it to be "satisfied" ' (1987: 10). The second half of Recanati's claim here has affinities with my suggestion that the full meaning of a promise is teleologically suspended until it is made good. Recanati goes on to defend Austin's distinction[16] between the 'meaning' and the 'illocutionary force' (promising, for example) of an utterance:

If, in virtue of the meaning it expresses, an utterance presents itself as having a particular illocutionary force, there is no certainty that it really does have the force that it has (more or less explicitly) attributed to itself. Taken in Austin's sense, the force of an utterance must always go beyond its meaning; the latter includes a 'projection' of the utterance's illocutionary force, not the force itself, which must be inferred by the hearer on the basis of the supposed intentions of the speaker. (27)

For a promise to be uttered successfully, the intention expressed in uttering it must be satisfied. Putting oneself under an obligation to bring about what one has promised is a central feature of promising.[17] In the case of God's promises, this implicates not only his faithfulness to his covenant with creation but also his faithfulness to himself. God's promises are fully meaningful only if the state of affairs they represent holds, and this is dependent on God's carrying out the intention expressed in (the illocutionary force of) the utterances.

The teleological suspension of full meaning can be considered from the perspective of the utterer and the addressee. For example, in making a promise the utterer puts themselves under obligation to carry through the intention expressed in the promise by bringing about the promised state of affairs. In receiving and acting upon the promise, the addressee trusts the utterer to bring about some state of affairs relevantly and intelligibly connected with the promise's semantic meaning. These two perspectives coincide in Jesus. The word of address from heaven at Jesus' baptism was also a commissioning to the vocation of divine sonship: Jesus took on himself responsibility to bring the divine promise to fulfilment through his own words and deeds.[18] He lived in faith that he had been addressed by God at his baptism and was therefore the recipient of God's promises; he acted in trust that God's promises were being fulfilled in and through him.

So Jesus was constrained both to hear God and to obey God's word. But he could be certain neither that he heard correctly – that he was

---

[16] See Austin 1975²: 100.   [17] See also Alston 2000: 70–1.
[18] See Matt. 3:13–4:17 and cf. 17:5; Mark 1:9–15, cf. 9:7; Luke 3–4, cf. 9:35; John 1:29–34. On Jesus' sonship as divinely commissioned agency, see A. E. Harvey 1982: 158–73, especially 161ff.

not a Messianic pretender – nor therefore that his obedience was not a misrepresentation of God. Hence the divine and human aspects of the teleological suspension of full meaning also coincide in Jesus. His speech acts and the actions by which he asserted the presence of God's Kingdom through his ministry were performed in faith that they constituted God's self-utterance in fulfilment of his covenant promise. For him, as for his contemporary followers, it was essential to trust that God would vindicate him and reveal the full meaning of his promise that appeared to be being enacted in and by him.[19]

The speech acts attending Jesus' crucifixion show how sharp and close is the relationship between teleological and semantic meaning and how full meaning – for God's people and, insofar as their humanity is representative, for all people – is suspended until God fulfils his eternal purpose. The act of trust performed by Abraham and all the other men and women of faith 'who did not receive what was promised' (Heb. 11:39) is brought to the highest tension in Jesus' passion. Jesus had been irrevocably committed to God's faithfulness to his word of promise. But at Calvary – according to Matthew and Mark – it came to seem to him that his trust in God's word to him and his own (speech) actions might have been mistaken.

'My God, my God, why have you forsaken me?' (Matt. 27:46, Mark 15:34) With these words of anguish and despair, solid confidence that God had commissioned Jesus to fulfil his promise is shattered. The filial intimacy of 'Abba' is eclipsed by Jesus' oneness with lost humanity.[20] For him, for those who had trusted in him, and for all humanity, the meaning of God's promise is still teleologically suspended.[21] His cry is an expressive speech act which as such carries no direction of fit between word and world.[22] It asserts neither that God is there nor that he is not there; that question, and with it that of the meaning of meaning, is left open. However, the cry also paradoxically posits the denial of the very direction of fit it must presuppose if it is true: if God will hear him, it must be the case that he has not been abandoned. But for now, the narrative is of death and of the dark clouds of divine judgement.[23] At his death, the teleological suspension of full meaning to which Jesus' words are subject is brought to a new

---

[19] Cf. John 7:14–52.   [20] Cf. Mark 14:36.
[21] Cf. Luke 24:21a. Here Luke attests the disciples' abandoned hope despite his more 'pious' account of Jesus' death (23:44ff).
[22] Since Jesus' cry is uttered as a question, it could be construed as a directive speech act requesting God to inform him of the reason for his abandonment. However, considering the circumstances, this seems implausible.
[23] See Mark 15:33; cf. Hooker 1991:375f.

pitch: 'the one who was God's Word in the world is dumb' (von Balthasar 1989: 209).

Jesus was now apparently abandoned by God as the blasphemer he had been accused of being; his words and deeds appeared to be empty. His speech's full meaning and the faith which had elicited it were in abeyance. Jesus' deeds and the words he had uttered – words of judgement and forgiveness which had seemed to be speech acts by which the world was brought into conformity with the word of God's promised Kingdom – hung over the abyss, their full meaning suspended. The representative nation's expressive jeers at the crucified one presupposed the falsehood of the claims they mocked: that Jesus was *not* the Messianic King and agent of God's salvation,[24] that his God was not God, and that his words could therefore be safely consigned to the desert winds.

As I suggested in chapter 6, in Jesus' death Christians can recognize humanity's failure to represent God in not offering him the worship which is his due and hence also the nadir of humanity's experience of unmeaning. To repeat the suggestion made there: the philosophical crisis of linguistic representation is taken up into the theological crisis of representation between God and sinful humanity. Nietzsche's *The Gay Science* illustrates the alternative. When the madman rushed into the market place, crying 'God is dead, and we have killed him' (1974: §125), was this an assertive or a declaration? Perhaps it is best understood in the same way as preaching: as an assertion of something's being the case, on the basis of which a declaration is made which brings about a new state of affairs. Yet in Nietzsche's case this new state of affairs is precisely its own self-subversion, for it is the wiping away of 'the entire horizon', the straying of humanity 'as through an infinite nothing' (§125). It is the annihilation of meaning. But to recall chapter 6 again, the annihilation of meaning is only expressible on the basis of the presumption that meaning is possible. So perhaps we should understand the madman's cry as an expressive which thereby presupposes its truth? But again the result is self-subverting, for on this interpretation the madman illustrates the impossible possibility of meaninglessness meaningfully uttered. So perhaps the teleological suspension of full meaning *is* humanity's real fate, and just as, to his frustration, the madman spoke before his time had come,[25] so we too must forever wonder if our words will always be wiped away...?[26]

[24] Cf. Luke 23:35f.   [25] Cf. Nietzsche 1974: §125.

[26] Rorty appeals to Nietzsche and explicitly repudiates teleology in his argument against representative and therefore realist views of language (1989: 3–20, especially 20; cf. Trigg 1992).

Derrida, the teleological suspension of meaning, and the fulfilment of God's promise

This, of course, is one way to read Derrida's detailed analysis of and attack on (Austin's) speech act theory in 'Signature Event Context' (1988: 1–23).[27] Derrida does not deny the existence of conscious intentions in relation to speech acts or the importance of convention in interpreting them, but, against Austin, he denies that these things can be taken for granted as unproblematic. Thus Derrida argues that the context of a speech act cannot be defined sufficiently narrowly to allow us to delimit precisely the range of possible meanings the act might have. A speaker's intention cannot be present in the transmitting and receiving of their speech act in such a way that we can finally decide what they mean.[28] '[T]he intention animating the utterance will never be through and through present to itself and to its content' (18). Part of the reason for this is that language is 'iterable': it consists of 'arbitrary' signs which can be transferred from one context to another. However, these pre-exist, and so cannot be limited by, the conscious intention of the utterer of a speech act. Now, this iterability is necessary for there to be communication, but it also opens up the possibility that the utterer's illocutionary act, together with the propositional content of that act, might not be successfully communicated. The possibility of what Derrida calls 'infelicitous' speech acts is always present and cannot, *contra* Austin, be ruled out a priori.

The risk of infelicity is, as Derrida puts it, 'a necessary possibility' (15, cf. 17). The context in which a speech act is issued, transmitted, and received cannot be wholly governed or determined and therefore 'communication . . . is not the means of transference of meaning, the exchange of intentions and meanings, discourse and the "communication of consciousness" ' (20). In other words, no speech act is so uttered, transmitted, and received as to allow 'the decoding of a meaning or truth' (21). To think that there can be such a decoding involves assuming as a reality 'a philosophical "ideal" ', an ideal Derrida thinks he has exposed to be non-actual, that is, 'the presence to self of a total context, the transparency of intentions, the presence of meaning . . . to the absolutely singular uniqueness of a speech act' (17).

Derrida's argument has important implications for my account of the meaning of God's speech acts, for it seems to imply that their meaning, just as much as that of human ones, is always and always will be, in my own terms, teleologically suspended, never to be conclusively fulfilled.

---

[27] Searle's reply to Derrida is summarized in Derrida 1988: 25–7.
[28] See 1988: 14f.

Ex hypothesi, we can admit that there was an intention in the issuing of the speech act, but because the iterations of its propositional content cannot be tied to the consciousness which gave it its illocutionary force, there cannot be any end to the chain of iterations of the original speech act which will allow us to say that it has now been fulfilled. The force of the speech act, along with the intention which gave it that force, is always liable to be lost in the necessary possibility of infelicity. If Derrida is right, his argument lends credence to the view that Jesus (or anybody else) cannot be understood as God's revelatory word. Indeed, the very idea of there being a singular, incarnate revelatory word of God seems incoherent.

Yet there is another option to be considered, and to see this we need to turn to John's Gospel. As a narrative, the Gospel is heavily teleological, and although from the first lines of the Prologue the outcome of the drama is never in doubt, John's use of irony ensures that the question of the identity of God and of Jesus' identity with the Father is never allowed to recede from view. Was Jesus 'I am' before Abraham (8:58)? Is he a blasphemer on account of such statements, or has the Father sanctified and sent him into the world (10:36)? When will his 'hour' come and will it be both his glorification and the glorification of the Father? Is this 'hour' the reason, the 'purpose', of his coming (John 12: 23, 27ff (RSV); cf. 17:1)? Beneath this unfolding drama lies the question as to the truth of the Prologue's suggestion that Jesus is the logos who was with God and was God from the beginning.

Commentators have made many suggestions as to the best translation of *logos* in the Prologue; one of the most interesting and coherent is G. B. Caird's. He proposes understanding it as 'purpose' (1980: 102). So the question is, Was Jesus sent to accomplish God's purpose by showing the primordial intra-trinitarian unity of the Father and the Son and by bringing the world into unity with God (cf. 17:20ff)? Is Jesus the culmination of the purpose of God expressed in the promises made to Abraham and Moses and the prophets (cf. 8:31–59, 1:45, 5:46, 9:28f)? Has God indeed issued a promise whose semantic meaning he has upheld teleologically through all the vicissitudes of history in such a way that Jesus could receive it and act upon it obediently? If Derrida's understanding of speech acts is correct, then this question cannot be settled. Yet despite the necessary possibility of infelicitous transmission of the promise and our inability to delimit the range of meanings the promise might have, perhaps God has been at work in such a way as to sustain the promise's teleological meaning?

Derrida's attack on logocentrism and his denial of the transcendental signified defer all possibility of the play of signifiers finding an ultimate stable ground in a self-present consciousness. He seems to think that this does away with not just metaphysics but also Christian theology and therewith, John's logos. If correct, this would make it impossible to understand God as working in such a way as to sustain the meaning of his promise and bring it to fulfilment. However, in his study of *Postmodern Theory and Biblical Theology* (1995) Brian Ingraffia argues that this conclusion need not be drawn.[29] He argues that 'by deconstructing the metaphysics of presence, [Derrida] claim[s] to have deconstructed ontotheology, both Greek metaphysics and Christian theology. But', Ingraffia continues,

> the logos of biblical theology is radically different from the logos of Greek philosophy and modern rationalism ... What sets the biblical God apart from the god of ontotheology is that the God of the Bible has revealed himself in human history. The God revealed in the Bible, revealed in Jesus, is not simply the negation of the finite, the human, the material. (1995: 237, 227, cf. 228)

To develop Ingraffia's point: the logos of Christian faith, the Johannine logos, is first and foremost the presence of God to himself in his eternal resolve to be faithful to himself. In the intra-trinitarian perichoresis of the divine persons, God is fully 'self-present' in his aseity. We can therefore go further and suggest that the logos is God's presence in the fulfilment in history of his own promise – that promise expressed in God's being faithful to himself: *ehyeh asher ehyeh*. God is fully present to himself in his works *ad extra*.

Ingraffia also suggests that Derrida has 'deconstructed only the human logos, and only "the name of god ... *as it is pronounced within classic rationalism*" ... only the god who acts as a metaphysical ground for the operations of the independent and autonomous ego' (1995: 221 quoting Derrida 1976: 71, Ingraffia's italics).[30] This is not, however, the ego of Christ, for he is 'God from God'; all that he has and is he shares with the Father even though the Father is greater than him.[31] Therefore, insofar as he is the word (*logos*) of God, he is this in the mutuality of the Trinity; the Son's identity consists in his being sent to reveal the Father with whom he is one.[32] The incarnate Son is therefore also one with the Father in his being

---

[29] See also Wolterstorff 1995: 155–65. Wolterstorff, a Christian philosopher, thinks that his difference with Derrida has to be left as 'a fundamental clash of intuitions' and 'emotions' (1995: 164f). It is a sign of the impoverishment of a Christian philosophy that it effectively disregards theology and doesn't seriously attempt to rebut Derrida by appeal to it.

[30] Ingraffia suggests that Derrida's deconstruction of the self-presence of consciousness and therewith of the divine word involves 'a "leap of unfaith"' (1995: 220). Catherine Pickstock concurs: 'Without faith, Derrida is correct' (1998: 265).

[31] John 3:35, 13:3, 14:28.   [32] John 8:42, 10:30. See Jenson 1997: 108ff.

the bringing to effect of God's promise, and he is one also with God's elect creature in being the beneficiary of that promise. So at his crucifixion, as John attests it, when Jesus says 'It is finished' (John 19:30), it is this work of bringing the purposes of God to completion that is in view. Jesus' words are a declaration that '[w]hat God has decreed has been accomplished' (Raymond E. Brown 1971: 931). Now, declarations have world-to-word direction of fit: the world is brought into conformity with the purpose that had been expressed in God's word. In John's telling of Jesus' crucifixion, then, Jesus' last words show that he and the Father are indeed one, for this is the hour of his glorification when the glory he has shared all along with the Father is revealed.

There are several important conclusions to be drawn from this. First, in going down into the realm of death and decay in the man Jesus Christ, God is most intimately and lovingly engaged with the reality of his creation. In Jesus' resurrection from the dead, the unity of purpose expressed in his filial relationship with the Father, and therewith, God's independence from his creation, is brought to full expression. Precisely because he is the independently real *ens realissimum*, nothing that we can think or do can banish God from his creation or thwart his love for it. Second, in this event of crucifixion and resurrection the identity of the Son and the Father is fully revealed, and with it the true fulfilment of God's promise. God's promises have found their 'Yes' in Christ.[33] Here the story of the word of God in human history is proleptically completed: the promise now has a narrative meaning, for, as Jenson argues in his theological meditation on God's narrated identity, 'It holds ... primally ... with God: a story is constituted by the outcome of events' (1997: 66).

Thus, third, against Derrida we can say that although the full meaning of God's promise had (from the perspective of its human recipients) been teleologically suspended, God has indeed been faithful to his word. His word has accomplished that which he purposed.[34] Through the story of the fulfilment of his promissory word in Christ, God has contradicted Derrida's avowed 'final intention' of 'undermining ... the meaning of language as the full continuity of speech' (1976: 70). God's intention has been conserved despite the obduracy and disobedience of his people. Despite the many unpropitious contexts in which it had seemed impossible for the semantic meaning of the promise to be preserved and despite the many occasions for infelicitous transmission of the promise, God has overseen the course of history in such a way that his promise has indeed been brought to fruition. *Contra* Derrida, the intention (*logos*) animating God's utterance has been

[33] 2 Cor. 1:20.   [34] Isa. 55:11.

'through and through present to itself and its content' (1988: 18). *Contra*
Catherine Pickstock – who argues against deconstruction that 'the optimum
site of this restoration [sc. of 'meaning to language'] is the integration of
word and action in the event of the Eucharist' (1998: 253) – meaning never
needed to be restored to the language in which God addressed humanity:
it only appeared this way to those who were unwilling to trust that it was
teleologically suspended. Word and action have always been one in the
teleological enactment of God's promises. Nor was meaning ever lost to
human language use: it had only appeared that way to the thought of those
unwilling to acknowledge that Christ 'is before all things, and in him all
things hold together' (Col. 1:17) – including the possibility of meaningful
human discourse. The resurrection of Christ reveals that word and action
are integrated primordially in God's promissory assertion to be faithful to
himself and his covenant with his creature.

CHAPTER 9

Realism: conformed to the conforming word

CHRISTOCENTRIC REALISM AND REALITY UNDER A DESCRIPTION

Against metaphysical realism

A running theme throughout this book has been the idea that Christians only ever have reality under a description. We know God as he gives himself to us in Jesus Christ and by his Holy Spirit grants us faith. So to say that we have his reality only under a description is emphatically not to imply that the description constructs a reality that would not have any existence apart from it.[1] However, it is to say that it is not possible for us to adopt a stance external to this (or any other) perspective so as to give a complete metaphysical description of the universe and its creator. Such metaphysical claims as Christians can make – whether about the creator or the creature – are those opened up by this perspective.[2]

To put the point positively, this is because, as we saw in chapter 1, if our speech is to be about God, then we must begin where God has given himself to be the object of our knowledge and speech. This is why a Christian realism will be Christocentric. We can begin at no other place than where God has dwelt among us, where he has judged our sinfulness and graciously healed us, where he has been heard by us in the man Jesus Christ, where obedient human deeds and speech about God have been vindicated, and where the Holy Spirit has been given so that we too can tell of God 'in our own native language' (Acts 2:8).

Negatively, to say that we only have reality under a description is a methodological counsel against idolatry. If we assume that we can have a neutral view of reality, unrestricted by creaturely limitations, then we risk failing to recognize how our own interests – distorted as they are by sin, the fear of death, and a desire to master the contingencies of life – can lead to

---

[1] I return to this important point later.   [2] Cf. Bruce Marshall 2000: 116.

our suppressing the truth about God and his world. As we saw in chapter 2 in our discussion of suffering, human beings tend to seek an ideal *locus standi* from which to survey the world and reconcile its contingencies in an explanatory metaphysical system.

Now, the philosophical position known as metaphysical realism seeks to give just such an orderly account of things. For example, Roger Trigg, a Christian philosopher, argues that '[metaphysical] realism can ... give us confidence that our small part of [the physical universe] may not be an area of order in a sea of disorder' (1998: 82). To establish this, the metaphysical realist must show that 'the world consists of some fixed totality of mind-independent objects'. It follows from this that the metaphysical realist's goal is to arrive at the 'one true and complete description of "the way the world is"' (Putnam 1981: 49). This is why the correspondence theory of truth is much favoured by metaphysical realists: they want to obtain an account of the world which is in the closest possible correspondence with the facts, and not just some of them – all of them. A consequence of this is that we should not explicate truth in terms of our knowledge, for to do so runs the risk of confusing our beliefs about and conceptions of things with things as they are independently of us – that is, of going anti-realist. This is why it is definitive of metaphysical realism that it 'is concerned with the objective character of reality, independent of judgements, beliefs, concepts, language and so on' (Trigg 1998: 65). It is also why a metaphysical realist will seek to rebut the claim that we only have reality under a description, for this, he will argue, is to set out on an anti-realist path confusing concepts with reality.

However, as Putnam points out, a metaphysically realist account of mind-independent reality seems to require that we can attain 'epistemically ideal conditions ... apart from all possible observers' (Putnam 1981: 55).[3] That is, if metaphysical realism is to attain the objectivity it seeks, we need to have a God's-eye view untainted by our biological, psychological, historical, theological, social, and, as many would now stress, ideological circumstances.[4] In other words, metaphysical realism requires that we abandon creatureliness and become like Gods. But, Putnam contends, for human beings '[t]here is no God's Eye point of view that we can know or usefully imagine; there are only the various points of view of actual persons reflecting various interests and purposes that their descriptions and theories subserve' (1981: 50).

---

[3] Michael Dummett criticizes realism on similar grounds; see, for example, 1978: 146.

[4] Cf. Trigg, who criticizes Gordon Kaufman's 'repudiation of realism' because it appears to leave us 'imprisoned within whatever conceptual scheme we happen to hold at the time. There is no question of transcending the special conditions of our culture' (1998: 187).

The Christian will disagree with the implication that there is no know-able God who can have a God's-eye view; however, she will agree with Putnam's appeal to the fact that human points of view are ineluctably situ-ated and embodied. And she will add that our various creaturely points of view are also corrupted and distorted by sin. Left to ourselves, we 'suppress the truth' about God, our 'senseless minds [are] darkened', and we lapse into idolatry (Rom. 1:18, 21, 23ff). Commenting on these themes, the Chris-tian philosopher Merold Westphal urges Christians to acknowledge their cognitive equipment's 'persistent propensity toward malfunctioning'. He suggests that one of the noetic effects of sin is that 'in spite of what God truly is, our sinfully corrupted receiving apparatuses generate gods conve-niently suited to our demands' (1993b: 177). This line of thought should give Christians pause before assuming that they must be committed to metaphysical realism. If we are after *the* objective truth about reality, then we seek a privileged position that is only God's by right, ours only by wish-ing to be like God, and we seek it by means of faulty equipment. But God's thoughts are not our thoughts, and his ways are not our ways (Isa. 55:8f). Westphal concludes his argument by asking

Could it be that realism/hostility toward antirealism in our account of human knowledge tends to blind us to the noetic effects of sin and encourages us to treat as episodic (empirical) error what needs to be seen as systematic (a priori) suppression of the truth? (1993b: 179)

A creaturely perspective on realism

In spite of these caveats, my argument for the mind-independent reality of the triune God might appear to be a version of metaphysical realism. After all, I am arguing for the truth of a metaphysical claim: that the triune God exists independently of our minds and that he is knowable. But re-member our starting point. We began not by seeking to discover whether God is a possible item on an inventory of all existing mind-independent objects; we began from an ontological commitment to the triune God. My Christocentric transcendental argument has shown that since this God is the self-revealing *ens realissimum*, we should not take the project of attain-ing epistemic access to him as the exclusive ground for truth about him or as a model of theological truth, for this would be to epistemize truth and so turn anti-realist. Rather, in Jesus Christ God has found us, become an epistemic subject for us, judged our sinfulness, and begun to restore our noetic equipment. This is why we only have reality under a description:

God's reality is known to us as we participate in the story of his saving dealings with his creation unfolded in Jesus Christ. Our capacity to represent him depends on our accepting our creatureliness and not seeking to evade suffering – whether in hedonism, high culture, metaphysics, or theology – for it is in the redemption of suffering humanity that God has shown his independent reality.

But what about non-human created reality? What account of realism does my argument imply for it? The triune God reveals himself through salvation history as the creator of a good creation who holds its orderly, contingent existence in being.[5] This implies that Christians should be realists about the everyday world of what philosophers call 'medium-size dry goods'. However, I do not believe that a Christocentric realism need have any ontological commitments about the ultimate metaphysical constitution of the created universe. For example, I see no theological objection to the Catholic philosopher of science Bas van Fraassen's constructive empiricism; in fact, insofar as it questions 'the metaphysical authority of science', it has quite a lot in its favour.[6] We can admit scepticism or uncertainty about what might exist independently of our minds in a theoretical, unobservable world without loss to a properly theological account of realism.

It is often objected that the view that we have reality under a description leads to a form of relativism according to which what exists is relative to our conceptual schemes or our descriptions.[7] In the sense that I deny our having a God's-eye point of view which will allow us to adjudicate between all competing truth claims made in our world, it would be correct to see my argument as leading to a theologically disciplined version of relativism.[8] But perhaps it is not necessary for us to be able to make such an adjudication; perhaps we don't need objectivity of the kind sought by those who, catching a whiff of relativism, detect imminent apostasy. If God, the *ens realissimum*, has granted us knowledge of himself, and part of that knowledge is that he is the creator of the one world shared by human beings who are defined as such by having been made in his image, then Christian faith has a concept of a common world and a common humanity. If God has shown us the way of salvation and a vision of the human good in the life of the church – as he has – then Christian faith is not spiritually and morally all at sea.

---

[5] See chapter 7, pp. 171–5.
[6] See his 1980: 204–15, 1994a, b, and 1999. See also Hesse 1998. McGrath (2001: 74) suggests that philosophers and theologians who have not been inducted into scientific 'experimental culture' are not qualified to enter the debate about scientific realism.
[7] This criticism is frequently made of Putnam's 'internal' realism; see, for example, Alston 1996: 132ff, 162–87.
[8] Cf. chapter 5, pp. 134–7 above. See also Niebuhr 1960: 37 and Kallenberg 2000.

So to say that a Christocentric realism only has reality under a description is not to endorse a radically relativistic attitude that 'anything goes'. It is to relativize other truth claims to the truth of God in Christ. It is to say against Protagoras that God, not humanity, is the measure of all things.

Nor does the view that we have reality only under a description commit us to claiming that any religious perspective is just as good/bad/indifferent as any other, or that if there is a religious truth of the matter, it is finally hidden from us. This might be a consequence of epistemological defences of religious realism, for then our ontological claims would be relative to our conceptual schemes. Just such an approach leads John Hick to pluralism about 'the [noumenal] Real' which the phenomena of all religions 'intend'. He writes that

> Our awareness of the world is necessarily an awareness of it as it impinges upon us and becomes meaningfully organised by our consciousness. All awareness, whether of our immediate or of our more ultimate environment, is ... formed in terms of conceptual systems embodied in the language of particular societies and traditions. We can therefore only experience the Real as its presence affects our distinctively human modes of consciousness, varying as these do in their apperceptive resources and habits from culture to culture and from individual to individual. (1989: 173)

There is nothing in my argument that implies this kind of epistemizing of realism. Putnam repudiates metaphysical realism because it has the consequences that we must take truth to be '*radically non-epistemic*' (1978: 125). It is his alternative *epistemic* understanding of truth that leads to conceptual relativity, and this is illustrated by the moves Hick makes.[9] By contrast (and apart from its theological rationale), my starting with an ontological commitment to the triune God's being the *ens realissimum* and my transcendental argument for a Christocentric realism obviate the need for an epistemic approach to realism. My argument has not been that we inevitably distort reality by accommodating it to our conceptual schemes, but that this is the best we can get. Rather, it has been that in Christ, God has accommodated himself to us without ceasing to be God; he has relativized our conceptual schemes to himself.

REALISM AND NARRATIVE

I suggest that the description under which God's independent reality is mediated to us is that of the narrative of salvation history. This story,

---

[9] Richard B. Miller (1986) shows that the epistemological approach to realism advocated by theological realists leads to pluralism. In his account of the epistemology of religious experience, Alston cautiously admits that 'Hick's position has much to be said for it' (1991: 265).

whose consummation is expressed in different but complementary ways by the Gospel writers – especially Matthew, Luke, and John[10] – shows us primarily who God is, that God's creatures are loved by him, that he has made the human world to be their home, that he is the 'three mile an hour God' (in Kosuke Koyama's helpful image) who walks alongside them, picks them up when they stumble, and that therefore humans can 'do justice ... love kindness, and ... walk humbly with [their] God' (Mic. 6:8). So a Christocentric realism will also be a narrative realism: God's reality as *ehyeh asher ehyeh* is shown in the story of his conforming human affairs to his loving will and thereby bringing his purposes to fulfilment. In other words, the realism that is appropriate to the Christian faith is one in which God's reality is shown under the narrative description offered in the Bible.

Many recent theologians have suggested that the Bible, and especially the Gospels, are self-involving narratives.[11] This is stressed in a particularly interesting way by David Ford in his paper on 'System, Story, Performance' (1989) in which, influenced by Frei and Lindbeck, he stresses the 'middle distance realism' of the gospels.[12] The concept 'middle distance realism' is drawn from the literary critic J. P. Stern's work *On Realism* (1973) and indicates 'that [literary] focus which best does justice to the ordinary social world of people in interaction' (Ford 1989: 195).[13] This avoids focussing either too closely on the subject and concentrating on their inner world, or too broadly and losing the particularities of the subject in generalizations. In Ford's view, this is a helpful way of understanding the Gospels as what Frei calls 'realistic narratives'; that is, narratives which work in a 'descriptive mode' (Ford 1989: 197) to render the unsubstitutable identity of Jesus Christ.

Alongside the descriptive mode there is also a 'realism of assessment' (197). This works in two ways. First, there is an internal assessment in the Gospels in that Jesus' resurrection is presented as the verdict on his life. Ford suggests that

In literary terms, the role of the resurrection in the story might even be seen to be an affirmation of the primacy of [the middle distance] perspective. If this man is alive again, raised from the dead by God and rightly called 'Lord', then the primary perspective on reality must be one that helps to identify and recognize him. (197–8)

[10] I have in mind here the ways in which these writers consciously set the story of Jesus in the wider context of God's dealings with Israel and also, in John's case, the *kosmos*.
[11] See especially Thiselton 1992: 272–312, 565f.
[12] Narrative accounts of the realism of Christian faith have also been suggested by Kenneth Surin (1989b: 41–56) and John Milbank (1990: 382–8, cf. 259–76, 339–47).
[13] The classic discussion of this is Auerbach's *Mimesis* (1968: see especially 24–49).

A consequence of this is the second kind of realism of assessment: the reader is involved in the narrative in that they are called upon to make an assessment of Jesus' life. What Auerbach says of Mark's Gospel is true of them all: 'the story speaks to everybody; everybody is urged and indeed required to take sides for or against it. Even ignoring it implies taking sides' (1968: 48). Assessment should, though it does not always or perhaps even usually, elicit a faithful, responsive 'performance'. A realism of assessment 'pivots between life and literature in a way that helps translate one mode of experience [story] into another [performance]' (Ford 1989: 198). The Gospel narratives not only identify God in Christ, but also call upon us to show his reality in our lives. More importantly, since the Gospels bring the narrative of scripture to its culminating point and open out into the (narratively substructured[14]) teaching of the epistles, they show that the world that God has made is habitable by and hospitable to human beings.

So my Christocentric narrative realism is less far-reaching than a metaphysical realist might desire in that it does not seek to 'transcend all practices and local assumptions to talk of what is "really" the case' (Trigg 1998: 134). Nevertheless, I believe that it is a theologically, spiritually, and morally appropriate realism because, in its commitment to God's self-revelation in the man from first-century Nazareth and the covenant practices he instituted, it seeks to uphold the independent reality of the triune Lord and his knowability and representability.

However, the narrative approach raises important questions. Consider the following line of thought: to argue that the realism of Christian faith is shown as humans are involved by God in the narrative world of the Bible is to suppress the fact that the Bible is the work of human story-tellers, tradents, writers, compilers, editors, and canonizers. Have not these people used their imaginations to *construct* a story of God? And if they have done this, then should not the description under which we have reality lead us to speak not of our *finding* reality, but of our *fashioning* it?[15] So is our account finally anti-realist? Have we not made God out of words, just as the Sea of Faith Network suggests? Should we not join them in celebrating our autonomy and with them ' "explore and promote religious faith as a human creation" ' (quoted in Boulton 1997: 3, no source cited)?

Much of Donald MacKinnon's philosophical theology is marked by his 'hostility to any form of idealism', by which he means, 'a view of spiritual activity as autonomous, as in fact creating its own objects' (1979: 24). A dominant theme in his work is the exposure of anti-realist lines of thought

---

[14] See Ford 1989: 202–4 and Hays 1983.   [15] See also Ford 1989: 196f.

in philosophers and especially theologians. He insists that we cannot and should not use metaphysics to transcend the exigencies and limitations of experience – especially the experience of suffering – for to do so is to miss the fact that the transcendent has entered human history.

> At the foundation of the [Christian] faith there lies a deed done, an incarnating of the eternal in the stuff of human history. It is not the delicate subtlety of our imaginative interpretations that is constitutive of this penetration of our human lot; what these interpretations seek to represent is the *act* that sets our every essay in conceptualization in restless vibration. (1979: 22)

So, how can we show that the Bible is indeed representation and not imaginative construction and hence that a Christocentric narrative realism really is realism?[16]

With these questions in mind, we now pick up our use of speech act theory in the last chapter in order to show how the Bible can be understood as a paradigm case of the way in which human words are conformed to the 'world' that is the reality of God. Then, in the final section we look at how our human world is conformed to the word of God so that we can faithfully represent him.

CONFORMING THE WORD TO THE WORLD

Where is the meaning of the Bible?

One of the most important questions in contemporary hermeneutics concerns where the *meaning* of the Bible is located. Current scholarly debate suggests that there are three places where it might be found. The historical-critical method locates it in the events about which the Bible was written, that is, in terms of the metaphors the debate trades in, *behind* the Bible.[17] This method has come under considerable criticism from within the guild of biblical scholars as well as those outside it.[18] Of the latter, perhaps the most important and influential has been Hans Frei,[19] who argued that

---

[16] For fruitful interaction with MacKinnon on these themes, see Lash 1982.

[17] In dogmatic theology, Pannenberg has offered a sophisticated defence of this. See, for example, 1970: 15–80, 96–136.

[18] The New Testament scholar N. T. Wright has developed a 'critical realist' epistemology and combined this with a version of traditional historical criticism (1992: 3–118). In my view, Wright's position collapses into a version of idealism (see my 'What's Wrong About (N. T.) Wright: Christ, Faith, and History' (forthcoming)).

[19] See Frei 1974 in particular. Assessments of Frei relevant to the present argument include Comstock 1986; Vanhoozer 1990: 148–89; Wallace 1990: 41–5, 89–110; Bruce Marshall 1992: 176–8; Watson 1994: 19–29, 46, 135, 224.

historical-criticism attached the meaning of the Bible to the (critically reconstructed) events that the Bible is about, rather than to the text itself. As
a result, the meaningfulness of the Bible came to depend on its historical
veracity,[20] or on our divining its authors' intentions. The upshot is that in
the attempt (from the eighteenth century onwards) to fit the Bible into the
world of empiricism, rationalism, and deism, it is treated in a way that leads
to either scepticism or a psychologizing and spiritualizing of its meaning.
It was assumed that a world of (religious) meaning was already in place and
that the Bible had to be understood in this world's general terms, rather
than its own particular terms. Thus 'the great reversal had taken place;
interpretation was a matter of fitting the biblical story into another world
with another story rather than incorporating that world into the biblical
story' (Frei 1974: 130). In Ford's terms, the focus of middle-distance realism
had been lost and replaced with a broad one; in my terms, we might say that
the biblical word had been conformed to the narrative world of a nascent
scientific naturalism rather than that revealed in Christ.

To correct this, Frei proposes that we should read the Bible as a 'realistic'
or 'history-like narrative'. Thus,

If one uses the metaphorical expression 'location of meaning', one would want to
say that the location of meaning in narrative of the realistic sort is the text, the
narrative structure or sequence itself ... For ... in narrative of the sort in which
character, verbal communications, and circumstances are each determinative of the
other and hence of the theme itself, the text, the verbal sense, and not a profound,
buried substratum underneath constitutes or determines the subject matter. (1974:
280)

The Bible is therefore to be read according to its 'literal sense',[21] that is, for
its *surface* meaning:

For the *sensus literalis* ... the *descriptive* function of language and its conceptual
adequacy are shown forth precisely in the kind of story that does not refer beyond
itself for its meaning ... the kind of story in which the 'signified', the identity of
the protagonist, is enacted by the signifier, the narrative sequence itself. It is an
instance of literary literal sense. (Frei 1993: 112)

Frei's work is massively important in two respects: first, for urging the
church to attend to the Bible as it stands with its own capacity to re-present
God as its ascriptive subject and, in the Gospels, 'the individual, specific,

---

[20] With regard to my criticisms of theological realism, it is worth noting Frei's observation that after
the eighteenth century, 'Theory of meaning is virtually identical with the theory of the knowledge
of reality' (1974: 138).

[21] On the literal sense, see in particular Frei 1993: 117–52.

unsubstitutable identity of Jesus' (1975: 49), and second, for quietly insisting that the church turn away from misconceived apologetic strategies. However, there is a grain of truth in Comstock's criticism that Frei makes 'The meaning of these narratives ... autonomous; they refer only to themselves' (1986: 120). Frei's work fails to show that the narrative refers to extratextual reality as the text itself purports to do.[22] As Stanley Hauerwas argues:

> the demand that what Jesus was not be different than how we have come to know him in the gospels is not based on some external demand of historical truth, but rather because the very nature of the story of Jesus itself demands that Jesus be the one who in fact the church said and continues to say he is. (1977: 72, *sic*)

To do this need not be to deny that we only ever have reality under a description and that the world narrated by scripture is the world as it really is, but it does demand more attention to ontology than Frei gives.

If hermeneutical strategies that seek to find meaning on the *surface* of the text or *behind* it are unsuccessful, perhaps we shall fare better if we seek it *in front of* the text. This approach is associated in contemporary theological hermeneutics particularly with Paul Ricoeur's doctrine that poetic language and metaphor have a disclosive power that arises from the surplus of meaning they generate and which enables human beings to explore their 'ownmost possibilities' in the world that discourse 'projects'.[23] 'For me', he writes, 'the world is the ensemble of references opened up by every kind of text ... that I have read, understood, and loved' (1976: 37). This means that the real world is the one that the text opens up for us: the biblical word is conformed to a possible world shaped by its interaction with human imagination.[24]

> The sense of a text is not behind the text, but in front of it. It is not something hidden, but something disclosed. What has to be understood is not the initial situation of the discourse, but what points towards a possible world, thanks to the non-ostensive reference of the text. (87)[25]

Ricoeur regards this 'pointing towards' as revelatory. However, his understanding of the hermeneutics of revelation in theology is an application of his general philosophical theory, and this allows *any* text to be revelatory

---

[22] Frei does not, as his critics frequently allege, deny that the Bible refers to extratextual reality: see his writings on the resurrection, e.g., 1993: 200–12; cf. 113f.
[23] For discussions of Ricoeur's work from a variety of theological perspectives, see Vanhoozer 1990; Fodor 1995; Frei 1993: 124–33; Wallace 1990.
[24] For theological development of this view see especially Tracy 1981.
[25] For a good analysis of Ricoeur's distinction between discourse and sense, see Wolterstorff 1995: 133–40.

in the sense that it projects a possible world.[26] Thus he reads the Bible in the light of his own general theory rather than allowing it to govern his hermeneutics, and he downplays the particularity and finality of God's self-revelation in Jesus Christ. He allows the text to become autonomous in disclosing the possibilities of its (metaphorical) language. Moreover, by giving metaphor this revelatory function, he severs the link between Christian language and the revelatory events which gave rise to it in the real world of salvation history to which it purports to refer. In its place Ricoeur puts a more idealist and constructivist emphasis on an ontology of *human* possibility.[27]

It may well be that metaphors have a disclosive function in Christian language, but if so, on my argument this needs to be grounded in an ontology determined by the proleptic accomplishment of God's purposes in Christ. The possible world towards which Christian language points is the real one disclosed in God's self-revelation attested in the Bible – not 'the ensemble of references opened up by every kind of text ... that I have read, understood, and loved'. On Ricoeur's account, the meaning of the Bible is too nearly what its readers make it mean. But the ontological possibilities the Bible projects are not just any ontological possibilities; the real world it opens up is not to be equated with those opened up by anything from C. S. Lewis to John Le Carré, even if we pass through *Crime and Punishment* on the way.[28] The Bible projects the ontological possibilities that are coming into being in the new creation because God's promissory word has been fulfilled in actuality.[29] Because God's word is living and active it is able to conform us to the real world that God is bringing into being, and it is this that is witnessed to in scripture. For these theological reasons, Ricoeur's search for the Bible's meaning in front of the text cannot be accepted.

To be more precise I should have said that we cannot accept seeking the meaning of the Bible *exclusively* in front of the text. Ricoeur wants to secure the contemporary kerygmatic value of the text, and this is clearly vital; the problem is that he appears to sacrifice historical actuality in the process. As Thiselton agues, Ricoeur 'leaves us ... trapped within our intralinguistic

---

[26] Ricoeur 1981: 73–118; cf. Vanhoozer 1990: 155, 180; Wolterstorff 1995: 144f.

[27] Ricoeur rejects the polarity of realism versus idealism: see his review of Nelson Goodman's *Ways of Worldmaking* (1978) in Valdés 1991: 200–15.

[28] For a stimulating account of eschatological possibilities in relation to literature and Christian faith, see Fiddes 2000.

[29] I allude to Jüngel's important paper 'The World as Possibility and Actuality: The Ontology of the Doctrine of Justification' (1989: 95–123), in which he argues for the ontological priority of possibility over actuality, but in a way which is fully grounded in Christian eschatology. His doctrine of metaphor is another interesting foil to Ricoeur, grounded as it is in his ontology (see 1989: 16–71).

world in which the traditional notion of "reference" has been transposed into an internal relation within a phenomenological system' (1992: 360). By contrast, historical criticism seeks an ontological commitment to the actuality of deeds done, but at the cost of excessive scepticism, diminished kerygmatic value, and an obsolete ontology.[30] Frei, on the other hand, gains what historical criticism loses but loses what it wishes to gain. In other words, what we need if we are to be both Christians and realists is the strengths of these three approaches without their weaknesses: ontological commitment to the actuality of God's bringing into being the new creation in Christ, respect for the text of the Bible in its canonical form, and commitment to the actualization of God's word in the present through preaching. We need to see the Bible as a witness to both the conforming of the fallen world to God's word and the conforming of human words to God's 'world'. How can we secure these things?

Scripture and teleology

I suggest that a teleological reading of scripture will help. Historical critical method tends so to fragment the text as to obliterate any impression of teleology (unless it is of the historicist kind Wellhausen imposed on the Pentateuch), but both Frei and Ricoeur have teleological outlooks. In his exposition of Ricoeur, Vanhoozer writes that for him

the world of the text, much like the referent of metaphor, should not be confused with the empirical world ... Freed from the burdens of ostensive reference and empirical description, texts can project *meaningful* worlds ... In both metaphor and narrative, then, there is a production of meaning that is the work of creative imagination. Narratives create sense and order where previously there was only nonsense and chaos. (1990: 89–90)

The order which narrative creates is teleological because 'A plot, which is the soul of narrative, *invents* an ordered and intelligible whole' (Vanhoozer 1990: 93, my italics) with a beginning, middle, and end. I italicized the word 'invents' to draw attention to the fact that for Ricoeur teleology is not immanent in God or in extratextual reality, but is *imposed* on the world by an autonomous text. Once again, Ricoeur's view seems to me to be mistaken: (1), his position seems defenceless against deconstruction,[31] (2), he appears

---

[30] Cf. C. Stephen Evans's (1999) critique of N. T. Wright's methodological naturalism.

[31] And not only against deconstruction, but also against readings such as Frank Kermode's, which – legitimately, given his presuppositions – finds that the Gospels' opening chapters 'lack the great mnemonic, plot' (1979: 113).

to presume that until reality is textualized, it is nonsensical and chaotic, and (3), his view of the Bible's plot seems to be rather too tidy. So far as the Bible can be spoken of as having a beginning, middle, and end, these are not like those of a well-formed nineteenth-century novel. It begins in chaos, at its middle stand failure and death, and its end is at worst incomprehensible and at best proleptic and open – even to the eye of faith. 'World and book ... are hopelessly plural, endlessly disappointing; we stand alone before them, aware of their arbitrariness and impenetrability, knowing that they may be narratives only because of our impudent intervention' (Kermode 1979: 145). Against these views I suggest that we need to find the teleology of the Bible not in the text itself, or in the interventions of autonomous readers, but in God and his relationship to the text.

Hans Frei is sympathetic to pre-critical reading of the Bible which (and here he has in mind Calvin, who, he thinks, believed that 'we have reality only under [biblical] description' (1974: 36)) was dominated by a teleo-logical outlook that sought spiritually to combine a literal reading with a sensitivity to the typological or 'figurative' relationship between different episodes in its 'history-like narrative'. This 'emerges solely as a function of the narrative itself. It is not imprinted on the text by the interpreter' (34–5). He continues,

The meaning pattern of reality is inseparable from its forward motion; it is not the product of the wedding of that forward motion with a separate backward perspec-tive upon it, i.e. of history and interpretation joined as two logically independent factors. Rather, the meaning of the full sequence emerges in the narration of the sequence ... The unity of literal and figural reading depended ... on the convic-tion that the narrative renders temporal reality in such a way that interpretative thought can and need only comprehend the meaning that is, or emerges from, the cumulative sequence and its teleological pattern, because the interpreter himself is part of that real sequence. (36–7)

Like Ricoeur, Frei finds teleology emerging as a function of the text, but unlike him, he thinks that it is yoked to the temporal reality it narrates, and he holds this view for particular theological reasons rather than general philosophical ones. In his discussion of Kermode,[32] Frei shows that he, like the Reformers, is concerned not to 'seek God beyond the text' lest he find 'that sinister force of devouring consummation' rather than the God of grace (1993: 163). Frei wishes to stand alongside the Reformers. For them '[t]he text did not refer to, it *was* the linguistic presence of God, the fit

[32] 1993: 106–10, 158–62.

embodiment of one who was himself "Word" ' (108), and this means that he finds the text's own teleology inseparable from God.

The Bible as perlocutionary effect of God's speech acts

Now, although I do not think that we can or should reintroduce a premodern reading of the Bible,[33] I suggest that there are some important clues in Frei's position for how we might argue for the kind of Christocentric narrative realism I am proposing. To see how this might work, we need to recall that speech acts have perlocutionary effects. These are 'what we bring about or achieve by doing something' (Austin 1975[2]: 109). For example, to over-simplify vastly, God's declarative speech act of covenant making in accordance with his promissory word has the perlocutionary effect of bringing about human salvation and his own glorification.

The Bible is, as many have stressed, *testimony*, principally to God's act in his Christ, the promised one. Just so, the apostles were called by Jesus and equipped by the Holy Spirit to witness to the Gospel of repentance and forgiveness and to Jesus' dying and rising.[34] In terms of speech act theory, they were called to testify to the effectiveness of God's declarative speech act in Christ by which he has brought the world into conformity with his word. The first point to note here is that the gift of the Holy Spirit effects salvation in the life of the apostle (as in all believers) and so enables their testimony to be a perlocutionary effect of God's speech acts in Christ. Their being witnesses is the conforming of their words to the new world that God has brought into being in Christ. This being the case, it is reasonable to suggest that we should regard the deposit of that witness in the New Testament as a paradigm case of the possibility of the meaningfulness and referential success of human speech about God.[35] This needs explaining.

John Searle suggests that some declarative speech acts can be understood as 'assertive declarations'. These are assertives 'issued with the force of declarations' (1979: 20, 19).[36] Now, declarations 'bring about some alteration of the status or condition of the referred to object or objects solely in virtue of the fact that the declaration has been successfully performed' (Searle 1979: 17). Remember also that declarations have both directions of fit: they are

---

[33] See here Charles Wood's excellent small book on hermeneutics (1981).

[34] Luke 24:44ff; Acts 1:8.

[35] The Old Testament can be argued to be a perlocutionary effect of God's speech acts, especially of promising; its wider role as witness to, and its being a perlocutionary effect of, salvation history follows from Christ's use of it, such passages as Luke 24:27, and the wider use made of the Old Testament by the composers of the New.

[36] See chapter 8, p. 200.

word-to-world and world-to-word. They assert the facts and hence their words are conformed to the world, but they also bring the world into conformity with the words used in the declaration. For example, a judge makes a factual claim when he says 'you are guilty' – he asserts how the world is; his words are conformed to the world. And, 'if the judge declares you guilty (and is upheld on appeal), then for legal purposes, you are guilty' (Searle 1979: 19). So his words have the force of a declaration: the world is brought into conformity with the judge's word and the guilty person punished.

Now, here we are concerned with God's self-declarative act in Christ. In Christ's crucifixion God's judgement on sin is declared: 'for our sake [God] made him to be sin who knew no sin'. Yet he does this 'so that' by being made alive with him in his resurrection 'we might become the righteousness of God' (2 Cor. 5:21): God's declaration of judgement and forgiveness in Christ brings about human salvation. Insofar as God makes Christ to be sin in our place, God's judgement is an assertion of the facts of human disobedience; his assertion has word-to-world direction of fit. And because Christ is judged in our place, God's declaration of forgiveness makes us 'the righteousness of God'; his declaration has world-to-word direction of fit. In virtue of God's judgement of sin and his declaration of forgiveness, God's word is brought to effect and the world is brought back under the liberating sovereignty of his word. This means that the perlocutionary effectiveness of the apostolic testimony to Christ is dependent on God's self-declarative action. That which it asserts is only a *witness* if their words are conformed to the world. Thus, only if God has indeed acted in the cross and resurrection of Christ in such a way as to have judged sin and pronounced his life-giving 'Yes' to humanity can the apostolic word be conformed to the world. The verdict and the forgiveness they declare are not their own, but God's; the story they tell is not their own, but God's.

Why does it matter that the Gospel story be told faithfully? Not principally to satisfy sceptics who separate the text's meaning from its truth as God's appointed testimony. Rather, the responsibility of the witnesses is to God's act in Jesus Christ so that by his grace their human words and interpretations may become God's interpretation of us and the means whereby he gives us fellowship with himself.[37] The effectiveness of the Bible depends on its being a faithful testimony to the consummation of God's teleological purposes in Christ; it is not effective intrinsically and apart from his action. It can only produce fellowship with him if he wills it. We have to trust that

[37] See 1 John 1:1–4.

what we have under a description in the Bible is indeed reality – that the witnesses' words are conformed to the world. The testimony of the church is that when the Bible is read with expectant, obedient faith, it becomes God's living word through which he reveals himself, exposes and judges our sin, sends forth his Holy Spirit, and conforms us, here and now, to himself. It is this that gives confidence that the text is related truthfully to extratextual reality and that '[a]t the foundation of the [Christian] faith there lies a deed done, an incarnating of the eternal in the stuff of human history' (MacKinnon 1979: 22). To see how this is so, we need to look in more detail at how God conforms the world to his word.

CONFORMING THE WORLD TO THE WORD

Teleology, story, worship

We can begin by noting that because the Lord is as he is for his people in their present and will be for them in their future, the Bible is testimony to what he has done and what he will do. Thus, the narrative unity of the Bible is found in the dialectic of promise and fulfilment and its teleology is grounded in God's nature and self-revealed name, *YHWH*, *ehyeh asher ehyeh*. Robert Jenson argues that, 'In the Bible the name of God and the narration of his works ... belong together. The descriptions that make the name work are items of the narrative. And conversely, identifying God, backing up the name, is the very function of the narrative' (1982: 7). This is correct, but although the primary function of the narrative is to identify God, its secondary function is, as we have just seen, to bring us into fellowship with him and to enable us to glorify him – to conform our world to his word.

It is a commonplace of much contemporary theology that narrative is an especially fitting means of theological reflection because of the way in which it allows 'the telling of a story whose meaning unfolds through the interplay of characters and actions over time' (Goldberg 1991[2]: 35). This kind of view presumes that the identity of an agent is neither constituted by a non-material essence behind their actions nor found in 'an arbitrary sequence of physical events' (Kelsey 1975: 47). Identity is not to be understood on either essentialist or behaviourist lines; rather it lies in the interaction of the public and the private. This implies a middle-distance, descriptive literary realism, for 'identity can only be described by recounting the characteristic patterns in [a person's] intention–action sequences' (47). I have argued that God's intentions and actions in the world are perfectly integrated in a way which is not characteristic of mortals,[38] and this means that God's self-expression through his word is uniquely apt to be rendered as a narrative.

We therefore have further reason to hold that the Bible's expression of God's word is properly regarded as having a teleological, narrative structure insofar as he uses it as a means of acting in the church. Thus, despite the range of historical contexts in which its writings were composed, the varying theological interests of its redactors, and the plurality of genres embraced by the canon, so far as they witness in their particular ways to *ehyeh asher ehyeh*'s relationship with humanity they can be said to be embraced by the single, over-arching narrative of the Bible's temporal sequence from creation to consummation. This sequence is brought into being because God's promises have what in the previous chapter I called a 'narrative meaning' in virtue of their fulfilment in Christ. In the words of Charles Wood, the canon of scripture is 'a story in which real events and persons are depicted in such a way that it discloses their relationship to God and God's purposes' (1981: 100). Thus, against Ricoeur, the Bible's teleology is neither *invented* by the narrative itself nor *fashioned* by the reader's constructive imagination. It is *found* by the church as its reading of the scriptures is quickened by God's Spirit and they become a word of revelation. So the church's reading of scripture is teleological in the double sense that it reads with the purpose of knowing God in his teleological action. Furthermore, in so reading scripture, the church is drawn into his purposes for his world – purposes of which the church is both anticipation and herald.[39] In this reading, the testimony of scripture transforms us into 'a letter of Christ . . . written not with ink but with the Spirit of the living God, not on tablets of stone but on tablets of human hearts' (2 Cor. 3:3).[40] The Bible becomes the living word of God that conforms us to his image and likeness and so enables us to represent him.

In a much-cited passage from his famous comparison of the Bible and the literature of classical antiquity, Erich Auerbach states that

> Far from seeking, like Homer, merely to make us forget our own reality for a few hours, [the Biblical narrative] seeks to overcome our reality: we are to fit our own story into its world, feel ourselves elements in its structure of universal history. (1968: 15)

This suggestion (and other of Auerbach's observations) lies behind much narrative theology. For example, recall Lindbeck's claim that 'no world is

---

[38] See pp. 167f above.

[39] For a more directly theological consideration of this topic, see John Webster's excellent 1998b. *The* primary text for teleological hermeneutics is Augustine's *De doctrina Christiana* (1958).

[40] Cf. 2 Cor. 3:3–4:7 *passim*.

more real than the one [the canonical writings] create. A scriptural world is thus able to absorb the universe' (1984: 117). Now, in his 'intratextualism' Lindbeck is concerned not just with our having that interpretative grid which gives us reality as it is; he wishes also to argue that the believer is 'to be conformed to the Jesus Christ depicted in the narrative' (120). This suggestion is very helpful, but, as we saw in chapter 5, Lindbeck's account is deficient in that it seriously downplays the significance of the Lord's present activity in the church. He – like Wolterstorff, who makes a similar proposal[41] – seems to think that, rather than being constituted by the living one to whom the story bears witness, '[t]he church's identity [is] *story-constituted*' (Wolterstorff 2001: 205). Because they do not take into consideration God's present work in sustaining the life of the church, these proposals can produce a rigid conservatism. Again, Francis Watson has argued for an 'intratextual realism' in relation to his call for a renewed biblical theology.[42] But a similar conservative ecclesiasticism will result if we accept his assertion of 'the fundamental hermeneutical significance of the reading community as the location from which the text derives its being and rationale' (1994: 3). Against these views, it seems to me vital that we maintain that the being, rationale, and meaning of the Bible *qua* scripture of the church depend on God's teleological action.

It is not (just our reading of) the text that brings us into conformity with Jesus Christ. Rather, if the Bible is a perlocutionary effect of God's declarative speech act in Christ crucified and risen, and if its effectiveness is backed up by that declaration, then it is reasonable to believe that, as the Holy Spirit makes the Lord present to the church in its reading of the scriptures and celebration of the sacraments, so the same Lord brings the church into conformity with himself.

But how does this conforming come about? We need to remember that the Holy Spirit has been given to indwell God's people. He heals and renews them – corporately and individually – so that they can offer the Lord true worship and show his independent reality through their words and deeds. This process is mediated by divinely instituted covenant practices that glorify God by bringing the world – represented by the church – into conformity with God's word. To unpack this and return to themes developed elsewhere (particularly in chapters 5 and 7): we can understand the life of the world and human participation in it as a story – a *single* story – because all the individual stories of human living, of human accomplishments and human wickedness, are redeemed and revealed as *a* story in

---

[41] See his 2001.   [42] See his 1994: 151f, 224f.

the Gospel story.[43] In liturgical worship, the story of God's love is told in a variety of ways – in absolution, in hearing scripture, in singing God's praise, in preaching, in professing the faith of the church, in prayer, and in celebration of the sacraments. In response to this telling of the divine story, the human story is capable of being told in a variety of speech acts: through the individual members of the church making corporate confession, in the praises and laments rehearsed in the recitation of the psalms, in the church's intercessions for the world, and in the sending out in mission. As the 'word' of the human story is told under the impetus of the great declaratives of the divine story – those great *faits accomplis* of salvation history – so the new world revealed in Jesus Christ comes into being in the church. The human world is conformed to the word of God's love in Christ.

(That worship should be liturgical needs emphasis here. One of the problems with non-liturgical or 'pick-and-mix' worship in the Church of England is that it frequently attenuates the range of biblical allusion and quotation found in liturgical worship and so gives reduced scope for expressing the story of God's love. Moreover, since this style is often less congregational than liturgical worship, it gives correspondingly less opportunity to integrate our stories with the biblical story. When combined with preponderantly affective and subjective 'spiritual songs' that have been wrenched from their wider scriptural and theological context (and are often sung repeatedly to the point where one wonders whether the congregation is not at risk of 'vain repetition'), this style of worship is worryingly close to Cupittian expressivism.)

In the life of the individual Christian this process of conformation goes on in private devotion and obedient living. But the corporate, worshipping life of the church is indispensable, and here conformation is especially focussed in preaching and the celebration of the covenantal sacraments instituted by Jesus. Considered as speech acts, the propositional content of preaching and sacraments is 'the word of the cross ... [which] is the power of God' (I Cor. 1:18).[44] Thus, both word and sacrament derive their meaning from the reconciliation accomplished between God and humanity in Christ's death and resurrection and the new participation in the divine reality thereby effected. Thiselton uses speech act theory in a helpful way to elucidate the operation of the word of the cross. He writes that

The language of *atonement* makes *assertions* about the finished work of Christ, in which direction of fit is from *word-to-world*: the word of the cross, in this context, communicates and asserts the reality of what God *has done*. That it is *past* is part of

---

[43] Compare my observations concerning the story of the people of Israel on p. 172 above.
[44] Cf. Rom. 10:14–17, 1:1–6, 6:1–11; 1 Cor. 11:20–31.

the logic of its description as a *completed* work to which humankind can contribute nothing. But the language of *participation* is bound up with *promise, commitment, declaration, and directive*: it is *world-to-word* in that it *shapes the identity* of the Christian and *creates the reality of the new creation.* (1992: 303, corrected)

Some exegetes try to drive a wedge between the logic of Paul's atonement language and that of his language of participation, but Thiselton cautions against this. From a theological point of view he is correct: both belong within the ambit of God's covenant, for it is this relationship – broken by sin but, by the grace of God, restored – that grants us participation in the life of God.

So we turn now to examine how, animated as they are by the word of the cross, preaching and sacraments conform us to God's word. We shall see that the idea of being sent and of being decentred are fundamental to this as well as to how Christian language can be meaningful. But before doing so, it will be helpful to bear in mind that since he is the word of God incarnate, Jesus' command to preach and celebrate the sacraments is a *directive* intended to enable Jesus' disciples to re-present God's consummation of his purposes in him: to reveal his glory through their sanctification; to conform their self-expression in deed and word to the reality of his word by allowing his word to shape their words and deeds. The effectiveness of this directive is underwritten by God's accomplishment of his purposes in Christ, and this is why, as I suggested in chapter 5, God, by his word and Spirit in the church, can be said to be the intended grammar of Christian faith.[45] That is, he is directly present to those practices, sustaining them and enabling them to show his independent, transcendent reality.[46]

The sending of the word

Preaching and sacraments are speech acts of both praise and prophecy. Inspired and animated by the Holy Spirit, they are founded in the completed work of Christ. As praise, they assert both the saving reality of God revealed in Christ and the truth of his speech. Because praise is offered to the God who will be the Lord of all in his coming Kingdom, praise is also prophetic, and prophetic speech is fundamentally promissory: it foretells the final conforming of the world to the word of God, and so enables the church to witness to it.

---

[45] See pp. 118–22 above.
[46] For a profound discussion of God's transcendence in the context of Christian practices, see Anderson 1975: 227–305.

Now of course, none of this would be possible had Christ not been raised from the dead, and this means that Christian speech is utterly dependent on God as its *alpha* and *omega*; it has full meaning and reference only insofar as God grants it participation in his teleological work. This dependency is of a similar kind to that Jesus experienced. As we saw in the last chapter, Jesus knew himself to have been commissioned – or, in Johannine language, sent – to bring the word of God to effect by conforming the world to it. His identity and mission were shaped both by trust that God had sent him and by the commensurate responsibility to bring about the state of affairs expressed in God's promise.[47] In John's terminology, this state of affairs is the glorification of the Father and 'eternal life' for humanity. '[A]nd this is eternal life, that they may know you, the only true God, and Jesus Christ whom you have sent' (John 17:3). Moreover, as Jesus prays to the Father, '[a]s you have sent me into the world, so I have sent them [sc. his disciples] into the world ... As you, Father, are in me and I am in you, may they also be in us, so that the world may believe that you have sent me ... and have loved them even as you have loved me' (17:18, 21). So the church's speech is like Jesus' in that it is speech which results from having been sent forth in mission.

The church is called to participate in the teleological work of the Lord, but its dependency is different from Jesus' because God's work has been proleptically finished in him and the church can add nothing to it. However, in being sent out in mission, it participates in bringing to present effect that conforming of the world to God's word that Christ has already achieved. And for this task it needs to find its identity as Jesus did: in being sent. Paul emphasizes that the preaching of the church arises from its being sent, and claims that when this occurs 'faith comes from what is heard, and what is heard comes through the word of Christ' (Rom. 10:17, cf. 15). The genitive in the verse just quoted is taken by many commentators to be subjective. For example, Cranfield paraphrases 'through the word of Christ' as 'through Christ's speaking the message by the mouth of his messengers' (1979: 537). The significance of this is that Paul thinks it is possible for human speech acts to be divine speech acts and that for this reason they are effective in producing faith and obedience.[48]

But isn't there a problem here? What about Derrida's deconstructive arguments against the felicitous transmission of the content of speech acts?[49]

[47] See John 6:57, 7:29, 8:49.
[48] See Wolterstorff's (1995: 37–57, 288–96) stimulating discussion of how human speech acts can be divine speech acts.
[49] See chapter 8, pp. 209–13 above.

Well, remember that Derrida's argument only works against the logos of rationalism, and then only from the perspective of disbelief. For this reason Brian Ingraffia points out that 'The logos of the Bible does not found the self-presence of the conscious subject, but unsettles the desire of humanity to establish truth and meaning within a realm of one's own' (1995: 185). We have noted elsewhere the unsettling effect of the logos incarnate in Jesus. This precipitated anxious questions as to the meaning and truth of his discourse and in the end brought about the attempt to annihilate him. We shall return to Jesus' unsettling – or, as I shall put it, decentring – effect. For the moment, remember also that Jesus' consciousness of his identity as the accomplishment of the divine promissory word was constituted by his being *sent* by the Father. He could do nothing on his own authority; he came not to do his own will but the will of the one who sent him; and his teaching was not his own but his who sent him.[50] Moreover, the middle-distance realism of the Gospels presents Jesus in the strength of his active obedience and the powerlessness of his suffering; it does not give us the materials we would need to talk about Jesus' inner consciousness.[51] This itself is significant against Derrida's attack on logocentrism. But so far as we are able to mythologize the Gospel narrative in Derridean terms, the key point is that Jesus did not find his identity in being self-consciously present to *himself*. His identity was not centred on himself; it was decentred by the demands of obedience to the Father. Jesus found his identity not by using language to generate a realm of meaning in which he could fully realize his own will but by being fully at the disposal of the word of the Father. As Hans Frei points out in his discussion of the enacted intention of Jesus:

His obedience exists solely as a counterpart to his being sent and has God for its indispensable point of reference. Jesus' very identity involves the will and purpose of the Father who sent him. He becomes who he is in the story by consenting to God's intention and by enacting that intention in the midst of the circumstances that devolve around him as the fulfilment of God's purpose. (1975: 107)

Because he was obedient, Jesus' speech acts could have full meaning. His being raised from the dead was the verdict that in his whole being he had been faithful to God's word.

In a similar way – similar and *only* similar: Christians are not second Christs[52] – the Christian's identity is not founded on their own self-presence in their utterances; it is found in dying to one's self in obedience to the word of Christ. 'If any want to become my followers, let them deny themselves

---

[50] John 5:30, 7:16.   [51] See Frei 1975: 105ff.   [52] See Outka 1987: 150–1.

and take up their cross and follow me. For those who want to save their life will lose it, and those who lose their life for my sake, and for the sake of the gospel, will save it' (Mark 8:34f). Only in this act of self-denial for Jesus' sake do human beings become who they truly are. This is sacramentally enacted in baptism. Here God acts interruptively in the life of the church and brings to present effect in the life of the convert what he did once and for all in Christ: 'when you were buried with him [sc. Christ] in baptism, you were also raised with him through faith in the power of God, who raised him from the dead' (Col. 2:12). To this objective and passive pole of baptism there corresponds a subjective and active pole: 'As many of you as were baptized into Christ have clothed yourselves with Christ' (Gal. 3:27). So the practice of baptism is the beginning of a person's new life as a disciple and redeemed *imago Dei*.

And because baptism is dying and being raised with Christ, we can speak of the disciple as one who lives a decentred life.[53] Jesus unsettles the life of his disciples so that the centre of their life is not themselves but him. The structure of the letter to the Colossians clearly reflects the dynamic relationship between the objective-and-passive and the subjective-and-active aspects of baptism.[54] Expounding the latter, the author writes: 'So if you have been raised with Christ, seek the things that are above, where Christ is, seated at the right hand of God. Set your minds on things that are above, not on things that are on earth, for you have died, and your life is hidden with Christ in God' (Col. 3:1–3).[55] Baptismal language might be taken to enunciate primarily an ontological and moral decentring, but this passage indicates that the Christian life also involves a conceptual and epistemological decentring in which the true nature of reality is discovered by setting one's mind on things that are above.

If baptism is the once and for all sacrament of initiation into Christ so that we live from and for him rather than ourselves, it is the eucharist which sustains that life. Its meaning is chiefly constituted by Jesus' self-offering to the Father for our sake on the cross. However, by reminding us that we belong to him and to one another in his body, the Lord of the eucharist trains the Christian to live a decentred life in him. We have seen that this is epistemological and conceptual, but because it is moral and ontological it also involves the 'form' of our agency – our embodiment.

---

[53] For the philosophical and phenomenological dimensions of this, see Westphal 1992.

[54] The teaching on baptism (2:6–15) functions as a hinge between the author's doctrinal teaching about what God has done and his moral teaching about how Christians should therefore live.

[55] The antithesis between 'above' and 'on earth' does not mean that matter is evil, nor does 'setting one's mind on things that are above' imply an other-worldly religiosity.

Thus remembrance of the broken body of the Lord and our feeding on his body and blood decentre our sense of our bodily existence and what constitutes our well-being. Our body is 'not [our] own' but 'a temple of the Holy Spirit'; how we think of our body and use it should reflect our acknowledgement that we were 'bought with a price' (1 Cor. 6:19f).

To return to the Wittgensteinian idiom used in chapters 4 and 5, Christians learn the grammar of 'body' in the context of the eucharist. To say that God himself is the grammar of Christian practices – that it is he who shows himself through them and sustains them – is (amongst many other things) to say that '[t]he Body and Blood of Christ ... are verily and indeed taken and received by the faithful in the Lord's Supper'.[56] It is not to commit ourselves to transubstantiation as Catherine Pickstock, a recent writer on these themes, does. Nor therefore is it to say that 'transubstantiation [is] the condition of possibility for all meaning' (Pickstock 1998: 261). That would be to argue transcendentally but in a way that risks by-passing the completed work of Christ and focussing on the 'how' rather than the 'that' of Jesus' real presence. It is God's verdict in raising Christ that warrants our breaking bread and sharing the cup; it is only because that verdict has been declared that we can take and eat and drink Christ's body and blood. Unless this is kept clearly in view, we risk falling into a conservative ecclesiasticism such as we found implicit in Lindbeck's, Watson's, and Wolterstorff's understanding of scripture. The church is not constituted primarily by scripture or by the sacraments; it is constituted by Jesus Christ, who meets us in and through them. As we saw in chapter 6 in particular, the condition of possibility of all meaning is the crucifixion and resurrection of Christ, for it is in these events that God abolishes our self-annihilating 'No' against him and declares his verdict of 'Yes' for human language use in Christ. But the question remains, How is it that *our* language use here and now can be meaningful?

At the end of the eucharist we are sent out in mission. Incorporated into Christ, worshippers offer their whole being as a living sacrifice and pray to be sent out in the power of the Spirit to live and work to his praise and glory.[57] Mission dramatizes and draws to a focus every aspect of decentring by the risen Lord, for it calls us to follow him and encounter with our whole being that which is other than ourselves culturally and morally, epistemologically and conceptually, ontologically and bodily (the latter especially if we work as overseas mission partners). In this sense, the eucharist is incomplete if it

[56] From the Catechism in *The Book of Common Prayer*.
[57] See *Common Worship*, p. 182, for example.

does not lead into mission.[58] The God who shows his independent reality through the word preached, the bread broken, and the wine shared is the one who goes out of himself for the sake of the world and commissions us to participate in this movement. So through this encounter with, and for the sake of, the other we learn afresh to find the centre of our lives in Christ rather than ourselves. It is just such experience that leads Paul to the extraordinary statement that 'I have been crucified with Christ; it is no longer I who live, but it is Christ who lives in me. And the life I now live in the flesh I live by faith in the Son of God, who loved me and gave himself for me' (Gal. 2:19–20). Only in trust that this is indeed happening dare a Christian say that the Lord uses our lives to represent his independent reality.

Paul found himself moved to speak in this way as a result of his being sent out in mission so that God could use him as his ambassador and make his appeal through him.[59] For this reason, Paul's identity consisted in his being sent out for the Lord.[60] Christians are sent by Christ as Christ was sent from the Father. By God's Spirit they declare and enact God's conforming the world to his word. Just as Jesus' identity was constituted by his being sent rather than by his presence to himself, so too for the disciple, her identity is found in the decentring experience of being sent. In her being conformed to the conforming word of Christ, she is able to bear effective witness to God's declaration in Christ. Thus, because she has been incorporated into Christ, the bringing into effect of the promises of God the Christian announces in her words (and deeds) does not – *contra* Derrida – depend on her preventing all possible infelicities in their transmission, for she, like Jesus, is one who is sent to proclaim *God's* word, not her own. In Christ he has undertaken to make her words useful and meaningful in his purposes. And insofar as anything she says is said 'in Christ', it too will be meaningful.[61]

I said that the Bible and Christian preaching are perlocutionary effects of God's fulfilment of his promises in Christ and that God is directly present to Christian practices as their grammar. Thus a Christocentric narrative realism is committed to the claim that the meaning and truth of the Bible is to be found where God is doing his teleological work. It is therefore to be found in front of the text in God's work here and now, in and through the body of Christ. It is this isomorphism between what God is doing and that

---

[58] Mission is here broadly conceived as what any Christian does in virtue of their vocation to participate in God's saving work for his world.

[59] 2 Cor. 5:20f; note that Paul uses the first person plural here to include all believers.

[60] See 2 Cor. 4:5–12; cf. Col. 1:24ff.   [61] Cf. James 1:19–27.

to which scripture testifies that warrants our confidence that this meaning and truth is more a finding than a fashioning, that the Bible's story is indeed realistic, and that it is ontologically related to what lies behind it. Confirmation of this depends on God's fully and finally conforming the world to his word. We have this confidence proleptically on the basis of the work of Christ and through his Spirit drawing us into the love of the Father.

Christians are in the same position as Hilary Putnam – 'a practising Jew … for whom the religious dimension of life has become increasingly important'. Although he is thinking of mundane language use, his words are also applicable to the theological case: 'our language game rests not on proof or on Reason but *trust*' (1992: 1, 177). God vindicated Christ's trust, so in him Christian speech about God is bold, confident that 'the ordinary language in which it is cast will miraculously suffice' (Frei 1993: 212). If we are able to show God's independent reality in our lives and speak faithfully of him, this is through his grace in Jesus Christ and under the guidance of the Holy Spirit; whether we have done so will be known fully only when the Book of Life is opened.

References

All quotations from the Bible are from the NRSV unless otherwise stated.

Abraham, W. J. and S. W. Holtzer (eds.). 1987. *The Rationality of Religious Belief: Essays in Honour of Basil Mitchell*. Oxford: Clarendon Press.

Achtemeier, P. Mark. 1994. 'The Truth of Tradition: Critical Realism in the Thought of Alasdair MacIntyre and T. F. Torrance', *Scottish Journal of Theology*, 47/3, pp. 355–74.

Alston, William P. 1989. *Divine Nature and Human Language: Essays in Philosophical Theology*. Ithaca: Cornell University Press.

1991. *Perceiving God: The Epistemology of Religious Experience*. Ithaca: Cornell University Press.

1992. 'Foundationalism', in Dancy and Sosa 1992, pp. 144–7.

1993. 'On Knowing that We Know: The Application to Religious Knowledge', in Evans and Westphal 1993, pp. 15–39.

1995a. 'Realism and the Christian Faith', *International Journal for Philosophy of Religion*, 38, pp. 37–60.

1995b. 'Taking the Curse off Language-Games: A Realist Account of Doxastic Practices', in Tessin and von der Ruhr 1995.

1996. *A Realist Conception of Truth*. Ithaca: Cornell University Press.

2000. *Illocutionary Acts and Sentence Meaning*. Ithaca: Cornell University Press.

Ambrose, Alice (ed.). 1979. *Wittgenstein's Lectures, Cambridge 1932–1935, from the notes of Alice Ambrose and Margaret Macdonald*. Oxford: Blackwell.

Anderson, Ray S. 1975. *Historical Transcendence and the Reality of God: A Christological Critique*. London: Geoffrey Chapman.

Anselm of Canterbury. 1979. *Proslogion* (trans. and introduced by M. J. Charlesworth). Notre Dame: Notre Dame University Press.

Aquinas, Thomas. 1964. *Summa theologiae*, Vol. 111 (trans. etc. Herbert McCabe). London: Eyre & Spottiswoode.

Aronson, J., R. Harré, and E. Way. 1995. *Realism Rescued: How Scientific Progress is Possible*. Chicago: Open Court.

Arrington, Robert L. 2001. '"Theology as Grammar": Wittgenstein and Some Critics', in Arrington and Addis 2001, pp. 167–83.

Arrington, Robert L. and Mark Addis (eds.). 2001. *Wittgenstein and Philosophy of Religion*. London and New York: Routledge.

Auerbach, Erich. 1968. *Mimesis: The Representation of Reality in Western Literature.* Princeton: Princeton University Press.

Augustine of Hippo. 1958. *On Christian Doctrine.* Indianapolis, Indiana: Bobbs-Merrill Educational Publishing (The Library of Liberal Arts).

1974². *The Essential Augustine* (selected by Vernon J. Bourke). Indianapolis, Indiana: Hackett.

1978. *The Confessions of St Augustine* (trans. F. J. Sheed). London: Sheed and Ward.

Austin, J. L. 1975². *How to Do Things with Words.* Oxford: Oxford University Press.

Baelz, Peter. 1972. 'A Deliberate Mistake?', in Sykes and Clayton 1972, pp. 13–34.

Baker, G. P. and P. M. S. Hacker. 1980. *Wittgenstein: Meaning and Understanding: An Analytical Commentary on the* Philosophical Investigations, *Volume 1.* Oxford: Blackwell.

1984. *Scepticism, Rules and Language.* Oxford: Blackwell.

1985. *Wittgenstein: Rules, Grammar and Necessity: An Analytical Commentary on the* Philosophical Investigations, *Volume 2.* Oxford: Blackwell.

Balthasar, Hans Urs von. 1989. *The Glory of the Lord: A Theological Aesthetics, Volume VII: Theology: The New Covenant.* Edinburgh: T. & T. Clark.

Bambrough, Renford (ed.). 1965. *New Essays on Plato and Aristotle.* London: RKP.

Banner, Michael C. 1990. *The Justification of Science and the Rationality of Religious Belief.* Oxford: Clarendon Press.

1999. *Christian Ethics and Contemporary Moral Problems.* Cambridge: CUP.

Barbour, Ian G. 1966. *Issues in Science and Religion.* London: SCM.

1974. *Myths, Models and Paradigms: The Nature of Scientific and Religious Language.* London: SCM.

1990. *Religion in an Age of Science: The Gifford Lectures for 1989–1991, Volume 1.* London: SCM.

Barr, James. 1993. *Biblical Faith and Natural Theology: The Gifford Lectures for 1991.* Oxford: Clarendon Press.

Barrett, Charles K. 1971². *A Commentary on the First Epistle to the Corinthians.* London: A. & C. Black.

Barrigar, Christian J. 1991. 'Protecting God: The Lexical Formation of Trinitarian Language', *Modern Theology,* 7/4, pp. 299–310.

Barth, Karl. 1933. *The Resurrection of the Dead.* London: Hodder & Stoughton.

1935. *The Word of God and the Word of Man.* London: Hodder & Stoughton.

1954. *Against the Stream: Shorter Post-War Writings 1946–52.* London: SCM.

1956. *Church Dogmatics, Volume I: The Doctrine of the Word of God, Second Half-Volume.* Edinburgh: T. & T. Clark.

1957. *Church Dogmatics, Volume II: The Doctrine of God, First Half-Volume.* Edinburgh: T. & T. Clark.

1958. *Church Dogmatics, Volume III: The Doctrine of Creation, Part One.* Edinburgh: T. & T. Clark.

1960a. *Anselm: Fides Quaerens Intellectum: Anselm's Proof of the Existence of God in the Context of his Theological Scheme.* London: SCM.

1960b. *Church Dogmatics, Volume III: The Doctrine of Creation, Part Three.* Edinburgh: T. & T. Clark.

1961a. *The Humanity of God.* London: Collins.

1961b. *Church Dogmatics, Volume IV: The Doctrine of Reconciliation, Part Three, First Half.* Edinburgh: T. & T. Clark.

1962. *Church Dogmatics, Volume IV: The Doctrine of Reconciliation, Part Three, Second Half.* Edinburgh: T. & T. Clark.

1966. *Dogmatics in Outline.* London: SCM.

1975. *Church Dogmatics, Volume I: The Doctrine of the Word of God, Part One.* Edinburgh: T. & T. Clark.

1979. *Evangelical Theology: An Introduction.* Edinburgh: T. & T. Clark.

1986a. 'Fate and Idea in Theology', in Rumscheidt 1986, pp. 25–61.

1986b. *Witness to the Word: A Commentary on John 1.* Grand Rapids, Michigan: Eerdmans.

1991. *The Göttingen Dogmatics: Instruction in Christian Religion, Volume I.* Grand Rapids, Michigan: Eerdmans.

Bauckham, R. 1992. 'The Worship of Jesus', in Freedman et al. 1992, Vol. III, pp. 812–20.

1998. *God Crucified: Monotheism and Christology in the New Testament.* Carlisle: Paternoster Press.

Baudrillard, Jean. 1997. 'The Illusion of the End', in Jenkins 1997, pp. 39–46.

Beasley-Murray, G. R. 1974. *The Book of Revelation.* London: Oliphants/Marshall, Morgan and Scott.

Beeck, Frans Jozef van, SJ. 1994. *God Encountered: A Contemporary Catholic Systematic Theology. Volume Two/2: The Revelation of the Glory, Part II: One God, Creator of All That Is.* Collegeville, Minnesota: The Liturgical Press.

Bell, Richard H. (ed.). 1988. *The Grammar of the Heart: New Essays in Moral Philosophy and Theology.* San Francisco: Harper & Row.

1995. 'Religion and Wittgenstein's Legacy: Beyond Fideism and Language Games', in Tessin and von der Ruhr 1995, pp. 215–47.

Beller, Mara. 1998. 'The Sokal Hoax: At Whom are we Laughing?', *Physics Today*, 51/9, pp. 29–34.

Berkhof, Hendrikus. 1989. *Two Hundred Years of Theology: Report of a Personal Journey.* Grand Rapids, Michigan: Eerdmans.

Bethge, Eberhard. 1970. *Dietrich Bonhoeffer: Theologian, Christian, Contemporary.* London: Collins.

Bhaskar, Roy. 1975. *A Realist Theory of Science.* Leeds: Leeds Books.

Blackburn, Simon. 1993. *Essays in Quasi-Realism.* New York and Oxford: Oxford University Press.

Bockmuehl, Markus. 1998. ' "To Be or Not To Be": The Possible Futures of New Testament Scholarship', *Scottish Journal of Theology*, 51/3, pp. 271–306.

Boghossian, Paul. 1996. 'What the Sokal Hoax Ought to Teach us: The Pernicious Consequences and Internal Contradictions of "Postmodernist" Relativism', *Times Literary Supplement*, 13 December 1996, pp. 14–15.

Boulton, David. 1997. *A Reasonable Faith: Introducing the Sea of Faith Network*. Loughborough: Sea of Faith.

Boyd, Richard N. 1979. 'Metaphor and Theory Change: What is "Metaphor" a Metaphor for?', in Ortony 1979, pp. 356–408.

1984. 'The Current Status of Scientific Realism', in Leplin 1984, pp. 41–82.

1985. '*Lex Orandi est Lex Credendi*', in Churchland and Hooker 1985, pp. 3–34.

Braaten, Carl and Robert Jenson (eds.). 1984. *Christian Dogmatics, Volume 2*. Philadelphia, Pennsylvania: Fortress Press.

Braithwaite, R. B. 1971. 'An Empiricist's View of the Nature of Religious Belief', in Mitchell 1971, pp. 72–91.

Brown, Colin (ed.). 1978. *The New International Dictionary of New Testament Theology*, Vol. III. Grand Rapids, Michigan: Zondervan.

Brown, Raymond E. 1971. *The Gospel According to John*, 2 vols. London: Geoffrey Chapman.

1982. *The Epistles of John*. Garden City, New York: Doubleday.

Brueggemann, Walter. 1997. *Theology of the Old Testament: Testimony, Dispute, Advocacy*. Minneapolis, Minnesota: Fortress Press.

Buckley, Michael J. 1987. *At the Origins of Modern Atheism*. New Haven: Yale University Press.

Bultmann, Rudolf. 1985. *New Testament and Mythology and Other Basic Writings*. London: SCM.

Byrne, Peter. 1995. *Prolegomena to Religious Pluralism: Reference and Realism in Religion*. London: Macmillan.

Cahn, Steven M. and David Shatz (eds.). 1982. *Contemporary Philosophy of Religion*. Oxford: Oxford University Press.

Caird, G. B. 1980. *The Language and Imagery of the Bible*. London: Duckworth.

Calvin, John. 1960. (trans. Ford Lewis Battles; ed. John T. McNeill). *Institutes of the Christian Religion*. Philadelphia, Pennsylvania: Westminster Press.

Caygill, Howard. 1995. *A Kant Dictionary*. Oxford: Blackwell.

Childs, Brevard S. 1974. *Exodus: A Commentary*. London: SCM.

1985. *Old Testament Theology in a Canonical Context*. London: SCM.

1992. *Biblical Theology of the Old and New Testaments: Theological Reflections on the Christian Bible*. London: SCM.

Churchland, Paul M. and Clifford A. Hooker (eds.). 1985. *Images of Science: Essays on Realism and Empiricism, with a Reply from Bas C. van Fraassen*. Chicago: Chicago University Press.

Clark, Kelly James (ed.). 1993. *Philosophers Who Believe: The Spiritual Journeys of Eleven Leading Thinkers*. Downers Grove: Inter Varsity Press.

Clark, S. R. L. 1998. *God, Religion and Reality*. London: SPCK.

Clayton, Philip. 1989. *Explanation from Physics to Theology: An Essay in Rationality and Religion*. New Haven: Yale University Press.

1997. *God and Contemporary Science*. Edinburgh: Edinburgh University Press.

Coakley, Sarah and David A. Pailin (eds.). 1993. *The Making and Remaking of Christian Doctrine: Essays in Honour of Maurice Wiles*. Oxford: Clarendon Press.

Common Worship: Services and Prayers for the Church of England. London: Church House Publishing, 2000.

Comstock, Gary. 1986. 'Truth or Meaning: Ricoeur versus Frei on Biblical Narrative', *Journal of Religion*, 66, pp. 117–40.

Cook, Francis. 1993. 'Zen and the Problem of Language', in Runzo 1993, pp. 61–76.

Coward, Harold and Toby Foshay (eds.). 1992. *Derrida and Negative Theology*. Albany: State University of New York Press.

Craig, Edward. 1993. 'Understanding Scepticism', in Haldane and Wright 1993, pp. 215–31.

1997. 'Meaning and Privacy', in Hale and Wright 1997, pp. 127–45.

Cranfield, C. E. B. 1975. *A Critical and Exegetical Commentary on The Epistle to the Romans, Volume I*. Edinburgh: T. & T. Clark.

1979. *A Critical and Exegetical Commentary on The Epistle to the Romans, Volume II*. Edinburgh: T. & T. Clark.

Crombie, I. M. 1971. 'The Possibility of Theological Statements', in Mitchell 1971, pp. 23–52.

Crowder, Colin (ed.). 1997. *God and Reality: Essays on Christian Non-Realism*. London: Mowbray.

Culler, J. 1982. *On Deconstruction*. Ithaca: Cornell University Press.

Cupitt, Don. 1980. *Taking Leave of God*. London: SCM.

1984a. *The Sea of Faith: Christianity in Change*. London: BBC.

1984b. 'A Reply to Rowan Williams', *Modern Theology*, 1/1, pp. 25–31.

1985². *Christ and the Hiddenness of God*. London: SCM.

1990. *Creation Out of Nothing*. London: SCM.

1992. *The Time Being*. London: SCM.

1993. 'Changing Our Beliefs: A Response to D. Z. Phillips', in Runzo 1993, pp. 117–18.

1997. 'Free Christianity', in Crowder 1997, pp. 14–25.

1998. *The Religion of Being*. London: SCM.

2001. *Reforming Christianity*. Santa Rosa: Polebridge Press.

Curtis, Edward M. 1992. 'Idol, Idolatry', in Freedman et al. Vol. III, pp. 376–81.

Dalferth, Ingolf U. 1988. *Theology and Philosophy*. Oxford: Blackwell.

1989. 'Karl Barth's Eschatological Realism', in Sykes 1989, pp. 14–45.

1992. 'God and the Mystery of Words', *Journal of the American Academy of Religion*, 40/1, pp. 79–104.

1999. 'Creation – Style of the World', *International Journal of Systematic Theology*, 1/2, pp. 119–37.

Dancy, Jonathan and Ernest Sosa (eds.). 1992. *A Companion to Epistemology*. Oxford: Blackwell.

Davies, G. Henton. 1967. *Exodus: Introduction and Commentary*. London: SCM.

Davis, Stephen T. 1983. *Logic and the Nature of God*. London: Macmillan.

1995. 'Anselm and Phillips on Religious Realism', in Tessin and von der Ruhr 1995, pp. 79–93.

D'Costa, Gavin (ed.). 1996. *Resurrection Reconsidered*. Oxford: Oneworld.

Derrida, Jacques. 1976. *Of Grammatology*. Baltimore, Maryland: Johns Hopkins University Press.

    1988. *Limited Inc*. Evanston, Illinois: Northwestern University Press.

    1992. 'How to Avoid Speaking: Denials', in Coward and Foshay 1992, pp. 73–142.

Devitt, Michael. 1991². *Realism and Truth*. Oxford: Blackwell.

Diamond, Cora. 1991. *The Realistic Spirit: Wittgenstein, Philosophy, and the Mind*. Cambridge, Massachusetts: MIT Press.

    1996. 'Wittgenstein, Mathematics and Ethics: Resisting the Attractions of Realism', in Sluga and Stern 1996: 226–60.

Dickinson, Emily. 1959. *Selected Poems* (ed. James Reeves). London: Heinemann.

Doctrine Commission of the Church of England, The. 1987. *We Believe in God*. London: Church House Publishing.

Drees, Willem B. 1996. *Religion, Science and Naturalism*. Cambridge: Cambridge University Press.

    1998. 'Should Religious Naturalists Promote a Naturalistic Religion?', *Zygon*, 33/4, pp. 617–33.

Dummett, Michael. 1978. *Truth and Other Enigmas*. London: Duckworth.

    1991. *The Logical Basis of Metaphysics*. London: Duckworth.

    1994. 'Reply to McGuinness' in McGuinness and Oliveri 1994, pp. 350–61.

Dunn, J. D. G. 1985. *The Evidence for Jesus: The Impact of Scholarship on Our Understanding of How Christianity Began*. London: SCM.

Durrant, Michael. 1989. 'Reference and Critical Realism', *Modern Theology*, 5/2, pp. 133–43.

    1992. 'The Meaning of "God" – I', in Warner 1992, pp. 71–84.

Eagleton, Terry. 1983. *Literary Theory: An Introduction*. Oxford: Blackwell.

Eicher, P. 1977. *Offenbarung: Prinzip neuzeitlicher Theologie*. Munich: Kösel.

Endean, Phillip. 1996. 'Rahner, Christology and Grace', *Heythrop Journal*, 37/3, pp. 284–97.

Ernst, Cornelius. 1979. *Multiple Echo*. London: DLT.

Evans, C. Stephen. 1998. *Faith Beyond Reason*. Edinburgh: Edinburgh University Press.

    1999. 'Methodological Naturalism in Historical Biblical Scholarship', in Newman 1999, pp. 180–205.

Evans, C. Stephen and Merold Westphal (eds.). 1993. *Christian Perspectives on Religious Knowledge*. Grand Rapids: Eerdmans.

Evans, Donald. 1963. *The Logic of Self-Involvement: A Philosophical Study of Everyday Language Use with Special Reference to the Christian Use of Language about God as Creator*. London: SCM.

Fee, Gordon D. 1987. *The First Epistle to the Corinthians*. Grand Rapids, Michigan: Eerdmans.

Feigl, H. and G. Maxwell (eds.). 1962. *Minnesota Studies in the Philosophy of Science, Volume III*. Minneapolis: University of Minnesota Press.

Ferguson, Niall (ed.). 1997. *Virtual History: Alternatives and Counterfactuals*. London: Picador.

Fergusson, David. 1990. 'Meaning, Truth, and Realism in Bultmann and Lindbeck', *Religious Studies*, 26, pp. 183–98.
Feyerabend, Paul. 1994. 'Quantum Theory and our View of the World', in Hilgevoord 1994, pp. 149–68.
Fiddes, Paul S. 1989. Review of Bruce Marshall 1987, *Journal of Theology Studies*, 40/2, pp. 700–3.
  2000. *The Promised End: Eschatology in Theology and Literature*. Oxford: Blackwell.
Fine, Arthur. 1996². *The Shaky Game: Einstein, Realism and the Quantum Theory*. Chicago: University of Chicago Press.
Flew, A. and A. MacIntyre (eds.). 1955. *New Essays in Philosophical Theology*. London: SCM.
Flint, Thomas P. (ed.). 1990. *Christian Philosophy*. Notre Dame, Indiana: Notre Dame University Press.
Fodor, James. 1995. *Christian Hermeneutics: Paul Ricoeur and the Refiguring of Theology*. Oxford: Clarendon Press.
Ford, David. 1989. 'System, Story, Performance: A Proposal about the Role of Narrative in Christian Systematic Theology', in Hauerwas and Jones 1989, pp. 191–215.
  1992. 'Hans Frei and the Future of Theology', *Modern Theology*, 8/2, pp. 203–14.
  1995. 'What Happens in the Eucharist?', *Scottish Journal of Theology*, 48/3, pp. 359–81.
Forsman, Rodger. 1990. ' "Double Agency" and Identifying Reference to God', in Hebblethwaite and Henderson 1990, pp. 123–42.
Foster, M. B. 1934. 'The Christian Doctrine of Creation and the Rise of Modern Natural Science', *Mind*, 43/172, pp. 446–68.
Fraassen, Bas van. 1980. *The Scientific Image*. Oxford: Clarendon Press.
  1985. 'Empiricism in the Philosophy of Science', in Churchland and Hooker 1985, pp. 245–308.
  1993. 'Three-sided Scholarship: Comments on the Paper of John R. Donahue SJ', in Stump and Flint 1993, pp. 315–25.
  1994a. 'The World of Empiricism', in Hilgevoord 1994, pp. 114–34.
  1994b. 'Discussion', in Hilgevoord 1994, pp. 255–94.
  1999. Response to John Haldane: 'Thomism and the Future of Catholic Philosophy', in *New Blackfriars* 80/938 (April 1999), pp. 177–81.
Freedman, David Noel et al. (eds.). 1992. *The Anchor Bible Dictionary*. 6 Vols. New York: Doubleday.
Freeman, Anthony. 1993. *God in Us: A Case for Christian Humanism*. London: SCM.
Frei, Hans W. 1974. *The Eclipse of Biblical Narrative: A Study in Eighteenth and Nineteenth Century Hermeneutics*. New Haven: Yale University Press.
  1975. *The Identity of Jesus Christ: The Hermeneutical Bases of Dogmatic Theology*. Philadelphia, Pennsylvania: Fortress Press.
  1990. 'Epilogue: George Lindbeck and *The Nature of Doctrine*', in Bruce D. Marshall 1990a, pp. 275–82.

1992. *Types of Christian Theology* (ed. George Hunsinger and William C. Placher). New Haven: Yale University Press.

1993. *Theology and Narrative: Selected Essays* (ed. George Hunsinger and William C. Placher). New York: Oxford University Press.

Gasché, Rodolphe. 1994. *Inventions of Difference: On Jacques Derrida*. Cambridge, Massachusetts: Harvard University Press.

Geach, Peter. 1992. 'The Meaning of "God" – II', in Warner 1992, pp. 85–90.

Goldberg, Michael. 1991². *Theology and Narrative: A Critical Introduction*. Philadelphia, Pennsylvania: Trinity Press International.

Gooch, Paul W. 1996. *Reflections on Jesus and Socrates: Word and Silence*. New Haven: Yale University Press.

Goodman, Nelson. 1978. *Ways of Worldmaking*. Indianapolis: Hackett Publishing Company.

Gould, Stephen Jay. 2001. *Rocks of Ages: Science and Religion in the Fullness of Life*. London: Jonathan Cape.

Greco, John. 1993. 'Is Natural Theology Necessary for Theistic Knowledge?', in Zagzebski 1993, pp. 168–98.

Greco, John and Ernest Sosa (eds.). 1999. *The Blackwell Guide to Epistemology*, Oxford: Blackwell.

Green, Garrett (ed.). 1987. *Scriptural Authority and Narrative Interpretation: Essays on the Sixty-Fifth Birthday of Hans W. Frei*. Philadelphia, Pennsylvania: Fortress Press.

Grisez, Germain. 1983. *The Way of the Lord Jesus, Volume 1: Christian Moral Principles*. Chicago: Franciscan Herald Press.

Gunton, Colin. 1991. *The Promise of Trinitarian Theology*. Edinburgh: T. & T. Clark.

Gutting, Gary. 1982. *Religious Belief and Religious Skepticism*. Notre Dame, Indiana: Notre Dame University Press.

1985. 'Scientific Realism versus Constructive Empiricism: A Dialogue', in Churchland and Hooker 1985, pp. 118–31.

Hacker, P. M. S. 1993. *Wittgenstein: Meaning and Mind: Part II: Exegesis §§243–427. Volume 3 of an Analytic Commentary on the Philosophical Investigations*. Oxford: Blackwell.

1996. *Wittgenstein's Place in Twentieth-Century Analytic Philosophy*. Oxford: Blackwell.

1997. *Insight and Illusion: Themes in the Philosophy of Wittgenstein*. Bristol: Thoemmes Press.

Hacking, Ian. 1983. *Representing and Intervening: Introductory Topics in the Philosophy of Natural Science*. Cambridge: Cambridge University Press.

1985. 'Do We See through a Microscope?', in Churchland and Hooker 1985, pp. 132–52.

1999. *The Social Construction of What?* Cambridge, Massachusetts: Harvard University Press.

Halbertal, Moshe and Avishai Margalit. 1992. *Idolatry*. Cambridge, Massachusetts: Harvard University Press.

Haldane, John. 1996. 'On Coming Home to (Metaphysical) Realism', *Philosophy*, 71, pp. 287–96.

Haldane, John and Crispin Wright (eds.). 1993. *Reality, Representation, and Projection*. New York: Oxford University Press.

Hale, Bob and Crispin Wright (eds.). 1997. *A Companion to the Philosophy of Language*. Oxford: Blackwell.

Hanson, A. T. 1987. *The Paradox of the Cross in the Thought of St Paul*. Sheffield: JSOT Press.

Hanson, R. P. C. 1988. *The Search for the Christian Doctrine of God: The Arian Controversy 318–381*. Edinburgh: T. & T. Clark.

Hare, R. M. 1992. *Essays on Religion and Education*. Oxford: Clarendon Press.

Harries, Richard. 1994. *The Real God: A Response to Anthony Freeman's God in Us*. London: Mowbray.

Harris, Roy. 1996. *The Language Connection: Philosophy and Linguistics*. Bristol: Thoemmes Press.

Hart, David A. 1993. *Faith in Doubt: Non-Realism and Christian Belief*. London: Mowbray.

1995. *One Faith?: Non-Realism and the World of Faiths*. London: Mowbray.

Hart, Kevin. 1989. *The Trespass of the Sign: Deconstruction, Theology and Philosophy*. Cambridge: Cambridge University Press.

Harvey, A. E. 1982. *Jesus and the Constraints of History*. London: Duckworth.

1996. *Renewal Through Suffering: A Study of 2 Corinthians*. Edinburgh: T. & T. Clark.

Hauerwas, Stanley (with Richard Bondi and David Burrell). 1977. *Truthfulness and Tragedy: Further Investigations in Christian Ethics*. Notre Dame: University of Notre Dame Press.

Hauerwas, Stanley and L. Gregory Jones (eds.). 1989. *Why Narrative? Readings in Narrative Theology*. Grand Rapids, Michigan: Eerdmans.

Hays, Richard B. 1983. *The Faith of Jesus Christ: An Investigation of the Narrative Substructure of Galatians 3:1–4:11*. Chico, California: Scholars Press.

Hebblethwaite, Brian. 1982. ' "True" and "False" in Christology', in Hebblethwaite and Sutherland 1982, pp. 227–38.

1988. *The Ocean of Truth: A Defence of Objective Theism*. Cambridge: Cambridge University Press.

1993. 'Reflections on Realism vs. Non-Realism', in Runzo 1993, pp. 209–11.

Hebblethwaite, Brian and Edward Henderson (eds.). 1990. *Divine Action: Studies Inspired by the Philosophical Theology of Austin Farrer*. Edinburgh: T. & T. Clark.

Hebblethwaite, Brian and Stewart Sutherland (eds.). 1982. *The Philosophical Frontiers of Christian Theology: Essays Presented to D. M. MacKinnon*. Cambridge: Cambridge University Press.

Helm, Paul. 1988. *Eternal God: A Study of God without Time*. Oxford: Clarendon Press.

1994. *Belief Policies*. Cambridge: Cambridge University Press.

1997. *Faith and Understanding*. Edinburgh: Edinburgh University Press.

Hempel, Carl G. 1965. *Aspects of Scientific Explanation and Other Essays in the Philosophy of Science*. New York: The Free Press.

1966. *Philosophy of Natural Science*. Englewood Cliffs, New Jersey: Prentice-Hall.

Hensley, Jeffrey. 1996. 'Are Postliberals Necessarily Antirealists?: Reexamining the Metaphysics of Lindbeck's Postliberal Theology', in Phillips and Okholm 1996, pp. 69–80.

Hesse, Mary. 1998. 'Is Science the New Religion?', in Watts 1998, pp. 120–35.

Hibbs, Thomas S. 1995. *Dialectic and Narrative in Aquinas: An Interpretation of the Summa Contra Gentiles*. Notre Dame, Indiana: Notre Dame University Press.

Hick, John. 1966². *Faith and Knowledge*. London: Macmillan.

1989. *An Interpretation of Religion: Human Responses to the Transcendent*. London: Macmillan.

1993. 'Religious Realism and Non-Realism: Defining the Issue', in Runzo 1993, pp. 3–16.

Hilary of Poitiers. 1954. *The Trinity* (trans. Stephen McKenna, CSSR). Washington, DC: Catholic University of America Press.

Hilgevoord, J. (ed.). 1994. *Physics and our View of the World*. Cambridge: Cambridge University Press.

Himmelfarb, Gertrude. 1997. 'Telling it as you Like It: Post-Modernist History and the Flight from Fact', in Jenkins 1997, pp. 158–74.

Holmer, Paul. 1988. 'The Grammar of Faith', in Bell 1988, pp. 3–20.

Hooker, Morna. 1991. *The Gospel According to St Mark*. London: A. & C. Black.

Hunsinger, George. 1991. *How to Read Karl Barth: The Shape of his Theology*. New York and Oxford: Oxford University Press.

Huyssteen, Wentzel van. 1988. 'Experience and Explanation: The Justification of Cognitive Claims in Theology', *Zygon*, 23/3, pp. 247–61.

1989. *Theology and the Justification of Faith: Constructing Theories in Systematic Theology*. Grand Rapids, Michigan: Eerdmans.

1997. *Essays in Postfoundationalist Theology*. Grand Rapids, Michigan: Eerdmans.

1999. *The Shaping of Rationality: Toward Interdisciplinarity in Theology and Science*. Grand Rapids, Michigan: Eerdmans.

Incandela, Joseph M. 1985. 'The Appropriation of Wittgenstein's Work by Philosophers of Religion: Towards a Re-evaluation and an End', *Religious Studies*, 21, pp. 457–74.

Ingraffia, Brian. 1995. *Postmodern Theory and Biblical Theology*. Cambridge: Cambridge University Press.

Jenkins, Keith (ed.). 1997. *The Postmodern History Reader*. London: Routledge.

Jenson, Robert W. 1982. *The Triune Identity: God According to the Gospel*. Philadelphia, Pennsylvania: Fortress Press.

1992. ' "The Father, He..." ', in Kimel 1992, pp. 95–109.

1995. 'What is the Point of Trinitarian Theology?', in Schwöbel 1995, pp. 31–43.

1997. *Systematic Theology – Volume One: The Triune God*. New York and Oxford: Oxford University Press.

2000. 'The Hidden and Triune God', in *International Journal of Systematic Theology*, 2/1, March 2000, pp. 5–12.

Jones, Serene. 1995. *Calvin and the Rhetoric of Piety*. Louisville, Kentucky: Westminster John Knox Press.

Jüngel, Eberhard. 1976. 'The Truth of Life: Observations on Truth as the Interruption of the Continuity of Life', in McKinney 1976, pp. 231–6.

1983. *God as the Mystery of the World: On the Foundation of the Theology of the Crucified One in the Dispute Between Theism and Atheism*. Edinburgh: T. & T. Clark.

1989. *Theological Essays* (ed. J. B. Webster). Edinburgh: T. & T. Clark.

2001a. *God's Being Is in Becoming: The Trinitarian Being of God in the Theology of Karl Barth* (trans. John Webster). Edinburgh: T. & T. Clark.

2001b. *Justification: The Heart of Christian Faith*. Edinburgh: T. & T. Clark.

Kallenberg, Brad. 2000. 'The Gospel Truth of Relativism', *Scottish Journal of Theology*, 53/2, pp. 177–211.

Kant, I. 1933. *Critique of Pure Reason* (trans. Norman Kemp Smith). London: Macmillan.

1960. *Religion Within the Limits of Reason Alone* (trans. T. M. Greene and H. H. Hudson). New York: Harper & Row.

1978. *Lectures on Philosophical Theology* (trans. Allen M. Wood and Gertrude E. Clark). Ithaca: Cornell University Press.

Käsemann, Ernst. 1964. *Essays on New Testament Themes*. London: SCM.

1969. *New Testament Questions of Today*. London: SCM.

Kasper, Walter. 1983. *The God of Jesus Christ*. London: SCM.

Kaufman, Gordon. 1993. *In Face of Mystery: A Constructive Theology*. Cambridge, Massachusetts: Harvard University Press.

Keck, Leander. 2000. *Who is Jesus? History in Perfect Tense*. Columbia: University of South Carolina Press.

Kelly, J. N. D. 1969. *A Commentary on the Epistles of Peter and of Jude*. London: A. & C. Black.

Kelsey, David H. 1975. *The Uses of Scripture in Recent Theology*. London: SCM.

Kermode, Frank. 1979. *The Genesis of Secrecy: On the Interpretation of Narrative*. Cambridge, Massachusetts: Harvard University Press.

Kerr, Fergus. 1986. *Theology After Wittgenstein*. Oxford: Blackwell.

1989. 'Idealism and Realism: An Old Controversy Dissolved', in Surin 1989a, pp. 15–33.

Kimel, Alvin F., Jr (ed.). 1992. *Speaking the Christian God: The Holy Trinity and the Challenge of Feminism*. Grand Rapids, Michigan: Eerdmans.

Knight, Christopher C. 2001. *Wrestling with the Divine: Religion, Science, and Revelation*. Minneapolis: Fortress Press.

Kreider, Alan. 1995. *Worship and Evangelism in Pre-Christendom*. Cambridge: Grove Books.

Kripke, Saul. 1980². *Naming and Necessity*. Oxford: Blackwell.

1982. *Wittgenstein on Rules and Private Language: An Elementary Exposition*. Oxford: Blackwell.

Lash, Nicholas. 1982. 'Ideology, Metaphor and Analogy', in Hebblethwaite and Sutherland 1982, pp. 68–94.

1986. 'Considering the Trinity', *Modern Theology*, 2/3, pp. 183–96.

1988. 'Observation, Revelation, and the Posterity of Noah', in Russell et al. 1988, pp. 203–15.

1996. *The Beginning and End of 'Religion'*. Cambridge: Cambridge University Press.

2001. 'Renewed, Dissolved, Remembered: MacKinnon and Metaphysics', *New Blackfriars*, 82/969, pp. 486–98.

Laudan, Larry. 1984. 'A Confutation of Convergent Realism', in Leplin 1984, pp. 218–49.

Leplin, J. (ed.) 1984. *Scientific Realism*. Berkeley and Los Angeles, California: University of California Press.

Lewis, Charles M. (ed.). 1995. *Relativism and Religion*. London: Macmillan.

Lindbeck, George A. 1984. *The Nature of Doctrine: Religion and Theology in a Postliberal Age*. London: SPCK.

1996. 'A Panel Discussion', in Phillips and Okholm 1996, pp. 246–53.

Lonergan, Bernard. 1996. *A Second Collection*. Toronto: University of Toronto Press.

Louch, Alfred. 1993. 'Saying is Believing', in Runzo 1993, pp. 109–14.

Loughlin, Gerard. 1996. *Telling God's Story: Bible, Church and Narrative Theology*. Cambridge: Cambridge University Press.

Luhrmann, T. M. 1989. *Persuasions of the Witch's Craft: Ritual Magic and Witchcraft in Present-Day England*. Oxford: Blackwell.

McAuley, James. 1981. 'An Art of Poetry: To Vincent Buckley', in *The New Oxford Dictionary of Christian Verse* (ed. Donald Davie). Oxford: Oxford University Press, pp. 293–4.

McClendon, James W. Jr and James W. Smith. 1994. *Convictions: Defusing Religious Relativism*. Valley Forge, Pennsylvania: Trinity Press International.

McClendon, James W. Jr, and Brad J. Kallenberg 1998. 'Ludwig Wittgenstein: A Christian in Philosophy', *Scottish Journal of Theology*, 51/2, pp. 131–61.

McCormack, Bruce L. 1995. *Karl Barth's Critically Realist Dialectical Theology: Its Genesis and Development 1909–1936*. Oxford: Clarendon Press.

McFague, Sallie. 1982. *Metaphorical Theology: Models of God in Religious Language*. London: SCM.

McGinn, Colin. 1997. 'Is Wittgenstein Losing his Hold?', *Times Literary Supplement*, 3 January 1997, pp. 9–10.

McGrath, Alister. 1990. *The Genesis of Doctrine: A Study in the Foundations of Doctrinal Criticism*. Oxford: Blackwell.

1996. *A Passion for Truth: The Intellectual Coherence of Evangelicalism*. Leicester: Apollos.

1998. *The Foundations of Dialogue in Science and Religion*. Oxford: Blackwell.

1999. *T. F. Torrance: An Intellectual Biography*. Edinburgh: T. & T. Clark.

2001. *A Scientific Theology, Volume I: Nature*. Edinburgh: T. & T. Clark.

McGuinness, Brian and Gianluigi Oliveri (eds.). 1994. *The Philosophy of Michael Dummett*. Dordrecht: Kluwer Academic Publishers.

MacIntyre, Alasdair. 1955. 'Visions', in Flew and MacIntyre 1955, pp. 254–60.
McKinney, R. W. A. (ed.). 1976. *Creation, Christ and Culture: Studies in Honour of T. F. Torrance*. Edinburgh: T. & T. Clark.
MacKinnon, Donald. 1948. 'The Christian Understanding of Truth', *Scottish Journal of Theology*, 1/1, pp. 19–29.
  1965. 'Aristotle's Conception of Substance', in Bambrough 1965, pp. 97–119.
  1968. *Borderlands of Theology and Other Essays*. London: Lutterworth Press.
  1972.' "Substance" in Christology – A Cross-Bench View', in Sykes and Clayton 1972, pp. 279–300.
  1979. *Explorations in Theology 5*. London: SCM.
  1987. *Themes in Theology: The Three-fold Cord*. Edinburgh: T. & T. Clark.
McMullin, Ernan. 1984. 'A Case for Scientific Realism', in Leplin 1984, pp. 8–40.
  1985. 'Realism in Theology and Science: A Response to Peacocke', *Religion and Intellectual Life*, 2/4, pp. 39–48.
  1994. 'Enlarging the Known World', in Hilgevoord 1994, pp. 79–113.
Malcolm, Norman. 1993. *Wittgenstein: A Religious Point of View?* (edited with a response by Peter Winch). London: Routledge.
Marion, Jean-Luc. 1991. *God Without Being: Hors-Texte*. Chicago: Chicago University Press.
Markham, Ian. 1998. *Truth and the Reality of God: An Essay in Natural Theology*. Edinburgh: T. & T. Clark.
Marshall, Bruce D. 1987. *Christology in Conflict: The Identity of a Saviour in Rahner and Barth*. Oxford: Blackwell.
  1990a (ed.). *Theology and Dialogue: Essays in Conversation with George Lindbeck*. Notre Dame, Indiana: Notre Dame University Press.
  1990b. 'Absorbing the World: Christianity and the Universe of Truths', in Bruce D. Marshall 1990, pp. 69–102.
  1992. 'Meaning and Truth in Narrative Interpretation: A Reply to George Schner', *Modern Theology*, 8/2, pp. 173–9.
  2000. *Trinity and Truth*. Cambridge: Cambridge University Press.
Marshall, I. Howard. 1978. *The Epistles of John*. Grand Rapids, Michigan: Eerdmans.
Mavrodes, George I. 1995. 'Polytheism', in Senor 1995, pp. 261–86.
Maxwell, Grover. 1962. 'The Ontological Status of Theoretical Entities', in Feigl and Maxwell 1962, pp. 3–27.
Mendenhall, G. E. and G. A. Herion. 1992. 'Covenant', in Freedman et al. 1992, Vol. 1, pp. 1179–1202.
Mettinger, T. N. D. 1988. *In Search of God: The Meaning and Message of the Everlasting Names*. Philadelphia, Pennsylvania: Fortress Press.
Michalson, Gordon E. Jr. 1988. 'The Response to Lindbeck', *Modern Theology*, 4/2, pp. 107–20.
  1999. *Kant and the Problem of God*. Oxford: Blackwell.
Milbank, John. 1990. *Theology and Social Theory: Beyond Secular Reason*. Oxford: Blackwell.

Milbank, John and Catherine Pickstock. 2001. *Truth in Aquinas*. London: Routledge.
Miller, Richard B. 1986. 'The Reference of "God"', *Faith and Philosophy*, 3/1, pp. 3–15.
Mitchell, Basil (ed.). 1971. *The Philosophy of Religion*. Oxford: Oxford University Press.
Moltmann, Jürgen. 1974. *The Crucified God*. London: SCM.
Monk, Ray L. 1996. 'Only Sentences', *London Review of Books*, 31 October 1996, pp. 30–1.
Moore, Andrew. 1999. 'Rebuilding the Boat: The Church and the Sea of Faith', *Anvil*, 16/3, pp. 187–200.
  2000. 'Theological Realism and the Observability of God', *International Journal of Systematic Theology*, 2/1, pp. 79–99.
  2001. 'Philosophy of Religion or Philosophical Theology?', *International Journal of Systematic Theology*, 3/3, pp. 309–28.
Moore, G. E. 1922. *Philosophical Studies*. London: RKP.
Morris, Thomas V. (ed.). 1994. *God and the Philosophers: The Reconciliation of Faith and Reason*. New York and Oxford: Oxford University Press.
Moser, Paul K. 1999. 'Realism, Objectivity, and Skepticism', in Greco and Sosa 1999, pp. 70–91.
Moule, C. F. D. 1977. *The Origin of Christology*. Cambridge: Cambridge University Press.
  1982. 'The Borderlands of Ontology in the New Testament', in Hebblethwaite and Sutherland 1982, pp. 1–11.
Murphy, Nancey. 1988. 'From Critical Realism to a Methodological Approach: Response to Robbins, van Huyssteen, and Hefner', *Zygon*, 23/3, pp. 287–90.
  1990. *Theology in the Age of Scientific Reasoning*. Ithaca: Cornell University Press.
  1994. 'What has Theology to Learn from Scientific Methodology?', in Rae et al. 1994, pp. 101–26.
Murphy, Nancey and James W. McClendon Jr. 1989. 'Distinguishing Modern and Postmodern Theologies', *Modern Theology*, 5/3, pp. 191–214.
Newman, Carey C. (ed.). 1999. *Jesus and the Restoration of Israel: A Critical Assessment of N. T. Wright's* Jesus and the Victory of God. Carlisle: Paternoster Press.
Newton-Smith, W. H. 1981. *The Rationality of Science*. London: RKP.
  1989. 'Modest Realism', in A. Fine and J. Leplin (eds.), *Philosophy of Science Association 1988*. East Lansing, Michigan: Philosophy of Science Association, pp. 179–89.
Niebuhr, H. Richard. 1960. *The Meaning of Revelation*. New York: Macmillan.
Nielsen, Kai. 1982. 'Wittgensteinian Fideism', in Cahn and Shatz 1982, pp. 237–54.
Nietzsche, Friedrich. 1974. *The Gay Science, with a Prelude in Rhymes and an Appendix in Songs*. New York: Vintage Books.
Noth, Martin. 1962. *Exodus*. London: SCM.
Nussbaum, Martha. 1990. *Love's Knowledge: Essays on Philosophy and Literature*. Oxford: Oxford University Press.

O'Donovan, Joan F. 1986. 'Man in the Image of God: The Disagreement between Barth and Brunner Reconsidered', *Scottish Journal of Theology*, 39/4, pp. 433–59.

O'Donovan, Oliver. 1978. 'The Natural Ethic', in David F. Wright 1978, pp. 19–35.

1986. *Resurrection and Moral Order: An Outline For Evangelical Ethics*. Leicester: IVP.

O'Neill, Colman. 1985. 'The Rule Theory of Doctrine and Propositional Truth', *The Thomist*, 49/3, pp. 417–42.

Origen. 1965. *Contra Celsum* (trans. Henry Chadwick). Cambridge: Cambridge University Press.

Ortony, A. (ed.). 1979. *Metaphor and Thought*. Cambridge: Cambridge University Press.

Outka, Gene. 1987. 'Following at a Distance: Ethics and the Identity of Jesus', in Green 1987, pp. 144–60.

Pannenberg, Wolfhart. 1968. *Jesus – God and Man*. London: SCM.

1970. *Basic Questions in Theology, Volume One*. London: SCM.

1971. *Basic Questions In Theology: Collected Essays, Volume Two*. Philadelphia, Pennsylvania: Fortress Press.

1991. *Systematic Theology, Volume I*. Edinburgh: T. & T. Clark.

Pascal, Blaise. 1995. *Pensées* (trans. A. J. Krailsheimer). Harmondsworth: Penguin Books.

Patrick, Dale. 1999. *The Rhetoric of Revelation in the Hebrew Bible*. Minneapolis: Fortress Press.

Patterson, Sue. 1993. 'Janet Martin Soskice, Metaphor and a Theology of Grace', *Scottish Journal of Theology*, 46/1, pp. 1–26.

1999. *Realist Christian Theology in a Postmodern Age*. Cambridge: Cambridge University Press.

Peacocke, Arthur. 1971. *Science and the Christian Experiment*. Oxford: Oxford University Press.

1979. *Creation and the World of Science*. Oxford: Clarendon Press.

1984. *Intimations of Reality: Critical Realism in Science and Religion*. Notre Dame, Indiana: Notre Dame University Press.

1988. 'Science and Theology Today: A Critical Realist Perspective', *Religion and Intellectual Life*, 5/3, pp. 45–58.

1993[2]. *Theology for a Scientific Age: Being and Becoming – Natural, Divine and Human*. London: SCM.

1994. 'The Religion of a Scientist: Explorations into Reality (*Religio Philosophi Naturalis*)', *Zygon*, 29/4, pp. 639–59.

Penelhum, Terence. 1983. *God and Skepticism: A Study in Skepticism and Fideism*. Dordrecht: D. Reidel Publishing Company.

Phillips, D. Z. 1965. *The Concept of Prayer*. London: RKP.

1970. *Faith and Philosophical Enquiry*. London: RKP.

1976. *Religion Without Explanation*. Oxford: Blackwell.

1985. 'The Friends of Cleanthes', *Modern Theology*, 1/2, pp. 91–104.

1988a. *Faith After Foundationalism*. London: Routledge.

1988b. 'Grammarians and Guardians', in Bell 1988, pp. 21–35.

1993a. *Wittgenstein and Religion*. London: Macmillan.

1993b. 'Great Expectations: Philosophy, Ontology and Religion', in Runzo 1993, pp. 203–7.

1995a. 'At the Mercy of Method', in Tessin and von der Ruhr 1995, pp. 1–16.

1995b. 'Where are the Gods Now?', in Lewis 1995, pp. 1–15.

1995c. 'Philosophers' Clothes', in Lewis 1995, pp. 135–53.

Phillips, Peter. 1998. 'George Steiner's Wager on Transcendence', *Heythrop Journal*, 39, pp. 158–69.

Phillips, Timothy R. and Dennis L. Okholm (eds.). 1996. *The Nature of Confession: Evangelicals and Postliberals in Conversation*. Downers Grove, Illinois: Inter Varsity Press.

Pickstock, Catherine. 1998. *After Writing: On the Liturgical Consummation of Philosophy*. Oxford: Blackwell.

Plantinga, Alvin. 1983. 'Reason and Belief in God', in Plantinga and Wolterstorff 1983, pp. 16–93.

1993. *Warrant and Proper Function*. New York and Oxford: Oxford University Press.

2000. *Warranted Christian Belief*. New York and Oxford: Oxford University Press.

Plantinga, Alvin and Nicholas Wolterstorff (eds.). 1983. *Faith and Rationality: Reason and Belief in God*. Notre Dame, Indiana: Notre Dame University Press.

Polkinghorne, John. 1991. *Reason and Reality: The Relationship between Science and Theology*. London: SPCK.

1996. *Scientists as Theologians: A Comparison of the Writings of Ian Barbour, Arthur Peacocke and John Polkinghorne*. London: SPCK.

1998. *Belief in God in an Age of Science*. New Haven: Yale University Press.

Pritchard, Paul. 1997. *Deep Play: A Climber's Odyssey from Llanberis to the Big Walls*. London: Bâton Wicks.

Puddefoot, John. 1994. ' Response' [to Murphy 1994] in Rae et al. 1994, pp. 137–47.

Putnam, Hilary. 1978. *Meaning and the Moral Sciences*. London: RKP.

1981. *Reason, Truth and History*. Cambridge: Cambridge University Press.

1983. *Realism and Reason: Philosophical Papers, Volume 3*. Cambridge: Cambridge University Press.

1992. *Renewing Philosophy*. Cambridge, Massachusetts: Harvard University Press.

1994. 'Sense, Nonsense, and the Senses: An Inquiry into the Powers of the Human Mind', *Journal of Philosophy*, 41/9, pp. 445–517.

Quinn, Phillip L. and Charles Taliaferro (eds.). 1997. *A Companion to Philosophy of Religion*. Oxford: Blackwell.

Rad, Gerhard von. 1975. *Old Testament Theology, Volume I: The Theology of Israel's Historical Traditions*. London: SCM.

Rae, Murray, Hilary Regan, and John Stenhouse (eds.). 1994. *Science and Theology: Questions at the Interface*. Edinburgh: T. & T. Clark.

Rahner, Karl. 1978. *Foundations of Christian Faith: An Introduction to the Idea of Christianity*. London: DLT.

Ramsey, Ian. 1974. *Christian Empiricism* (ed. Jerry H. Gill). Grand Rapids, Michigan: Eerdmans.

Ramsey, Paul. 1950. *Basic Christian Ethics*. Chicago: Chicago University Press.

Recanati, François. 1987. *Meaning and Force: The Pragmatics of Performative Utterances*. Cambridge: Cambridge University Press.

Redhead, Michael. 1995. *From Physics to Metaphysics*. Cambridge: Cambridge University Press.

Rhees, Rush. 1969. *Without Answers*. London: RKP.

Ricoeur, Paul. 1976. *Interpretation Theory: Discourse and the Surplus of Meaning*. Fort Worth: Texas Christian University Press.

　1981. *Essays on Biblical Interpretation* (edited with an Introduction by Lewis S. Mudge). London: SPCK.

Rogers, Eugene F., Jr. 1996. *Thomas Aquinas and Karl Barth: Sacred Doctrine and the Natural Knowledge of God*. Notre Dame, Indiana: Notre Dame University Press.

Rorty, Richard. 1980. *Philosophy and the Mirror of Nature*. Oxford: Blackwell.

　1989. *Contingency, Irony, and Solidarity*. Cambridge: Cambridge University Press.

　1992. 'Is Derrida a Transcendental Philosopher?', in Wood 1992, pp. 235–46.

Ruben, David-Hillel. 1990. *Explaining Explanation*. London: Routledge.

Rumscheidt, H. Martin (ed.). 1986. *The Way of Theology in Karl Barth: Essays and Comments*. Allison Park, Pennsylvania: Pickwick Publications.

Runzo, Joseph (ed.). 1993. *Is God Real?* London: Macmillan.

Russell, R. J., W. R. Stoeger, and G. V. Coyne (eds.). 1988. *Physics, Philosophy, and Theology: A Common Quest for Understanding*. Vatican City: Vatican Observatory, distributed outside Italy by Notre Dame University Press.

Ryle, Gilbert. 1954. *Dilemmas: The Tarner Lectures 1953*. Cambridge: Cambridge University Press.

　1963. *The Concept of Mind*. Harmondsworth: Penguin Books.

Sayre-McCord, Geoffrey (ed.). 1988. *Essays on Moral Realism*. Ithaca: Cornell University Press.

Schleiermacher, Friedrich. 1928. *The Christian Faith* (ed. H. R. Mackintosh and J. S. Stewart). Edinburgh: T. & T. Clark.

Schnackenburg, Rudolf. 1980. *The Gospel According to St John, Vol. 1* . London: Burns & Oates.

Schwöbel, Christoph (ed.). 1995. *Trinitarian Theology Today: Essays on Divine Being and Act*. Edinburgh: T. & T. Clark.

Schwöbel, Christoph and Colin Gunton (eds.). 1991. *Persons, Divine and Human: King's College Essays in Theological Anthropology*. Edinburgh: T. & T. Clark.

Scott, Michael. 2000. 'Wittgenstein and Realism', *Faith and Philosophy*, 17/2, pp. 170–90.

Scott, Michael and Andrew Moore. 1997. 'Can Theological Realism be Refuted?', *Religious Studies*, 33/4, pp. 401–18.

Searle, John R. 1969. *Speech Acts: An Essay in the Philosophy of Language*. Cambridge: Cambridge University Press.

1979. *Expression and Meaning: Studies in the Theory of Speech Acts*. Cambridge: Cambridge University Press.

1983. *Intentionality: An Essay in the Philosophy of Mind*. Cambridge: Cambridge University Press.

1995. *The Construction of Social Reality*. Harmondsworth: Allen Lane.

Seitz, Christopher R. 1998. *Word Without End: The Old Testament as Abiding Theological Witness*. Grand Rapids, Michigan: Eerdmans.

Selby, Peter. 1997. 'The Reality of Power and the Power of Reality', in Crowder 1997, pp. 71–84.

Senor, Thomas D. (ed.) 1995. *The Rationality of Belief and the Plurality of Faith: Essays in Honour of William P. Alston*. Ithaca, New York: Cornell University Press.

Sherry, Patrick. 1989. 'Modes of Representation and Likeness to God', in Surin 1989a, pp. 34–48.

Shields, Phillip R. 1993. *Logic and Sin in the Writings of Ludwig Wittgenstein*. Chicago: Chicago University Press.

Shiffer, Stephen R. 1987. *Remnants of Meaning*. Cambridge, Massachusetts: MIT Press.

Sluga, Hans and David G. Stern (eds.). 1996. *The Cambridge Companion to Wittgenstein*. Cambridge: Cambridge University Press.

Smalley, Stephen. 1984. *1, 2, 3, John*. Waco, Texas: Word Books.

Sokal, Alan and Jean Bricmont. 1998. *Intellectual Impostures: Postmodern Philosophers' Abuse of Science*. London: Profile Books.

Sonderegger, Katherine. 1997. 'Gordon Kaufman: An Attempt to Understand Him', *Scottish Journal of Theology*, 50/3, 1997, pp. 321–44.

Soskice, Janet Martin. 1985. *Metaphor and Religious Language*. Oxford: Clarendon Press.

1987. 'Theological Realism', in Abraham and Holtzer 1987, pp. 105–19.

1988. 'Knowledge and Experience in Science and Religion: Can we be Realists?', in Russell et al. 1988, pp. 173–84.

Stackhouse, John G., Jr. 2000. 'Evangelical Theology Should Be Evangelical', in John G. Stackhouse Jr. (ed.). 2000. *Evangelical Futures: A Conversation on Theological Method*. Leicester: Apollos, pp. 39–58.

Stead, Christopher. 1994. *Philosophy in Christian Antiquity*. Cambridge: Cambridge University Press.

Steiner, George. 1989. *Real Presences: Is There Anything* in *What we Say?* London: Faber & Faber.

1996. *No Passion Spent: Essays 1978–1996*. London: Faber & Faber.

Stern, J. P. 1973. *On Realism*. London: RKP.

Stern, Robert (ed.). 1999. *Transcendental Arguments: Problems and Prospects*. Oxford: Clarendon Press.

Stout, Jeffrey. 1981. *The Flight from Authority: Religion, Morality, and the Quest for Autonomy*. Notre Dame, Indiana: Notre Dame University Press.

Stump, Eleonore and Thomas P. Flint (eds.). 1993. *Hermes and Athena: Biblical Exegesis and Philosophical Theology*. Notre Dame, Indiana: Notre Dame University Press.

Surin, Kenneth. 1986. *Theology and the Problem of Evil*. Oxford: Blackwell.

    1989a. (ed.). *Christ, Ethics and Tragedy: Essays in Honour of Donald MacKinnon*. Cambridge: Cambridge University Press.

    1989b. *The Turnings of Darkness and Light: Essays in Philosophical and Systematic Theology*. Cambridge: Cambridge University Press.

Swinburne, Richard. 1977. *The Coherence of Theism*. Oxford: Clarendon Press.

    1991^2. *The Existence of God*. Oxford: Clarendon Press.

    1992. *Revelation: From Metaphor to Analogy*. Oxford: Clarendon Press.

    1993. 'The Vocation of a Natural Theologian', in Clark 1993, pp. 179–202.

    1994. *The Christian God*. Oxford: Clarendon Press.

Sykes, S. W. (ed.). 1979. *Karl Barth: Studies of his Theological Method*. Oxford: Clarendon Press.

    1989. (ed.). *Karl Barth: Centenary Essays*. Cambridge: Cambridge University Press.

Sykes, S. W. and J. P. Clayton (eds.). 1972. *Christ, Faith and History: Cambridge Studies in Christology*. Cambridge: Cambridge University Press.

Tanner, Kathryn. 1988. *God and Creation in Christian Theology: Tyranny or Empowerment?* Oxford: Blackwell.

Taylor, Charles. 1985. *Human Language and Agency: Philosophical Papers, Volume I*. Cambridge: Cambridge University Press.

    1989. *Sources of the Self: The Making of the Modern Identity*. Cambridge: Cambridge University Press.

Tessin, Timothy and Mario von der Ruhr (eds.). 1995. *Philosophy and the Grammar of Religious Belief*. London: Macmillan.

Thiel, John E. 1994. *Nonfoundationalism*. Minneapolis, Minnesota: Fortress Press.

Thiemann, Ronald F. 1985. *Revelation and Theology: The Gospel as Narrated Promise*. Notre Dame, Indiana: Notre Dame University Press.

Thiselton, Anthony C. 1978. 'Truth', in Colin Brown 1978, pp. 874–902.

    1992. *New Horizons in Hermeneutics*. London: HarperCollins.

    1995. *Interpreting God and the Postmodern Self: On Meaning, Manipulation and Promise*. Edinburgh: T. & T. Clark.

    2000. *The First Epistle to the Corinthians: A Commentary on the Greek Text*. Grand Rapids: Eerdmans and Carlisle: Paternoster Press.

Tilley, Terrence W. 1989. 'Incommensurability, Intratextuality, and Fideism', *Modern Theology*, 5/2, pp. 87–111.

Tillich, Paul. 1953. *Systematic Theology, Volume I*. London: Nisbet & Co.

Tomlin, Graham. 1999. *The Power of the Cross: Theology and the Death of Christ in Paul, Luther and Pascal*. Carlisle: Paternoster Press.

Torrance, Alan. 1996. *Persons in Communion: An Essay on Trinitarian Description and Human Participation with Special Reference to Volume One of Karl Barth's Church Dogmatics.* Edinburgh: T. & T. Clark.

Torrance, T. F. 1969. *Theological Science.* Oxford: Oxford University Press.

  1981. *Divine and Contingent Order.* Oxford: Oxford University Press.

  1982. *Reality and Evangelical Theology.* Philadelphia, Pennsylvania: The Westminster Press.

Tracy, David. 1981. *The Analogical Imagination: Christian Theology and the Culture of Pluralism.* New York: Crossroad.

  1985. 'Lindbeck's New Program for Theology', *The Thomist,* 49/3, pp. 460–72.

Trigg, Roger. 1973. *Reason and Commitment.* Cambridge: Cambridge University Press.

  1989². *Reality at Risk: A Defence of Realism in Philosophy and the Sciences.* Hemel Hempstead: Harvester Wheatsheaf.

  1992. 'Reason and Faith – II', in Warner 1992, pp. 33–43.

  1997. 'Theological Realism and Antirealism', in Quinn and Taliaferro 1997, pp. 213–20.

  1998. *Rationality and Religion: Does Faith Need Reason?* Oxford: Blackwell.

Valdés, Mario J. (ed.). 1991. *A Ricoeur Reader: Reflection and Imagination.* Hemel Hempstead: Harvester Wheatsheaf.

Vanhoozer, Kevin J. 1990. *Biblical Narrative in the Philosophy of Paul Ricoeur: A Study in Hermeneutics and Theology.* Cambridge: Cambridge University Press.

  1998. *Is There a Meaning in This Text? The Bible, the Reader and the Morality of Literary Knowledge.* Leicester: Apollos.

Vass, George. 1985a. *A Theologian in Search of a Philosophy: Understanding Karl Rahner, Volume 1.* London: Sheed and Ward.

  1985b. *The Mystery of Man and the Foundations of a Theological System: Understanding Karl Rahner, Volume 2.* London: Sheed and Ward.

Wainwright, Geoffrey. 1988. 'Ecumenical Dimensions of Lindbeck's Nature of Doctrine', *Modern Theology,* 4/2, pp. 121–32.

Wallace, Mark I. 1990. *The Second Naiveté: Barth, Ricoeur, and the New Yale Theology.* Macon, Georgia: Mercer University Press.

Ward, Keith. 1982. *Holding Fast to God: A Reply to Don Cupitt.* London: SPCK.

Warner, Martin (ed.). 1992. *Religion and Philosophy: Royal Institute of Philosophy Supplement: 31.* Cambridge: Cambridge University Press.

Watson, Francis. 1994. *Text, Church and World: Biblical Interpretation in Theological Perspective.* Edinburgh: T. & T. Clark.

Watts, Fraser (ed.). 1998. *Science Meets Faith.* London: SPCK.

Webster, John. 1992. 'Locality and Catholicity: Reflections on Theology and the Church', *Scottish Journal of Theology,* 45/1, pp. 1–17.

  1995. *Barth's Ethics of Reconciliation.* Cambridge: Cambridge University Press.

  1998a. *Theological Theology.* Oxford: Clarendon Press.

  1998b. 'Hermeneutics in Modern Theology: Some Doctrinal Reflections', *Scottish Journal of Theology,* 51/3, pp. 307–41.

Weinandy, Thomas G., OFM, Cap. 2000. *Does God Suffer?* Edinburgh: T. & T. Clark.

Wessels, Linda. 1993. 'Scientific Realism and Quantum Mechanical Realism', *Midwest Studies in Philosophy*, 18, pp. 317–41.

Westermann, Claus. 1974. *Creation*. London: SPCK.

Westphal, Merold. 1990. 'Taking St Paul Seriously: Sin as an Epistemological Category', in Flint 1990, pp. 200–26.

1992. 'Religious Experience as Self-Transcendence and Self-Deception', *Faith and Philosophy*, 9/2, pp. 168–92.

1993a. *Suspicion and Faith: The Religious Uses of Modern Atheism*. Grand Rapids, Michigan: Eerdmans.

1993b. 'Christian Philosophers and the Copernican Revolution', in Evans and Westphal 1993, pp. 161–79.

Whitaker, Andrew. 1996. *Einstein, Bohr and the Quantum Dilemma*. Cambridge: Cambridge University Press.

White, Graham. 1984. 'Karl Barth's Theological Realism', *Neue Zeitschrift für Systematische Theologie und Religionsphilosophie* 26, pp. 54–70.

White, Stephen Ross. 1994. *Don Cupitt and the Future of Christian Doctrine*. London: SCM.

Williams, Michael. 1993. 'Realism and Scepticism', in Haldane and Wright 1993, pp. 193–214.

Williams, Rowan. 1979. *The Wound of Knowledge: Christian Spirituality from the New Testament to St John of the Cross*. London: DLT.

1984. ' "Religious Realism": On Not Quite Agreeing with Don Cupitt', *Modern Theology*, 1/1, pp. 3–24.

1997. 'Foreword', in Crowder 1997, pp. v–ix.

2000. *On Christian Theology*. Oxford: Blackwell.

Williams, Stephen N. 1988. 'Lindbeck's Regulative Christology', in *Modern Theology*, 4/2, pp. 173–86.

1995. *Revelation and Reconciliation: A Window on Modernity*. Cambridge: Cambridge University Press.

Wittgenstein, Ludwig. 1961. *Tractatus Logico-Philosophicus* (trans. D. F. Pears and B. F. McGuinness, with an Introduction by Bertrand Russell). London: RKP.

1966. *Lectures and Conversations on Aesthetics, Psychology and Religious Belief*, (compiled from Notes taken by Yorick Smythies, Rush Rhees, and James Taylor; ed. Cyril Barrett). Oxford: Blackwell.

1969. *On Certainty* (ed. G. E. M. Anscombe and G. H. von Wright, trans. Denis Paul and G. E. M. Anscombe). Oxford: Blackwell.

1969². *The Blue and Brown Books: Preliminary Studies for the 'Philosophical Investigations'*. Oxford: Blackwell.

1974. *Philosophical Grammar* (ed. R. Rhees, trans. A. J. P. Kenny). Oxford: Blackwell.

1978³. *Philosophical Invesitgations* (trans. G. E. M. Anscombe). Oxford: Blackwell.

Wobbermin, Georg. 1929. *Richtlinien evangelischer Theologie zur Uberwindung der gegenwartigen Krisis*. Göttingen: Vandenhoeck and Ruprecht.

Wolff, Hans Walter. 1974. *Anthropology of the Old Testament*. London: SCM.

Wollheim, Richard. 1959. *F. H. Bradley*. Harmondsworth: Penguin Books.

Wolterstorff, Nicholas. 1987. *Lament for a Son*. Grand Rapids, Michigan: Eerdmans.

   1995. *Divine Discourse: Philosophical Reflections on the Claim that God Speaks*. Cambridge: Cambridge University Press.

   1998. 'Is it Possible and Desirable for Theologians to Recover from Kant?', in *Modern Theology*, 14/1, pp. 1–18.

   2001. 'Living within a Text', in Yandell 2001, pp. 202–13.

Wood, Charles M. 1981. *The Formation of Christian Understanding: An Essay in Theological Hermeneutics*. Philadelphia, Pennsylvania: Westminster Press.

Wood, D. (ed.). 1992. *Derrida: A Critical Reader*. Oxford: Blackwell.

Wood, James. 1999. *The Broken Estate: Essays on Literature and Belief*. London: Jonathan Cape.

Woods, G. F. 1958. *Theological Explanation: A Study of the Meaning and Means of Explaining in Science, History, and Theology, based upon the Stanton Lectures delivered in the University of Cambridge, 1953–6*. Welwyn: James Nisbet & Co.

Wright, David F. (ed.). 1978. *Essays in Evangelical Social Ethics*. Exeter: Paternoster Press.

Wright, N. T. 1991. *The Climax of the Covenant: Christ and the Law in Pauline Theology*. Edinburgh: T. & T. Clark.

   1992. *The New Testament and the People of God*. London: SPCK.

   1996. *Jesus and the Victory of God*. London: SPCK.

Yandell, Keith (ed.). 2001. *Faith and Narrative*. Oxford and New York: Oxford University Press.

Zagzebski, Linda (ed.). 1993. *Rational Faith: Catholic Responses to Reformed Epistemology*. Notre Dame, Indiana: Notre Dame University Press.

Zimmermann, W.-D. and R. Gregor Smith (eds.). 1966. *I Knew Dietrich Bonhoeffer*. London: Collins.

Zizioulas, John D. 1991. 'On Being a Person: Towards an Ontology of Personhood', in Schwöbel and Gunton 1991, pp. 33–46.

   1995. 'The Doctrine of the Holy Trinity: The Significance of the Cappadocian Contribution', in Schwöbel 1995, pp. 44–60.

Zorn, Hans. 1995. 'Grammar, Doctrines, and Practice', *Journal of Religion*, 75, pp. 509–20.

Index of scripture references

Index of names and subjects